State Trading in the Twenty-First Century

SiE *Studies in International Economics* includes works dealing with the theory; empirical analysis; political, economic, and legal aspects; and evaluation of international policies and institutions.

Keith E. Maskus, Peter M. Hooper, Edward E. Leamer, and J. David Richardson, Editors
Quiet Pioneering: Robert M. Stern and His International Economic Legacy

Bjarne S. Jensen and Kar-yiu Wong, Editors
Dynamics, Economic Growth, and International Trade

Kala Marathe Krishna and Ling Hui Tan
Rags and Riches: Implementing Apparel Quotas under the Multi-Fibre Arrangement

Alan V. Deardorff and Robert M. Stern
Measurement of Nontariff Barriers

Thomas Cottier and Petros C. Mavroidis, Editors
The World Trade Forum, Volume I: State Trading in the Twenty-First Century

Rajesh Chadha, Sanjib Pohit, Alan V. Deardorff, and Robert M. Stern
The Impact of Trade and Domestic Policy Reforms in India: A CGE Modeling Approach

Alan V. Deardorff and Robert M. Stern, Editors
Constituent Interests and U.S. Trade Policies

Gary R. Saxonhouse and T. N. Srinivasan, Editors
Development, Duality, and the International Economic Regime: Essays in Honor of Gustav Ranis

WORLD TRADE FORUM, VOLUME I

State Trading in the Twenty-First Century

Thomas Cottier and Petros C. Mavroidis,
Editors

Krista Nadakavukaren Schefer, Associate Editor

Ann Arbor

THE UNIVERSITY OF MICHIGAN PRESS

Copyright © by the University of Michigan 1998
All rights reserved
Published in the United States of America by
The University of Michigan Press
Manufactured in the United States of America
♾ Printed on acid-free paper

2001   2000   1999   1998   4   3   2   1

A CIP catalog record for this book is available from the British Library.

ISBN: 0-472-10996-0
ISSN: 1520-3476

1003244574

The World Trade Forum

The World Trade Forum was founded in 1997 to offer an opportunity for an international in-depth discussion of issues facing the world trading system. The Forum is organized through the cooperation of the Universities of Bern and Neuchâtel (Switzerland) and the financial support of the Silva Casa Foundation of Bern. Forum participants include academics, practitioners, and professionals from government and from international non-government organizations. Representing both the legal and economic communities, the participants bring a wide variety of perspectives to the issues of debate.

Each year, one particular topic is chosen as the focus of that year's forum. The participants invited to the conference are requested to prepare a paper on that topic, and then to present the paper for discussion. Question-and-answer sessions follow each presentation, and a short analysis by an appointed discussant following the presentation of each groups of papers allows for a synthesis of the ideas. At the end of all sessions, a roundtable discussion takes place, in which participants may either make comments on the overall problems of the topic or address questions and suggestions to the other participants in light of the entire series of papers presented.

Following the conference, the authors of the papers revise their submissions for publication in the series of books that accompany the World Trade Forum conferences. An introduction and conclusory analysis by the editors furthers the synthesis of the topic at hand and aids the reader in determining the overall results of the scholarship. A transcript of the roundtable discussion is included as an annex.

We are most grateful to the Silva Casa Foundation in Bern, Switzerland for its generous financial support that allow the conferences to take place as well as for its encouragement to pursue the idea of the World Trade Forum and to the University of Bern.

The World Trade Forum series has been founded in order to help spread the ideas that arise from the careful consideration of the issue presented to interested persons throughout the world. We sincerely hope that this volume achieves this goal.

Contents

Part V: Conclusions

Abbreviations and Acronyms

ACTPN	Advisory Committee for Trade Policy and Negotiations (U.S.)
AD	Antidumping
ALIC	Agriculture and Livestock Industries Corporation (Japan)
AT&T	American Telephone and Telegraph, Inc.
BCE	Bell Canada Enterprises
BISD	Basic Instruments and Selected Documents (GATT/WTO)
BRI	Brewer's Retail Inc. (Canada)
CAA	Agreement on Trade in Civil Aircraft (WTO)
CBFS	Carbon Black Feedstock
CCC	Commodity Credit Corporation (U.S.)
CDN	Canadian Dollars
CIS	Commonwealth of Independent States
CN	Canadian National Railroad Company
COCOM	Coordinating Committee for Export Controls (Japan)
CRTC	Canadian Radio-Television and Telecommunications Commission
CVD	Countervailing Duty
DOD	U.S. Department of Defense
DOE	U.S. Department of Energy
DSU	Understanding on the Rules and Procedures Governing the Settlement of Disputes (WTO)
DT	Deutsche Telekom
EC	European Community
ECJ	European Court of Justice
ECR	European Court Reports
ECT	European Community Treaty (Treaty of Rome)
EEC	European Economic Community
EIT	Economy in Transition
EPC	European Patent Convention
EU	European Union
FDIC	Federal Deposit Insurance Corporation (FDIC)
FERC	Federal Energy Regulation Commission (U.S.)
FHP	Federal Helium Program (U.S.)
FIRA	Foreign Investment Review Act (Canada)
FSU	Former Soviet Union
FTC	Foreign Trade Corporation (China)
FTO	Foreign Trade Organization (Russia)
GAO	U.S. General Accounting Office

GATS	General Agreement on Trade in Services (WTO)
GATT	General Agreement on Tariffs and Trade (WTO)
GDP	Gross Domestic Product
GPA	Agreement on Government Procurement (WTO)
IGC	Intergovernmental Conference
IMF	International Monetary Fund
IPO	Initial Public Offering
IPRs	Intellectual Property Rights
ITC	International Trade Commission (U.S.)
JTI	Japan Tobacco Inc.
LIPC	Livestock Industry Promotion Corporation (Japan)
MAFF	Ministry of Agriculture, Forestry and Fisheries (Japan)
MAI	Multilateral Agreement on Investment (OECD)
MFER	Ministry of Foreign Economic Relations (Russia)
MFN	Most-Favoured Nation
MHW	Ministry of Health and Welfare (Japan)
MITI	Ministry of International Trade and Industry (Japan)
MOFTEC	Ministry of Foreign Trade and Economic Cooperation (China)
NAFTA	North American Free Trade Agreement
NEDO	New Energy and Industrial Technology Development Organization (Japan)
NTE	National Trade Estimate (U.S.)
OECD	Organization for Economic Cooperation and Development
PRC	People's Republic of China
PTTNS	Public Telecommunications Transport Networks and Systems
QR(s)	Quantitative Restriction(s)
R&D	Research and Development
RBP	Restrictive Business Practice
RTC	Resolution Trust Company (U.S.)
SAA	Statement of Administrative Action (U.S.)
SIA	Sole Import Agency
SOE	State-Owned Enterprise
STA	State Trading Agreement
STE	State Trading Enterprise
STM	State Trading Monopoly
TEU	Treaty on Economic Union
TRIMs	Agreement on Trade-Related Investment Measures (WTO)
TRIPs	Agreement on Trade-Related Aspects of Intellectual Property Rights (WTO)
TVA	Tennessee Valley Authority (U.S.)
UK	United Kingdom
UNCTAD	United Nations Conference on Trade and Development

US	United States
USC(A)	United States Code (Annotated)
USDA	U.S. Department of Agriculture
USEC	U.S. Enrichment Corporation
USSR	Union of Soviet Socialist Republics
USTR	United States Trade Representative
VCLT	Vienna Convention on the Law of Treaties
VERs	Voluntary Export Restrictions
WTO	World Trade Organization

Authors and Conference Participants

Authors

FREDERICK ABBOTT, Professor, Chicago-Kent College of Law, Chicago, USA

ICHIRO ARAKI, WTO Legal Affairs Officer, Geneva, Switzerland

CHRISTIAN BACH, Assistant Professor, University of Copenhagen, Denmark

JACQUES H.J. BOURGEOIS, Attorney, Akin, Gump, Strauss, Hauer & Feld, Brussels, Belgium; College of Europe, Brugge, Belgium

THOMAS COTTIER, Professor, University of Bern, Bern, Switzerland

WILLIAM DAVEY, Director, WTO Legal Affairs, Geneva, Switzerland

VLADIMIR DREBENTSOV, Economist, World Bank, Washington, D.C., USA

CRAWFORD FALCONER, Head of Division, OECD, Paris, France

TONI HANIOTIS, Administrator, Federal Department of External Economic Affairs, Bern, Switzerland

KRISTIN HEIM MOWRY, O'Melveny and Myers, Washington, D.C., USA

BERNARD M. HOEKMAN, Counsellor, World Bank; CEPR, Washington, D.C., USA

GARY N. HORLICK, Attorney, O'Melveny and Myers, Washington, D.C., USA

HENRIK HORN, WTO, Geneva, Switzerland

ROBERT HOWSE, Professor, University of Toronto, Toronto, Canada

PATRICK A. LOW, Counsellor, WTO Services Division, Geneva, Switzerland

WILLIAM MARTIN, Development Research Group, The World Bank, Washington, D.C., USA

MITSUO MATSUSHITA, Seikei University, Seikei, Japan; Member, WTO Appellate Body, Geneva, Switzerland

AADITYA MATTOO, WTO Services Division, Geneva, Switzerland

PETROS C. MAVROIDIS, Professor, University of Neuchâtel, Neuchâtel, Switzerland

PATRICK MESSERLIN, Professor, Institut d'Etudes Politiques, Paris, France

CONSTANTINE MICHALOPOULOS, Special Economic Advisor, WTO, Geneva, Switzerland

STILPON NESTOR, Counsellor, OECD, Paris, France

N. DAVID PALMETER, Attorney, Powell, Goldstein, Frazer & Murphy LLP, Washington, D.C., USA

ERNST-ULRICH PETERSMANN, Professor, University of Geneva; Legal Advisor, WTO, Geneva, Switzerland

ANDRÉ SAPIR, Professor, Université Libre de Brussel; European Community Commission, Brussels, Belgium

DIANE P. WOOD, Judge, U.S. Court of Appeals for the Seventh Circuit; Senior Lecturer, University of Chicago, Chicago, USA

WERNER ZDOUC, Legal Affairs Officer, WTO, Geneva, Switzerland

Other Conference Participants

REMO ARPAGAUS, Research Fellow, University of Bern, Bern, Switzerland

PATRICK BLATTNER, University of Neuchâtel, Neuchâtel, Switzerland

MARCO C.E.J. BRONCKERS, Attorney, Stibbe Simont Monahan Duhot, Brussels, Belgium

CLAUS D. EHLERMANN, Professor, European University Institute, Florence, Italy; Member, WTO Appellate Body, Geneva, Switzerland

YVAN FAUCHERE, Research Fellow, University of Neuchâtel, Neuchâtel, Switzerland

CHRISTOPH GRABER, Research Fellow, University of Bern, Bern, Switzerland

MAYA HERTIG, Research Fellow, University of Bern, Bern, Switzerland

ALWIN KOPSE, Research Fellow, University of Bern, Bern, Switzerland

MAX BEAT LUDWIG, Chairman, Silva Casa Stiftung, Bern, Switzerland

KRISTA NADAKAVUKAREN SCHEFER, Research Fellow, University of Bern, Bern, Switzerland

DAMIEN NEVEN, Professor, University of Lausanne, Lausanne, Switzerland

REINHARD QUICK, Verband der chemischen Industrie, Brussels, Belgium

FABIENNE RUBIO, Research Fellow, University of Neuchâtel, Neuchâtel, Switzerland

CHRISTOPH SCHELLING, Secretary, Silva Casa Stiftung, Bern, Switzerland

LAURENT SIGISMONDI, Research Fellow, University of Neuchâtel, Neuchâtel, Switzerland

DANIEL WUGER, Research Fellow, University of Bern, Bern, Switzerland

Preface

On September 12 and 13, 1997, twenty-seven trade professionals met in the alpine village of Gerzensee near Bern, Switzerland for the first annual World Trade Forum Conference. The topic established for the 1997 Conference was how the world trading system, and in particular the World Trade Organization (WTO), regulates property ownership within states and to what extent it should do so in the future.

As is clear from the contributions to this volume, the basic question is one of determining the role of the state as an actor in international trade operations. This in turn requires an examination of areas such as state trading, the granting of exclusive rights, and competition policy.

The theme of state trading is particularly timely in view of the proposed accessions to the WTO of countries such as China and Russia, that have traditionally relied on state-owned or state-controlled enterprises as major components of their trading systems. The subject, however, is also of great importance to market economies that are already WTO members. Their traditional regulation of "public sectors" that have great domestic importance is often accomplished by a grant of a monopoly to either a government-owned or controlled enterprise or by such a grant to a private company. The extent to which the liberalization or de-monopolization of these sectors is or should be subject to WTO rules makes the topic of this year's Conference just as relevant for them as it is for the applicants to the WTO.

The World Trade Forum could not have taken place without the active involvement and support of the participants. We want to once again thank the participants, the Silva Casa Foundation, and the directors of the Gerzensee Conference Center for making the 1997 Conference a success.

The Editors

Part I: Introduction

State Trading in the Twenty-First Century:
An Overview

Petros C. Mavroidis and Thomas Cottier

Participants in the World Trade Forum dealt with a question that so far has not attracted the attention it deserves: to what extent has trade liberalisation, as we have experienced it over the last fifty years, prejudged property ownership? Trade liberalisation has not occurred in a vacuum; the General Agreement on Tariffs and Trade (GATT) constitutes its regulatory framework. The GATT has not imposed on its members any particular obligations with respect to property ownership. Essentially, its proposition in this respect is twofold: on the one hand, members of the GATT are free to regulate on this issue; on the other, in case they opt for state trading, members must respect the basic GATT principle of non-discrimination.

The WTO agreements, succeeding to the GATT regime, did not substantially modify the picture. With respect to Article XVII GATT, which regulates the field of state trading, no modifications or amendments are reported. With respect to the WTO Agreement on Subsidies, there is now a more comprehesive framework in place, but it does not directly affect property ownership in the sovereignties of the WTO Members.

This is, however, hardly surprising. The Treaty of Rome, which was supposed to regulate the much more intensive integration process of the European Community (EC), proclaims in Article 222 its ideological neutrality with respect to property ownership. Under these circumstances, and taking into account the state of play in the mid-forties when the GATT was negotiated and agreed, it would be odd to expect an "Article 222 Plus" provision in the context of the GATT.

An analysis at this level, though, is superficial. At the end of the day it is the actual everyday life of the agreement that matters most and not its original drafting. It is the way any given international regime can and does influence choices at the domestic level and the way choices at the domestic level influence the shaping of international regimes that should be analysed. This interaction (the look "inside out" and "outside in" as Keohane has aptly put it)[1] is crucial for the study at hand. In this context, the examination of state practice is of primary importance.

Such examination is particularly relevant in the EC context, where the process of deregulation can be instituted at both the state and the supranational level. If we use time as the relevant criterion, we observe that some intrusions by the European Court of Justice (ECJ) in the field of property ownership beyond the ideological neutrality of Article 222 were met with a lot of scepticism in different corners and indirectly obliged the ECJ to retreat from its original thoughts, as its subsequent jurisprudence shows.

In the WTO context, there is not much jurisprudence on this issue. This should not come as a surprise either. In a context of looser integration than that of the EC, one should expect more respect for sovereign choices, especially for choices in sensitive areas like property ownership. State trading though is present in a number of WTO agreements. A de-codification of the totality of the relevant provisions is the necessary condition for a thorough discussion of the issue.

Necessary but not sufficient. A discussion on property ownership is to a large extent circumscribed by the time-element. Economic theory has evolved on this issue through the years and so has political reality. This does not mean, however, that there is a direct correlation between the two. Economic theory can offer more useful insights on the question concerning the optimal extent of states. To what extent economic theory can attract the attention of the political establishment remains an open question. At this stage, the WTO is facing one of its more formidable tasks: the eventual accession of China and Russia. Both countries share, or at least are perceived to share, an element of direct relevance to the question we are treating in this book: extensive state trading.

State trading has been one of the most often recurring themes in the negotiations on accession of both China and Russia and it recently attracted a lot of attention among the existing WTO members. The institutional expression of such attention found its form in the establishment of a WTO Working Party on state trading enterprises, which aims precisely at re-visiting the existing multilateral regime in order to examine its adequacy to deal effectively with state trading.

In order to provide a sufficient overview of the regulation of state trading in the GATT/WTO regime, but also in order to advance thoughts on its future shaping, the authors of this volume examined the regulatory framework and state practice. Some contributors focused solely on conceptual issues.

The papers presented in the conference can be broadly classified in three categories: first, papers which aim at presenting the WTO legal framework for state trading enterprises; second, the papers dealing with regional experience in the field of state trading; and third, the papers concerned with conceptual issues. The organisers of the conference insisted that a "synergy" between lawyers and economists be the "dominant strategy" in all three categories of papers presented.

First Category: WTO Legal Framework for STEs

In the first category, papers were presented by Davey, Mattoo, Petersmann, Horlick and Heim Mowry, Palmeter, and Abbott. Zdouc provided the comment for all of them.

Davey dealt essentially with three issues: first he explores why the GATT/WTO regime needs special rules dealing with state trading enterprises; then he offers his explanation of the nature of the existing GATT rules and how they have evolved; and lastly, he touches briefly on the problem of the accession of non-market economies. With respect to the first point, Davey argues that GATT rules assume the existence of market-based economies where enterprises make decisions on the basis of economic factors, and not on the basis of economic directives. It is clear to the author that GATT rules on non-discrimination and fair trading would be easily circumvented if there were no controls on state trading. With respect to the second issue, the author says that the GATT provisions on state trading (the most important being Article XVII GATT) can be used to prevent state trading enterprises from countering market access and non-discrimination rules especially when used in conjunction with general GATT provisions that may be applicable because of state involvement in state trading enterprises. The reasons why some up-front clarity with respect to Article XVII GATT is now an issue has to do most likely with the wish of governments to leave little room for discretion to the international decision-maker called to consider such issues. Drawing on past experience, Davey argues in the context of the third issue that in the case of China it seems likely that the protocol will require a quick phase-out of its limitations on companies permitted to engage in foreign trade.

The objective of Mattoo's paper is to assess the adequacy of multilateral rules dealing with monopolies and state trading enterprises, particularly in the domain of services. He argues that since these rules depend largely on the other obligations undertaken by Members, a variety of exemptions and exclusions have weakened the rules considerably. Furthermore, liberalisation of services trade, aided by negotiations under the General Agreement on Trade in Services (GATS), is leading to changes in market structure and the pattern of ownership. These changes imply that government-mandated monopolies or non-competing oligopolies are disappearing from the infrastructure services for which Article VIII GATS is most relevant. The behaviour of those dominant suppliers that often remain does not fall within the scope of Article VIII GATS and has been addressed by creating other disciplines.

Mattoo addresses how much emphasis needs to be placed on pro-competitive regulation to ensure competitive market conditions and argues that there is need to strengthen Article VIII GATS and widen its scope to deal with certain generic problems.

Petersmann, whose paper is complementary to the one by Davey, explains in detail the mechanics of Article XVII GATT, paying particular attention to its evolution. Petersmann discusses thoroughly both procedural and substantive issues. With respect to the first set of issues, he seems to share Bhagwati's belief in the "Dracula principle" — that for a problem to be solved, first ample light needs to be thrown at it. This is why the author insists on the notification requirements under Article XVII GATT. He notices that in GATT history, under Article XVII GATT 1994, the obligation to notify (necessary in order to achieve transparency) has been consistently neglected by the contracting parties. He then goes on to suggest that unless something is done in this area, the problem could be even bigger in the future with the eventual accession of countries with large state trading sectors. With respect to substantive issues, the author makes two important points: first, he focuses his attention on what he considers to be a negative evolution: the "working definition" of state trading enterprises in the WTO Understanding seems to be narrower than that in Article XVII GATT. He expresses the view that this definition should be construed as a temporary definition for the work assigned to the WTO Working Party on state trading enterprises but that it should not prejudge the future evolution of Article XVII GATT. Second, the author underlines the need for clarifying the obligations of Article XVII GATT. In the absence of rich case-law in the field and since a formal amendment is difficult to achieve, the author proposes that such clarifying and strengthening of the obligations under Article XVII GATT could be anticipated by including precise legal obligations in future Protocols of Accession to the WTO with state trading countries. Petersmann's proposal is particularly interesting with respect to the eventual accession of China and Russia.

Horlick and Heim Mowry, Palmeter, and Abbott deal with state trading in three specific instances: subsidies, antidumping, and intellectual property. Horlick and Heim Mowry examine the interaction of Article XVII GATT with the provisions on subsidies of the WTO Agreement on Agricultural and the WTO Agreement on Subsidies and Countervailing Measures. The authors notice that the very nature of state trading enterprises creates the possibility for provisions of subsidies (especially export subsidies in the agricultural field). They further point out that the largest number of state trading enterprises notified involve agricultural products such as grains and dairy. Most of the time such subsidisation occurs either through statutory or regulatory marketing boards. With respect to state trading countries about to accede to the WTO, the authors notice that the role of state trading in non-market economies is larger than in most market economies. They notice, however, that if active WTO Members have trouble meeting the notification requirements of Article XVII GATT, it can hardly be expected that an applicant to the WTO will be able to communicate exactly how its state trading regime will fit into Article XVII requirements. Moreover, the situation would be drastically different if current applicants were admitted as developing countries to the WTO.

Palmeter essentially argues that the WTO Agreement on Antidumping does little to assist economies in transition from state planning to the free market. The author reaches his conclusion by delving into the language of the Agreement as well as in a series of proposals by former state trading GATT contracting parties to amend it. He concludes that the real antidumping reform for the economies in transition might not come until reform comes for the entire WTO which, in the author's view, is unlikely to be any time soon.

Abbott points out the ambiguous perspective of WTO members regarding highly protective rules protecting intellectual property rights on the one side, and the interest in promoting technological equivalence in the developing countries on the other. In the eyes of the author, the current WTO mainstream political view appears to favour high level of intellectual property rights' protection as of equal interest to both developed and developing country economies. The entry of new members such as China into the WTO, might, according to Abbott, result in a modification of the balance of perspectives. Both perspectives could be eventually accomodated within the literal scope of WTO legal texts.

Zdouc's comments essentially focus on the discrepancies between the economic logic and the legal drafting of Article XVII GATT. Zdouc points out that the economist's paper (Mattoo's) in this respect clearly shows dissatisfaction with respect to the interpretation of Article XVII GATT through GATT case-law. The current understanding of Article XVII GATT, in the economist's eyes, does not suffice to deal with contemporary problems in the context of state trading. Zdouc argues that the lawyers' papers in this context agree that case-law in this field has not provided the necessary input as far as the desired coverage of Article XVII GATT is concerned. At the same time though, he notices that the wording of Article XVII GATT leaves ample room for interpretation. The question consequently becomes whether such a "daring" understanding of Article XVII GATT should be the privilege of the interpreter, or conversely, whether an amendment to Article XVII GATT is necessary.

Second Category: Regional Experience in State Trading

Papers by Bourgeois, Howse, Wood, Sapir, Matsushita, Nestor, Martin and Bach, and Drebentsov and Michalopoulos were presented in the second category where Araki provided the overall comment.

The purpose of Bourgeois' contribution is to examine whether the European Community experience in dealing with import and export monopolies, state enterprises, and enterprises to which Members States grant special or exclusive rights could be relevant for the WTO. After reviewing the relevant legal developments in the EC, this contribution compares the EC and the WTO rules and argues that steps should be taken to strengthen the enforcement of the WTO rules.

Howse's paper is intended to provide a *tour d'horizon* of the interaction between the interaction of state trading practices in Canada with the world trading system, past, present, and emerging. According to the author, Article XVII GATT appears as an untenable half-way house between the national treatment obligation on the one hand and the kind of comprehensive code to ensure market contestability where state trading enterprises are present in the market on the other. But, as Howse points out, the idea of evolving Article XVII GATT into such a code seems overtaken by the multiple initiatives to clarify and develop the rules of the game where state trading enterprises are part of the picture (e.g., telecoms, financial services). As a result, Howse concludes, protective measures that now sustain, for example, Canadian marketing boards, are largely beyond challenge under existing trade law.

Wood, for her part, notices that the role of state trading at both the federal and the State government levels in the United States is for more sectors negligible. Depending on how strictly one applies the criteria laid down in Article XVII GATT to define a state trading enterprise, one could end up with a minimum of one and a maximum of twelve state trading enterprises. The existing programs in the United States are, according to the author, normally not exclusive; corporations do not have monopoly power or notable special privileges and activities have little effect on international trade flows. Wood makes the point that a simple antitrust analysis would reveal which companies were even capable of threatening the harms against which Article XVII GATT was directed; such companies are obliged to behave in a WTO-conform way not only because of the Article XVII GATT discipline, but also because of the constitutional jurisprudence of the U.S. Supreme Court. Accordingly, Wood concludes, the interest in state trading in the United States continues to manifest itself in a more defensive posture, in the sense that private traders fear that state trading practices elsewhere will put them at a disadvantage.

Sapir's paper analyses the role performed by Articles 37 and 90 ECT in the creation of a single European market in utilities, focusing on actions by the Commission and the ECJ pursuant to these two articles. It finds that the success of Community actions based on Articles 37 and 90 ECT in bringing about a single market in utilities is a mixed one. The paper contrasts the situation in telecommunications services with that of the other utilities sectors, and argues that the success in telecommunications is probably an exception rather than a forerunner of future developments toward the integration of other EC utilities markets. This pessimistic view rests on two observations. First, the telecommunications sector is characterised by a feature shared at the moment by no other utilities. Second, the Commission and the ECJ are far from enjoying the support of other Community institutions for pursuing the liberalisation of politically-sensitive utilities sectors, which would be required to ensure the legitimacy of their actions.

Matsushita analyses state trading in Japan by starting with Article 22 of the Japanese Constitution, which states that freedom of occupation (and thus trade) may be restricted for the purposes of promoting public welfare. Hence, the interpretation of public welfare becomes crucial in this context. State trading in Japan exists in a number of sectors (leaf tobacco, salt, opium, alcohol, rice, wheat and barley, milk products, and raw silk). Matsushita notices that the state trading system is currently under review in Japan in the context of deregulation of the economy. Although it is difficult to predict the future role of state trading in Japan, the author points out it is foreseeable that the state's role will decrease. Matsushita believes that this will be the case especially in the agricultural sector which is characterised by inefficiencies and high prices.

Nestor's paper presents the privatisation model proposed by the Organization for Economic Cooperation and Development (OECD). The OECD experience is particularly relevant in non-market economies where the OECD has been advising the governments of largely state trading economies on how to privatise. The author stresses the importance of unequivocal government support for the success of privatisation programmes and notes that it is important to separate *ex ante* public policy and the protection of public interest from commercial operations in large natural monopolies about to be privatised by placing firmly all regulatory functions outside the industry and minimising regulatory capture risks. Nestor underlines that high levels of transparency might help in achieving regulatory neutrality.

Martin and Bach notice that the trading regime in China has changed dramatically from the system of state trading monopolies prevailing prior to 1978. Although firms must obtain approval to trade, this has been given very liberally. A small set of products, including grains and mineral oil, is reserved for state trading monopolies and designated firms. China has committed to fully liberalise trading rights following WTO accession, including a phase-out of designated trading, but plans to retain state trading.

Drebentsov and Michalopoulos note that today in Russia trade is primarily conducted by private firms. The role of state trading has shrunk considerably, and in some respects is the last vestige of central planning, according to the authors. In support of their argument, the authors point out that Russia is applying for accession to the WTO without seeking any special consideration for state trading activities. The new regime inherited, but gradually decreased, the importance of state trading (in Russian parlance, Foreign Trade Organizations or FTOs) to sector specific FTOs, companies engaging in barter with other CIS (Commonwealth of Independent States) countries and FTOs which may enjoy certain privileges. The total value of state trading activity in Russia, the authors submit, is estimated to be twenty-four percent of total trade (exports plus imports). The authors conclude that Russia has made tremendous progress in privatising its economy and operating enterprises on a commercial basis.

Araki notes that while each state trading regime is different in its details from that of other regimes elsewhere, one common element in these different regimes is the political sensitivity of the sectors affected. There is no denying, the author notes, that state trading enterprises are used as a tool for protecting domestic industries from foreign competition. At the same time, in order to be able to benefit from such protection, the particular sector must have a political clout. Araki goes on to say that it is not surprising to see many state trading activities occur in the agricultural sector, which has strong influence in the political process of any country. He concludes that, although it is difficult to assess the overall impact of state trading enterprises in the multilateral trading system, one could hope that the global trend of regulatory reform would bring about more competition in areas which have been traditionally protected by state trading.

Third Category: Conceptual Issues of State Trading

The third category consisted of papers by Haniotis, Mavroidis and Messerlin, Hoekman and Low. Horn and Neven acted as discussants.

Economic theory typically suggests that tariffs represent superior ways of regulating trade when compared to quotas. This conclusion is based on the assumption that the quotas are distributed in some administrative fashion, for instance according to historical market shares or on a first come, first serve basis. A main message of Haniotis' paper is that quotas need not be inferior to tariffs if the quotas are distributed through auctions. A distinguishing feature of auctions, at least when conducted under full information, is that they imply competition between bidders, and as a result can be both an effective means of extracting revenue, as well as a method to efficiently allocate the sold objects. Haniotis' argument rests on three pillars. First, he provides theoretical motivations for why auctions may be socially preferred to tariffs, observing that such auctions may both extract government revenue in an efficient manner, and may avoid the inefficiencies that arise when a quota applies to products of different qualities. Secondly, Haniotis argues that auctions of quotas are legal under the existing GATT regime since they are non-discriminatory (unless explicit preferences are granted to domestic relative to foreign bidders). Thirdly, Haniotis uses some observations concerning the Swiss auctions of tariff-quotas for wine in order to argue that auction-quotas also work empirically.

In his comment on the theoretical part of Haniotis' paper, Horn discusses the restrictiveness of some of the assumptions upon which the analysis rests. Particular attention is focused on what Horn sees as an implicit assumption underlying the claim that auction quotas are socially superior to tariffs: that revenue is more socially valuable in the hands of the government than in the hands of the private sector from where it originates. While not denying this possibility, Horn expresses certain scepticism concerning the empirical plausibility of this assumption, in particular with regard to the situation in many less developed countries and economies in transition, which are the type of countries to which Haniotis' analysis is specifically meant to be applied. Horn also questions whether the Swiss experience from the auctioning of tariff quotas provides much empirical support for the superiority of auction quotas over tariffs. First, the theoretical part of the paper deals with the auctioning of regular quotas, and not tariff-quotas. Secondly, the Swiss protection of wine production might be driven by other concerns than the collection of government revenue, and the success of the auctioning must be measured with these other motives in mind.

The paper by Mavroidis and Messerlin is to a large extent complementary to the paper by Bourgeois. The authors start from the original architecture of the Treaty on the European Community (ECT) and then proceed to examine the way case-law in this field has evolved. Their analysis however, focuses on undertakings entrusted with acting in the public interest. The authors set for themselves the task of de-codifying the EC practice in this field to determine to what extent it can serve as an example for the multilateral setting. They notice that the original neutrality in Article 222 ECT as far as property ownership is concerned has been undermined by the case-law of the European Court of Justice (ECJ). The ECJ in its early case-law may have gone too far and tested the tolerance of some Member and then had to retrieve to more acceptable positions. The authors point out that especially in the later judgement, the ECJ's position is rather irreconcilable with sound economic theory (referring to the relationship between cross-subsidisation and "creaming off"). They lastly put forward the question of whether a court of is best placed to address the issue of property ownership, or whether such choices are best left to the discretion of the executive. Without providing an answer to this question, the authors alert the reader to the extra difficulty presented when the context is an international one with looser integration (like the WTO), and one where judges are called to address issues such as defining the national general interest and how it interferes with trade liberalisation.

Hoekman and Low explore alternative approaches to rule making for entities with exclusive rights. They note that state trading has been poorly attended to in the history of the GATT, not least because it was considered a relatively minor aspect of policy among the original signatories of the GATT, and in any event was most prevalent in agriculture — a sector that remained largely outside the purview of the multilateral system. They suggest that the situation is changing though, mainly because of the entry into force of the GATS and the eventual WTO accession of many economies in transition. The authors propose to further develop behavioural disciplines or alternatively to seek commitments from governments in the style contemplated by GATS, where state trading could be eliminated through negotiated commitments. They further suggest that where government policy *per se* is not the root of the problem, competition policy questions enter the picture. They strongly reject the idea, however, of addressing state trading-related problems through countervailing mechanisms of a self-help nature.

In his comments, Neven notes that Hoekman and Low effectively argue that Article XVII GATT is not powerful enough and they consider various ways in which it can be improved. One popular candidate is to make Article XVII GATT subject to competition rules at the supranational level, but these authors reject this approach because they do not want to prejudge the debate on the introduction of antitrust rules in the WTO. Yet, what the EC has done is precisely to make state trading enterprises subject to competition rules. Hence, the paper by Mavroidis and Messerlin, in Neven's view, offers particularly useful evidence for the debate on the appropriate scope of antitrust rules in the WTO. Article 90(2) ECT is, as the author notes, too general to be applied as such. Neven notes that Mavroidis and Messerlin convincingly argue that its implementation cannot and should not be left to national courts. This, in Neven's view, is right but it is only the tip of the iceberg. The existing case-law is, in the author's mind, really not very significant relative to the potential conflict that could arise across jurisdictions if Article 90 ECT were to be interpreted by national courts in the area of universal services. Serious conflicts could arise between national regulators, national courts, and the EC. Neven makes the point that Mavroidis and Messerlin would like to do away with Article 90 ECT altogether, given that in their view the scope for public services is narrow and shrinking. Neven does not share this conclusion. In his view, Article 90 ECT should be clarified possibly through a directive (given the powers attributed to the Commission under Article 90(3) ECT). The Commission, in the author's view, should define the scope of services of general interest and offer guidelines about appropriate ways of financing them. Neven lastly remarks that the notion of services of general interest should also be grounded in the twin concepts of market failures and essential services.

Conclusions

The overall conclusion that emerges from all papers presented in the conference as well as from the discussions which took place is that state trading for a number of reasons has not until recently attracted the attention it deserves, but that the picture is changing dramatically. The new disciplines committed to the multilateral system as well as the likely accession of states like Russia and China have re-focused the attention of trading nations on state trading. There was no disagreement among the participants that the way the basic disciplines on state trading have so far been interpreted in the GATT system cannot adequately address the new challenges. It is debatable however, whether imaginative reading of the existing multilateral obligations can provide a solution or whether a strengthening of the existing regime has to be sought. This discussion is closely linked to the more general discussion on the role of the international judge. Trading nations have historically preferred a limited role for the international judge. Regardless of which approach is chosen, experiences concerning state trading in other fora could prove valuable for WTO members. The participants in the conference advanced a series of such proposals as summarised above that could prove a very useful tool to WTO negotiators.

NOTE

1. See Robert Keohane, After Hegemony (Princeton, N.J.: University of Princeton Press, 1984).

Part II: The Relevant Legal Framework

CHAPTER 1

Article XVII GATT: An Overview

William J. Davey[*]

Historically, Article XVII on state trading enterprises has been one of the less well known provisions of the General Agreement on Tariffs and Trade (GATT). Recently, more attention has been paid to it, in large part because (i) such enterprises play an important role in agricultural trade, which became subject to stricter disciplines in the Uruguay Round negotiations, and (ii) the pending accession negotiations of China and Russia, where state trading still plays an important economic role. This overview of Article XVII will set out some background information on the use and importance of state trading by World Trade Organization (WTO) Members, explain the reasons why GATT needs special rules dealing with state trading enterprises, describe the existing GATT rules on state trading enterprises and their evolution, and touch briefly on the problem of the accession of non-market economies. The aim of the chapter is to provide background information on Article XVII, as other chapters will focus on a critical analysis of the provision.[1]

1. The Use and Importance of State Trading Enterprises

Governments make use of state trading enterprises for a variety of reasons. The WTO Secretariat's background paper on "Operations of State Trading Enterprises as They Relate to International Trade"[2] sub-divides state trading enterprises into several major categories: marketing boards; fiscal monopolies; canalizing agencies; foreign trade enterprises; and nationalized industries. A study of notifications to GATT revealed that most state trading enterprises are in the agricultural sector, where such enterprises are used to achieve a variety of agricultural-related policy objectives. In addition, state trading enterprises are found in industrial sectors. In the past, such enterprises have been particularly important in developing economies and in centrally planned, non-market economies.

[*]Director, Legal Affairs Division, World Trade Organization; Professor of Law, University of Illinois College of Law (on leave). The views expressed are personal and should not in any way be attributed to the World Trade Organization or its Secretariat. I would like to thank Elizabeth Shaffer of the WTO Secretariat for helpful comments on an earlier draft of the article.

State Trading Enterprises in Agriculture

State trading enterprises in the agricultural sector are used to achieve a number of policy objectives, such as (i) income support, (ii) price stabilization, (iii) expansion of domestic output, (iv) security of the food supply and (v) rationalization and control of foreign trade in order to achieve economies of scale and improve the terms of trade.[3] Such enterprises, which often take the form of marketing boards, are viewed as allowing flexible management of imports and exports so as to achieve one or more of the above-mentioned goals. The powers of marketing boards vary considerably. They often have a monopoly on the export of a product and they may also have a monopoly on (or some significant control of) the domestic market for the product. They may participate in the market directly or through private entities. A cursory review of the sixty-eight notifications (counting the EC notification as containing fifteen notifications) on state trading enterprises filed since the establishment of the WTO indicates that twenty-nine of the thirty-eight notifications indicating the existence of state trading enterprises include state trading enterprises dealing with agricultural products.

The involvement of such enterprises in export trade is significant. Recently published statistics by the U.S. Department of Agriculture show the following average annual export values of major state trading enterprises in the agricultural sector (for the years 1992–1994 or 1993–1995)[4]:

Canadian Wheat Board (wheat)	$2.9 billion
New Zealand Dairy Board	$1.8 billion
Australian Wheat Board	$1.4 billion
Queensland Sugar Corporation	$0.9 billion
China COFCO (corn)	$0.7 billion
China COFCO and others (sugar)	$0.4 billion
New South Wales Rice Board	$0.4 billion
China Native Products (tea)	$0.3 billion
Canadian Wheat Board (barley)	$0.3 billion
South Africa Deciduous Fruits Board	$0.3 billion

There are also state trading enterprises that are particularly important on the import side in agricultural trade, particularly in developing countries, but also in such countries as Japan.

One of the reasons that the issue of state trading enterprises has generally become more visible in recent years is due to concern on the part of some WTO Members, especially the United States, but also the EC, that marketing boards may distort competition unfairly. More specifically, there is a fear that these enterprises may engage in practices that were supposed to be controlled by the Uruguay Round Agreement on Agriculture. For example, according to a recent article published by the Economic Research Service of the U.S. Department of Agriculture:[5]

> [T]he lack of transparency in the pricing and operational activities of agricultural state trading enterprises (STE's) has generated growing concern that some World Trade Organization (WTO) member countries will use STE's to circumvent Uruguay Round commitments on export subsidies, market access, and domestic support.
>
> . . .
>
> The chief concern with export-oriented STE's is whether they use their exclusive power of domestic monopsony (operating as the sole purchaser of domestic production) and/or export monopoly (operating as the sole exporter of domestic supply) to engage in unfair trading competition. The lack of transparency which characterizes the operations of STE's makes it difficult to determine whether they win sales because of true competitive advantage or because of practices such as excessive price cutting. This contrasts with the explicit export subsidies of the U.S. and the European Union, which will be reduced significantly by 2001 in accordance with provisions of the Uruguay Round.
>
> Grains and dairy products are the chief exports of the agricultural STE's reported to the WTO — 16 STE's export wheat and 10 export dairy products. Two of the major export STE's — the Canadian and Australian Wheat Boards — accounted for more than 30 percent of world wheat exports from 1992 to 1995. By comparison, the U.S. and EU share 50–60 percent of world wheat trade.
>
> For dairy products, STE's reported to the WTO by Australia, Canada, New Zealand, Poland and the U.S. controlled 30–40 percent of world skim milk powder exports and about 25 percent of world cheese exports in 1993. The chief world cheese exporter is the EU with a 50 percent share of the world market in 1993. The EU also accounts for about 30 percent of world skim milk powder exports.

State Trading Enterprises in Other Sectors

State trading enterprises also exist in industrial sectors. The WTO/GATT notifications suggest that such enterprises typically deal with products important for strategic or other reasons or have resulted from nationalizations.[6]

This category includes products that are subject to so-called fiscal monopolies, such as alcoholic beverages, tobacco, salt, and matches and other inflammables. Such monopolies typically have a regulatory function, as well as providing government revenue. Other products often subject to the control of state trading enterprises for similar reasons (i.e., domestic regulatory and government revenue) are energy and minerals. A review of the WTO notifications shows that state trading enterprises in the alcohol and tobacco sectors occur in both developed and developing countries, while those in energy and minerals tend to be in developing countries.

State Trading Enterprises in Developing Economies

Studies have shown that many developing countries use various forms of state trading. A 1987 United Nations Conference on Trade and Development (UNCTAD) study of trade control measures of developing countries found that a majority of them used a single channel for imports, i.e., either a state trading monopoly (STM) or a sole import agency (SIA), for at least some products.[7] As the following table indicates, such measures were found in all regions:

Region	STM or SIA	No STM or SIA
Africa	29	22
Americas	17	19
West Asia	8	8
S/SE Asia	14	7
Oceana	0	9

Although dated, the study is a useful indicator of the pervasiveness of state trading.

Many developing and least developed country WTO Members have never made notifications to GATT or the WTO of their state trading enterprises. Of those thirteen that have made such notifications and that reported no state trading enterprises, it is noteworthy that eight are shown as not having any such enterprises in the UNCTAD study as well, while five were shown as having had such enterprises in 1987.[8] The UNCTAD study indicates that the extent of state trading in individual developing countries ranged from only one product to virtually all products. While the products were often agricultural, there was a wide variety of products listed — from pharmaceuticals to cement to playing cards.

State Trading Enterprises in Non-Market Economies

In non-market economies, it is common to have enterprises with monopoly rights over foreign trade, either generally or in respect of specific products. With the decline in the number of non-market economies, especially among the WTO membership, this type of state trading enterprise has become less common. Where such enterprises exist in countries wishing to accede to the WTO, the status of such enterprises may be a major subject in the accession negotiations.

The case of China is instructive as an example of the decline, although not the elimination, of state trading in former non-market economies.[9] Until 1978, foreign trade was subject to a centralized state planning process. Once the plan was established, it was implemented by twelve foreign trade corporations, each of which had exclusive rights as to the import and/or export of certain products.[10] Since 1978, there has been considerable change in the Chinese economy and now planning in respect of foreign trade has been largely eliminated. At the end of 1993, less than twenty percent of total imports (involving fourteen products) and about fifteen percent of exports were subject to canalization, i.e., trade was required to be conducted through a limited number of specific foreign trading enterprises. It remained the case, however, that other imports and exports could generally be imported or exported only by enterprises authorized to engage in foreign trade. However, the number of foreign trade enterprises had increased from 12 to 8,800 and in addition some 80,000 foreign-funded enterprises had trading rights in respect of specific products.[11]

2. Why Does GATT Need Special Rules on State Trading Enterprises?

In the first instance, it is important to consider the question: why does GATT need special rules on state trading enterprises? The answer is straightforward. In essence, GATT needs special rules on state trading enterprises because GATT rules often assume the existence of a market-based economy where enterprises make decisions on the basis of economic factors, not government directives. If one examines the basic GATT rules on non-discrimination, market access, and fair trading, it is clear that evasion of those rules would be easily possible if there were no controls on state trading enterprises.[12]

For example, the basic GATT rules on non-discrimination are the most-favored nation clause of Article I and the national treatment clause of Article III. A state trading enterprise could choose to ignore commercial considerations and favor particular exporting countries or national competitors of imports through its purchasing and resale decisions. If it did so, it would effectively subvert GATT's non-discrimination requirements.

To take the example of market access, the basic GATT rules are the prohibition of quotas in Article XI and the procedures for binding tariffs in Article II. GATT assumes that in an economy without quantitative restrictions, an agreement to bind tariffs at non-prohibitive levels and reduce them over time will allow increased access for imported products. Where a state trading enterprise has a monopoly on the importation of a product, that result cannot be assured in respect of that product. The effect of a quota may be duplicated by the purchasing decisions of the state trading enterprise even if there is technically no government decision limiting imports. The effect of a bound tariff may be undercut by decisions of the state trading enterprise concerning the resale price it charges for the imported product. That is, it may set the price high so as to curtail demand for it.

The basic GATT rules on fair trading — Article VI on antidumping and the rules dealing with the use of subsidies — are also difficult to apply to state trading enterprises, particularly in countries where state trading is the rule.[13] In the case of dumping, there may be no valid home-market prices or costs to serve as a basis for the dumping calculations. In the case of subsidies, it may not be meaningful to speak of subsidies in an economy where state control is pervasive. The export subsidy commitments of the Uruguay Round Agreement on Agriculture may be difficult to enforce if a state trading enterprise in the agricultural sector operates both domestically and internationally. Determining whether a subsidy on exports is being granted may involve difficult accounting issues.

The problems discussed above may differ in intensity depending on whether the individual state trading enterprise is situated in an economy that is predominantly market-oriented or in an economy that is predominantly a non-market economy. While the nature of the problems is the same, the problems are obviously more significant when state trading is pervasive in an economy.

3.   The GATT Rules on State Trading Enterprises

The General Agreement addresses the problem of state trading mainly in Article XVII, and the specific situation of import monopolies in Article II:4. Article XVII provides as follows:

State Trading Enterprises

1.   (a)   Each Member undertakes that if it establishes or maintains a State enterprise, wherever located, or grants to any enterprise, formally or in effect, exclusive or special privileges, such enterprise shall,

in its purchases or sales involving either imports or exports, act in a manner consistent with the general principles of non-discriminatory treatment prescribed in this Agreement for governmental measures affecting imports or exports by private traders.

The provisions of sub-paragraph (a) of this paragraph shall be understood to require that such enterprises shall, having due regard to the other provisions of this Agreement, make any such purchases or sales solely in accordance with commercial considerations, including price, quality, availability, marketability, transportation and other conditions of purchase or sale, and shall afford the enterprises of the other Members adequate opportunity, in accordance with customary business practice, to compete for participation in such purchases or sales.

No Member shall prevent any enterprise (whether or not an enterprise described in sub-paragraph (a) of this paragraph) under its jurisdiction from acting in accordance with the principles of sub-paragraphs (a) and (b) of this paragraph

The provisions of paragraph 1 of this Article shall not apply to imports of products for immediate or ultimate consumption in governmental use and not otherwise for resale or use in the production of goods for sale. With respect to such imports, each Member shall accord to the trade of the other Members fair and equitable treatment.

The Members recognize that enterprises of the kind described in paragraph 1 (a) of this Article might be operated so as to create serious obstacles to trade; thus negotiations on a reciprocal and mutually advantageous basis designed to limit or reduce such obstacles are of importance to the expansion of international trade.

4.   (a)   Members shall notify the [WTO] of the products which are imported into or exported from their territories by enterprises of the kind described in paragraph 1 (a) of this Article.

A Member establishing, maintaining or authorizing an import monopoly of a product, which is not the subject of a concession under Article II, shall, on the request of another Member having a substantial trade in the product concerned, inform the [WTO] of the import mark-up* on the product during a recent representative period, or, when it is not possible to do so, of the price charged on the resale of the product.

The [WTO] may, at the request of a Member which has reason to believe that its interest under this Agreement are [sic] being adversely affected by the operations of an enterprise of the kind described in paragraph 1 (a), request the Member establishing, maintaining or authorizing such enterprise to supply information about its operations related to the carrying out of the provisions of this Agreement.

The provisions of this paragraph shall not require any Member to disclose confidential information which would impede law enforcement or otherwise be contrary to the public interest or would prejudice the legitimate commercial interests of particular enterprises.

Paragraphs 3 and 4 were added as a result of the 1955 Review Session.

The text of Article XVII directly addresses some of the problems discussed in the preceding section. However, there are a number of other problems that have arisen over the years. These include, *inter alia*,

1. the problem of defining the scope of application of Article XVII (i.e., what is a state trading enterprise);

2. what are the general principles of non-discriminatory treatment mentioned in Article XVII:1(a) GATT;

3. what does the phrase "commercial considerations" mean in Article XVII:1(b) GATT;

4. what is the significance to state trading enterprises of Article II:4 and the interpretative note to Articles XI *et seq.* GATT;

5. what is the scope of the obligation in the last phrase of Article XVII:1(b) GATT (i.e., "afford the enterprises of the other Members adequate opportunity, in accordance with customary business practice, to compete for participation in such purchases or sales"); and

6. what is the scope of the transparency provisions of Article XVII:4 GATT?

This chapter will address each of these issues in turn.

Definition of State Trading Enterprise

First, there is a problem of definition. Article XVII:1 GATT is not very precise. By its terms, it covers (i) state enterprises and (ii) enterprises granted exclusive or special privileges.[14] The original draft U.S. charter provided: "[f]or purposes of this Article, a State enterprise shall be understood to be any enterprise over whose operations a Member government exercises, directly or indirectly, a substantial measure of control".[15] This definition was not included in the final version of Article XVII. It appears that some countries were concerned that it was too broad. This concern is also reflected in other discussions of Article XVII, where Jackson concludes that there were some countries who feared that the U.S. proposals would place greater restrictions on state traders than on private enterprises.[16]

At the Havana conference, the relevant negotiating sub-committee noted that "it was the general understanding that the term [state enterprise] includes, inter alia, any agency of government that engages in purchasing and selling".[17]

In 1960, the Contracting Parties adopted a report on "Notifications of State-Trading Enterprises", in which some additional precision was given to the definition for the purpose of clarifying the enterprises subject to the notification requirement.

> [T]he Panel did not use the word "enterprise" [in connection with the scope of the notification requirements] to mean any instrumentality of government. There would be nothing gained in extending the scope of the notification provisions of Article XVII to cover governmental measures that are covered by other articles of the General Agreement. The term "enterprise" was used to refer either to an instrumentality of government which has the power to buy or sell, or to a non-governmental body with such power and to which the government has granted exclusive or special privileges.[18]

However, the actual experience with notifications of state trading enterprises clearly showed that different GATT contracting parties interpreted the term differently. By and large, there were relatively few such notifications in any event.[19]

The 1994 Understanding on the Interpretation of Article XVII includes the following working definition for notification requirements:

> Governmental and non-governmental enterprises, including marketing boards, which have been granted exclusive or special rights or privileges, including statutory or constitutional powers, in the exercise of which they influence through their purchases or sales the level or direction of imports or exports.

There remains some vagueness. For example, the scope of the phrase "exclusive or special rights or privileges", and the degree of "influence" required.[20] This vagueness may be reduced over time, however, since the Understanding provided for the establishment of a working party on state trading enterprises, which, inter alia, is to develop an illustrative list showing the kinds of relationships between governments and enterprises, and the kinds of activities engaged in by these enterprises, which may be relevant for purposes of Article XVII. The illustrative list has not yet been agreed upon, but the United States and New Zealand have put forward specific proposals for it.

It should be noted in conclusion that most of the work on defining the term "state trading enterprise" has been aimed at establishing clearer rules for notification. The definitional issue has not yet been considered by dispute settlement panels.

Article XVII:1(a) GATT – General Principles of Non-Discriminatory Treatment

Paragraph 1(a) of Article XVII addresses the problem of discriminatory behavior by state trading enterprises by requiring Members to undertake that their state trading enterprises shall act in a manner consistent with the general principles of non-discriminatory treatment prescribed in GATT. This provision is somewhat oddly worded in that *Members* undertake that *enterprises* shall act in a given way. Typically, WTO obligations are concerned with governmental behavior only. In this connection, it is interesting to note that paragraph 1(c) of Article XVII provides that Members shall not prevent *any* enterprise from acting in accordance with the principles of paragraphs 1(a) and 1(b) of Article XVII.[21]

More significantly, however, there has been disagreement over whether the phrase "general principles of non-discriminatory treatment" refers only to most favored nation treatment and not to national treatment. The drafting history can be read to suggest that only MFN treatment is required. For example, in the original U.S. proposal only MFN treatment was required, and there is an explicit statement in the relevant sub-committee that this was the intention.[22] This interpretation also finds support in two panel reports.[23] A U.S. proposal in the Uruguay Round to explicitly subject state trading to the national treatment obligation was not accepted, although the 1994 Understanding does state in its preamble that "Members are subject to their GATT 1994 obligations in respect of those governmental measures affecting state trading enterprises".

This definitional uncertainty would not be of great significance to the degree that other GATT articles, such as Article III, apply to state trading. In this regard, it should be noted that one of the panels suggesting that there is no national treatment obligation in Article XVII, did apply Article III to the challenged measure.[24] However, a panel will be able to apply Article III only if the challenged action may be viewed as a governmental measure, i.e., a "law, regulation or requirement". When this is the case, the definitional uncertainty will not be important. It is not clear, however, that this will often be the case, which means that this definitional issue remains an important shortcoming in the application of Article XVII.

Article XVII:1(b) GATT – Commercial Considerations

Paragraph 1(b) of Article XVII specifies that it is understood that the provisions of subparagraph (a) require state trading enterprises to make their purchases and sales in accordance with commercial considerations. This provision appears to address the possibility that state trading enterprises could negate the results of tariff negotiations by indirectly imposing quantitative restrictions through their purchasing decisions or offsetting the effect of a tariff binding through their pricing policies. The scope of this provision may be narrower than it appears at first blush, however, as one panel has noted that this requirement is stated to be an interpretation of the non-discrimination provisions of subparagraph (a), and as a result the panel considered that it is applicable only if the action at issue falls within the scope of the general principles of non-discriminatory treatment.[25] This interpretation obviously reduces the potential of Article XVII to prevent state trading enterprises from engaging in market access limiting activities.

As to the meaning of the phrase "commercial considerations", the interpretative notes and the drafting history indicate that Article XVII:1(b) would not preclude the charging by a state trading enterprise of different prices in different export markets[26]; nor consideration of the advantages of receiving a "tied loan" in connection with a purchase[27]. Moreover, it was understood that the phrase "customary business practice" as used in Article XVII:1(b) was intended to cover business practices customary in the respective line of trade.[28]

Article II:4 and the Interpretative Note to Article XI *et seq.*

There are two GATT provisions other than Article XVII that are particularly important in limiting the possibility that state trading enterprises may offset market access commitments through their business decisions. First, the interpretative note to Articles XI, XII, XIII, XIV and XVIII of GATT states that "[t]hroughout [those] Articles . . ., the terms 'import restrictions' or 'export restrictions' include restrictions made effective through state-trading operations". This provision provides a basis on which to attack quota-like restrictions implemented through state trading enterprises, and panels have so used it.[29] For example, in one case the interpretative note was applied to find that certain practices, followed by certain state trading enterprises, that discriminated against imported products violated Article XI, thus effectively imposing a national treatment obligation on the state trading enterprises in question.[30] It should be noted, however, that those enterprises were government agencies.

The second provision, Article II:4, explicitly provides that an import monopoly shall not operate so as to afford protection on the average in excess of the amount of protection provided for in the relevant schedule. It reads as follows:

> If any Member establishes, maintains or authorizes, formally or in effect, a monopoly of the importation of any product described in the appropriate Schedule annexed to this Agreement, such monopoly shall not, except as provided for in that Schedule or as otherwise agreed between the parties which initially negotiated the concession, operate so as to afford protection on the average in excess of the amount of protection provided for in that Schedule.

An interpretative note to Article II:4 provides that it shall be applied in light of the provisions of Article 31 of the Havana Charter, which in relevant part provides as follows with respect to the quantities to be imported:

> 5. With regard to any product to which the provisions of this Article apply, the monopoly shall, wherever this principle can be effectively applied and subject to the other provisions of this Charter, import and offer for sale such quantities of the product as will be sufficient to satisfy the full domestic demand for the imported product. . . .[31]

As to the price to be charged:

> 4. The import duty negotiated . . . shall represent the maximum margin by which the price charged by the import monopoly for the imported product (exclusive of internal taxes . . ., transportation, distribution and other expenses incident to the purchase, sale or further processing, and a reasonable margin of profit) may exceed the landed cost. . . .

Dispute settlement panels examining the practices of Canada's provincial liquor boards have had occasion to apply these rules and have concluded that they prevent an import monopoly from charging prices in excess of costs plus a reasonable margin of profit.[32] Thus, although there has only been limited use of this provision, it does provide a basis on which import monopolies may be prevented from restricting import levels inappropriately, either through their purchasing or pricing practices.[33]

Purchasing By State Trading Enterprises

Paragraph 1(b) of Article XVII contains what appears to be an obligation in respect of government procurement. It provides that state trading enterprises shall "afford the enterprises of the other Members adequate opportunity, in accordance with customary business practice, to compete for participation in such purchases or sales". As noted above, the scope of Article XVII is understood to extend to any government agency that engages in purchasing and selling. That government procurement is subject to Article XVII is confirmed by paragraph 2 of Article XVII, which contains an exception similar to that in Article III:8 for government procurement:

The provisions of paragraph 1 of this Article shall not apply to imports of products for immediate or ultimate consumption in governmental use and not otherwise for resale or use in the production of goods for sale. With respect to such imports, each Member shall accord to the trade of the other Members fair and equitable treatment.

The requirement of "fair and equitable treatment" derives from the original U.S. proposal, which would have covered government procurement more generally.[34] That proposal was ultimately not accepted, although the limited obligation of Article XVII:1(b) was retained. Given the view discussed earlier that the obligations of paragraph 1(b) are only in the nature of MFN obligations, the "fair and equitable treatment" obligation may be viewed as requiring a form of MFN treatment in government procurement. There has never been a dispute settlement panel interpretation of this obligation.

Transparency Obligations of Article XVII

Paragraph 4 of Article XVII requires Members to inform the WTO of the products that are imported into or exported from their territories by state trading enterprises.[35] Under a 1962 GATT decision[36], Members are to submit "new and full" notifications every three years and to submit updating notifications in each of the intervening two years. The "new and full" notifications are intended to provide a complete record of a Member's state trading activities, while the updating notifications are to report changes that have occurred in between the new and full notifications. These obligations have often been overlooked in the past, as relatively few notifications have been filed. Between 1982 and 1994, for example, notifications ranged from six to eleven per year.[37]

In 1995, in order to start the notification process under the WTO and in order to permit the Working Party on State Trading Enterprises to conduct its work in a timely manner on the basis of complete information, the Council for Trade in Goods decided that notifications in 1995 on state trading enterprises should be new and full notifications.[38] This decision resulted in an improvement in the number of Members complying with the notification requirement. To date, sixty-eight full notifications have been received (counting the EC notification as fifteen), while there were forty-two updated notifications filed in 1996 (including the EC) and fifteen in 1997.

The format of the notifications is set out in a 1960 GATT decision, which establishes a questionnaire to be answered in respect of state trading enterprises.[39] The 1960 questionnaire is divided into six parts:

First, it requires the listing of products (or groups of products) for which a state enterprise is maintained or for which an enterprise has exclusive or special privileges.

Second, it requires the purpose for introducing and maintaining the enterprise to be given for each product.

Third, for each product ("item"), it requires a description of (i) whether the enterprise deals with exports and/or imports; (ii) whether private traders are allowed to export and/or import and any conditions, and whether there is free competition between the private traders and the state trading enterprise; (iii) the criteria used to determine the quantities to be exported or imported; (iv) how export prices are determined, how the mark-up on imported products is determined and how export and import resale prices compare with domestic prices; and (v) whether long-term contracts are used.

Fourth, it requires statistics for each product in respect of imports, exports, and national production for the last three years, broken down to show trade by the state trading enterprise and other trade.

Fifth, it requires an explanation of why no foreign trade in the product has taken place, if that is the case.

Sixth, it requests any additional information as appropriate.

The scope of the information requested is rather broad, and there have been complaints about the usefulness of the information notified.

The Working Party on State Trading Enterprises, established by the 1994 Understanding, is working to improve the notification process, and a series of drafts of a revised questionnaire have now appeared. In general, the drafts aim at providing more specific and detailed information, which would be relevant to assessing the activities of state trading enterprises in light of

GATT rules. In addition, the Working Party serves as a forum for the review of the notifications and has established a procedure under which written questions about a notification and responses thereto are circulated to Members generally. This process has led in some cases to more enterprises being added to notifications.

Summary

It was noted above that one potential problem with state trading enterprises in the GATT system is that they could effectively undermine GATT non-discrimination provisions through their purchasing and selling decisions. They could, for example, undermine the MFN clause by choosing to buy a product from only Member A and not from Member B, even though A and B offered comparable products, or undermine the national treatment clause by choosing a domestic supplier rather than either A or B. Article XVII:1(a) deals directly with the MFN part of this problem. As interpreted to date, it may not, however, deal with the national treatment aspect. To the extent that Article III applies in any event (e.g., when a state agency is involved or where the actions challenged can be considered to be governmental measures), the lack of inclusion of a specific national treatment obligation in Article XVII:1(a) is not so serious. However, in cases where there is no governmental measure involved (in terms of Article III), there is a lacuna in the GATT rules on state trading.

The second potential problem noted in respect of state trading enterprises was that they could undermine a Member's market access commitments through their purchasing and pricing policies. For example, they could simply refuse to purchase products or purchase only limited quantities, thereby effectively imposing a quota that would not be permitted under Article XI.[40] Similarly, they could price imported products at such a level as to discourage their resale on the domestic market. To the extent that GATT precedents have interpreted the requirement in Article XVII:1(b) to act in accordance with "commercial considerations" to apply only in repect of the Article XVII:1(a)'s non-discrimination requirement, Article XVII:1(b) cannot be relied upon to address these problems. As noted above, however, the application of Articles III and XI directly to state trading enterprises where their actions may be viewed as governmental, the interpretative note to Article XI and the rules on import monopolies in Article II:4 provide a means to address them.

The third potential problem noted in respect of state trading enterprises was that they made WTO rules on "fair trade" difficult to apply. Article XVII does not address the problems that state trading enterprises present, particularly in non-market economies, for the application of antidumping duties and rules relating to subsidies, except through its transparency provisions. The problem of subsidies is of particular concern and explains what appears to be a renewed interest in the topic of state trading. With the extensive involvement of marketing boards in international agricultural trade, as outlined above, there are concerns in some quarters that state trading enterprises could be used to evade commitments in the Agreement on Agriculture on export subsidies and market access.

4. The Problems of Accession of Non-Market Economies

The foregoing discussion concerns rules that apply to a single state trading enterprise. The same rules, of course, would apply to a country with many state trading enterprises. However, the problems caused by allowing countries with non-market economies and many state trading enterprises into GATT and the WTO has raised special concerns, not in the least because of a sense that the rules described above are not sufficient to deal with such economies.

The initial U.S. proposal for an International Trade Organization, out of which only GATT emerged, contained a provision in the state trading chapter as follows:

> Any Member establishing or maintaining a complete or substantially complete monopoly of its foreign trade with other Members shall [*inter alia*] . . . undertake to import in the aggregate over a period products of other Members valued at not less than an amount to be agreed upon. This purchase arrangement will be subject to periodic adjustment.[41]

This provision was not included in GATT.

Starting in the late 1960s, three countries with non-market economies — Poland, Romania, and Hungary — negotiated their accessions to GATT. In each case, there was concern that Article XVII was not adequate to deal with the problems of a non-market economy and that additional commitments were needed to ensure that the market access of those countries would not be offset indirectly.[42]

In the 1960s when Poland negotiated its accession to the WTO, consideration was given to requiring it to commit (i) to import certain quantities of certain products, (ii) to use its increased export earnings to expand imports, and (iii) to increase its imports by a certain percent annually. The third mechanism was chosen, and Poland's 1967 accession protocol provided in Annex B, "Poland shall . . . undertake to increase the total value of its imports from the territories of contracting parties by not less than 7 per cent per annum".[43]

In practice, this provision proved to be unworkable because Poland lacked the necessary foreign exchange to implement it. In addition, as a result of a concern over whether their exports to Poland would in fact increase as a result of Poland's market access commitments, the protocol permitted the other GATT contracting parties to maintain their existing quotas on Polish goods (subject to an undefined phase-out) and to apply selective safeguard measures on Polish imports that caused or threatened serious injury. There were supposed to be annual reviews of the Polish protocol, but these were often not held. In 1990 Poland requested that the protocol be renegotiated, but it never was.[44]

In the case of Romania, it argued that as a developing country it should be subject to less demanding terms of accession than Poland. The Romanian protocol of accession provided that Romania

> will develop and diversify its trade with the contracting parties as a whole, and firmly intends to increase its imports from the contracting parties as a whole at a rate not smaller than the growth of total Romanian imports provided for in its Five-Year Plans.[45]

As in the case of Poland, the protocol permitted the maintenance of quotas by existing contracting parties on Romanian imports (with a 1974 target for removal) and for the possibility to apply selective safeguards on Romanian exports. In the reviews of the protocol, both sides expressed dissatisfaction with its implementation.[46]

In the case of Hungary, it claimed that its customs tariff was a significant factor in regulating imports and that it should therefore be allowed to accede on the basis of its tariff commitments, without any special import commitment. While this claim was accepted, the protocol did contain provisions allowing other contracting parties to maintain quotas on Hungarian imports and did subject Hungarian exports to selective safeguards.[47] There was also dissatisfaction expressed by both sides in reviews of this protocol.

Two former non-market economies have acceded to the WTO — Bulgaria and Mongolia. In both cases they had, prior to their accession, liberalized their foreign trade regimes so that any business is permitted to engage in importation and exportation. In both cases, they had also undertaken extensive privatization programs. Generally speaking, they committed in their accession protocols to comply with WTO rules and were not made subject to special additional obligations. Their commitments, it should be mentioned, were often expressed in rather detailed terms as to when and how they would remove WTO-inconsistent measures.

For the moment, the WTO continues to face the problem of how best to deal with the accession of non-market economies. The problem has taken on

particular importance because of the economic importance to world trade of
two of the accession applicants — China and Russia.[48]

NOTES

1. See in particular E.-U. Petersmann, "Article XVII GATT on State Trading Enterprises: Critical Evaluation and Proposals for Reform," in this volume; A. Mattoo,
"Dealing with Monopolies and State Enterprises," in this volume.

2. G/STR/2 (26 October 1996) (hereinafter "Secretariat Background Paper").

3. Secretariat Background Paper, paras. 4–8.

4. K. Ackerman, P. Dixit, and M. Simone, "State Trading Enterprises: Their Role in
World Markets," in: U.S. Department of Agriculture, Economic Research Service,
Agricultural Outlook (June 1997) at 11, 12. Based on WTO notifications, except for
China.

5. Id. at 11.

6. Secretariat Background Paper, para. 5.

7. United Nations Conference on Trade and Development, *Handbook of Trade Control Measures of Developing Countries 1987* (New York: UNCTAD, 1997).

8. The definition used by UNCTAD was not the WTO definition and may well have
been broader. In the case of two of the five countries reporting no state trading enterprises, questions were raised in the Working Party as to the accuracy of the notifications.

9. See generally W. Martin & C. Bach, "State Trading in China," in this volume.

10. World Bank, *China: External Trade and Capital* 18–19, 22–23 (Washington,
D.C.: World Bank, 1988).

11. Tseng, Khor, Kochhar, Mihaljek & Burton, *Economic Reform in China: A New
Phase* (IMF, No. 1994).

12. See generally J. Jackson, *World Trade and the Law of GATT* 331 (1969); J.
Jackson, W. Davey & A. Sykes, *Legal Problems of International Economic Relations* 1140–1142 (3rd ed. St. Paul: West Publishing, 1995).

13. See generally G. Horlick and K. Heim Mowry, "The Treatment of Activities of
State Trading Enterprises Under the WTO Subsidies Rules," in this volume; D.
Palmeter, "The WTO Antidumping Agreement and the Economies in Transition," in
this volume.

14. An interpretative note to Article XVII indicates that this definition covers marketing boards that purchase and sell but not those that only regulate the purchase and
sale of a product.

15. Quoted in GATT, *Analytical Index* 473 (6th rev. ed. Geneva: WTO, 1995).

16. Jackson, op. cit., 334.

17. Havana Reports, 114, para. 10, quoted in *Analytical Index*, op. cit., 473.

18. Adopted on 24 May 1960, BISD 9S/179, 183–184, paras. 21–23.

19. Under GATT, from 1980 to 1994, the number of notifications ranged from eighteen (1981) to six (1985). Secretariat Background Paper, Annex. There were 85 contracting parties to GATT in 1980, 128 in 1994.

20. The phrase "exclusive or special privileges" in Article XVII:1(a) does not encompass governmental measures to ensure quality and efficiency in external trade or certain privileges granted for the exploitation of natural resources. Interpretative note to Article XVII:1(a). In addition, it appears from the drafting history that the phrase was not intended to include certain tax exemptions. *Analytical Index*, op. cit., 474–475.

21. For reasons discussed below, this provision has been interpreted to apply only to the non-discrimination obligations found in paragraph 1(a), as the requirements of paragraph 1(b) have been viewed as limited to interpreting paragraph 1(a).

22. See *Analytical Index*, op. cit., 475.

23. Belgian Family Allowances, adopted on 7 November 1952, BISD 1S/59, 60, para. 4; Canada - Administration of the Foreign Investment Review Act, adopted on 7 February 1984, BISD 30S/140, 163, para. 6.16.

24. Canada - Administration of the Foreign Investment Review Act, id.

25. Id.

26. Interpretative note to Article XVII:1.

27. Interpretative note to Article XVII:1(b).

28. *Analytical Index*, op. cit., 477.

29. Canada - Import, Distribution and Sale of Alcoholic Drinks by Canadian Provincial Marketing Agencies, adopted on 22 March 1988, BISD 35S/37, 89, para. 4.24; Japan - Restrictions on Imports of Certain Agricultural Products, adopted on 2 February 1988, 35S/163, 229, paras. 5.2.2.1–5.2.2.2; Republic of Korea - Restrictions on Imports of Beef - Complaint by the United States, adopted on 7 November 1989, BISD 36S/268, 301–302, paras. 114–115.

30. Canada - Import, Distribution and Sale of Alcoholic Drinks by Canadian Provincial Marketing Agencies, id. A later panel examining similar practices found that they violated Article III and that it was therefore unnecessary to decide if they violated Article XI. Canada - Import, Distribution and Sale of Certain Alcoholic Drinks by Provincial Marketing Agencies, adopted on 18 February 1992, BISD 39S/27, 74–75, paras. 5.3–5.4.

31. There is an exception applicable if the product is rationed.

32. Canada - Import, Distribution and Sale of Alcoholic Drinks by Canadian Provincial Marketing Agencies, adopted on 22 March 1988, BISD 35S/37, 87–88, paras. 4.13–4.19; Canada - Import, Distribution and Sale of Certain Alcoholic Drinks by Provincial Marketing Agencies, adopted on 18 February 1992, BISD 39S/27, 80–82, paras. 5.17–5.22.

33. Article II:4 is only applicable where there is a scheduled concession. As a result of the Uruguay Round, the percentage of products subject to tariff bindings has increased considerably, although coverage is certainly not universal. Paragraph 4(b) of Article XVII provides that where a product is not subject to a concession, a Mem-

ber shall inform the WTO of the mark-up on the product if requested to do so by a Member having a substantial trade in the product.

34. See generally Annet Blank & Gabrielle Marceau, "A History of Multilateral Negotiations on Procurement: From ITO to WTO," in: Bernard M. Hoekman & Petros C. Mavroidis (eds.), *Law and Policy in Public Purchasing: The WTO Agreement on Government Procurement* (Ann Arbor: University of Michigan Press, 1997).

35. In addition, on request Members are to inform other Members of the mark-ups charged by state trading enterprises and of other information concerning their operation, subject to confidentiality considerations.

36. Subsidies and State Trading: Procedures for Notifications and Review, Decision of 9 November 1962, BISD 11S/58.

37. Secretariat Background Paper, Annex.

38. G/C/M, pp. 5–6 (27 March 1995).

39. BISD 9S/179, 184–185.

40. Similar trade distortion could be effected on the export side.

41. Described in *Analytical Index*, op. cit., 478.

42. See generally M. Kostecki, *East-West Trade and the GATT System* (New York: St. Martin's Press, 1978).

43. Protocol for the Accession of Poland, BISD 15S/46, 52.

44. See Jackson, Davey & Sykes, op. cit., 1150–1151.

45. Protocol for the Accession of Romania, BISD 18S/5, 10.

46. Jackson, Davey & Sykes, op. cit., 1151–1152.

47. Jackson, Davey & Sykes, op. cit., 1152. See Protocol for the Accession of Hungary, BISD 20S/3.

48. See generally W. Martin & C. Bach, "State Trading in China," in this volume; V. Drebentsov & C. Michalopoulos, "State Trading in Russia," in this volume.

CHAPTER 2

Dealing with Monopolies and State Enterprises: WTO Rules for Goods and Services

Aaditya Mattoo[*]

Multilateral trade rules on monopolies and state trading enterprises (STEs) do not create any general obligations to change either the market structure or the pattern of ownership. Nor are these rules primarily designed to prevent anticompetitive behaviour in order to achieve economic efficiency. Rather, their purpose is to prevent monopolies and STEs from behaving in a way that undermines the multilateral market access obligations undertaken by governments. This concern arises because such enterprises may be subject to government control or, in the case of monopolies, because market power creates scope for autonomous behaviour which has the effect of subverting multilateral rules.

The rules that apply to monopolies and STEs, however, are not the same in the domains of goods and services. To an extent, this is not surprising since the problems that can arise in the two domains are different. In the case of goods, concern has been raised primarily by the operation of STEs which are exclusive buyers (sellers) abroad on the behalf of domestic consumers (producers). The perishability of most services largely precludes such intermediation. At the same time, in services there is much greater concern about monopoly control over essential facilities. This is because, first, such control is more frequently observed in services, such as telecom and transport networks and terminals, than in goods. Secondly, the same perishability of services reduces the scope for arbitrage and enables monopolistic discrimination in segmented markets in a way that is seldom possible with goods.

There are, however, also similarities in the concerns that arise in goods and services. In both domains there are examples of exclusive or non-competing final producers, for instance in energy production and distribution, communications, health, or education services, that often constitute the only or major source of demand for the producers of certain specialized inputs. The lack of competition in the markets for their output may allow

---

[*]The views expressed in this chapter are those of the author and should not be ascribed to the WTO Secretariat. This chapter has benefited from the comments of the conference participants and of Rolf Adlung, Julian Arkell, Pierre Latrille, and Adrian Otten.

them to deviate from strictly commercial considerations in their input purchases. The objective of this chapter is to assess the adequacy of multilateral rules in addressing these concerns, with an emphasis on the problems arising in the domain of services where such rules are relatively new. The next section undertakes a comparison of GATS Article VIII dealing with monopolies and GATT Article XVII dealing with STEs, highlighting the difference in the domains and disciplines of these two articles. Section 2 focuses on the limitations of GATS Article VIII, and Section 3 shows how it has been necessary to modify and elaborate on its rules to deal with sector-specific issues in telecommunications and maritime transport. Section 4 assesses the scope for addressing anticompetitive practices in services under existing rules, and Section 5 presents a simple framework to analyze the implications for trade and regulatory policy of alternative technological situations. Section 6 concludes the chapter.

1. Comparing GATS Article VIII with GATT Article XVII

Table 1 juxtaposes certain elements of Article XVII of the GATT 1994, as well as the Uruguay Round Understanding on the Interpretation of Article XVII of GATT 1994, with Article VIII of the GATS.

Scope

The domain of GATT Article XVII is significantly wider than that of GATS Article VIII, both in terms of the entities covered and their activities. GATT Article XVII, which contains the substantive disciplines on STEs, covers all state enterprises and those private enterprises which have been granted exclusive or special privileges.[1] The Understanding on the Interpretation of Article XVII, which is relevant only for notification purposes, narrows the scope to enterprises (public or private) that have been granted exclusive or special rights or privileges. Thus, state enterprises which are not recipients of privileges or rights need not be notified even though they continue to be subject to GATT Article XVII disciplines.

GATS Article VIII resembles the Understanding in taking a market structure-based view as opposed to an ownership-based view, but is still narrower in scope. Its domain includes only monopolies (i.e., sole suppliers) and those oligopolies which behave like monopolies. Some form of government involvement is a necessary condition insofar as it is required that the monopoly or non-competing oligopoly be "authorized or established formally or in effect" by a member (GATS Article XXVIII:h). Natural monopolies and oligopolies which exist without any facilitating government action are outside the scope of GATS Article VIII.[2]

It is notable that Article VIII refers to the supply of the monopoly service "in the relevant market". This concept has received significant attention in competition law, but here it is sufficient to note that a judgement of what constitutes the relevant market may, therefore, be necessary to establish whether or not a "monopoly" exists. For instance, the government may provide exclusive rights to a private supplier to operate a particular port or a particular highway. If the relevant market is defined narrowly in geographical terms, then the operators would be considered monopolists. However, a wider view, taking into account the competition offered by proximate ports or alternative routes, may suggest that the exclusive rights do not amount to a monopoly.

An important respect in which the scope of GATS Article VIII differs from that of GATT Article XVII is that obligation in the former relates only to the "supply of the monopoly service" and not to "purchases or sales" as in the latter. The implication is that under the GATS, a monopoly's behaviour in its input market is not subject to any disciplines.

GATT Article XVII excludes from the scope of its main disciplines "imports of products for immediate or ultimate consumption in governmental use and not otherwise for sale or use in the production of goods for sale".[3] The line dividing government procurement from state trading is not always clear, but the language here implies that any government purchases which are sold either directly or indirectly would be covered by the disciplines of Article XVII.[4] It is also relevant that Ad Article XVII states that the term "goods" is not intended to include the purchase or sale of services. This would seem to suggest that the purchase of goods for use in the production of services is not covered by Article XVII. Hence, taking stock of all the exclusions, we find that neither GATT Article XVII nor GATS Article VIII deals with the purchases by covered entities of goods or services to produce services, or the purchase of services to produce goods.

Disciplines

In the WTO context, Article XVII of GATT 1994 and Article VIII of GATS have an unusual aspect: they both apply to the behaviour of enterprises, not to government rules of general application. Thus GATT Article XVII requires that any covered enterprises acts in a manner consistent with the general principles of non-discriminatory treatment (in its purchases or sales). This obligation has been interpreted in some instances only to imply an MFN obligation, i.e., a prohibition of discrimination between imports on the basis of country of origin, and not a national treatment obligation (see

Jackson 1992:284). The reasons for this narrow interpretation are not clear because the "general principles of non-discriminatory treatment prescribed in this Agreement" would seem to include national treatment. It is also specified, in Article XVII:1(b), that such enterprises shall make any

> purchases or sales solely in accordance with commercial considerations, including price, quality, availability, marketability, transportation and other conditions of purchase or sale, and shall afford foreign enterprises adequate opportunity, in accordance with customary business practice, to compete for participation in such purchases or sales.

Disciplines on STEs in the goods context are also contained in other Articles of GATT 1994. Thus, import monopolies are required not to operate so as to afford protection above the level of tariff bindings (Article II:4) and STEs cannot be used to give effect to import or export restrictions inconsistent with the general rules of the GATT on such measures (Ad Articles XI, XII, XIII, XIV and XVIII).

In some respects, the disciplines in Article VIII of the GATS resemble those in Article XVII of GATT 1994. The basic obligation is that the monopoly supplier of a service should not, in the supply of the monopoly service in the relevant market, act in a manner inconsistent with a member's MFN obligation and specific commitments. There are, however, some important differences with the Article XVII obligation. Consider, for instance, the requirement that a monopoly service supplier must respect the specific commitments under GATS on both market access and national treatment. Yet both only apply in scheduled sectors and there too are subject to limitations. The scope of the Article VIII disciplines, therefore, crucially depends on the extent to which members have made liberalizing specific commitments. Under GATT 1994, this is mirrored to an extent by the requirement that mark-ups on imported goods charged by STEs should not violate tariff bindings, the extent and level of which differs between members. However, while the rules against quantitative restrictions apply more generally in GATT 1994 than in the GATS (which allows quantitative market access limitations), the obligation on STEs to provide national treatment apparently does not apply at all in GATT 1994 but does in the GATS to the extent members have made specific commitments in this respect.

It is, however, the different implications of the MFN obligation that are perhaps the most interesting. GATT Article XVII does not prevent a state enterprise from practising price discrimination in its sales. Notably, Paragraph 1 Ad Article XVII states:

The charging by a state enterprise of different prices for its sale of a product in different markets is not precluded by the provisions of this Article, provided that such different prices are charged for commercial reasons, to meet conditions of supply and demand in export markets.

On the other hand, the charging by a monopolist telecom supplier of different prices for termination services to foreign telecommunications suppliers, or by a monopolist port operator of different rates to different foreign ships, could in principle be held to be inconsistent with Article VIII:1. Why does this difference arise? One argument could be that in the goods case, price discrimination pertains to behaviour in export markets, whereas in the case of essential intermediate services, price discrimination would lead to discrimination between imports from different foreign sources. The latter presumably raises more serious concerns than the former.[5]

Transparency of Existence and Behaviour

It has been recognized that it is difficult to enforce the disciplines on state enterprises since the required monitoring of their *behaviour* (rather than rules of general application) is rarely feasible. The creation of transparency has therefore received emphasis. GATT Article XVII only required a notification of products imported or exported from their territory by covered enterprises. The Understanding created a requirement to notify all enterprises which had been granted exclusive or special rights. In the GATS, a certain degree of transparency is achieved by the requirement to specify measures inconsistent with Article XVI in scheduled sectors with respect to bound modes. Thus, if a member wishes to maintain a monopoly or any other restriction on the number of suppliers, this must be specified in its schedule. Furthermore, in Article VIII there is a requirement to notify monopoly rights granted after the entry into force of the WTO Agreement that affect the supply of a service covered by specific commitments. A gap in information arises with respect to sectors not included in the schedules, or if the relevant mode of supply (commercial presence) is unbound.

Both Agreements create similar obligations with regard to the transparency of operations. Members may, at the request of a member which has reason to believe that its interests under the Agreement are being adversely affected by the operations of a covered enterprise, request the member establishing, maintaining, or authorizing such an enterprise to supply information concerning relevant operations.

GATT Article XVII goes further in requiring a member establishing, maintaining, or authorizing an import monopoly of a product which is not subject to a tariff to inform members of the import mark-up on the product concession (or, when this is not possible, of the resale price) upon the request by a member having a substantial trade in the product. Moreover, the Understanding creates an obligation on each member to conduct a review of policy to ensure maximum transparency in its notifications so as to permit a clear appreciation of the manner of operation of the enterprises and the effect of their operations on international trade.

Table 1. A Comparison of GATT Article XVII and GATS Article VIII

	GATT Article XVII and the Understanding on the Interpretation of Article XVII	GATS Article VIII
Scope	All state enterprises, and any enterprise granted, formally or in effect, exclusive or special privileges. Understanding: Governmental and non-governmental enterprises that have been granted exclusive or special rights or privileges in the exercise of which they influence the level or direction of imports or exports through their purchases or sales.	Any monopoly supplier: any person, public or private, that is authorized or established formally or in effect by that member as the sole supplier of such service in the relevant market of the territory of a member; and exclusive service suppliers: where a member, formally or in effect, (a) authorizes or establishes a small number of service suppliers; and (b) substantially prevents competition among those suppliers in its territory.
Disciplines	In its purchases or sales involving either imports or exports, act in a manner consistent with the general principles of non-discriminatory treatment. Shall make any purchases or sales solely in accordance with commercial considerations, and shall afford foreign enterprises adequate opportunity, in accordance with customary business practice, to compete for participation in such purchases or sales.	In the supply of the monopoly service in the relevant market, act in a manner consistent with that member's obligations under Article II (MFN) and specific commitments. If the monopoly supplier competes in the supply of a service outside the scope of its monopoly rights and which is subject to specific commitments, the supplier shall not abuse its monopoly position to act in its territory in a manner inconsistent with such commitments.
Transparency of existence	Requirement to notify products that are imported or exported by covered enterprises. Understanding: requirement to notify enterprises under new definition. Also provision for counter-notification.	Requirement to notify monopoly rights regarding the supply of a service covered by specific commitments granted after the entry into force of the WTO Agreement.
Transparency of behaviour	A member establishing, maintaining or authorizing such an enterprise may be requested	A member establishing, maintaining, or authorizing such a supplier may be requested to

	to supply information about its operations if a member has reason to believe that its interests under the Agreement are being adversely affected by such operations. And shall, on the request of a member having a substantial trade in a product, which is not subject to a tariff concession, inform members of the import mark-up on the product or, when this is not possible, of the resale price. Understanding: each member is required to conduct a review of policy to ensure maximum transparency in its notifications so as to permit a clear appreciation of the manner of operation of the enterprises and the effect of their operations on international trade.	provide specific information concerning the operations of a monopoly supplier if a member has reason to believe that the monopoly supplier is acting inconsistently with Article VIII:1 or 2.

The Approach to Eliminating the Restrictive Effect of STEs and Monopolies

Both the GATT and the GATS allow members to maintain STEs and monopolies. As noted above, the Agreements themselves create no obligations to change either the pattern of ownership (from public to private) or the market structure.[6] GATT Article XVII:3 does contain a collective recognition that STEs might be operated so as to create serious obstacles to trade, and recognizes the importance of negotiations designed to reduce such obstacles. Such negotiations between members have usually pertained to aspects of the behaviour of STEs, such as the level of mark-ups on imports, but recent accession negotiations have also been concerned with the elimination of exclusive rights.[7]

However, what is an exception in the goods context is the rule in the services context. GATS defines trade to include the supply of services through establishment of commercial presence which could be through foreign ownership of existing (government-owned) suppliers or through new entry into markets which were previously the subject of monopoly rights. Changes in ownership and market-structure have, therefore, been central to the negotiations. The collective commitment to progressive liberalization contained in the GATS could be expected to translate into a further reduction in the scope of state-owned entities and state-mandated monopolies.

Privatization and liberalization, however, do not always go hand-in-hand. In several cases, state-owned monopolies have been replaced, at least temporarily, by private monopolies. For instance, in Pakistan's basic telecommunications schedule, the government has committed to privatizing part of the state provider, but has maintained its exclusive rights for a period of seven years. Similarly, an entry for Italy in the GATS schedule of the European Union states that exclusive rights may be granted to, or maintained for, newly-privatized companies. One reason why governments find this pattern tempting is that privatization may be more easily accomplished or may yield greater revenue if liberalization is delayed.

2. An Assessment of GATS Article VIII

This Section argues that GATS Article VIII in itself is of limited current relevance. First, what the article covers may well be less important than what it excludes. Government-mandated pure monopolies or non-competing oligopolies are disappearing from the infrastructural services for which Article VIII is most relevant, notably telecommunications. The behaviour of the dominant suppliers that often remain does not fall within its scope and must be disciplined through other means (which include the Annex on Telecommunications and the additional commitments undertaken in basic telecommunications and maritime transport discussed in the next Section). Furthermore, the exclusion of purchasing behaviour of non-competing public enterprises may not be innocuous.[8]

Secondly, since the article's disciplines depend exclusively on the other obligations undertaken by members, a variety of exemptions have weakened Article VIII in key areas. These include the understanding that accounting rates in basic telecommunications would not be an issue for dispute settlement for some time, the suspension of the MFN obligation for the maritime sector and the limited specific commitments in the sector, and finally, the exclusion of air traffic rights from the scope of the GATS.

Where Are the Monopolies?

First, consider the existing domain of Article VIII. Where are the monopolies (or non-competing oligopolies) to be found whose *supply* behaviour merits concern? The answer is most commonly in "locational services" like transport, telecommunications, and energy distribution which frequently require specialized distribution networks, such as roads, rails, cables, pipes, and satellites (see UNCTAD and World Bank, 1995). There may also be need for specialized equipment for transmitting or receiving the service, such as telephone exchanges, railway stations, airports, and ports. Even though it is usually possible to introduce competition in certain segments of the markets for such services, the high barriers to entry due to the need for large initial investment in other segments may lead to the existence of natural monopolies. Thus, while different airlines may compete with each other on the same route, they are usually obliged to use the same airport, as is the case with maritime transport companies and ports. It has also been easier to introduce competition in long-distance telephone calls than in the provision of local calls, where technologies which reduce the optimal scale of operation have only recently emerged. Similarly, while some countries have introduced competition in electricity generation, electricity distribution is still subject to (regional) monopolies. In many of these situations, therefore, monopolistic market structures are a consequence of the state of technology, without the need for supporting government action. However, such action often exists as well, if only to extend the scope of the monopoly beyond what would be technologically necessary.

What about monopolies in areas where there is no technological reason for their existence? As noted in the section on transparency, Article XVI obliges members to indicate in scheduled sectors, with respect to the modes of supply that they choose to bind, if certain restrictions on market access are maintained, including limitations on the number of service suppliers. Table 2 contains the results of an examination of the GATS schedules of commitments for sectors other than basic telecommunications where members have indicated that a monopoly is or exclusive rights are maintained. The sparseness of the table probably reflects an absence of commitments by members in sectors where government-mandated monopolies exist, and the table should be seen as illustrative rather than exhaustive.

Again, the focus in this section is on monopolies whose supply behaviour causes concern. Non-discriminatory access to placement and supply services of personnel may be important for locally established foreign firms which are obliged to hire local personnel by restrictions on the movement of labor. The monopolies in the supply of pharmaceutical goods (i.e., pharmacists), tobacco, and certain retailing services do not reflect the existence of a single seller, but rather the need to fulfil certain conditions in order to qualify as a supplier of these products. These monopolies may have implications for the non-discriminatory distribution of foreign goods rather than services.

Table 2. Monopolies or Exclusive Rights Scheduled as Limitations on Market Access

Sector	Countries
Business services	
Supply of pharmaceutical goods to the general public (pharmacists)	Belgium, Denmark, Spain, France, Greece, Italy, Luxembourg, Portugal
Placement and supply services of personnel	Belgium, France, Italy, Spain, Norway
Legal services	Iceland (exclusive rights)
Communication services	
Value-added telecom services	Turkey
Computerized airline reservation services	Mexico
Construction services	
Construction and maintenance of highways and Rome airport	Italy (exclusive rights)
Maintenance of highways	Portugal (exclusive rights)
Distribution services	
Wholesale trade service	Spain, Italy, Portugal
State monopoly on tobacco	
Retailing services	Spain, France, Italy
Environmental services	
Refuse disposal services	Norway
Some categories of waste	
Control services of exhaust gas from cars and trucks	Norway, Sweden
Recreational, cultural, and sporting services	
Gambling and betting services	Senegal
Transport services	
Cargo handling	Aruba, Benin, Ghana, Netherlands, Antilles
Storage and warehouse services	Benin, Ghana
Container station and depot services	
Supporting services for air transport	Mexico
Rail transport services	Turkey
Management of highways	Italy, Portugal (exclusive rights)
Management of Rome airport	Italy (exclusive rights)
Road transport	Iceland (exclusive rights)
Financial services	
Motor vehicle insurance	Canada (Quebec, Manitoba, Saskatchewan, British Columbia)

Sector	Countries
	Australia (in most States and Territories)
Fire and natural damage insurance on buildings	Switzerland (in nineteen cantons)
Workers compensation	Australia (Southern Australia, Queensland, Victoria)
Mandatory or facultative reinsurance	Brazil
Residential property disaster insurance	New Zealand
Management of pension funds of public and para-public institutions	Canada (Quebec)
Registration of securities	Norway
Securities custodial depository services	Singapore
Settlement and clearing services	Turkey, Italy
Public utilities	
Sector coverage variable	EU Member States, Slovenia, Turkey

Source: Compiled from GATS Schedules

The monopolies in financial services mostly pertain to certain mandatory insurance services. Among the most significant instances of monopolies are those in public utilities, which certainly exist in many more members than have chosen to indicate their existence. The EU schedule notes that services considered as public utilities at a national or local level may be subject to public monopolies or to exclusive rights granted to private operators. According to the schedule, public utilities exist in sectors such as environmental services, health services, transport services, and services auxiliary to all modes of transport.

The basic telecommunications sector merits a separate examination. In the recently concluded negotiations on basic telecom under the GATS, sixty-nine governments made multilateral commitments, in many cases granting significantly liberalized access to their markets to foreign services and service suppliers (table 3). Taking into account both immediate liberalization (L) and phased-in liberalization (P), fifty-five governments committed to competition among infrastructure-based operators (defined here as permitting two or more) in public local voice telephony, fifty-two in domestic long-distance, and fifty-six in international service. Forty-two governments will allow simple resellers to offer public voice telephony. It is true that nearly half the WTO members did not make any commitments on basic telecommunications, and that in many of these markets there is a persistence of monopoly. But in terms of world market share, network competition will be allowed in eighty percent of the market by the beginning of 1998, and in an additional six percent by the year 2005. On the whole, there is overwhelming evidence that the development of modern telecommunication technologies, characterised by relatively small optimal scales of production combined with liberalization of access, has overturned conventional wisdom about telecom infrastructure being inevitably monopolised.

Table 2 shows that monopolies in transport services may appear in terminal services, such as cargo handling, and networks, such as railroads and highways. It may also be useful to consider the commitments which members have made regarding supporting services for various transport services. These may reveal the extent to which there are policy restrictions on the supply of terminal services for various modes of transport. In maritime transport, only eleven members have made commitments in the area of port services, of which just two (Australia and Gambia) have fully liberalized access to foreign service suppliers. In supporting services for air transport, thirty-three members have made commitments, of which only five (Bulgaria, Cuba, Gambia, Nicaragua, Sierra Leone) have fully liberalized the right of foreign suppliers to establish commercial presence. Only five members have made commitments with respect to supporting services for road and rail transport, with four (Gambia, Guyana, Iceland, Norway) and two (Nicaragua, Norway), respectively, imposing no restrictions on the establishment of commercial presence.

To sum up, pure monopolies in the sense of Article VIII (i.e., those with facilitating government action), are disappearing from telecommunications — in part, due to the success of GATS negotiations in liberalizing telecom markets. Where they persist, or are replaced by dominant suppliers, it is often due to the nature of the technology. Certain aspects of transport services, relating to terminals, roads, and railway tracks, and aspects of energy distribution have similar technological features. However, the lack of GATS commitments in these areas suggests that the government may have a role in the persistence of monopolies beyond areas where it is a technological necessity.

Table 3. Results of the Basic Telecommunications Negotiations

Participant	Local	Dom'stic long distance	Internat'l	Resale	Add'l. comms. Ref. Paper (2) (6)
Antigua & Barbuda			P		+
Argentina	P	P	P	P	+
Australia (3)	L	L	L	L	+
Bangladesh	L	L			

Participant	Local	Dom'stic long distance	Internat'l	Resale	Add'l. comms. Ref. Paper (2) (6)
Belize					+
Bolivia	L	P	P	P	
Brazil (3) (5)					
Brunei Darussalam	(6)		L		+
Bulgaria	P	P	P		+
Canada	L	L	P	L	+
Chile		L	L	L	+
Colombia	L	L	L		+
Cote d'Ivoire	P	P	P	P	+
Czech Republic	P	P	P	P	+
Dominica					+
Dominican Republic	L	L	L	L	+
Ecuador					
El Salvador	L	L	L	L	+
European Union (4)	L	L	L	L	+
Ghana	L (6)	L (6)	L (6)		+
Grenada	P	n.a.	P	P	+
Guatemala	L	L	L	L	+
Hong Kong	L	n.a.	L	L	+
Hungary	P	P	P	P	+
Iceland	L	L	L	L	+
India	L	L (6)	(6)		+
Indonesia	L (6)	L (6)	L (6)		+
Israel (5)	(6)	(6)	L (6)		+
Jamaica	P	P	P		+
Japan	L	L	L	L	+
Korea	L	L	L	P	+
Malaysia	L	L	L		
Mauritius	P	P	P		
Mexico	L	L	L	L	+
Morocco	P	P	P		
New Zealand	L	L	L	L	+

Participant	Local	Dom'stic long distance	Internat'l	Resale	Add'l. comms. Ref. Paper (2) (6)
Norway	L	L	L	L	+
Pakistan	P	P	P	P	+
Papua New Guinea					+
Peru	P	P	P	P	+
Philippines	L	L	L		
Poland	L	P	P	P	+
Romania	P	P	P	P	+
Senegal					+
Singapore	P	n.a.	P		+
Slovak Republic	P	P	P	P	+
South Africa	P (6)	P (6)	P (6)	P	+
Sri Lanka					+
Switzerland (3) (5)					+
Thailand					
Trinidad & Tobago	P	P	P	P	+
Tunisia	P				
Turkey					
United States	L	L	L	L	+
Venezuela	P	P	P		
Total schedules (55)	41	38	42	28	0
Total governments (69)	55	52	56	42	14

Source: WTO

Explanatory Notes for Table 3

(1) L indicates that the service will be "liberalized" (i.e., can be supplied by at least two suppliers) as of 1 January 1998. P indicates that liberalization will be phased-in at a later date.

(2) + indicates that the member incorporated the Reference Paper on regulatory principles with few, if any, modifications.

(3) Commitments made conditional upon the passage of relevant national legislation.

(4) Phase-in of facilities-based voice service applies for Greece, Ireland, and Portugal.

(5) Where no public voice telephone commitments are indicated, voice over closed user groups is nonetheless committed.

(6) Commits to review the possibility of allowing market access for additional suppliers.

Do the Exclusions Matter?

As noted above, neither GATT Article XVII nor GATS Article VIII covers the purchases by covered entities of goods or services to produce services, or the purchase of services to produce goods. Furthermore, firms operating in a competitive environment are excluded from the scope of GATS Article VIII regardless of whether they are privately- or publicly-owned. Some of these exclusions are covered by the plurilateral Agreement on Government Procurement, but only twenty-three WTO members are signatories to this Agreement, and its coverage, particularly of services, is limited in certain respects.

For the purchasing decision of an enterprise to evoke concern, two conditions need to be fulfilled: first, the firm does not operate in a competitive market for its output; second, its purchases of a particular good or service are large compared to domestic supply.

An enterprise operating in a competitive market is unlikely to be able to afford the luxury of procuring intermediate service inputs from any but the most competitive seller. Thus, non-competitive product markets would seem to be a necessary condition for distorted purchase decisions. The source of the distortion could then be either government influence or anticompetitive practices by a firm enjoying significant market power. Creating disciplines on government action or influence would fall clearly within the domain of the GATS. But it would seem unnecessary to impose disciplines on public enterprises operating in competitive conditions, and may even lead to inefficiencies.[9] At the same time, there may be a need for disciplines on private enterprises operating in non-competitive environments. Thus, market structure in the final goods market is a more important consideration than the nature of ownership.

Even though operating in a non-competitive product market is a necessary condition for a firm to be able to deviate from strictly commercial considerations in its purchases, it may not be sufficient to merit concern. Baldwin (1970, 1984) and Baldwin and Richardson (1972) are among those who have shown that if non-discriminating demand is sufficiently large and if domestic and foreign goods are perfect substitutes, then in a perfectly competitive context, extending preferential treatment to domestic industry by a particular entity neither reduces imports nor increases domestic price, output, or employment. Discriminatory procurement is ineffectual because shifting demand toward domestic products by a particular entity tends to increase their prices and, therefore, generates an equal and opposite shift in the demand of non-discriminating entities toward imports.

This result can be qualified in certain important respects. Perhaps most importantly, the discriminating entities' demand may be a large part of total domestic demand.[10] More precisely, if the discriminating entities' demand is larger than the quantity supplied domestically in the non-discriminatory equilibrium, then shifting their demand towards domestic producers can clearly have real effects — such as increased domestic output and reduced imports. Thus, a revealing empirical test would involve comparing the magnitude of such entities' demand with the quantity supplied domestically at the notional free trade price in order to determine when discriminatory purchases are likely to affect trade and output.

Consider the two questions in turn: first, where do enterprises (public or private) continue to operate in non-competitive environments? In the case of goods, inadequate access to the upstream market for goods has evoked significant concern in energy generation and other utilities. In the area of services, large non-competing government enterprises still exist in the health and education sectors, as well as in the transport and communications sectors. The question that arises is whether the purchases of such enterprises qualify as government procurement. If they do, such purchases are excluded from the scope of the disciplines of both GATT 1994 and GATS. Furthermore, the line between employment and purchases of services (say of doctors and teachers) may be blurred. In a splintered world, there is clearly greater scope for competition between suppliers than in a vertically integrated world.

The second question, regarding the importance of purchases of goods and services by non-competing entities relative to domestic supply, is not easy to address. Data on procurement, which is sufficiently disaggregated to make the homogeneity assumption plausible, is difficult to find. At a somewhat aggregated level, Francois et al. (1995) find that in the United States purchases by state enterprises in total demand tends to be small. The share of state purchases is largest in maintenance and repair construction, but even there it is less than ten percent of aggregate demand. A key variable, in terms of the test identified above, is the share of public enterprise purchases in total domestic production. Again, even aggregate non-defence procurement (including purchases for own use and by enterprises) accounts for a substantial share of domestic output only in construction-related services and in the ophthalmic and photographic equipment sector.

The relative insignificance of purchases by state enterprises is probably not generalizable to countries other than the United States. In contrast to many other countries, the United States does not have a telecommunications monopoly, a state-owned airline, or full state ownership of utilities. Thus, Francois, et al. (1995, table 9) show that public ownership of the type found in certain European Union states would imply significant government presence in the markets for engines, turbines, transportation equipment, communications, pipelines, air transport, rail and motor freight services, communications equipment, computer and data processing services, as well as financial and non-medical professional services.

It seems, therefore, that the conditions for discriminatory purchases to adversely affect imports may be fulfilled in certain areas. If a fuller empirical examination confirms this, then the challenge would be to create effective disciplines in the areas where they are needed without creating unnecessarily burdensome regulation in areas where they are not.

The Problem of Weakened Disciplines

Accommodating Accounting Rates in Telecommunications

As discussed above, monopolies (or non-competing oligopolies), whose supply behaviour merits concern, are to be found most commonly in "locational services" like transport and telecommunications. If one were to identify the central purpose of Article VIII, it would be to prevent national monopolies from undermining the MFN obligation through price-discrimination. Interestingly, the accounting rate system in basic telecommunications is the most obvious example of such price-discrimination, but it has been virtually exempted from the scope of GATS disciplines. Furthermore, unilateral measures designed to counter the system may themselves fall foul of the MFN obligation.

The accounting rate system was adopted to compensate carriers for the costs of providing international telephone calls. It is widely recognized that the accounting rates negotiated with carriers located in non-competitive markets are substantially above costs and that they discriminate between different countries of origin according to "what the market will bear". This discrepancy between costs and rates has widened due to technological development in the telecommunication industry. This means that the cost of international telephone calls have remained higher than they would in competitive conditions.[11] The strongest justification of the system is that it helps generate revenues for developing country telecommunication operators. Such revenues are needed to fund investment in domestic systems and provide a useful source of hard currency.

The MFN obligation would have prevented price-discrimination, but it would allow the charging of a uniform monopoly price. Furthermore, the implications for global welfare of the shift from the former to the latter are ambiguous. A discriminating monopolist sets prices which would be inversely related to the respective elasticities of demand. The move to uniform pricing, which an MFN obligation would necessitate, is bound to make the monopolist worse off because the uniform price it is now obliged to charge in each segment could at worst also have been charged in segmented markets. Consumers in low elasticity markets are adversely affected by price discrimination and prefer the uniform price; consumers in high elasticity markets prefer price discrimination.[12] Price discrimination causes the marginal rates of substitution to differ among consumers and is therefore socially inferior to uniform prices if aggregate output is unchanged in the two situations. Thus, a necessary condition for price discrimination to increase welfare is that it raise total output — that is, that it reduce the distortion caused by monopolistic pricing.[13]

Not surprisingly, five countries (Bangladesh, India, Pakistan, Sri Lanka, and Turkey) that have telecom monopolies in international services listed MFN exemptions to cover the application of differential accounting rates. In order to prevent a spate of such exemptions being listed, an understanding was reached, reflected in the Report of the Group on Basic Telecommunications. Agreement was reached so that application of such accounting rates would not give rise to action by members under dispute settlement in the WTO. This understanding is to be reviewed no later than commencement of the next comprehensive round of services negotiations (due to begin no later than the year 2000).

Suspension of Key Disciplines in Maritime Services and
Air Transport Services
Even though the maritime transport sector is an integral part of the GATS, for the moment it is not subject to its full disciplines. First, the application of the MFN obligation to this sector has been temporarily suspended. Secondly, since it has not yet been possible to reach a negotiated agreement on the level of specific commitments that members are willing to make, the existing market access and national treatment commitments are limited to those which certain members have been willing to make unilaterally.

The suspension of the MFN obligation was prompted by the difficulty in eliminating MFN-inconsistent measures in the maritime sector.[14] One example of such measures are the bilateral cargo-sharing arrangements — such as those under the United Nations Code of Conduct for Liner Conferences — which favour the trading partner at the expense of third countries. A somewhat different example of an MFN-inconsistent measure are unilateral retaliatory actions taken by a member against trading partners who, in its perception, resort to restrictive foreign trade practices.

International air transport services are for the most part governed by arrangements negotiated under the Chicago Convention. The Annex on Air Transport Services in the GATS specifically excludes the Chicago Convention's complex network of bilateral agreements on air traffic rights from the new services rules. Consequently, the GATS applies at present only to aircraft repair and maintenance services, the selling and marketing of air transport services (a function defined as not including the pricing or conditions of transport services), and computer reservation systems as far as the air transport sector is concerned.[15] A provision for review of developments in the air transport sector to be undertaken at least once in every five years leaves the door open for a possible future extension of GATS commitments in the sector.

In sum, if the MFN principle does not apply to key service areas, and if members have made no or limited commitments, then Article VIII's function of ensuring that monopoly suppliers do not undermine a member's obligations loses much of its meaning. Of course, it remains possible that GATS disciplines will be extended to these areas. If so, and if government-mandated monopolies persist, then Article VIII may again assume relevance.

3. Going beyond Article VIII: Developing Alternative Disciplines

Telecommunications

The telecommunications sector is the focus of two additional sets of rules: the generally applicable Annex on Telecommunications and the Reference Paper which has been incorporated into the schedules of commitments by around sixty WTO members.[16] At the risk of some oversimplification, we can see the Annex as primarily a response to the central role of telecommunications as a medium of transporting services. Similarly, the Reference Paper can be viewed as a response to the particular difficulties in achieving liberalization in a sector characterized by significant network externalities.

The Annex on Telecommunications: Reinforcing Access Guarantees for Users

The Annex on Telecommunications was drafted during the Uruguay Round by negotiators who realized that despite Article VIII, telecom operators were in a unique position of having the potential to undermine commitments undertaken in schedules — not only on telecom but on any service sector in which telecommunicating was essential to doing business. Three aspects of the Annex make it a much more powerful defender of the rights of users of telecommunications services than Article VIII. First, it is silent about market structure and therefore applies regardless of whether the services in question are supplied by a monopoly or through competition. This reflects the fact that not just monopolies, but also dominant operators in a more competitive regime might engage in unfair practices restricting access and use.

Secondly, the Annex contains its own non-discriminatory disciplines on telecom service suppliers and, unlike Article VIII, does not depend on the sector-specific obligations undertaken by members. The Annex requires governments to ensure that other member's suppliers are afforded reasonable and non-discriminatory access to and use of public telecommunications transport networks and services (PTTNS) for the supply of a service included in its schedule.[17] The term "non-discriminatory" refers to most-favoured nation and national treatment as defined in the Agreement, as well as to sector-specific usage of the term to mean "terms and conditions no less favourable than those accorded to any other user of like public telecommunications transport networks or services under like circumstances". The suppliers of any service listed in a government's schedule, for example financial services, are thus assured of non-discrimination with respect to access to and use of telecom services even if a member has not committed to national treatment with respect to that particular service.

Finally, the Annex offers greater specificity in certain areas than Article VIII. For instance, it elaborates further on transparency obligations for the sector. It requires members to ensure that relevant information on conditions affecting access to and use of public telecom transport networks and services is publicly available. It also lists examples of such measures. These include tariffs and other terms and conditions of service, specifications of technical interfaces with such networks and services, and conditions applying to attachment of terminal or other equipment.

The Reference Paper: Ensuring Competition in the Supply of Telecom Services

In the basic telecommunications negotiations, there was concern that despite the commitments to liberalize both trade and investment, telecommunications markets would still frequently be characterized by dominant suppliers that controlled bottleneck or essential facilities. This could be because this sector has for a long time been monopolised, and despite efforts to break-up these monopolies, control over key infrastructural facilities will not immediately be diversified. Or it could be that large fixed-costs and economies of scale render some markets inherently incontestable (i.e., given the minimum efficient scale of operation, the market was simply not large enough to accommodate more than one or two suppliers). In any case, the concern was that dominant players in the telecom market, left free to make decisions about how to treat other suppliers, would be capable of frustrating the market access and national treatment commitments made by governments in the negotiations.[18]

Furthermore, participants felt that neither Article VIII nor the Telecom Annex would be adequately equipped to deal with potential anticompetitive practices. First, Article VIII did not cover dominant suppliers who may face limited competition. While the Annex was wider in scope, there were some doubts over whether the interconnection guarantees it contained applied to rival telecom suppliers and not just to the users of telecom services. Secondly, there was concern that the disciplines contained in Article VIII and the Annex were too general to guard sufficiently against the possible anticompetitive practices. For example, the Annex contained no clear disciplines, beyond "reasonableness", over the pricing or promptness of access or on bundling practices.

In anticipation of these problems, some sixty governments participating in the basic telecommunication negotiations made additional commitments under Article XVIII of the GATS to apply certain regulatory principles contained in a Reference Paper.[19] The Reference Paper is wider in scope than Article VIII and its domain is clearer than that of the Annex. Its disciplines apply to any "major supplier". This term is defined as one who

> has the ability to materially affect the terms of participation (having regard to price and supply) in the relevant market for basic telecommunications services as a result of: (a) control over essential facilities; or (b) use of its position in the market.

"Essential facilities" are defined to mean facilities of a public telecommunications transport network or service that (a) are exclusively or predominantly provided by a single or limited number of suppliers; and (b) cannot feasibly be economically or technically substituted to provide a service. Notably, the conditions to qualify as a "major supplier", and therefore to be subject to the disciplines in the Reference Paper, do not include government responsibility for its existence, unlike in the case of Article VIII monopolies. The Reference Paper also makes clear that its adherents must ensure that major suppliers will allow linking with *other suppliers* of public telecommunications transport networks or services, an issue on which the Annex was apparently not adequately clear.

The disciplines of the Reference Paper can also be seen as going beyond those contained in Article VIII and the Annex. In the current context, the most interesting relate to *interconnection* and *competition safeguards*.[20] Interconnection must be on non-discriminatory, transparent and reasonable terms, conditions (including technical standards and specifications), and rates; of a quality no less favourable than that provided for its own like services or for like services of non-affiliated service suppliers or for its subsidiaries or other affiliates; at cost-oriented rates; in a timely fashion; sufficiently unbundled so that a supplier need not pay for network components or facilities it does not require; at any technically feasible point in the network; and upon request, at points in addition to the network termination points offered to most users (albeit allowing for charges that reflect the construction cost of necessary additional facilities). The requirement to offer interconnection at "cost-oriented rates", for instance, goes much further than anything in the Annex or Article VIII.

Competition safeguards oblige members to prevent a major supplier from abusing control over information, or engaging in anticompetitive cross-subsidization. The safeguards are to prevent a major supplier from using profits made in one segment of the market to subsidize its *output* sales in another segment and thus drive out rival suppliers. Certain disciplines against cross-subsidization can already be read in Article VIII:2, however there the discipline is curtailed by reference to a member's territory and commitments.

Maritime Transport Services

The failed negotiations on maritime transport services also illustrated a recurrent theme in the GATS context: the difference between liberalizing access for foreign service *suppliers* to supply a service and ensuring that foreign *users* of the service are given non-discriminatory access. This issue is illustrated by a curious switch in the manner of scheduling commitments with regard to port services. Port services were initially treated as a sub-sector — under supporting services for maritime transport — in which members could make specific commitments on market access and national treatment. Thus, if a member scheduled this sub-sector and did not impose prohibitive restrictions, it would be possible for the suppliers of another member to provide these services.

Later negotiators developed a "draft schedule" which focused on the three pillars of the maritime transport sector: international shipping; maritime auxiliary services; and access to and use of port facilities. In the draft schedule, while commitments on the first two pillars are scheduled under Article XVI (market access) and Article XVII (national treatment), commitments on the third pillar are scheduled under Article XVIII (additional commitments). However, differences in the way that the additional commitments are phrased may imply significantly differing obligations. Some have simply stated that port services shall be made available to international maritime transport suppliers on reasonable and nondiscriminatory terms, while others have stated that no governmental measure will be taken which prevents the availability of port services on such terms. It would seem that in the former case, a member has undertaken to ensure that even private suppliers do not discriminate in the provision of these services and thus has committed itself to pro-competitive regulation.

In some respects, the approach to port services can also be seen as "essential facilities" often controlled by "major" or monopoly suppliers. As such it was analogous to the approach for basic telecommunications networks.

However, the draft schedule structure does not include the possibility of allowing the service suppliers of another member to provide port services. In effect, it is concerned only with the rights of consumers of port services (suppliers of international shipping services, rather than the rights of suppliers of port services).[21] Thus, while in telecom we have both access guarantees and liberalization of supply itself, in maritime, there is currently scope for providing guarantees on access but not for liberalizing foreign entry into the sector.[22]

4. Anticompetitive Practices, Article IX and MFN

This chapter has focused for the most part on GATS Article VIII, at the expense of the other article which deals with anticompetitive practices, Article IX. The scope of Article IX is wider, dealing as it does with "certain business practices of service suppliers, other than those falling under Article VIII, [which] may restrain competition and thereby restrict trade in services", but its disciplines are much weaker. In effect, the only obligations imposed relate to consultation and information-sharing.

Even though it is evident that the GATS itself contains only limited obligations on members to curtail anticompetitive practices, the question arises of whether it leaves members adequate scope to take action against the anticompetitive practices of the service suppliers of other members.

An interesting issue arose in the context of the basic telecommunications negotiations pertaining to international services. Some members were reluctant to grant unconditional MFN access to their liberalized markets to operators originating from non-liberalized markets. Apart from the desire to retain negotiating leverage, there were two main concerns. The first was the fear of anticompetitive cross-subsidization. The second was the problem of "one way monopoly by-pass".[23] The first concern is relatively straightforward, and not unlike certain concerns about predatory pricing that have been raised about the dumping of goods. The concern is that the competitive structure of the liberalized market could be undermined if an operator from a closed home-market were to subsidize its activity in the liberalized market using revenues generated in the closed home market, including revenue from excessively high accounting rates. This problem highlights the limitations of Article VIII:2 since it only requires that a member ensure that a monopoly supplier "does not abuse its monopoly position to act *in its territory* in a manner inconsistent with [a member's *specific*] *commitments*" (emphasis supplied). The behaviour at issue is not taking place in a member's territory and is not inconsistent with its specific commitments.

The second concern was that the operator from the closed market would be able to by-pass the accounting rate system by establishing commercial presence and its own facilities in the liberalized market and using this to terminate its own calls. Operators of the liberalized market would, meanwhile, still have to depend on the closed-market operator to terminate their calls. The imbalance in payments between the two would worsen, since the liberalized market operators would no longer be able to offset some of their payments for out-going calls with receipts from in-coming calls. Furthermore, foreign carriers from closed-markets operating in the liberalized market would be able to offer cheaper international calls from the liberalized market to their country of origin, being able to circumvent the high termination charge imposed on other carriers.

Several solutions were considered for the problem of achieving MFN-based liberalization while allowing members the freedom to deal with possible anticompetitive practices by exclusive operators from closed markets. One was taking measures *ex ante*, to limit market access for operators capable of engaging in anticompetitive practices because their home-markets were closed. A second was taking measures *ex post*, after market access is granted, if there was evidence of actual anticompetitive practices. And finally, the possibility of commitments by non-liberalizing members to restrain exclusive operators from engaging in anticompetitive practices in international services was raised. The limited time available did not permit a full exploration of the alternatives, and eventually it was the second option which seems to have been adopted by default.[24]

The ability to exercise national competition policy depends on the interpretation of the MFN obligation. Is a long-distance call provided at a low price by a subsidiary of a protected monopolist like a long-distance call provided by any other supplier? And is the subsidiary of a protected monopolist like any other supplier? If the reply to these questions is in the affirmative, then the MFN obligation would preclude any discrimination between these services and service suppliers, including on the basis of competition policy considerations. Alternatively, it could be argued that if competition policy itself is based on non-discriminatory principles, then it would be acceptable for it to impact differentially on particular services or service suppliers in specific instances provided they themselves manifested the characteristics that aroused concern. For instance, if competition policy had general restrictions on cross-subsidization or on the expansion of dominant suppliers, then specific actions that happened to be directed against foreign services or service suppliers with these attributes would not constitute infringements of the MFN obligation. However, any discrimination in treatment, based not on competition policy related attributes of the service or the service supplier, but instead on unrelated attributes (such as the fact of protection in the home market) would seem to violate MFN.[25]

5. An Integrated Approach to Policy

The question arises as to where pro-competitive regulation is a necessary complement to trade liberalization (or at least temporarily required to facilitate the advent of market forces) and where the development of genuinely competitive conditions depends not so much on regulation as on complementary liberalization in areas like distribution services. The answer to these questions depends on the degree of contestability of certain markets. The traditional view that certain basic services are necessarily natural monopolies has changed significantly due to technological advances, but in certain areas the existence of significant economies of scale still precludes the emergence of competitive markets.

Table 4.

Nature of technology	Nature of policy	Liberalizing entry into all stages of production (distribution)	Enforcing non-discriminatory access to the use of facilities
Optimal scale of production at some stage of production (distribution) is small relative to demand	No advantage arising from vertical integration	Sufficient	Sufficient
	Advantage arising from vertical integration	Only way of ensuring competitive conditions	Does not ensure fully competitive conditions and may prevent economically efficient arrangements
Optimal scale of production at some stage of production (distribution) is large relative to demand	No advantage arising from vertical integration	Does not ensure competitive conditions	Only way of ensuring competitive conditions
	Advantage arising from vertical integration	Does not ensure competitive conditions	Creates increased competition but may prevent economically efficient arrangements

An analysis of the impact of monopolies and STEs can be conducted in the framework of multistage production, where one of the stages is the distribution of the product/service. The existence of a monopoly or STE has been cause for international concern when it has exclusive control over supply at any stage of production or over the supply of an essential input. Such exclusive control may be due to rights conferred by the government or some other form of government facilitating action. Alternatively, it may be a consequence of large economies of scale in production. In some cases the situation is more fuzzy. Such is the case where monopolies were originally government-mandated, but even after the end of the government mandate, more competitive situations are slow to emerge.[26]

It is when the exclusive supplier at any stage of production (of a particular input) chooses to discriminate against or between foreign suppliers at other stages of production that there is cause for international concern.[27] Why might this happen? One possibility is that the exclusive supplier may in some way be vertically linked to producers at another stage of production. This link may be policy-induced and based solely on nationality, as when an STE restricts purchases from foreign sources to protect national suppliers. Or the link may be deeper, taking the form of vertical integration, as when a telecommunications monopolist demands high interconnection charges from its rivals in order to ensure the profitability of its own downstream operations. Even if there is no national or own production to protect, the exclusive supplier may still choose to behave as a monopolist (pure or discriminating) simply to maximise its own profits.

Table 4 attempts to relate technological fundamentals to policy prescriptions. The first two columns describe alternative technological possibilities depending on whether there is scope for competition at all stages of production (inclusive of distribution) and whether there is an advantage arising from vertical integration. If economies of scale imply that a particular stage of production or distribution is monopolised, then the mere liberalization of entry is not sufficient and there is need for regulation to ensure non-discriminatory access to the monopolised facilities. On the other hand, where an advantage arises from vertical integration, as in the distribution of certain consumer durables, liberalization of entry is the only way of ensuring competitive conditions. Enforcing non-discriminatory access for all suppliers is then a sub-optimal instrument for achieving increased competition because it prevents gains from vertical integration from being realised.

These issues can be illustrated by referring to an area of tension between trade and competition policy which also demonstrates the interplay between liberalization and rules in the domains of goods and services. This involves the perceived denial of market access through vertical foreclosure. It has been argued that vertical linkages between manufacturers and distributors in certain countries make it difficult for foreign goods to reach consumers. In a way there is a parallel issue in the telecom context because again the problem, if any, arises from discrimination in the provision of a crucial input: service-distribution. The problem of vertical foreclosure in this form is a less extreme version of the concern about STEs, in that the concern is not about state entities and not necessarily about fully monopolised distribution. Some of the considerations raised in Section 2 are relevant in determining whether the problem genuinely merits concern. Nevertheless, insofar as it does, can it be addressed purely by trade liberalization or is there a need for the application of complementary pro-competitive regulation?

First, if the discrimination in distribution can in any way be attributed to government action, then there is scope for challenging this under Article III of GATT 1994 (dealing with national treatment on internal taxation and regulation). Article III:4 states that imports must be "accorded treatment no less favourable than that accorded to like products of national origin in respect of all laws, regulations and requirements affecting their internal sale, offering for sale, purchase, transportation, *distribution* or use" (emphasis supplied). Thus, in a sense Article III:4 is an access provision like those which have been created in telecom and maritime transport services, but it is a guarantee against discrimination through government regulations, not a protection from the practices of private and government firms.

If the discrimination is purely a consequence of private arrangements between local manufacturers and distributors, then the obvious question is, what prevents foreign suppliers from creating their own distribution networks?[28] Here a country's commitments under GATS are relevant.[29] In principle, liberalization of trade (understood in the wide GATS sense to include establishment of commercial presence) in distribution services could go a long way in addressing most difficulties. Of course, economies of scale may still limit the scope for competition — a small town may not be able to profitably accommodate more than one supermarket, or energy distribution may need to be monopolised at the regional level. Drawing an analogy from telecommunications, if economies of scale considerations force foreign sellers to rely on local distributors, then trade liberalization is not enough, and there would seem to be a case for application of pro-competitive regulation to prevent discrimination. What makes this different from the existing WTO approach is that pro-competitive disciplines would be applied in the domain of *services* to protect the integrity of market access commitments, not only in the domain of *services*, as is the focus of Article VIII, but in the domain of *goods*. This may be an example of the type of situation which has prompted calls for an international agreement on competition policy.

A particular problem could arise where the ability of the manufacturer to distribute his own product and provide post-sales service affects the competitiveness of his product (i.e., where vertical integration enhances efficiency). This is most obvious in the case of certain consumer durables, such as automobiles. If a foreign manufacturer is not allowed to enter the distribution and service industries and is forced to rely on local agents, he may be put at a competitive disadvantage vis-à-vis local manufacturers. It would be difficult to argue that the obligation under Article III:4 of GATT 1994 implies that a member is obliged to give access to the distribution sector to manufacturers where such access is necessary to ensure competitiveness. Nor is it clear how pro-competitive regulation would address this problem. Forcing all existing distributors to stock a range of products from different manufacturers may prevent the realization of benefits from efficient vertical arrangements. The only meaningful solution would seem to be the liberalization of entry into the distribution sector.

An analogous problem arose within the domain of services during in the negotiations on maritime transport. The form of transportation called multimodal transport services is an area of growing importance. Apparently it can be provided most efficiently by vertically integrated operators who control both the ocean and the inland means of transport. The willingness of some members to make additional commitments guaranteeing access and use to the inland mode, but not the right to own or control that mode, were deemed to be inadequate by others who felt that foreign suppliers would be put at a disadvantage relative to vertically integrated national suppliers. Progress in these negotiations will therefore depend heavily on the willingness of countries to liberalize foreign access to trucking and related services.

Perhaps the central point that emerges is that liberalization of trade and investment in both goods and services is frequently necessary to ensure effective competition. However, where there are intrinsic limitations on the contestability of markets because of scale considerations, pro-competitive regulation may well be required to ensure a competitive outcome in the market.

6. Conclusions

This chapter has argued that GATS Article VIII is of limited relevance today. What that Article currently covers may well be less important than what it excludes. Government-mandated pure monopolies or non-competing oligopolies are disappearing from the infrastructural services for which Article VIII is most relevant, notably telecommunications. The behaviour of the dominant suppliers which often remain does not fall within its scope. Furthermore, the exclusion of the purchasing behaviour of non-competing public enterprises from its scope may not be innocuous.

Furthermore, since GATS Article VIII's disciplines depend exclusively on the other obligations undertaken by members, a variety of exemptions have weakened Article VIII in key areas. These include: the understanding that accounting rates in basic telecommunications would not be an issue for dispute settlement; the suspension of the MFN obligation for the maritime sector, along with the limited specific commitments in the sector; and finally, the exclusion of air traffic rights from the scope of the GATS.

In telecommunications, one of the first areas under GATS where there were serious liberalizing negotiations, the limitations in the scope and disciplines of Article VIII needed to be addressed. The Annex reinforced the rights of users of telecommunications services, while the Reference Paper strengthened guarantees of market access for suppliers of liberalized services. In maritime transport, similar steps were taken in the form of additional commitments ensuring reasonable and non-discriminatory access to port services.

One basic question concerns how much emphasis should be placed on pro-competitive regulation to ensure competitive market conditions in other sectors, rather than simply to continue the process of trade and investment liberalization already underway. The answer, not surprisingly, depends on the technological features of the market. The existence of benefits from vertical integration, as in multimodal transport services or in car manufacture and distribution, makes access obligations such as those considered in maritime negotiations or contained in GATT Article III:4 an inferior substitute for liberalization of access to all stages of production and distribution. However, the existence of significant economies of scale at any stage of production or distribution relative to the size of demand, as in telecom and transportation networks and energy distribution, implies the need for some form of pro-competitive regulation to ensure non-discriminatory access to the relevant good or service.

It may well be that the specific conditions in each services area necessitates the creation of detailed sector-specific regulatory disciplines and makes cross-sectoral rules like those contained in Article VIII inevitably inadequate. Nevertheless, it may be desirable to strengthen Article VIII to deal with certain generic problems rather than to rely on developing regulatory disciplines for each sector. Such an approach would economise on negotiating effort and avoid the need to anticipate all the sector-specific problems that could arise.

How then could GATS Article VIII be strengthened? First, in recognition of the intrinsic limitations on the contestability of certain markets because of scale considerations, it would be desirable to extend the scope of Article VIII. Thus, its coverage could extend to major suppliers, as defined in the Reference Paper, in terms of control over essential facilities and without requiring some form of government responsibility as a condition for coverage. Second, it would be worth examining fully the empirical significance of the exclusion of the purchases of goods and services by services producers and of services by goods producers from both GATT Article XVII and GATS Article VIII. The challenge would be to design disciplines which are sufficiently discerning to be effective where these exclusions matter without being unnecessarily burdensome where they do not. Finally, while the MFN obligation is valuable in promoting allocative efficiency, real liberalization depends on the national treatment obligation. The application of the latter to STEs in the domain of goods is doubtful, and the application of both in all areas of services is riddled with holes. Remedying these gaps would automatically strengthen the disciplines under both articles.

One final question concerns how far it is possible to address anticompetitive practices under the GATS. The disciplines here are so weak that the relevant issue is not so much what GATS does as what GATS would allow in the form of unilateral remedies. The scope for national competition policies to address foreign anticompetitive practices is found to depend on the interpretation of the non-discriminatory obligations, especially relating to the notions of like services and service suppliers. It could be argued that if competition policy itself is based on non-discriminatory principles, then it would be acceptable for it to impact differentially on particular services or service suppliers in specific instances, provided that they manifested the relevant anticompetitive characteristics.

NOTES

1. While Article XVII is entitled "State Trading Enterprises", the text refers more widely to "state enterprises".

2. The words "in effect" could be interpreted to form the basis for a wider view whereby the failure of government to act in preventing the emergence of such market structures would constitute a form of governmental responsibility. But such a view is not convincing in that it would be so wide as to render superfluous the requirement of a member having "authorized or established" a monopoly, since the existence of most monopolies could then be attributed to government action or inaction. Perhaps the relevant question is, would a monopoly have existed even without government involvement?

3. Article XVII:2 states that "with respect to such imports, each contracting party shall accord to the trade of the other contracting parties fair and equitable treatment". The procurement of some twenty-two WTO members is subject to the disciplines of the Agreement on Government Procurement.

4. It is notable that the exclusion of government procurement from Article III disciplines refers to "products purchased for governmental purposes and not with a view to *commercial* resale" (emphasis supplied). The Article XVII exclusion of government procurement differs in omitting the word "commercial" from before "sale".

5. GATT Article I (MFN) is symmetric in its application of the non-discrimination principle to imports and to exports, while the MFN obligation in GATS is only defined in terms of treatment of foreign services and service suppliers, and thus excludes measures affecting exports.

6. In fact, Article XX(d) contains a general exception for measures necessary to secure compliance with laws or regulations which are not inconsistent with the provisions of the GATT, including those relating to "the enforcement of monopolies operated under paragraph 4 of Article II and Article XVII".

7. This shift in emphasis reflects that in many of the new acceding countries, like China and Russia, STEs have a major influence on trade.

8. One other area of exclusion from Article VIII relates to monopolies in professional services which exercise control over activities ranging from accounting, architecture, and legal services. Here the issue of monopoly control is related to the issue of professional standards and qualification requirements, which are being addressed in negotiations mandated by Article VI:4 of the GATS.

9. It has been argued that the procedural disciplines of the GPA have imposed excessive costs on public enterprises operating in competitive conditions and adversely affected their ability to compete with private enterprises which are not subject to similar disciplines.

10. Other qualifications of the neutrality result are that domestic and foreign goods and services may not be perfect substitutes and that markets are rarely perfectly competitive. The implications of these assumptions in discussed in Mattoo (1996).

11. According to the Financial Times, international calls in the United States cost more than six times as much as domestic long-distance calls (eighty-eight cents compared to thirteen cents per minute). Net outpayments from the U.S. to foreign carriers in 1995 were almost five billion dollars, corresponding to five percent of the U.S. trade deficit for goods and services.

12. It may be the case that when prices in different markets are not common knowledge and search is costly, all risk-averse consumers prefer uniform pricing to price discrimination. In these circumstances, a producer may have an incentive to create a reputation for uniform pricing.

13. If demand were linear, uniform pricing would socially dominate third-degree price discrimination since total output under the two situations would be the same.

14. Even though the GATS does permit members to seek temporary exemptions from the MFN obligations, the dominant view was that the continued suspension of the MFN obligation would avert the need for many countries to take MFN exemptions which may be more difficult to negotiate away once explicitly listed.

15. The WTO dispute settlement procedures can be invoked only in respect of obligations specifically assumed by members, and even then only after any bilateral or other procedures have been exhausted.

16. This Section draws upon Tuthill (1997).

17. In Annex definitions: 'Public telecommunications transport service' means any telecommunications transport service required, explicitly or in effect, to be offered to the public generally and typically involving the real-time transmission of customer-supplied information without any end-to-end change in its form or content. 'Public

telecommunications transport network' means the public telecommunications infrastructure permitting telecommunications between and among network termination
points.

18. For instance, a major supplier, with control over essential facilities, may allow
rivals to enter the local telephone call market but deny them dialling parity. That is,
while its own customers had seven-digit telephone numbers, those of the rival could
be allotted sixteen-digit numbers. We can imagine the impact a seemingly innocuous
"technical restriction" would have on the relative attractiveness for customers of the
two suppliers.

19. Governments had the flexibility to draw selectively from a common text. Fifty-
seven of the sixty-nine participants in the negotiations on basic telecommunications
adopted the Reference Paper in full or with fairly minor modifications as additional
commitments. However, six more participants scheduled selected elements of it or
drafted their own wording. Another six decided not to offer any additional commitments on regulation.

20. Other Reference Paper provisions provide for greater transparency and require
the creation of dispute resolution mechanisms. Governments who have scheduled the
Reference Paper must also ensure that a regulator of the sector will be separate from,
and not accountable to, any supplier of basic telecommunications services. The Reference Paper also specifies that the decisions of and the procedures used must be
"impartial with respect to all market participants".

21. This gap in the draft schedule may reflect pessimism about liberalizing commitments on access to port services. However, even if concentrated market structures
persist, many countries are in the process of privatizing port facilities and frequently
seek to attract foreign investment in these areas.

22. There is one other issue which the draft schedule approach raises, which is also
relevant to basic telecommunications. Article XXVIII(c)(ii) of the GATS states that
"'measures by Members affecting trade in services' include measures in respect of the
access to and use of, in connection with the supply of a service, services which are
required by those Members to be offered to the public generally". Thus, it could be
argued that non-discriminatory access to and use of port services is already assured
by the MFN principle in Article II. Why is there any need then for an explicit listing
of port services under additional commitments? Such an explicit listing does have an
independent value when the national treatment commitments are not comprehensive
— in which case the explicit listing would assure suppliers of another member at
least of reasonable and non-discriminatory access to port services, while they remain
vulnerable to other protective instruments. It could also be argued that Article
XXVIII(c)(ii) only covers access to services inputs and not non-services inputs (such
as water and electrical supplies) which are included in the draft schedule list of port
services.

23. This discussion draws upon Gamberale (1997).

24. At the end of 1996, the U.S. Federal Communication Commission (FCC) published a Notice of Proposed Rulemaking dealing with international accounting rates.
This notice presents a possible solution to the problem of exclusive operators taking
advantage of the combined effect of liberalization and the existing accounting rate
system. It sets "benchmarks" based on costs for accounting rates, which countries

should respect as a condition for their operators to be licensed in the U.S. market. The FCC makes provision for higher completion costs in poorer countries and proposes benchmarks which differ according to the level of development of countries. The Notice of Proposed Rulemaking was adopted as an Order by the FCC on 7 August 1997 and is due to come into force on 1 January 1998. The Order allows for gradual phase-ins conditional on the level of development. In effect, the FCC proposes to enforce the benchmarks by withdrawing or denying a license if an accounting rate above the benchmark is charged. Though some have expressed doubts over the consistency of the legislation with the MFN obligation, the United States has argued that these doubts are not justified since its actions are based on post-entry competition safeguards rather than on *ex ante* reciprocity.

25. There would seem to be an acknowledgement of this distinction in the case of maritime transport. This time the concern is that anticompetitive practices in the provision of port services in certain countries have hampered access of foreign maritime transport suppliers to their markets. How far these practices are facilitated by government action (or inaction) is subject to dispute. In this case, the MFN obligation was not a constraint on retaliatory action since the application of the obligation to the sector has been suspended. Indeed, one of the reasons the United States presented for seeking an MFN exemption when the application of the obligation was a possibility was precisely to preserve its right to retaliate against foreign restrictive practices. Recently, the United States imposed penalties on Japanese ships visiting United States ports because of the perceived persistence of anticompetitive practices in Japanese ports.

26. This may be because it takes time for competitors to create alternative production facilities, such as telecom networks, or for alternative technologies to develop that are not subject to large economies of scale.

27. Control over essential facilities may give rise to non-discriminating pure monopolist behaviour which has adverse welfare-effects, but this is as much a concern for national authorities as for foreign suppliers.

28. It could also be argued that private anticompetitive practices can be addressed under Article XXIII (dealing with nullification and impairment) of GATT 1994. The argument would be that the failure to enforce national competition law by a member has led to another member's benefits under GATT 1994 being nullified. It would, of course, be necessary to demonstrate that non-enforcement of competition law could not have been reasonably expected when certain market access commitments were made. If no specific commitments had been made, if competition law did not exist in a particular country, or if the level of enforcement had always been weak, then the non-violation argument would be weakened.

29. For instance, New Zealand, a country which has numerous market boards operating in agriculture, has excluded from the scope of their commitments on wholesale trade services those which pertain to CPC classes 6221 (wholesale trade services of agricultural raw materials and live animals), 6222 (wholesale trade services of food, beverages, and tobacco), and services relating to CPC classes 2613–2615 (wool and animal hair).

REFERENCES

Baldwin, R.E. 1970. "Restrictions on Governmental Expenditures." In R. Baldwin, *Nontariff Distortions of International Trade*. Washington, D.C.: Brookings Institution.
Baldwin, R.E. 1984. "Trade Policies in Developed Countries." In R.W. Jones and P.B. Kenen, eds. *1 Handbook of International Economics*. Amsterdam: North Holland. pp. 571–619.
Baldwin, R.E. and J.D. Richardson. 1972. "Government Purchasing Policies, Other NTBs, and the International Monetary Crisis." In H. English and K. Hay, eds. *Obstacles to Trade in the Pacific Area*. Ottawa: Carleton School of International Affairs.
Francois, J., D. Nelson, and N.D. Palmeter. 1997. "Public Procurement in the United States: A Post-Uruguay Round Perspective." In B.M. Hoekman and P.C. Mavroidis, eds. *Law and Policy in Public Purchasing: The WTO Agreement on Government Procurement*. Ann Arbor: University of Michigan Press.
Gamberale, C. 1997. "Competition Concerns in Telecommunications Services Liberalization." Mimeo.
Jackson, J.H. 1992. *The World Trading System: Law and Policy of International Economic Relations*. Cambridge, MA: MIT Press.
Mattoo, A. 1996. "Government Procurement Agreement: Implications of Economic Theory." World Economy 19: 695–720.
Tuthill, L. 1997. "The GATS and New Rules for Regulators." Telecommunications Policy, November *forthcoming*.

CHAPTER 3

GATT Law on State Trading Enterprises: Critical Evaluation of Article XVII and Proposals for Reform

*Ernst-Ulrich Petersmann**

1. GATT Law and State Trading Enterprises

STEs as a Systemic Challenge to the GATT System

GATT law proceeds from the principle of state sovereignty and recognizes (e.g., in Articles II:4, XVII, and XX:d) the right to establish or maintain trade monopolies and state enterprises, and to grant "any enterprise, formally or in effect, exclusive or special privileges" (Article XVII:1). In most countries, the government intervenes in the national economy not only as regulator but also as a direct participant in certain economic activities as producer, trader, or consumer of goods and services. Yet, most GATT rules address governments only in their role as regulator of economic activities. For instance, GATT Articles I to III and XI to XV limit the governmental use of tariffs, non-tariff trade barriers, and trade discrimination so as to enhance trade opportunities and protect non-discriminatory conditions of competition. Many GATT rules further assume that, as stated in GATT Article VII:2, "merchandise is sold or offered for sale in the ordinary course of trade under fully competitive conditions". GATT tariff bindings, for example, have been consistently construed in GATT dispute settlement practice as justifying reasonable expectations about competitive opportunities which must not be impaired by unforeseen subsequent governmental distortions of competition.

This focus of GATT law on rules for government conduct, and their frequent assumption that government interventions in the economy are separated from business activities, entail a systemic problem for the GATT legal system: how can the system ensure that state trading enterprises (STEs) do not undermine GATT commitments on the reciprocal liberalization of gov-

*Professor of Law at the University of Geneva and the Geneva Graduate Institute of International Studies. Former legal adviser to the German Ministry of Economic Affairs (1978–1981), the GATT (1981–1994) and the WTO (1994–1997). The author is grateful to Betsy Shaffer and Jeff Gertler from the WTO Secretariat for helpful comments on an earlier draft.

ernmental market access barriers and market distortions? If governments make use of their right to set up STEs or confer "exclusive or special privileges" to private enterprises, other GATT member countries and their trading firms may experience different kinds of problems.

Market Behaviour: Restrictive Business Practices By STEs
STEs may resort to numerous kinds of restrictive business practices (RBPs) that discriminate against foreign goods and services and possibly undermine the GATT commitments. For instance, if an STE:

- serves as exclusive importer/exporter of a product and — through its import or export decisions and its determination of resale prices, "mark-ups" and delivery terms — prevents other imports or exports at lower prices from particular traders or particular countries;

- administers import regimes (e.g., through allocation of import licences) or exchange control regimes, or otherwise determines prices and quantities of traded products, in a manner which discriminates against private competitors or against particular countries;

- uses government funds for subsidizing trade, domestic production, or distribution (e.g., of production inputs such as fertilizers and seeds) in a trade-distorting manner;

- purchases and procures all or part of a commodity from domestic producers notwithstanding more competitive offers from foreign suppliers;

- holds or disposes of stocks (e.g., of agricultural and strategic goods), or finances stockholding activities, in a manner discriminating against foreign goods;

- establishes or controls product standards, inspects imports and exports to see that they meet the established standards, or establishes and controls minimum prices in the domestic market in a manner favouring domestic products and discriminating against competition from abroad;

- owns and operates production and processing facilities which compete with imports and benefit from the special privileges of STEs.

Market Structure: Special Rights and Privileges of STEs
Rather than worrying about individual RBPs, GATT member countries might want to limit the underlying sources of such trade distortions, namely the special rights and privileges of STEs. These may include:

- exclusive or privileged rights of STEs to export, import, issue import or export licences, contract with foreign governments or with domestic importers/exporters in competition with private traders, produce, or distribute one or more products;

- exclusive or privileged rights of STEs to process domestic or imported commodities for domestic consumption or export;

- authority of STEs to participate in the administration of GATT market access commitments, for instance by controlling prices, quantities, and for distribution of imported agricultural products;

- exclusive or privileged access of STEs to governmental financial assistance for subsidizing imports, exports, the establishment of subsidiaries in export markets, or domestic production and distribution;

- authority of STEs to stabilize domestic supply, demand, and product prices through domestic purchases, stock-holdings, or sales;

- authority of STEs to establish and enforce product or production standards, including (phyto-) sanitary standards.

Legal Problems: Low Transparency, Inadequate Remedies
RBPs may often be difficult to prove due to lack of transparency in the pricing, operational activities, and "economies of scale" of STEs. The relationship between governments and STEs, and the special privileges conferred on STEs, may likewise not be publicly known. And trade-distorting practices may be difficult to challenge in GATT/WTO dispute settlement proceedings (for instance if the defendant government claims that discriminatory RBPs were not influenced by the government concerned and are neither inconsistent with GATT rules nor actionable in the intergovernmental GATT dispute settlement system).

Specific legal problems may arise from the fact that agriculture remains the most important sector of state trading and continues to benefit from special exceptions in GATT and WTO law. While prior to the entry into force of the WTO Agreement many GATT legal disciplines were not effectively applied and enforced in the field of agricultural trade, the WTO Agreement on Trade in Agriculture has introduced comprehensive new commitments on export subsidies, market access, and domestic support. Yet, STEs with monopolistic power as sole purchaser, sole importer, or sole exporter of domestic supply — such as the Australian and Canadian Wheat Boards, or the New Zealand Dairy Board, each of which controls annual commodity exports worth more than one billion U.S. dollars — may find it easy to undermine these Uruguay Round commitments by offering price and supply conditions that would be impossible for private traders. Moreover, STEs were established in the agricultural sector for public policy reasons, such as the provision of price support and food security, which are reflected in specific safeguard clauses of GATT/WTO law.

Outside the agricultural sector, the worldwide trend toward market economies, deregulation, and privatization of state enterprises tends to diminish the importance of the GATT and WTO legal disciplines on STEs. Yet the current negotiations on accession to the WTO of most former centrally planned economies — such as Russia and other republics of the former Soviet Union, China, and Vietnam — increase the systemic need for effective substantive and procedural GATT/WTO legal disciplines for the thousands of enterprises in these countries which, even if privatized, may continue to benefit from special rights and privileges.

GATT Approach: Eight Layers of STE Regulations

GATT Article XVII:3 explicitly recognizes that STEs "might be operated so as to create serious obstacles to trade". In order to deal with these problems, GATT includes specific provisions relating to STEs and import monopolies in Articles II, XI–XIV, XVII, XVIII, and XX(d). The basic purpose of these provisions is "to extend to state-trading the rules of the General Agreement governing private trade and to ensure that the contracting parties cannot escape their obligations with respect to private trade by establishing state-trading operations".[1] Another GATT panel likewise found:

> Articles II:4, XVII and the Note Ad Articles XI, XII, XIII, XIV and XVIII clearly indicated the drafters' intention not to allow contracting parties to frustrate the principles of the General Agreement governing measures affecting private trade by regulating trade through monopolies. Canada had the right to take . . . the measures necessary to secure compliance with laws consistent with the General Agreement relating to the enforcement of monopolies. This right was specifically provided for in Article XX(d) of the General Agreement. . . . The Panel found that Canada's right . . . to establish an import and sales monopoly for beer did not entail the right to discriminate against imported beer inconsistently with Article III:4 through regulations affecting its internal transportation.[2]

Article XVII defines state trading enterprises in the following manner:

- "a state enterprise, wherever located"; and
- "any enterprise" that has been granted, "formally or in effect, exclusive or special privileges";
- "marketing boards" (interpretative note to paragraph 1) and "import monopolies" (paragraph 4) are explicitly included in these two basic categories.

GATT's legal approach to STEs rests essentially on eight legal provisions and GATT practices. First, *Article II:4* seeks to protect the GATT schedules of concessions from being circumvented by import monopolies. According to Article II:4 of GATT,

> If any contracting party establishes, maintains or authorizes, formally or in effect, a monopoly of the importation of any product described in the appropriate Schedule annexed to this Agreement, such monopoly shall not, except as provided for in that Schedule or as otherwise agreed between the parties which initially negotiated the concession, operate so as to afford protection on the average in excess of the amount or protection provided for in that Schedule. The provisions of this paragraph shall not limit the use by contracting parties of any form of assistance to domestic producers permitted by other provisions of this Agreement.

An interpretative note to Article II:4 states that paragraph 4 "will be applied in the light of the provisions of Article 31 of the Havana Charter". Article 31 of the Havana Charter stated that an import duty bound in a Schedule

> shall represent the maximum margin by which the price charged by the import monopoly for the imported product (exclusive of internal taxes . . ., transportation, distribution and other expenses incident to the purchase, sale or further processing, and a reasonable margin of profit) may exceed the landed cost: provided that regard may be had to average landed costs and selling prices over recent periods. . . .

Second, as regards Articles XI, XII, XIII, XIV, and XVIII of GATT, it is clarified in an interpretative note (GATT Annex I) that

> [t]hroughout Articles XI, XII, XIII, XIV and XVIII, the terms 'import restrictions' or 'export restrictions' include restrictions made effective through state-trading operations.

No equivalent provision is to be found in the interpretative notes relating to the non-discrimination requirements in GATT Articles I and III. Notwithstanding the claim by one government that the interpretative note made it clear that provisions other than Article XVII applied to STEs by specific reference only, a GATT panel

> saw great force in the argument that Article III:4 was also applicable to state-trading enterprises at least when the monopoly of the importation and monopoly of the distribution in domestic markets were combined, as was the case of the provincial boards in Canada.[3]

The 1997 Annual Report of the WTO, in its special chapter devoted to trade and competition policies, likewise notes in respect of STEs:

> There is nothing in the rules to suggest that autonomous behaviour by enterprises in a manner contrary to the standards set out in the relevant WTO provisions would escape the scope of the obligations accepted by Members in those provisions.[4]

Third, *Article XVII* GATT seeks to regulate and limit the market behaviour of STEs by requiring WTO Members to comply with special non-discrimination requirements and notification requirements.[5] The concepts used in Article XVII — such as "STE", "general principles of non-discriminatory treatment", and "purchases or sales solely in accordance with commercial considerations" — were left vague. The drafters believed that more practical experience with the relatively new state trading practices during and after the exceptional war-time situation was needed for understanding how GATT legal disciplines could be effectively applied to STEs.

Fourth, according to the "general exceptions" in *Article XX*:

> nothing in this Agreement shall be construed to prevent the adoption or enforcement by any contracting party of measures . . . (d) necessary to secure compliance with laws or regulations which are not inconsistent with the provisions of this Agreement, including those relating to . . . the enforcement of monopolies operated under paragraph 4 of Article II and XVII.

The 1988 Panel report *on Japanese Import Restrictions on Certain Agricultural Products* clarified that the detailed GATT rules designed to preclude protective and discriminatory practices by import monopolies would become meaningless if Article XX(d) were interpreted to exempt such trading practices from the GATT obligations.[6]

Fifth, the GATT dispute settlement procedures (*Articles XXII, XXIII*) offer legal remedies for "nullification or impairment" of GATT rules and GATT benefits by STEs. They have been repeatedly used for the settlement of disputes over trade-distorting practices of STEs.[7]

Sixth, GATT *Article XVII:3* explicitly provides for "negotiations on a reciprocal and mutually advantageous basis designed to limit or reduce obstacles" to trade resulting from the operation of STEs.

GATT contracting parties have pursued this objective mainly in the context of negotiations on the accession to GATT by former state trading countries. When Poland, Romania, and Hungary acceded to the GATT[8], the accession protocols used different legal techniques and safeguard clauses for dealing with the problem that, in state trading countries, the level of imports and countertrade arrangements are determined more by governmental planning decisions than by tariff levels and other general trade policy instruments. Poland's 1967 accession protocol provided that "Poland shall . . . undertake to increase the total value of its imports from the territories of contracting parties by not less than 7 per cent per annum".[9]

The other GATT contracting parties also retained considerable discretion to impose selective safeguard measures on imports from Poland and to maintain their existing quotas on Polish goods during an undefined transitional period. The 1971 accession protocol of Romania provided that Romania

> will develop and diversify its trade with the contracting parties as a whole, and firmly intends to increase its imports from the contracting parties as a whole at a rate not smaller than the growth of total Romanian imports provided for in its Five-Year Plans.

GATT members were allowed to maintain quotas on Romanian products only up to their elimination by a target date of 1974, but they reserved the right to use selective safeguards against imports from Romania.[10] Hungary's 1973 accession protocol does not contain quantitative import commitments; as in the case of Romania, GATT members were allowed to maintain quotas on Hungarian products up to their elimination by 1974, and they also retained the right to use selective safeguards against imports from Hungary.[11] In the context of more recent negotiations on accession to the WTO, especially with former state trading countries, liberalization commitments have been sought not just on the behaviour of STEs but also on the existence of their exclusive "trading rights", i.e., the market structure itself.[12]

Seventh, the eight "GATT Rounds" of multilateral trade negotiations, based on *Article XXVIIIbis* of GATT, have so far led to relatively few concessions specifically relating to the liberalization of STEs. There have also been few attempts to strengthen the general legal GATT disciplines on STEs so as to protect market access rights and non-discriminatory conditions of competition more effectively. The 1994 WTO "Understanding on the Interpretation of Article XVII of the GATT 1994" is largely confined to the strengthening of the notification requirements of GATT Article XVII:4. As stated in the Preamble of the Understanding, it "is without prejudice to the substantive disciplines prescribed in Article XVII". In the 1996 WTO Working Party on State Trading Enterprises, the EC suggested widening the scope of activities beyond the review, strengthening of the notification requirements under Article XVII:4 of GATT, and examining the need for further strengthening the substantive obligations under Article XVII.[13] Especially in the field of the WTO negotiations on the liberalization of telecommunications and other services, the right of foreign service suppliers to establish in markets which are the subject of monopolies or exclusive rights has been a major issue of negotiation and commitments on market access (Article XVI GATS) and national treatment (Article XVII GATS).

Eighth, government procurement was exempted from the non-discrimination principles of GATT (see *Articles III:8* and *XVII:2*). The 1979 and 1994 Agreements on Government Procurement introduced additional transparency and non-discrimination requirements for the public purchasing and tendering procedures of those GATT and WTO member countries which accepted these "plurilateral agreements". The relationships between these various GATT provisions bearing on STEs have remained controversial in some respects. During the drafting of Article XVII,

> it was agreed that when marketing boards buy or sell they would come under the provisions relating to State-trading; where they lay down regulations governing private trade their activities would be covered by the relevant articles of the Charter. It was understood that the term 'marketing boards' is confined to boards established by express governmental action.[14]

This understanding was in part incorporated into the interpretative note to Article XVII:1, but one cannot infer that discretionary government involvement in STEs and RBPs by STEs (other than general "regulations governing private trade") are never covered by other relevant GATT Articles such as Articles II:4, III, XI, or XVI. Thus, it has been recognized in GATT practice[15] that:

- "mark-ups" by import monopolies may be inconsistent with Article II:4 regardless of whether the mark-ups were made effective through general regulations or individual transactions by STEs;

- import monopolies may act inconsistently with Article II:4 if they charge a profit margin which was on the average higher than that "which would be obtained under normal conditions of competition (in the absence of the monopoly)";

- import monopolies are obliged under Article II:4 to "import and offer for sale such quantities of the product [for which a concession had been granted] as will be sufficient to satisfy the full domestic demand for the imported product"; and that

- quantitative restrictions made effective through state trading operations may be inconsistent with Article XI even if they result from mere practices of STEs that are not laid down in general regulations.

2. GATT Practice: Critical Evaluation of Article XVII

The Scope of Article XVII

During the drafting of Part IV of the GATT in 1964, it was agreed that "there was nothing in Article XVII which prevents a contracting party from establishing or maintaining State-trading enterprises, nor does the General Agreement sanction discrimination against State-trading enterprises which are, in this regard, placed on the same basis as any other enterprise".[16] In GATT dispute settlement practice, it has been inferred from Article XVII that

[the] mere existence of producer-controlled import monopolies could not be considered as a separate import restriction inconsistent with the General Agreement. The Panel noted, however, that the activities of such enterprises had to conform to a number of rules contained in the General Agreement, including those of Article XVII and Article XI:1.[17]

In the London and New York Drafts of the Havana Charter, the article on non-discriminatory administration of STEs included an explicit definition of "state enterprise". This definition was deleted at Geneva based on the the view that in sub-paragraph 1(a), such enterprises were defined as precisely as practicable. The Sub-Committee at the Havana Conference, which considered the Charter articles on state trading, found that "the term 'state enterprise' in the text did not require any special definition; it was the general understanding that the term includes, inter alia, any agency of government that engages in purchasing or selling".[18]

The 1960 GATT panel on *Subsidies and State Trading*, in discussing which enterprises were covered by Article XVII, agreed, *inter alia*:

- "the requirements in paragraph 4(a) of Article XVII that contracting parties should notify products 'imported into or exported from their territories' should be interpreted to mean that countries should notify enterprises which have the statutory power of deciding on imports and exports, even if no imports or exports in fact have taken place";

- "[t]he term 'enterprise' was used to refer either to an instrumentality of government which has the power to buy or sell, or to a non-governmental body with such power and to which the government has granted exclusive or special privileges. The activities of a marketing board or any enterprise defined in paragraph 1(a) of Article XVII should be notified where that body has the ability to influence the level or direction of imports or exports by its buying or selling."[19]

Paragraph 1 of the WTO Understanding on the Interpretation of Article XVII of GATT 1994, which constitutes an integral part of GATT 1994, provides the following 'working definition' for the purposes of notification under Article XVII:

> Governmental and non-governmental enterprises, including marketing boards, which have been granted exclusive or special rights or privileges, including statutory or constitutional powers, in the exercise of which they influence through their purchases or sales the level or direction of imports or exports.

This definition is narrower than the definition in Article XVII:1(a): state-owned enterprises are excluded unless they satisfy two conditions: (1) they have a special right or privilege; and (2) the STEs influence the level or direction of trade through purchases or sales. According to the 1994 Understanding, this narrowing of the notification requirements "is without prejudice to the substantive disciplines prescribed in Article XVII".

The Non-Discrimination Requirements (Article XVII:1, 2)

"General Principles of Non-Discriminatory Treatment"
The drafting history of Article XVII and the pertinent GATT practice leave unclear whether the obligation of STEs, in their purchases or sales involving either imports or exports, to "act in a manner consistent with the general principles of non-discriminatory treatment prescribed in this Agreement for governmental measures affecting imports or exports by private traders" refers only to most-favoured nation treatment of trade with other countries (e.g., Article I:1) or also to national treatment of imported and like domestic goods (e.g., Article III).[20] The 1952 Panel report on *Belgian Family Allowances* noted:

> As regards the exception contained in paragraph 2 of Article XVII, it would appear that it referred only to the principle set forth in paragraph 1 of that Article, i.e. the obligation to make purchases in accordance with commercial considerations and did not extend to matters dealt with in Article III.[21]

Since Article XVII:2 is explicitly limited to the treatment of "imports" and does not refer to the treatment of "imported goods" in relation to domestic goods, this *obiter dictum* of the panel has hardly any precedential value for the question whether "the general principles of non-discriminatory treatment prescribed in this Agreement" (Article XVII:1) include also the principles in Article III. The same seems to be true for the references to Article XVII in the 1955 Working Party Report on the Haitian Tobacco Monopoly, which related to an import licensing scheme, operated in connection with an import and production monopoly. This Report did not examine the question of whether Article XVII:1 refers also to GATT Article III.[22]

In the panel proceeding relating to Canada's administration of its Foreign Investment Review Act, arguments were presented concerning both the issue of whether Article XVII:1 requires national treatment, and the distinct question of whether Article III applies directly to the administration of laws or regulations bearing on state trading enterprises. The 1984 Panel report notes:

> The Panel saw great force in Canada's argument that only the most-favoured-nation and not the national treatment obligations fall within the scope of the general principles referred to in Article XVII:1(a). However, the Panel did not consider it necessary to decide in this particular case whether the general reference to the principles of non-discriminatory treatment referred to in Article XVII:1 also comprises the national treatment principle since it had already found the purchase undertakings at issue to be inconsistent with Article III:4 which implements the national treatment principle specifically in respect of purchase requirements.[23]

The 1988 Panel report on *Canada - Import, Distribution and Sale of Alcoholic Drinks by Canadian Provincial Marketing Agencies* also examined this issue:

> The Panel . . . turned its attention to the relevance of Article XVII and in particular to the contention of the European Communities that the practices under examination contravened a national treatment obligation contained in paragraph 1 of that Article. The Panel noted that two previous panels had examined questions related to this paragraph. . . . The Panel considered, however, that it was not necessary to decide in this particular case whether the practices complained of were contrary to Article XVII because it had already found that they were inconsistent with Article XI.[24]

It is noteworthy that in the past, no GATT or WTO dispute settlement report has established a violation of Article XVII. The claims of GATT-inconsistent discrimination were always decided in favour of the complainants directly on the basis of Articles I, III, and XI rather than on Article XVII. For instance, since Article III:4 is applicable to "all laws, regulations and requirements affecting [the] internal sale, offering for sale, purchase, transportation, distribution or use" of imported and like domestic products, the *FIRA Panel* applied Article III:4 directly to purchase requirments without deciding on the additional applicability of Article XVII:1. This dispute settlement practice raises various questions such as:

- does the absence of dispute settlement findings on violations of Article XVII justify the conclusion that there is so far little evidence that the general GATT obligations (e.g., under Articles I to III, XI) have been seriously undermined through state trading operations?

- do the few dispute settlement cases relating to Article XVII suggest that GATT contracting parties preferred to settle their problems with foreign STEs by recourse to other remedies (such as the selective safeguard clauses in the accession protocols of some former state trading countries)?

- can one conclude from the text of Article XVII:1(b)[25] that STEs must respect "the other provisions of this Agreement" (such as GATT Article III) and, for instance, must avoid discrimination against imported products which is not justified by "commercial considerations"? Is there any convincing reason why the requirement "to act in a manner consistent with the general principles of non-discriminatory treatment prescribed in this Agreement" should not extend to the non-discrimination requirements in Article III?

The Non-Discrimination Requirement of Article XVII:1(c)
The obligation Article XVII:1(c) that contracting parties not "prevent any enterprise (whether or not an enterprise described in subparagraph (a) of this paragraph) under its jurisdiction from acting in accordance with the principles of subparagraphs (a) and (b) of this paragraph" has likewise not yet been clarified in GATT and WTO dispute settlement practice. The 1984 *FIRA* panel report notes that the United States requested the Panel to find that the purchase undertakings obliging investors to give less favourable treatment to imported products than to domestic products prevented the investors from acting solely in accordance with commercial considerations and that therefore they violated Canada's obligations under Article XVII:1(c). But the Panel did not consider it necessary to decide in this particular case whether the general reference in Article XVII:1 to the principles of non-discriminatory treatment also comprised the national treatment principle since it had already found the purchase undertakings at issue to be

inconsistent with Article III:4. The Panel clarified, however, the relationship between sub-paragraphs (a), (b), and (c):

> [T]hrough its reference to sub-paragraph (a), paragraph 1(c) of Article XVII of the General Agreement imposes on contracting parties the obligation to act in their relations with state-trading and other enterprises 'in a manner consistent with the general principles of non-discriminatory treatment prescribed in this Agreement for governmental measures affecting imports or exports by private traders'. This obligation is defined in sub-paragraph (b), which declares, inter alia, that these principles are understood to require the enterprises to make their purchases and sales solely in accordance with commercial considerations. The fact that sub-paragraph (b) does not establish a separate general obligation to allow enterprises to act in accordance with commercial considerations, but merely defines the obligations set out in the preceding sub-paragraph, is made clear through the introductory words 'The provisions of sub-paragraph (a) of the paragraph shall be understood to require' . . . For these reasons, the Panel considers that the commercial considerations criterion becomes relevant only after it has been determined that the governmental action at issue falls within the scope of the general principles of non-discriminatory treatment prescribed by the General Agreement.[26]

In the same *FIRA* panel proceeding, the United States also requested the Panel to find that the undertakings, which obliged investors to export specified quantities or proportions of their production, were inconsistent with Article XVII:1(c) because the export levels of companies subject to such undertakings cannot be assumed to be the result of a decision-making process based on commercial considerations. The panel found

> there is no provision in the General Agreement which forbids requirements to sell goods in foreign markets in preference to the domestic market. In particular, the General Agreement does not impose on contracting parties the obligation to prevent enterprises from dumping. Therefore, when allowing foreign investments on the condition that the investors export a certain amount or proportion of their production, Canada does not, in the view of the Panel, act inconsistently with any of the principles of non-discriminatory treatment prescribed by the General Agreement for governmental measures affecting exports by private traders. Article XVII:1(c) is for these reasons not applicable to the export undertakings at issue.[27]

The 1988 Panel report on *Japan - Trade in Semi-Conductors* clarified the legal relationship between Article XVII:1(c) and other GATT provisions by finding:

> The Panel . . . turned to the contention of the EEC that the measures by the Japanese Government were contrary to Article XVII:1(c). . . . The Panel considered that, once a measure had been found to be inconsistent with a specific provision of the General Agreement, it was no longer meaningful to address the question of whether or not the measure was also contrary to principles underlying that Agreement and therefore the Panel, having already found the Japanese measures to be inconsistent with Article XI, did not consider it necessary to examine them in the light of Article XVII:1(c).[28]

The wording of Article XVII:1(c) makes clear that the obligation in paragraph 1(c) applies not only in respect of STEs but with regard to "any enterprise" under the jurisdiction of the country concerned. Unlike Article XVII:1(b), Article XVII:1(c) therefore establishes an additional obligation to *allow* any enterprise to make its purchases and sales in accordance with the non-discrimination principles of GATT and on the basis of commercial considerations.

"Fair and Equitable Treatment" (Article XVII:2)
Similar to the exemption of government procurement from the national treatment obligation in Article III:8(a), the non-discrimination obligations of Article XVII:1 "shall not apply to imports of products for immediate or ultimate consumption in governmental use and not otherwise for resale or use in the production of goods for sale" (Article XVII:2). Yet, "with respect to such imports, each contracting party shall accord to the trade of the other contracting parties fair and equitable treatment" (Article XVII:2 second sentence). During the drafting of this provision, the U.S. delegate explained this clause by saying

> [The] most-favoured-nation treatment should also apply to the awarding of government contracts. But it could not be applied to government purchases with the same precision which was possible in the case of fiscal measures. That was why the phrase 'fair and equitable treatment' had been used in the Draft Charter.[29]

So far, no GATT or WTO dispute settlement panel has made a finding based on Article XVII:2. This might also be due to the fact that the 1979 and 1994

Agreements on Government Procurement have strengthened and enlarged the non-discrimination requirements relating to government procurement.

The Liberalization Objective (Article XVII:3)

Article XVII:3 GATT recognizes that STEs

> might be operated so as to create serious obstacles to trade; thus negotiations on a reciprocal and mutually advantageous basis designed to limit or reduce such obstacles are of importance to the expansion of international trade.

By acknowledging in its interpretative note that such negotiations "may be directed towards the reduction of duties and other charges on imports and exports or towards the conclusion of any other mutually satisfactory arrangement consistent with the provisions of this Agreement", Article XVII:3 reflects the fact that STEs may lead to non-tariff trade barriers not being effectively covered by the general GATT disciplines of Articles II, III, and XI.[30]

In contrast to the extensive tariff concessions bound under GATT Article II, commitments regarding state trading operations in GATT countries with market economies have been made only rarely in the various GATT Rounds (see Roessler 1978: 268). In GATT and WTO negotiations on the accession of former state trading countries, in contrast, commitments have been sought not only on the market behaviour of STEs but also on the liberalization of their exclusive trading rights so as to liberalize the market structure itself (demonopolization).

Notification and Information Requirements (Article XVII:4)

The procedures for notifications and reviews under Article XVII:4 were progressively improved in 1960, 1962, and 1994 (GATT Analytical Index: 482). The 1960 questionnaire on state trading is the format in which contracting parties and, since 1995, WTO Members are required to submit their notifications under Article XVII.[31] The problems of monitoring and enforcing Article XVII are illustrated by the fact that under GATT 1947 the majority of member countries appear not to have met their notification obligations. In the "new and full" notifications (as opposed to updating notifications) in 1990/93, for instance, seven GATT contracting parties responded to the request in 1990, one of them stating that it did not maintain any state trading enterprises; in 1993, eleven contracting parties responded, two of them indicating that they did not maintain any state trading enterprises. This unsatisfactory record of compliance with the notification requirements in the area of state trading increases the non-transparency in the trade conducted by STEs. According to a 1995 background paper by the WTO Secretariat,

> [t]he fact that there are very few recent Article XVII notifications from current or former non-market economy countries makes it difficult to meaningfully assess the current state trading situation in such countries as a whole.[32]

The same background paper also emphasizes "that Article XVII notifications often lack information on the precise operations of the identified state trading enterprises".

3. Problem Areas Needing Clarification by the WTO

Is the 1994 Understanding Definition Adequate?

The above-mentioned "working definition" of STEs, which applies only to the notification requirements under Article XVII, is narrower than the legal definition of STEs in Article XVII:1(a). Whereas Article XVII:1(a) includes any "state enterprise", the working definition covers "governmental enterprises" only if they "have been granted exclusive or special rights or privileges . . . in the exercise of which they influence through their purchases or sales the level or direction of imports or exports." Does this limitation of the definition, notification requirements, and transparency of STEs also risk limiting the effective scope of application of Article XVII:1?

The narrower working definition seems to reflect proposals during the Uruguay Round negotiations "that attention should be concentrated on the functions these enterprises fulfilled rather than on their form or ownership"[33] and

> that state ownership per se does not confer special powers or privileges, since many state-owned enterprises operate in a fully competitive environment, and that those which do so would not be subject to Article XVII disciplines, including the notification requirement.[34]

This latter claim appears contradictory for two reasons. First, even if it *should* be true that "many state-owned enterprises operate in a fully competitive environment" (*quod est demonstrandum!*), it does not follow that all of them do so. Since the purpose of the notification requirement is to provide transparency as to whether state-owned enterprises do in fact operate according to commercial considerations in a competitive environment, it would seem justifiable — at least in principle — that the notification requirements under Article XVII:4 of GATT 1947 applied to any "state enterprise". At least the burden of proof should remain with the country operating state-owned enterprises to show that its state ownership does not lead to discriminatory trade-distorting practices.

Second, it seems likewise incorrect to claim that state-owned enterprises are not "subject to Article XVII disciplines" if they operate in a "fully competitive environment". Since the 1994 Understanding on the Interpretation of Article XVII is explicitly "without prejudice to the substantive disciplines prescribed in Article XVII", the non-discrimination requirements of Article XVII:1 continue to be applicable to all "state enterprises" as defined in Article XVII:1, even if they are not covered by the new "working definition" which applies only to the notification requirements. The limitation of the definition of STEs in respect of the notification requirements (Article XVII:4) also risks limiting the effectiveness of the substantive non-discrimination obligations of "state enterprises" under Article XVII:1.

The limitation of the definition of STEs is therefore not the optimal policy instrument for resolving the practical problem that the notification requirements have been widely disregarded in GATT practice. A more effective approach has been chosen in paragraphs 4 and 5 of the WTO Understanding on the Interpretation of Article XVII, which provide for the possibility of bilateral consultations on the notification obligations, counter-notifications, and the setting-up of a WTO Working Party on STEs with the mandate

> to review notifications and counter-notifications. In the light of this review and without prejudice to paragraph 4(c) of Article XVII, the Council for Trade in Goods may make recommendations with regard to the adequacy of notifications and the need for further information. The working party shall also review, in the light of the notifications received, the adequacy of the above-mentioned questionnaire on state trading and the coverage of state trading enterprises notified under paragraph 1. It shall also develop an illustrative list showing the kinds of relationships between governments and enterprises, and the kinds of activities, engaged in by these enterprises, which may be relevant for the purposes of Article XVII.

The purpose of this illustrative list is thus not only to clarify the two key elements used in the "working definition": (1) whether enterprises have been "granted exclusive or special rights or privileges" in the exercise of which (2) "they influence through their purchases or sales the level or direction of imports or exports". The mandate of the Working Group goes, with good reason, beyond this task and includes "showing the kinds of relationships between governments and enterprises, and the kinds of activities, engaged in by these enterprises, which may be relevant for the purposes of Article XVII". The review of the adequacy of notifications under Article XVII, and the development of an illustrative list of relationships between governments and STEs, should also assist the WTO Council for Trade in Goods to review whether the narrow "working definition" in the 1994 WTO Understanding does not risk undermining the broader definition of STEs, and their correspondingly broad substantive obligations under Article XVII.

It remains to be clarified in particular which kinds of state ownership of enterprises justify the assumption underlying Article XVII:4 that purchases or sales by a "state enterprise" may not be made "solely in accordance with commercial considerations", as required by Article XVII:1(b), and therefore call for international notification, transparency, and surveillance. For example, if the STE (1) is a branch of a government ministry and is financed by government budget allocations, or (2) has another public law statute different from private law companies, or (3) the capital and management of a private law company are exclusively or predominantly controlled by the government (e.g., for the purposes of carrying out a government-determined program), it may be viewed *per se* as enjoying "special rights or privileges"; by recognizing that compared to private enterprises, certain forms and exercises of state ownership can be tantamount to a "special right or privilege", the narrow "working definition" of STEs could lead to the same results as the broader legal definition of STEs in Article XVII. With regard to these and other kinds of state ownership, the frequent lack of transparency in the relationships between governments and state-owned enterprises, and the ease of abusing the state ownership for discriminatory practices (e.g., by using foreign exchange controls, the allocation of quotas, subsidies or other discretionary government policies for the benefit of state-owned enterprises), seem to warrant the broader definition of STEs in Article XVII:1 and the broader notification requirements under the old Article XVII:4 of GATT 1947. Yet, such notification requirements might not be necessary and should be limited in the case of other kinds of state ownership, for instance if the government owns only part of the shares of a private law enterprise that is organized separately from the government and operates without major government involvement in a competitive environment.

Making Notification Requirements More Effective

In contrast to the unsatisfactory experience under GATT 1947 where only twenty-five contracting parties submitted substantive notifications under Article XVII from 1980 to 1995, sixty-eight WTO member countries had submitted "new and full" notifications under the WTO Understanding on the Interpretation of Article XVII by the end of 1997. In the area of updating notifications, forty-two had been received for 1996, but only fifteen for 1997. While this represents a remarkable increase in notifications compared to the GATT 1947, about half of the WTO member countries still fail to meet their notification obligations under Article XVII and the pertinent WTO Understanding. No counter-notifications have been received.

The negotiations on the revision of the 1960 questionnaire on state trading enterprises[35] appear to be close to reaching a consensus on a revised text in 1998; the outstanding differences center on the type of statistical information that should be requested in the questionnaire. The revision of the 1960 questionnaire is closely related to the additional task of the WTO Working Party on State Trading Enterprises, namely to develop an illustrative list showing the kinds of relationships between governments and STEs and the kinds of activities engaged in by STEs. Such an illustrative list should give priority to those relationships between governments and STEs, and to those activities engaged in by STEs, which have significant trade implications and, therefore, should be subject to more specific notification requirements and more rigorous review in the WTO. The objective of focusing the notification requirements under Article XVII:4 on the trade-related, and notably on trade-distorting, activities of STEs can be better achieved by a redefinition of the questionnaire on state trading and by a ranking of the notification requirements according to the "special privileges" and trade-distorting RBPs, than by a too limited redefinition of the legal concept of STEs. In the November 1997 meeting of the Working Party on State Trading Enterprises, for instance, the United States rejected the view that STEs which no longer had monopoly import rights were no longer STEs; in the U.S. view, monopoly import or export rights were not the only special rights and privileges that were covered by the definition of state trading enterprise.

Strengthening the Substantive Obligations of Article XVII

The need for clarifying and strengthening the legal limits of monopolies and STEs in national, regional, and worldwide foreign trade rules has been recognized for a long time.[36] In September 1996, the EC suggested continuing and widening the tasks of the Working Party on STEs; following the revision of the 1960 questionnaire and the clarification of the notification requirements, the Working Party should examine also whether Article XVII and the 1994 Understanding needed further strengthening in order to guarantee market access, non-discrimination, and a balance of rights and obligations of WTO Members. According to the EC, the number of former state trading countries currently seeking accession to the WTO increases the importance of Article XVII and the need to ensure that STEs do not undermine the market access rights and obligations of WTO Members. The EC suggested that the WTO Working Party on STEs could examine in particular:

- whether Article XVII can be reviewed so that its provisions are understood to ensure that trading monopolies of an *exclusive* kind have to be adjusted to guarantee that private traders may engage in parallel import or export trade of the product covered by an Article XVII exception;

- the scope of Article XVII of GATT (what entities are covered and which disciplines apply). In general, the relation between the obligation of non-discriminatory treatment and purchases or sales in accordance with commercial considerations on one hand, and competition-related principles on the other, could be re-examined. If necessary, a strengthening of Article XVII of GATT could be considered to guarantee competitive conduct.

This initiative followed an earlier proposal in an EC Expert Group Report on "Competition Policy in the New Trade Order: Strengthening International Cooperation and Rules". That Report states that

Article XVII of the GATT relating to the obligations of national monopolies or companies with 'exclusive or special privileges' would need to be strengthened in so far as these enterprises should generally be subject to the same rules as other enterprises exercising a commercial activity.[37]

Even though the EC proposal to broaden the mandate of the Working Party was not taken up at the WTO Ministerial Conference at Singapore in December 1996, several WTO Members supported the idea of strengthening not only the procedural notification requirements, but also the substantive non-discrimination obligations under Article XVII.

Proposals for the strengthening of Article XVII had already been discussed in the Uruguay Round Negotiating Group on GATT Articles. In order to reduce the uncertainty about the meaning and clarify the obligations of Article XVII, the United States, for instance, made the following four negotiating proposals[38]:

1. Agreement by contracting parties that Article XVII is a complementary discipline, and that the activities of state trading enterprises are subject to all GATT disciplines.

2. Agreement by contracting parties that (1) the national treatment obligation of Article III applies to state trading; (2) Article XI's prohi-

bition against quantitative and other restrictions, both formal and informal, applies to state trading; and (3) the subsidies disciplines embodied in Articles VI and XVI apply to state trading as well.

3. Agreement by Contracting Parties that the complementary discipline approach to state trading applies to all types of state trading enterprises, including all types of marketing boards. In other words, marketing boards are subject to all GATT disciplines.

4. Agreement by Contracting Parties to establish a working party which would (a) develop an illustrative list of practices associated with state trading, (b) review the state trading questionnaire and make necessary revisions, and (c) conduct periodic comprehensive reviews of notifications and provide a forum for discussion and clarificaton of state trading issues and problems.

Only the fourth proposal became part of the WTO Understanding on the Interpretation of Article XVII, and this with the too narrow "working definition" of STEs. As a consequence, the scope of the substantive obligations of Article XVII and their relationships with other GATT Articles (such as Articles III and XX(d) if a STE discriminates against imports through a monopoly of distribution in the importing country) remain uncertain in several respects. For instance, under what conditions does GATT Article III apply to discriminatory practices of distribution monopolies in the importing country? When are trade monopolies equivalent to quantitative restrictions prohibited by GATT Article XI? Which kinds of measures and exclusive trading rights can be justified by the exception in GATT Article XX(d) to take "measures necessary to secure the enforcement" of monopolies?

There is today increasing concern that access to markets for goods (e.g., agricultural goods controlled by state monopolies and marketing boards in the importing country) and services (e.g., basic telecommunication services) may be impaired by STEs, monopolies, or abuses of market power. In GATS negotiations (notably on telecommunications), and also in WTO accession negotiations with former state trading countries, WTO Members are increasingly seeking market access commitments not only in regard to the market conduct of STEs, but also regarding their exclusive "trading rights" and the "market structure". The so-called "Reference Paper", which forms part of the commitments made by many WTO Members in the 1997 GATS Protocol on Basic Telecommunications, includes specific competition rules so as to prevent major suppliers from engaging in anticompetitive RBPs (such as cross-subsidization and misuse of information). This "deregulation" and "competition law approach", which has also been actively used in European Community law for the liberalization of trade in goods and services (e.g., in the context of requirements, based on Articles 37 and 90 of the EC Treaty, to remove import monopolies and other exclusive rights), has obvious advantages over the traditional "GATT approach". By recourse to general competition policy principles, it is also likely to enhance the mutual coherence of WTO rules and government policies in different sectors.

It would therefore be desirable if the Working Party on STEs, after completing its task of revising the 1960 questionnaire and clarifying the notification requirements, would take up the above-mentioned and other proposals for clarifying and stengthening the substantive obligations under Article XVII. As the problems of STEs are also being examined in the context of various other WTO bodies, such as the Working Parties on the accession of former state trading countries and the WTO Working Group on the Interaction between Trade and Competition Policy, there is a need for ensuring the overall consistency of dealing with these problems in WTO accession protocols, GATS protocols on the liberalization of certain services sectors, and in GATT practice relating to Article XVII.

A "pragmatic approach" to the reform of Article XVII could focus on strengthened legal disciplines in future Protocols of Accession to the WTO for former state trading countries (like China, Russia, and Vietnam). This might be politically easier to achieve than any direct attempt at formally amending Article XVII or negotiating generally applicable reforms of Article XVII in the context of a future "WTO Round". Such a pragmatic approach might be criticized as unfair by former state trading countries negotiating their accession to the WTO. But it would offer an economically efficient and politically feasible approach to the task of strengthening the legal disciplines on STEs in former state trading countries, an approach certainly preferable to the alternative of unilateral uses of "unfair trade remedies" in response to perceived trade distortions caused by STEs.

4. Summary of Conclusions

The main conclusions of this chapter may be summarized as follows:

1. The "working definition" of STEs in the 1994 Understanding is narrower than the legal definition in Article XVII:1(a).

    This narrow definition was not convincingly explained and justified during the Uruguay Round negotiations. It seems doubtful whether the criteria used for the "working definition" — (1) "exclusive or special rights or privileges, including statutory or constitutional powers"; (2) "in the exercise of which they influence through their purchases or sales the level or direction of imports or exports" — cover all potential discriminatory RBPs by state-owned enterprises, especially if the discrimination does not result from governmental measures of general application, but from discretionary regulatory measures (such as exchange control measures, subsidies and tax benefits, administration of licenses and quotas). The "working definition" therefore does not seem to be the optimal policy instrument for dealing with the practical problem of the widespread non-compliance with the notification requirements under Article XVII. The resultant limitation of the scope of the legal notification requirements under Article XVII:4 risks undermining the substantive legal obligations for "state enterprises" under Article XVII:1(a), and the burden of proof on state-owned enterprises, in cases where the state enterprise is not covered by the "working definition" and the dispute is essentially about whether the government ownership has been abused for special privileges and trade distortions.

Without notification requirements and WTO surveillance of state-owned enterprises that are claimed not to be covered by the "working definition", the Article XVII disciplines — albeit not formally amended — risk becoming even less effective than before. The "working definition" should therefore be construed as a temporary, pragmatic definition for the work assigned to the WTO Working Party on STEs; it should not prejudge a future review and amendment of Article XVII GATT by WTO Members and, as explicitly recognized in the 1994 Understanding, "is without prejudice to the substantive disciplines prescribed in Article XVII".

2. Under GATT 1947, the majority of member countries did not meet their notification requirements under Article XVII:4.

Under the WTO, the number of new and full notifications has increased, yet the majority of WTO Members fail to make timely updating notifications. Trade conducted by STEs, and their compliance with GATT disciplines, often continue to lack transparency. This problem risks becoming larger with the increasing WTO membership of former state trading countries. The need for focusing the Article XVII:4 notification requirements on trade-distorting government-enterprise relationships and on RBPs of STEs can be better achieved by a revision of the questionnaire on state trading, and by giving priority to the notification of "special privileges" and trade-distorting RBPs, than by a too-limited redefinition of the legal concept of STEs. The elaboration, by the WTO Working Party on STEs, of an illustrative list of actually or potentially trade-distorting

RBPs and government relationships of STEs can render the notification requirements more effective and, at the same time, reduce the burden of notifying less problematic activities and relationships of STEs. In addition to the WTO Working Party on STEs, there might also be other WTO bodies (such as the WTO Trade Policy Review Body) which could strengthen their surveillance of compliance with the notification requirements for STEs.

3.   There is a need for clarifying and strengthening the substantive obligations of Article XVII and their relationships with other GATT Articles and WTO Agreements.

The mandate of the WTO Working Party on STEs should be enlarged to examine proposals made by WTO Members for strengthening the substantive legal disciplines of STEs and the liberalization of their exclusive trading rights, including the suggested clarification that Article XVII compliments the other GATT disciplines which, even if they do not specifically refer to STEs, apply not only to WTO Members but also to their STEs (including marketing boards). Since a formal amendment, or alternatively another "Understanding on the Interpretation of Article XVII", may be difficult to achieve, the proposals for clarifying and strengthening the substantive obligations of Article XVII could be anticipated by including them in future Protocols of Accession to the WTO with former state trading countries. Such a progressive inclusion in WTO law of stricter legal disciplines on STEs could facilitate a later consensus on a generally applicable reform of Article XVII of GATT. Apart from attempts at strengthening the general GATT legal disciplines on STEs, there is a strong case for negotiating additional competition rules and commitments for the deregulation of STEs and the progressive abolition of their special rights and privileges.

NOTES

1. BISD 35S/163, 229.

2. BISD 39S/27, 79–80.

3. BISD 35S/37, 90.

4. WTO, 1 Annual Report 1997 59 (Geneva: WTO, 1997).

5. The text of Article XVII GATT and of the WTO Understanding on Article XVII is reproduced in the Annex.

6. See BISD 35S/163, 229–230.

7. See the case law referred to in GATT 469 et seq.

8. For details see, e.g., Jackson, et al. 1150–1153. Note that Cuba and Czechoslovakia had joined the GATT at a time when they were still market economies. In the case of the former Yugoslavia, the country was considered to be sufficiently market-oriented so as not to necessitate additional GATT provisions on STE.

9. BISD 15S/46, 52.

10. BISD 18S/5–10.

11. BISD 20S/3–8.

12. Cf. WTO, Annual Report 1997 59.

13. See WTO document G/STR/W/33.

14. GATT 483.

15. For references see the GATT under Articles II:4 and XI:1.

16. L/2281, paras. 9–10.

17. BISD 36S/268, 301–302.

18. See GATT 473.

19. BISD 9S/179–184.

20. See the GATT 475.

21. BISD 1S/59, 60.

22. See BISD 4S/38, 39: "As the representative of Haiti informed the Working Party that the import licenses issued by the Régie may be used for purchases from any source, it was considered that the measure did not conflict with the provisions of Article XVII calling for non-discriminatory treatment".

23. BISD 30S/140, 163.

24. BISD 35S/37, 90.

25. "The provisions of sub-paragraph (a) of this paragraph shall be understood to require that such enterprises shall, having due regard to the other provisions of this Agreement, make any such purchases or sales solely in accordance with commercial considerations, including price, quality, availability, marketability, transportation and other conditions of purchase or sale, and shall afford the enterprises of the other contracting parties adequate opportunity, in accordance with customary business practice, to compete for participation in such purchases or sales."

26. BISD 30S/140, 163.

27. BISD 30S/140, 163.

28. BISD 35S/116, 159–160.

29. See GATT 481.

30. The 1989 Panel report on "United States - Restrictions on Imports of Sugar" followed from this interpretative note:

The negotiations foreseen in Article XVII:3 are thus not to result in arrangements inconsistent with the General Agreement, in particular not quantitative restrictions made effective through state-trading that are not justified by an exception to Article XI:1 . . . .

BISD 36S/222, 228.

31. BISD 9S/184–185.

32. G/STR/2, para.58.

33. See, e.g., MTN.GNG/NG7/4, at 6.

34. See the Note by the Chairman of the Uruguay Round Negotiating Group on GATT Articles, 2 February 1990, p. 3.

35. See BISD 9S/184–185.

36. See, e.g., D. Edward and M. Hoskins, "Article 90: Deregulation and EC Law," 32:1 Common Market L. Rev. 157–186 (1995) who emphasize the inherent limitations in judicial control and call for additional EC legislation to clarify the legal limits of monopolies and state regulation (e.g., if legal monopolies use "cross-subsidization" to undersell competitors in competitive markets, or if the universal supply obligations of the monopolist risk being economically undermined by profitable "creaming off" activities by specialized suppliers).

37. EC 1995: 23.

38. Document MTN.GNG/NG7/55 of 13 October 1989.

REFERENCES

EC. 1995. Competition Policy in the New Trade Order: Strengthening International Cooperation and Rules.

GATT. 1995. Analytical Index. Guide to GATT Law and Practice. Geneva: WTO.

Jackson, John H., William J. Davey, Alan Sykes. 1995. Legal Problems of International Economic Relations. St. Paul: West Publishing.

Petersmann, Ernst-Ulrich. 1993. "International Competition Rules for the GATT-WTO World Trade and Legal System." Journal of World Trade 27/6: 35.

Roessler, Frieder. 1978 "State Trading and Trade Liberalization." In M.M. Kostecki, ed. East-West Trade and the GATT System. London: Macmillan. pp. 261–284.

CHAPTER 4

The Treatment of Activities of State Trading Enterprises under the WTO Subsidies Rules

*Gary N. Horlick** and Kristin Heim Mowry***

1. Introduction

The World Trade Organization (WTO) Agreements establish the rules by which international trade is conducted throughout most of the world. The WTO rules are comprised of a number of separate agreements.[1] This chapter examines how the activities of state trading enterprises (STEs) relate to the subsidies provisions of the WTO, in particular through the interaction of Article XVII of GATT 1994, the Understanding on the Interpretation of Article XVII, the Agreement on Agriculture, and the Agreement on Subsidies and Countervailing Measures ("Subsidies Agreement").[2]

2. Historical Background on STEs

The activities of STEs are governed by Article XVII of GATT 1994, which requires the STEs of members to "act in a manner consistent with the general principles of non-discriminatory treatment," (1(a)), and to "make purchases or sales solely in accordance with commercial considerations," (1(b)). The 1994 WTO Understanding on the Interpretation of Article XVII established the working definition of STEs as:

> Governmental and non-governmental enterprises, including marketing boards, which have been granted exclusive or special rights or privileges, including statutory or constitutional powers, in the exercise of which they influence through their purchases or sales the level of direction of imports or exports.

A WTO member's obligations under Article XVII require that purchases and sales by STEs be made in accordance with commercial considerations. Ad-

---

*O'Melveny & Myers, LLP, Washington, D.C.; formerly Deputy Assistant Secretary, Import Administration, U.S. Department of Commerce.
**O'Melveny & Myers, LLP, Washington, D.C.; Georgetown University Law Center, *juris doctor* candidate, 1998; formerly of Office of Investigations, Import Administration, U.S. Department of Commerce.

herence to this requirement would allow enterprises from other member countries to compete with STEs on a commercial basis.

Principles of Non-Discriminatory Treatment

The phrase "in a manner consistent with the general principles of non-discriminatory treatment" has been much debated. The question is whether this phrase is intended to mean one or two of the fundamental principles of the GATT: most-favored nation (MFN) (Article I, GATT 1994) and national treatment (Article III GATT 1994).[3] While there is much agreement that the phrase includes MFN[4], it is disputed whether national treatment is required as well[5]. Most-favored nation and national treatment are the mechanisms that ensure the achievement of the overall goal of the GATT — more equal competitive opportunities through the reduction of tariffs and some other trade barriers.[6] The MFN principle requires that all trading partners receive equal treatment from a country. The principle of national treatment reflected in Article III requires that, once imported, a product from any member will receive equal treatment to domestic products.

Some light on the dispute may be shed by Article XVII. It allows for some exceptions for STEs to this non-discriminatory treatment obligation. It does not apply to government procurement, i.e., government purchase for government use.[7] This exception parallels the government procurement exception in Article III:8(a). Article XVII permits the receipt of a "tied loan" to be a "commercial consideration".[8] In addition, it permits export price discrimination provided the price differential is caused by varying market conditions in the export markets.[9] Some scholars have interpreted the permission of export price discrimination as an implicit prohibition of price discrimination in the domestic import market.[10]

The United States has taken the view that the phrase "general principles of non-discriminatory treatment" includes *both* MFN *and* national treatment.[11] In a GATT panel proceeding, the United States argued that Canada's Foreign Investment Review Act (FIRA) prevented investors from acting in accordance with commercial considerations.[12] Part of the U.S. argument included analysis of the term *principles* of non-discrimination, thereby implying that more than just MFN was at issue. Canada took the view that Article XVII only required MFN treatment, and included in its analysis an historical review of the documents leading up to Article XVII.[13] Ultimately the GATT Panel decided the FIRA issue on grounds that the Canadian measure was inconsistent with Article III, and therefore did not make its ruling on the basis of Article XVII. In stating that it was not the appropriate time to decide whether Article XVII imposed a national treatment requirement, the Panel went so far as to note that it "saw great force in Canada's argument that only the most-favored-nation and not the national treatment obligations fall within the scope of the general principles referred to in Article XVII.1(a)".[14]

Duty To Notify

Article XVII imposes upon members the obligation to notify the WTO (and previously the GATT) the activities of its STEs.[15] A questionnaire was developed in 1960 to elicit the appropriate STE information and thereby increase transparency.

Member countries are not required to include in their notifications any confidential information that would impede law enforcement, be contrary to the public interest, or prejudice the legitimate commercial interests of their STEs.[16] Nevertheless, this reporting requirement, while aimed at increasing transparency, has fallen far short of its goal.

A review of notifications from 1980 through 1994 revealed that only twenty-nine member countries submitted STE notifications, with eight of those reporting no STE activities at all. In 1981, the most successful year of STE reporting, seventy-nine percent of GATT contracting parties did not submit STE notifications.[17] Research conducted by the U.S. General Accounting Office revealed that parties gave the following reasons for not complying with the notification requirement:

a) confusion over the definition of STEs;

b) lack of a systematic review of notifications received;

c) apparent low priority given to STE notification requirement by some GATT members;

d) overall burden associated with GATT reporting requirements.[18]

The dearth of information on STEs and the apparently inconsistent reporting among those members that have complied with the notification requirements renders a complete analysis of STE activity unlikely. However, the WTO Working Party on STEs produced a Background Paper to examine the level and content of reporting, and the adequacy of the 1960 questionnaire.[19] This Background Paper provides the basis for an examination of how STE activities may be treated under the WTO subsidies rules.

The majority of problems with notification requirements has apparently been mitigated by the adoption of the Understanding. In 1995, 45 out of 108 members (the EU having submitted a single notification for its 15 members) submitted full STE notifications. Despite the increased participation, discrepancies concerning the interpretation of the Understanding remain.[20]

3. Can STEs Confer Subsidies?[21]

In order to examine whether and to what extent the activities of STEs will be covered by the Subsidies Agreement, it is necessary to review briefly 1) the definition of a subsidy and 2) the methods by which governments operate STEs.

In order to be a subsidy under the Subsidies Agreement, a law or program must provide either a financial contribution as described in Article 1.1(a)(1) or a price or income support.[22] In either case, it must provide a benefit. In examining the possibility of subsidies given by an STE, one would primarily look to the provision of goods or services, or to the purchase of goods under item (iii) or to price supports under item (a)(2). Nevertheless, other measures under Article 1.1, e.g., direct transfer of funds such as loan guarantees, or foregone revenue in the form of uncollected levies, should not be ignored.

The WTO Background Paper explains the activities of STEs under the following general categories: statutory, regulatory and export marketing boards; fiscal monopolies; canalizing agencies; foreign trade enterprises; and corporations resulting from nationalization of industries (e.g., the coal and steel, motor vehicles, and aluminum industries).[23]

The WTO Working Party on STEs also reported the following objectives of STEs identified by members: income support; price stabilization; expansion of domestic output; continuity in domestic food supply; increase in government revenue (or decrease in spending); rationalization and control of foreign trade operations; protection of public health; management of important domestic resources; fulfillment of international commitments on price and/or quantity.[24]

Finally, the Background Paper compiled a list of seventeen different STE operations.[25] For purposes of examining potential subsidization by STEs, we highlight the following types of operations: involvement in support schemes for domestic production; import and export operations (including possible monopoly of either or both); domestic distribution of imports; credit guarantees for producers and processors; granting of licenses (for import, export, or production); and intervention purchases and sales (based on floor and ceiling prices).[26]

The Agriculture Dilemma

The nature of STEs creates the possibility for the provision of an export subsidy. If a country decides to distort the trading pattern that would otherwise exist, an agency operating in the purchase and sale of the product would be in a perfect position to provide some benefit to the producer who exports rather than the one who sells domestically. Export subsidies are prohibited under the Subsidies Agreement (Article 3). However, Article 3.1 qualifies the prohibition with the following introduction, "except as provided in the Agreement on Agriculture".

Therefore, to the extent an STE does provide a trade distortive export subsidy, that subsidy may not be prohibited or even actionable under the Subsidies Agreement at the WTO level if the program under which it is provided is included in the member's export subsidy reduction commitments under the Agriculture Agreement.[27] However, even if the subsidy is not actionable at the WTO, it can be countervailable at the domestic level.[28]

The largest number of STEs notified involve agricultural products such as grains and dairy.[29] Ranked by value of agricultural products shipped, the four largest STEs dealing with agricultural products (agro-STEs) are the Canadian Wheat Board (CWB), the New Zealand Dairy Board, the Australian Wheat Board, and the Queensland Sugar Corporation.[30] Many countries believe that the United States should have notified the Commodity Credit Corporation (CCC) yearly. However, the United States did so only once prior to 1995.[31]

Unlike export subsidies, which are explicitly identified and subject to reduction under the Agreement on Agriculture, the export activities of an agro-STE are difficult to discern and, as is discussed below, often very difficult to measure.

A recent academic study of two-tiered pricing systems for milk indicates that such a system could result in a violation of Article 9 of the Agriculture Agreement which requires members to reduce their level of export subsidization.[32]

Several U.S. industries have raised concerns regarding agro-STEs in Australia,[33] New Zealand[34], and Canada.[35]

Measurement of Adequate Remuneration

The Subsidies Agreement, at Article 14, defines the issue in terms of "adequate remuneration". This phrase requires remuneration to be determined in relation to "prevailing market conditions for the good or service in question in the country of provision or purchase (including price, quality, availability, marketability, transportation, and other conditions of purchase or sale)".[36]

Prior to the WTO Agreement, the U.S. Commerce Department followed certain preferential pricing guidelines regarding the determination of whether a good or service was provided at preferential rates. Commerce would compare the price charged or paid by the government entity to a benchmark price, which normally would be the "nonselective prices the government charges to the same or other users of the good or service within the same political jurisdiction".[37]

Commerce developed the following alternative benchmarks, in order of preference:

1. the non-selective price, i.e., the price the STE charges for a good or service which is similar or related to the good or service in question, adjusted for any difference in variable cost of production;

2. the price charged by other sellers to buyers within the same political jurisdiction for an identical good or service;

3. the STE's cost of providing the good or service; or

4. the price paid for the identical good or service outside the political jurisdiction in question.

The first alternative should be relatively non-controversial — if the STE is selling at a lower price (adjusted for relevant cost differences) to selected companies or industries, the possibility of subsidy is apparent (and, obviously, parallel to the specificity requirement of Article 2).

The second alternative, also subject to the Article 2 specificity requirement, falls within the same parameters. The more difficult case is when the STE is the only seller — the mere fact of selling below cost by an STE is not automatically "non-commercial" within the meaning of Article XVII — in particular if one uses the protectionist measure of cost found in the WTO Antidumping Agreement.[38] Finally, the use of data from outside the jurisdiction is probably inconsistent with the Subsidies Agreement, which focuses (correctly) on benchmarks within the relevant unit[39] — except perhaps as "facts available" (in the spirit of Article 12.7 of the Subsidies Agreement) where the respondent in a subsidies case does not supply information within its control.

An example shows the complexity of these cases in practice. In a countervailing duty case involving carbon black from Mexico, the U.S. Department of Commerce found that there were too few users (two companies) in Mexico of an input product, carbon black feedstock (CBFS), to determine if the STE price was preferential. There were no other sellers, so alternative 2 in the preferentiality hierarchy would not be available. The STE failed to supply the data needed for alternative 3. Commerce correctly did not use the price of CBFS in another country (alternative 4). Instead, Commerce tried to compare the STE's mark-up over cost for CBFS to the same STE's mark-up over cost for sales of a very similar product, number six fuel oil. If the mark-up on CBFS were lower than the mark-up on number six fuel oil, there would be preferential pricing (or now, inadequate remuneration). Since the STE would not supply the necessary data, however, Commerce, as "best information available", compared the ratio of prices of number six fuel oil to CBFS in the United States.[40] Commerce made this decision on the theory that if the ratio of prices charged by the STE was greater than the ratio of prices in an open market, the STE price of CBFS in Mexico was inadequate.

The parameters of Article 14 of the Subsidies Agreement, while somewhat instructive, have not been refined to the point of predictability. The U.S. Department of Commerce has reserved its definition of adequate remuneration in its recently published proposed countervailing duty regulations. Commerce states in the preamble:

> we are reluctant to go beyond the terms of the statute and the [Statement of Administrative Action[41]]. . . . Instead, we intend to apply this new standard on a case-by-case basis.[42]

It should be noted, however, that Commerce does not close the door on the preferentiality hierarchy. "[W]e do not believe this precludes us from continuing to apply certain preferentiality based analyses we have used in the past."[43]

Commerce has received significant comments on this proposed regulations. Several commenters (including a law firm which typically represents complainants; a law firm representing Micron Technology, a frequent complainant; and a law firm which represents members of the steel pipe and tube industry) pointed out that the benchmark of adequate remuneration should include all costs associated with a good, including transport costs.[44] Others suggest that the effect, if any, of government involvement or participation in a particular market should be included in any analysis for an appropriate benchmark.[45] One commenter, a law firm typically representing complainants, noted that where an STE purchases or sells to the sole domestic producer/consumer, there could be no analysis of "market conditions" and therefore suggests that the benchmark be the world market price.[46]

One commenter, another law firm typically representing complainants, suggests that adequate remuneration means "the market price for the good or service at issue in the jurisdiction of the subsidizing government absent government intervention associated with a subsidy program".[47] This commenter further suggests that the benefit should be measured by comparing the price paid to a benchmark price, which should be "adjusted to the extent necessary to best reflect an un-subsidized or non-specific price". This same commenter also makes the point that this market-based standard would preclude using the price the government charges to other users as a benchmark. Assuming there is specificity, it is argued that there is no reason to believe that the government prices to other users reflect the market value.

Finally, envisioning a situation where all prices (for the good or service) in the jurisdiction are distorted by government intervention associated with a subsidy program, the benchmark should be "the least distortive price . . . in a neighboring jurisdiction". Distortion of the market by government involvement for this commenter means something more than thirty-five percent of the market receiving the subsidy. One may question why this commenter would suggest the price in a neighboring jurisdiction — query whether, if one were examining a price for goods in South Korea, it would be appropriate to choose Japan as a comparison market.

Commerce also received the suggestion from the government of Quebec that it should understand that "different users supplied solely by the government-owned company may legitimately have different rate structures".[48] These "sole source" situations should not automatically result in a countervailable benefit if, when there are differing rates for different industries, the rates take into account the market situations of the various users. The government of Quebec specifically refers to provision of electricity, water, and natural gas as examples of this type of sole source situation.

Commerce received comments from the Boeing Company that suggested Commerce specifically include those purchases made by a government monopoly in its regulation covering adequate remuneration for the purchase of goods.[49] Boeing suggests this be done in order to address the subsidization of an industry through the purchase of goods by indirect means.

At the time of printing this article, Commerce has not yet issued its final countervailing duty regulations that will include responses to the above comments.

Examples of Potentially-Subsidizing STEs

Statutory Marketing Boards
Statutory marketing boards are the most common form of STE for agricultural products such as grains and dairy. Statutory marketing boards are government or quasi-government agencies characterized by exclusive authority to purchase domestic production, control output, set consumer and producer prices, and control foreign trade.[50] There may also be an added benefit of the consolidation of marketing and transaction costs which the STE already has absorbed. The Background Paper cites as functions of STEs reduction of overhead costs, foreign market development, and quality control.[51] In addition, there may be an "economies of scale" advantage to consolidating ship-

ping costs, insurance, and other transaction costs. Agricultural products are generally characterized by inelastic demand and fluctuating supply. Marketing boards can operate as monopsonists (sole buyers) in their domestic market and oligopolists (one of few sellers) in external markets. The potential for engaging in unfair competition, which can result in trade effects, is significant for an export-monopsony or -monopoly.

In the most straightforward case, a grain board could purchase a domestically produced product at a higher rate than that for which it could sell it on the international market. Therefore, if an STE in country X buys from its farmers at $1 per bushel and sells for 95¢ per bushel in country Y, country Y, on behalf of its growers, may be able to challenge this under the Subsidies Agreement or start a countervailing duty (CVD) case and/or an antidumping (AD) case (as long as there is no double-counting).[52] Country Y will claim that the government of country X did not receive adequate remuneration from the customer for that product.

The difference in price is a financial contribution and the benefit is the difference between the price the domestic producer gets from the STE and the price at which it could sell on the world market if it had to act on its own.

Country Y could claim that it has suffered adverse effects as described in Article 5 because of Country X's actions. It could claim that its own industry had been injured by the STE's actions. It could also claim the inconsistency is a nullification or impairment of its bargained-for rights under the WTO.[53]

Country Y can claim it has suffered in its own market because of the subsidized imports, as well as in third markets because of increased competition abroad. This is not necessarily a predatory actor's model. Even if the world market price is such that it is perfectly competitive and country Y would not lose market share because X has priced its product lower, Y's argument will be that because the grower in X is receiving more than the grower in Y, X can produce a better grain (or have a higher yield) because of improved capital equipment accessible through the subsidy.

Country Y could claim that it has suffered serious prejudice under Article 6 of the Subsidies Agreement. Serious prejudice is presumed to exist where: the total ad valorem subsidization of a product exceeds five percent; subsidies are given to cover operating losses sustained by an industry; subsidies (other than one-time, non-repeatable measures for social purposes only) are given to cover the operating losses of an enterprise; or where there is direct forgiveness of debt.[54] The actions of an STE, when operating in accordance with Article XVII of the GATT, can result in serious prejudice. However, notwithstanding the requirements of Article XVII, if an STE shifts its imports for non-commercial reasons, the Subsidies Agreement states that serious prejudice cannot arise.[55]

In a CVD case, the producer from country Y would have to show that the amount paid to the grower was in excess of what would be adequate remuneration for the product.

Regulatory Marketing Boards

Unlike the statutory marketing boards, regulatory marketing boards do not participate in international trade operations. However, they are given the responsibility of setting the prices and/or quantity of either exports or imports. In this manner, one attribute of a statutory marketing board that regulatory marketing boards do not share are the economies of scale advantages. These types of STEs act only as a control on the price and/or quantity, but not on the transaction itself.[56]

Since the STE in this case is neither buying nor selling a good, it would be difficult to argue that there was a financial contribution. Further, it may be difficult to prove inadequate remuneration. However, the activities of this type of STE could certainly qualify as a price support and, in some cases therefore, a subsidy.[57]

This raises the question of how to determine the benefit of a price support. When there is no market price within the jurisdiction, the best approach would be to compare, as one would in an "adequate remuneration"-type inquiry, what a comparable or identical good costs on the world market. To the extent a price support program operates as a price floor with the government entity guaranteeing the difference if the market price fell below the floor, then the benefit would be the difference between the floor and the market price. It is necessary to consider whether the producers/growers have contributed to any kind of fund (in effect, insurance) in this regard.[58] However, if the price support does not act as a guarantee, but is simply an absolute price minimum, how can the benefit of such a program be measured? This question is especially valid when, in a given year, the actual prices fall below the minimum. The insurance analysis could possibly reveal a benefit but again it is very difficult to measure what benefit arises to the producer, especially if the STE follows a principle of national treatment.

4. State Trading in Nonmarket Economies and Economies in Transition

STEs in Nonmarket Economies

In nonmarket economies (NMEs), the role of STEs in the economy is far greater than in most market economy countries, so the operation of STEs in nonmarket economies is a source of considerable interest as major NMEs negotiate accession to the WTO.

The U.S. Department of Agriculture has identified the agro-STEs of China, Taiwan, Russia, and Vietnam as of interest to those countries' accession bids to the WTO.[59] One report suggests that in the Czech Republic, Slovakia, and Poland, STEs use export subsidies for agricultural products while private traders export the unsubsidized products.[60] Also an issue in Romania and Bulgaria is bulk procurement by STEs that regulate the subsequent sale in order to hold down prices.[61]

China, Russia, and the Ukraine have all submitted applications to become WTO members. One aspect of the negotiations for all three is the transition of their economies and the role of STEs in that transition.[62] These countries utilize STEs for significant portions of their economies. In the beginning of 1994, Ukraine still maintained STEs in such sectors as machine building, agriculture, coal, oil, and gas.[63] It has been suggested that the members of the former Soviet Union have made (or will make) efforts to follow the example of certain Eastern European countries and work on the transition away from the STE regimes in their countries.[64]

The path of the state trading regime in China is less clear. As discussed in the beginning of this chapter, many WTO member countries had failed to notify their STEs in part because they were unclear of the definition and scope of reporting requirements. It is possible that the concerns listed were superseded by the drafting of the Understanding on Article XVII. However, if active WTO members (and long-standing GATT members) have trouble clearly interpreting the requirements of the Article XVII reporting, it can hardly be expected that an applicant to the WTO will be able to communicate exactly how its state trading regime would fit into the Article XVII requirements, both in reporting and in application of STE activities.[65] Couple that with the fact that much of the world does not truly understand the full range of activities for which the state trading regime in China is responsible[66], and one could end up in protracted accession negotiations.

Any hesitation on the part of China to follow the example of the Eastern European countries does not necessarily indicate an unwillingness to reform. It has been noted that the Eastern European countries were much more heavily industrialized and continued subsidization of STEs posed a greater financial burden on the government.[67] In addition, the Eastern European economies were characterized by more centralized control than China's current system. Finally, China has been assisted by foreign investors (as well as Chinese investors), many with investment and economic development expertise.

There has been a trend in China towards collective ownership and joint-venture ownership, and away from state ownership. Ownership "by all the people" generally means more of a local or provincial focus rather than central planning. As of 1995, China still operated 118,000 state-owned enterprises.[68] However, not all of these would fall within the definition of STEs under Article XVII or the Understanding on Article XVII. While they are state controlled, many do not engage in trade related activities.

China's Accession to the WTO

The Republic of China was an original contracting party to the GATT. However, with the communist takeover in 1949, China withdrew from the organization. In 1986 China requested accession to the GATT (now the WTO). Since 1987, the preparations for negotiations for China's accession have taken place primarily in the Working Party on China's accession. Since the establishment of the WTO, China has continued to prepare for accession, now focusing on the necessary WTO commitments.[69] The United States and the European Union have expressed an interest in China's accession, but only on commercially meaningful terms.

China currently has in place a system of trading rights through which the state grants licenses for the ability to import or export a product. This area could be of major concern to WTO members because the foundation of the GATT/WTO trading system — reduction of tariffs — could be negated through the refusal by the Chinese government to grant an import license.

Another issue in Chinese accession is whether it should be classified as a developed or developing nation. This distinction carries with it great importance for the purposes of countervailing duty laws. If China is admitted as a developed country, and if and when it is found to be a market economy, then its *de minimis* level for purposes of measuring subsidies would be one percent, like other developed nations. If however, it is admitted as a developing country, it could gain advantage under the two percent de minimis level for developing countries.[70]

A second advantage for China in being admitted as a developing country is that it would enjoy the advantages of limited immunity from WTO actions under the Subsidies Agreement for export or import substitution subsidies.[71]

Measurement of Subsidies in Former NMEs

The United States' administration of CVD law has been characterized by the proposition that CVD law cannot be applied to imports from nonmarket economy countries.[72] This ruling stems from the characterization of a subsidy as a market distortion — if there are no market forces at work in an NME, then no government action can distort what is not there.

The same logic that applies to government action while a country is an NME should also apply *after* a country becomes a market economy — or even while it is still an economy in transition — to "subsidies" given, by an STE or other government entity, while it was still an NME. The question remains, however, how "subsidies" provided during the transition period should be treated.

Article 29 of the Subsidies Agreement establishes special rules for economies in transition (EIT). Countries transforming "from a centrally-planned into a market free-enterprise economy" are given a seven-year grace period during which they would enjoy the advantages of limited immunity from WTO actions under the Subsidies Agreement for export or import-substitution subsidies.[73] While the Agreement states that this grace period is calculated from the date of entry into force of the WTO, it is possible that the accession negotiations could provide for different terms. The insulation from WTO action on subsidization does not necessarily protect an EIT from being subject to countervailing duties.

NOTES

1. The Agreement establishing the WTO states that in the event of a conflict between a provision of the General Agreement on Tariffs and Trade (GATT) 1994 and any other Agreement in Annex 1A (which includes the Agreement on Subsidies and Countervailing Measures), the provision of the other Agreement shall prevail. See General Interpretive Note to Annex 1A.

2. As Tim Josling has pointed out, there are practical ways to resolve or eliminate some of the STE "problem" without recourse to Article XVII, such as by eliminating monopoly rights or expanding TRQ's to a point where the STE loses market power. T. Josling, "The Agenda for Further Reform of International Agricultural Trade Rules" 13–17 (mimeo, 1997).

3. General Agreement on Tariffs and Trade, opened for signature 30 October 1947, 61 Stat. A3, T.I.A.S. No. 1700, 55 U.N.T.S. 187, at Preamble.

4. See GATT, *Analytical Index: Guide to GATT Law and Practice* 475 (6th rev. ed. Geneva: WTO, 1995).

5. Id.

6. See Havana Charter for an International Trade Organization. U.N.Doc. E/Conf. 2178 (March 24, 1948), *reprinted in* U.S. Dep't of State, Pub. No. 3206 1948, [hereinafter Havana Charter], at Article 16 (MFN) and Article 18 (national treatment).

7. Article XVII:2.

8. Article XVII:1(b).

9. Article XVII:1.

10. See Edmond M. Ianni, "State Trading: Its Nature and International Treatment," 5 J. Int'l L. Bus 46, 56–57 (1983).

11. See Canada - Administration of the Foreign Investment Review Act, adopted on 7 Feb. 1984, BISD 30S/140 [hereinafter FIRA Panel Report].

12. Id. at 3.14–3.15.

13. Id. at 3.14, 3.16.

14. Id. at 5.16. The European Communities also argued that actions by an STE in Canada contravened its national treatment obligation in a GATT Panel proceeding involving the import, distribution, and sale of alcoholic drinks. That panel too declined to settle the debate on whether Article XVII required both MFN and national treatment.

15. A "full" notification is required every three years, with "update" notifications being provided in the intervening years.

16. Article XVII(4)(d).

17. "State Trading Enterprises: Compliance with the General Agreement on Tariffs and Trade," U.S. General Accounting Office Report to Congressional Requesters, GAO/GGD-95-208, at 6 (August 1995) [hereinafter GAO Report].

18. Id. Some member states indicated that they were withholding their STE notification until the notifications of the European Union and/or the United States were submitted. Id. at 13. This is a constraint on all of the WTO notification processes. See, e.g., Testimony of Terence P. Stewart, Esq. before the House Ways and Means Committee, Subcommittee on Trade, February 26, 1997.

19. "Operations of State Trading Enterprises As They Relate to International Trade," G/STR/2, October 26, 1995 [hereinafter Background Paper].

20. See Report (1996) of the Working Party on State Trading Enterprises, at paragraphs 9 and 14, [hereinafter 1996 STE Working Party Report].

21. The act of subsidization we are concerned with in this article is subsidization through the STE to a private party. As far as subsidies that could be provided to STEs, any of items (i) through (iv) of Article 1.1(1)(a) could provide a benefit, depending on the situation. For purposes of determining the benefit and/or the harm placed on other members' trade, it may not make a difference. For example, if a producer of coal is paid more than the value of the coal by the STE, then the STE can be said to have provided a benefit by giving more than adequate remuneration for that product. However, if a government passes legislation providing for reduced rail transportation rates for the transport of salt, then the STE for the salt industry is a recipient of a benefit in the form of foregone revenue by the government. This problem can be particularly acute when the STE both produces and purchases, and can therefore be both the recipient and provider of a subsidy in the same transaction, or arising from the same transaction. Presumably, the receipt of a subsidy by an STE would not be affected by Article XVII, which is concerned with the activities or actions of an STE. Therefore, we will limit our examination to subsidies conferred by STEs. This examination is limited to situations where and STE purchases goods, or sells goods or services, *other than those intended for immediate government consumption.*

22. Agreement on Subsidies and Countervailing Measures, Article 1.

23. Background Paper at 4. A 1996 GAO report also provides an excellent introduction to the structure of STEs. "Canada, Australia, and New Zealand: Potential Ability of Agricultural State Trading Enterprises to Distort Trade," U.S. General Accounting Office Report to Congressional Requesters, GAO/NSIAD-96-94 at 23–31 (June 1996).

24. Id. at 3. But see, e.g., the 1989 GATT Panel Report on "United States - Restrictions on Imports of Sugar" where the Panel found that arrangements negotiated under Article XVII were not to conflict with exceptions to quantitative restrictions under Article XI.

25. Id. at 15.

26. Id.

27. See Article 9 of the Agreement on Agriculture.

28. Compare Article 13(a) of the Agriculture Agreement (domestic support measures conforming with provisions of Annex 2 are not subject to countervailing duties) with Article 13(b) (domestic support measures conforming with provisions of Article 6 can be subject to countervailing duties upon a determination of injury or threat thereof and Article 13(c) (export measures conforming to provisions of Part V can be subject to countervailing duties only upon determination of injury or threat thereof).

29. The notifications reveal a combined 100 STEs in agricultural products. "World Agricultural Outlook Board: Agricultural Outlook Approved," IAC Newsletter Database, M2 Communications, June 4, 1997.

30. Id. For example, the Canadian Wheat Board at present mills and exports ninety-six to ninety-nine percent of all Canadian wheat. For the remainder, the CWB issues licenses and exports the wheat. The CWB's mandate .includes: maximizing grain sales at the best price, providing price stability; and ensuring that each producer obtains an equitable share of the grain market. Other agro-STEs have similar goals and many of the same activities such as storage, transportation and marketing of the product abroad.

31. The United States notified this organization once more in 1995. See State Trading, Notification of the United States, G/STR/N/1/USA (29 Sept. 1995).

32. "Two-tier milk pricing not 'WTO Compatible'," Dairy Markets Weekly, February 27, 1997 (study by Professor Frieder Roessler for DGVI of the EU). The study examined the current two-tiered pricing system in Canada and proposed systems in France and Denmark.

33. See United States Trade Representative, 1997 National Trade Estimate Report on Foreign Trade Barriers [hereinafter 1997 NTE Report] at page 20. Included in the complaints are the Australian Wheat Board and the Australian Diary Corporation (especially diary market support payments).

34. 1997 NTE Report, at 268–269. The U.S. industry identified the New Zealand Dairy Board and the meat and wool structures as STEs which should be closely examined.

35. Id. at 38 (referring to the Canadian Wheat Board).

36. Article 14(d) of the Subsidies Agreement. This language is repeated in the implementing legislation of both the United States and the European Union.

37. Notice of Proposed Rulemaking and Request for Public Comments. 19 CFR 355.44(f)(1), 54 Fed.Reg 23,366, 23,381 (1989).

38. Agreement on Implementation of Article VI of the General Agreement on Tariffs and Trade 1994, GATT, Article 2.2.1.1.

39. See, e.g., Article 14(d) "in the country of provision of good or service".

40. Carbon Black from Mexico: Final Results of Countervailing Duty Administrative Review, 51 Fed.Reg. 30385 (August 26, 1986).

41. Uruguay Round Agreements Act Statement of Administrative Action - Agreement on Subsidies and Countervailing Measures, *reprinted in* Message from the President of the United States Transmitting the Uruguay Round Trade Agreements, texts of Agreements Implementing Bill, Statement of Administrative Action and Required Supporting Statements, H.R. Doc. No. 316, 103rd Cong., 2d Sess. 1533 (1994). The Statement of Administrative Action (SAA) is the Administration's authoritative interpretation of the statute. On this subject the SAA says that the standards of Article 14 (less than adequate remuneration in the case of provision of goods and services, and more than adequate remuneration in the case of procurement of goods) replace the previous "preferentiality" standards.

42. 62 Fed. Reg. 8818, 8836 (February 27, 1997).

43. Id.

44. These comments appear in, respectively: *Letter from law firm of Collier, Shannon, Rill & Scott, PLLC, representing various domestic industries, to Robert S. LaRussa*, May 27, 1997, [hereinafter Collier Shannon Comments]; *Letter from law firm of Hale and Dorr, LLP, representing Micron Technology, to Robert S. LaRussa*, May 27, 1997 [hereinafter Hale and Dorr Comments]; and *Letter from law firm of Schagrin Associates, representing the Committee on Pipe and Tube Imports and the Weirton Steel Corporation, to Robert S. LaRussa*, May 27, 1997 [hereinafter Schagrin Comments].

45. See Schagrin Comments and Hale and Dorr Comments.

46. *Letter from law firm of Stewart and Stewart to Robert S. LaRussa*, May 27, 1997.

47. *Letter from law firm of Dewey Ballantine to Robert S. LaRussa*, May 27, 1997.

48. *Letter from the Government of Quebec to Robert S. LaRussa*, May 27, 1997.

49. *Letter from the Boeing Company to Robert S. LaRussa*, May 22, 1997.

50. This description could equally apply to Export Marketing Boards, which serve the same functions, but exclusively for exports.

51. Background Paper at 5.

52. See GATT Article VI:3.

53. That is, if the STE action affected tariff concessions made by country Y.

54. Article 6.1(a) through (d).

55. See Article 6.7(b).

56. Despite the decisions of the Commerce Department, such controls are not a financial contribution. But see, Collier Shannon Comments, *supra* at footnote 44, suggesting that the Commerce Department's regulations specifically state that export

restraints will continue to be treated as subsidies because they enable foreign producers to purchase goods at below market rates.

57. A statutory marketing board may also operate a price support if it establishes a price floor for certain products.

58. See Live Swine and Fresh, Chilled and Frozen Pork from Canada, 50 Fed. Reg. 25097 (June 17, 1985).

59. "World Agricultural Outlook Board: Agricultural Outlook Approved - Part 3," IAC Newsletter Database, M2 Communications, June 4, 1997. This report further states that little is known about the STEs in these countries.

60. Id.

61. Id.

62. China, Chinese Taipei, the Russian Federation, and Vietnam all participated as ob servers in the WTO Working Group on STEs. See, e.g., Report (1996) on the Working Party on State Trading Enterprises, G/L/128, 28 October 1996.

63. GAO Report at 17.

64. Id.

65. Even after the Understanding was issued, concerns about which activities to notify continued. See Report (1996) of the Working Party on State Trading Enterprises, at 2, para. 9.

66. GAO Report at 17.

67. See Robert F. Dodds, Jr., "State Enterprise Reform in China: Managing the Transition to a Market Economy," 27:3 L. & Pol. Int'l Bus., 695, 751 (1996).

68. *China Statistical Yearbook 1996*, 401.

69. Comments of WTO Director-General Renato Ruggiero at Beijing University, as reported in IAC newsletter database, M2 Presswire, April 22, 1997. See also, Congressional Press Release, February 12, 1997, where Reps Bill Barrett (R-Neb.) and David Minge (D-Minn.) requested that Secretary of State Madeleine Albright ensure that China fulfill disclosure requirements concerning its STEs prior to accession to the WTO. Congressional Press Releases, Federal Document Clearinghouse, Inc.

70. Articles 11.9 and 27.10(a) of the Subsidies Agreement.

71. Articles 27.2 and 27.3 of the Subsidies Agreement.

72. Georgetown Steel Corp. v. United States, 801 F.2d 1308 (Fed. Cir. 1986).

73. These types of subsidies, of course, are otherwise prohibited under Article 3 of the Subsidies Agreement.

CHAPTER 5

The WTO Antidumping Agreement and the Economies in Transition

*N. David Palmeter**

It is no exaggeration to say that the Uruguay Round Antidumping Agreement — formally, the Agreement on Implementation of Article VI of the General Agreement on Tariffs and Trade 1994 (hereinafter "Agreement") — provides little comfort to economies in transition from state planning to the free market. To the contrary, it probably would be an exaggeration to say that the Agreement provides *any* comfort to those economies.

In the first place, the Agreement does not even mention economies in transition, so any comfort there might be must be looked for indirectly, rather than directly. In this respect, the transition economies are not as favored as the developing countries, who are the beneficiaries at the very least of the platitudes of Article 15 of the Agreement:

It is recognized that special regard must be given by developed country Members to the special situation of developing country Members when considering the application of antidumping measures under this Agreement. Possibilities of constructive remedies provided for by this Agreement shall be explored before applying antidumping duties where they would affect the essential interests of developing country Members.

Undoubtedly, some, at least, of the transition economies may be considered developing countries, and therefore may merit whatever benefits Article 15 confers, but if so, it is because of their status as developing countries, not because of their status as economies in transition. Moreover, it is questionable whether Article 15 confers anything of concrete value. In the jurisdiction with which I am most familiar, the United States, it decidedly does not. Nothing in the antidumping provisions of Title VII of the Tariff Act requires the exploration of other remedies before the imposition of duties. The regulations of neither the Department of Commerce nor the International Trade Commission, the agencies that administer the law, provide "special regard" for developing countries. Indeed, any attempt by either agency to temper its determination on the explicit ground that it was

---

*Attorney with Powell, Goldstein, Frazer & Murphy LLP, Washington, D.C. At the time of the conference, the author was with the law firm of Graham & James, Washington, D.C.

dealing with a developing country would soon be overturned on appeal to the Court of International Trade — and properly so, under existing law.

Arguably, the Department of Commerce could be more willing to accept price undertakings, as provided for in Article 8 of the Agreement, from a developing country. However, neither the law nor the regulations makes reference to this consideration, and the relatively few price undertakings accepted by the United States so far appear to have had everything to do with the politics of the case, and nothing to do with whether the exporters concerned were from a developed or a developing country.

And this, to repeat, is for developing countries, a category that merely overlaps, but is not necessarily co-extensive with, transition economies.

The only legal provision in the Agreement pointing in the direction of transition economies is a roundabout one. Article 2.7 states, "[t]his Article is without prejudice to the second Supplementary Provision to paragraph 1 of Article VI in Annex I to GATT 1994". Thus, despite the fact that the Agreement is *lex specialis* to Article VI, the reader of the Agreement is directed back to Article VI, and a Supplemental Provision at that. There is nothing in Article 2.7 that would provide a clue that the second Supplemental Provision to paragraph 1 of Article VI in the Annex to GATT 1994 was in any way relevant to economies in transition. However, it is relevant — to a degree. The second Supplemental Provision states:

> It is recognized that, in the case of imports from a country which has a *complete or substantially complete monopoly of its trade* and where *all* domestic prices are fixed by the State, special difficulties may exist in determining price comparability for the purposes of paragraph 1, and in such cases importing contracting parties may find it necessary to take into account the possibility that a strict comparison with domestic prices in such a country may not always be appropriate [emphasis supplied].

This is the language used to justify special treatment of non-market economies in antidumping investigations. It dates from a proposal by Czechoslovakia in the 1950s to amend Article VI:1(b) to deal with situations in which all, or substantially all, trade was operated by a state monopoly.[1] A Working Party declined to recommend amendment to Article VI, but agreed to the Supplemental Provision as an interpretive note.[2]

A decade later, when Poland acceded to the GATT, the Working Party expressed its understanding that the second Supplemental Provision would apply, and went on to state:

> In this connexion it was recognized that a contracting party may use as the normal value for a product imported from Poland the prices which prevail generally in its markets for the same or like products or a value

for that product constructed on the basis of the price for a like product originating in another country, so long as the method used for determining normal value in any particular case is appropriate and not unreasonable.[3]

This language, recognizing the use of "a value for that product constructed on the basis of the price for a like product originating in another country", provided the basis for the surrogate country methodology widely used in non-market economy cases. Similar language appears in the Report of the Working Party on Accession of Hungary.[4]

The Working Party language, which is permissive, might seem to provide for transition from non-market to market economy treatment at the discretion of the importing country: the importing country "may" use prices in the exporting country, "or a value for that product constructed on the basis of the price for a like product originating in another country". However, the stronger case suggests that it does not apply to transition economies. The language is simply the language of a Working Party concerning the application of the second Supplemental Provision to Article VI:1, which is relevant only when a state has a complete or substantially complete monopoly of its trade, and when all domestic prices are fixed by the state.

While it may be arguable whether the degree of a less than complete state monopoly of trade is substantial, the word "all" with regard to control over domestic prices is quite specific. Unless the state fixes *all* prices, the Supplemental Provision does not apply. If it does not apply, Article 7 of the Agreement, which refers to it, is not relevant, and normal value, by the terms of the Agreement, must be determined in accordance with the remainder of Article 2. It is not at all clear that Article 2 permits the surrogate country methodology currently used in the United States for non-market economies that may be WTO Members, let alone transition economies.

Briefly, the surrogate country methodology favored in the United States is based on a market valuation of the factors of production utilized in the non-market economy. The hours of labor, the quantities of raw material, the units of energy, and capital costs are determined and then valued on the basis of their values in a market economy at a similar stage of development. For example, in a recent preliminary determination in an administrative review concerning *Tapered Roller Bearings from Romania*, the Department of Commerce concluded that Romania is a non-market economy, and based normal value on the value of the calculated factors in Indonesia.[5] Since Romania was not a WTO Member at the time of this action, no WTO issue is presented. However, should Romania accede to the WTO, the methodology would raise serious questions under Article 2.

Article 2.1 provides that a product is dumped when its export price "is less than the comparable *price*, in the ordinary course of trade, for the like product when destined for consumption *in the exporting country*" [emphasis supplied]. Since the surrogate methodology disregards the price in the exporting country, it is inconsistent with Article 2.1 unless the "ordinary course of trade" language provides an exception. The use of the phrase "ordinary course of trade" in the Agreement is very significant, but it is questionable whether it permits the surrogate methodology. It is the vehicle by which home market (or third country) sales are disregarded in calculating normal value, if those sales are at prices below total cost of production.[6] It does not appear to be relevant to the question of the calculation of normal value in a non-market economy or an economy in transition.

Article 2.2, however, offers two other grounds for disregarding home market sales: (1) "the particular market situation"; and (2) low volume. The phrase "particular market situation" is not defined or elaborated upon; it can be viewed reasonably as a euphemism for a state-controlled economy. Nevertheless, even accepting that the "particular market situation" permits the importing country to disregard sales in the home market of a non-market economy or economy in transition, it does not permit resorting to the surrogate country methodology. Article 2.2 provides that when home market sales are not in the ordinary course of trade, or when the "particular market situation" or the low volume of sales —

> do not permit a proper comparison, the margin of dumping shall be determined by comparison with a comparable price of the like product when exported to an appropriate third country . . . or with the cost of production in the country of origin plus a reasonable amount for administrative, selling and general costs and for profits.

Thus, Article 2 offers three options for calculation of normal value: (1) home market price; (2) third country price; (3) cost of production. Not only is there no mention of surrogate country, there is no room in Article 2 for the methodology.

The extent to which all of this will have legal significance in WTO dispute settlement proceedings is uncertain. The largest transition economies — China and Russia — are not WTO Members, so the requirements of the Agreement are not relevant to them. Moreover, it is possible that accession protocols may legitimize practices that otherwise would appear to be inconsistent with the Agreement. The real antidumping reform for the economies in transition, therefore, might not come until reform comes for the entire WTO — and that is unlikely to be any time soon.

NOTES

1. Article VI:1 provides:

1. The contracting parties recognize that dumping, by which products of one country are introduced into the commerce of another country at less than the normal value of the products, is to be condemned if it causes or threatens material injury to an established industry in the territory of a contracting party or materially retards the establishment of a domestic industry. For the purposes of this Article, a product is to be considered as being introduced into the commerce of an importing country at less than its normal value, if the price of the product exported from one country to another

(*a*) is less than the comparable price, in the ordinary course of trade, for the like product when destined for consumption in the exporting country, or,

(*b*) in the absence of such domestic price, is less than either

(i) the highest comparable price for the like product for export to any third country in the ordinary course of trade, or

(ii) the cost of production of the product in the country of origin plus a reasonable addition for selling cost and profit.

Due allowance shall be made in each case for differences in conditions and terms of sale, for differences in taxation, and for other differences affecting price comparability.

2. BISD 3S/222, 223, para. 6.

3. BISD 15S/109, 111, para. 13.

4. BISD 20S/34, 37, para. 18.

5. *Tapered Roller Bearings and Parts Thereof, Finished or Unfinished, From Romania; Preliminary Results of Antidumping Duty Administrative Review*, 62 Fed. Reg. 11,152 (March 11, 1997).

6. Article 2.2.1.

CHAPTER 6

Technology and State Enterprise in the WTO

Frederick M. Abbott[*]

Governments are intricately intertwined in the development and maintenance of technology. This involvement ranges from the most embedded
interest of government as provider of education, to its varietal allocation of
tax burden based on type of activity (e.g., research and development), to its
indirect subsidization of technology development through procurement activity (including in the military sector), to its direct subsidization of research
and development activity, to its provision of technology transport infrastructure, to its grant and deprivation of rights in intellectual property, and
to its imposition of technology transfer requirements in international trade.
The World Trade Organization (WTO), through its extension to the new
areas of services and TRIPS, and in conjunction with pre-existing GATT
coverage of subsidies, government procurement, and related areas, imposes a
substantial set of rules governing this technology complex.

From the standpoint of private intellectual property rights (IPRs) holders, governments and state enterprises become problematic, *inter alia,*
when they preempt commercial opportunities through the diversion of IPRs.[1]
Two of the circumstances in which such diversion is likely to occur are examined in this chapter.

The first of the circumstances is that in which the government or state
enterprise uses the IPRs of a private party without its authorization or consent. This chapter begins by examining the rules of the Paris Convention on
the Protection of Industrial Property (Paris Convention) and those of the
WTO Agreement on Trade-Related Aspects of Intellectual Property Rights
(TRIPS Agreement) that apply to the ownership by governments and state
enterprises of patents. It then examines the provisions of those two international agreements relating to the use by governments and state enterprises of
privately held patent rights without the consent of the rights holder. Though
all forms of IPR may be used as instruments to promote technology development, this chapter focuses on the patent grant because it is the major form
of IPR most specifically directed to the promotion of technology development in connection with private commercial exploitation. It is suggested that
the Paris Convention and TRIPS Agreement, taken together, afford consi-

[*]Professor of Law, Chicago-Kent College of Law.

derable leeway to governments in authorizing their state enterprises to make use of privately held patent rights without the consent or authorization of right holders.

Second, this chapter examines WTO rules regarding government-mandated transfers of technology to states, state enterprises, and contractors, particularly in the context of the aerospace sector. The aerospace sector is selected because private enterprises in that sector are among those that have been subject to the most visible demands for technology transfer by governments. This chapter concludes that there is some ambiguity in the relevant WTO provisions in this area. This ambiguity may be addressed in WTO accession negotiations with prospective new WTO members, such as China. Whether and to what extent WTO law permits members to mandate transfers of technology to state and other domestic enterprises is a question the answer to which may divide developed and developing members.

1. State Trading and Patents

Government as Patent Holder

The Paris Convention and National Legislation
Governments may hold title to patents either directly or as assignees, depending upon national laws relating to persons who are entitled to file for and obtain patents, and specific legislation relating to government patent rights. The Paris Convention requires that an inventor be mentioned in a patent[2], but it does not demand that an individual be the patent applicant or holder. The Paris Convention refers to "persons" and "nationals" who may apply for patents and hold patent rights[3], and does not draw a distinction between government or public rights holders, and private rights holders. Under the United States Patent Act, only natural person inventors may apply for a patent.[4] In the usual case a corporate employer or the federal government will be the assignee of an individual=s rights in the patent.[5] Under the European Patent Convention (EPC), a business entity may file for and hold title to a patent.[6]

Because of the high level of research and development (R&D) activity that takes place by or on behalf of governments and their instrumentalities, it is fair to assume that a substantial number of patents are held directly or indirectly by governments worldwide, though this writer is not at present aware of estimates of such holdings.

Though it might seem anomalous for the government as grantor of the patent monopoly in the public interest to act as monopoly rights holder itself, some conceptual justification for this may be possible. In the United States, the justification proffered in the legislative history of relevant legislation is that the government should obtain the maximum benefit from the expenditure of public funds on R&D, and seek to return any commercializable benefits to the public budget, rather than freely disperse technology to private enterprises capable of exploiting it.

Under U.S. law, the federal government as patent holder may license patented technology to private enterprises.[7] Thus through the expenditure of public funds, the government may indirectly subsidize the commercial activities of private entities in the commercial marketplace through the licensing of government-owned patented technology.[8] Though in the case of the United States there are few state trading entities to which the government might license its patented technology, in other countries in which state trading is more prevalent, such licensing activity might be quite significant.

The TRIPS Agreement and Patent Holders

As a general matter, the TRIPS Agreement does not distinguish between government/public and private rights holders.[9] The most significant exception relates to compulsory use and licensing, discussed in the following section. However, it is of some interest to note that the preamble to the TRIPS Agreement expressly refers to intellectual property rights as "private rights".[10]

It is probably the case that the reference to IPRs as "private rights" in the preamble was not intended to exclude the possibility of government or public ownership of IPRs for TRIPS Agreement protection and control purposes.[11] Most likely, the reference to IPRs as private rights was inserted in the preamble because of the unique characteristic of the TRIPS Agreement in regulating national laws governing privately held interests (*e.g.*, patents), in specifying remedies that are to be provided under national law for protecting such interests, and because of the unique place of IPRs in relation to their possibility to be affected in DSU compensation awards. In regard to the latter point, the withdrawal of trade concessions relating to IPRs such as patents may have uniquely harmful effects on private rights as compared to the withdrawal of other concessions, so that special attention should be paid in this area.[12]

The Paris Convention continues to apply in respect to patents under the TRIPS Agreement.[13] The TRIPS Agreement does not permit derogation from existing rights under the Paris Convention.[14] As governments and state trading enterprises are entitled to hold patents under the Paris Convention, they should be entitled to do so under the TRIPS Agreement.[15]

Compulsory Licensing and Compulsory Use

Paris Convention and TRIPS Agreement

Governments and state enterprises have the possibility to enter the commercial market place by the appropriation of private patent rights under Article 31 TRIPS Agreement. This appropriation is customarily referred to as "compulsory licensing", which is permitted under the terms of the Paris Convention.[16] The Paris Convention places few restrictions on the right of governments to legislate on the grant of compulsory licenses, except in the limited area of "failure to work". With respect to "failure to work", a time period of four years is required to elapse before a compulsory license may issue, and compulsory licenses are to be non-exclusive and in general non-transferable.[17] The Paris Convention does not mandate the payment of compensation to the patent holder whose rights have been licensed under compulsion.

TRIPS Agreement Article 31 adds conditions on the grant of the compulsory patent license. It notes that such licenses may be granted to governments or to "third parties authorized by the government".[18] The proposed user must have made efforts "to obtain authorization from the right holder on reasonable commercial terms and conditions and that such efforts have not been successful within a reasonable period of time".[19] This requirement may be waived in case of "national emergency", "other circumstances of extreme urgency", or "in cases of public non-commercial use". In the former two cases, the right holder "will be notified as soon as reasonably practicable". In the case of "public non-commercial use",

> where the government or contractor, without making a patent search, knows or has demonstrable grounds to know that a valid patent is or will be used by or for the government, the right holder shall be informed promptly.[20]

There are a number of additional conditions on compulsory licensing: (1) the scope of the license shall be limited to the purpose of the authorization, and semi-conductor patents may only be used for non-commercial purposes or to remedy anti-competitive practices; (2) the use shall be non-exclusive; (3) no assignment shall be made except with the relevant part of the business; (4) the use should be predominantly to supply the domestic market; (5) the use should be terminated when conditions which led to the authorization cease; (6) "the right holder shall be paid adequate remuneration in the circumstances of each case, taking into account the economic value of the authorization"; (7) decisions of government authorities shall be subject to independent judicial review. The aforementioned conditions do not apply when anticompetitive practices are being remedied.[21]

The Case of the United States

United States law permits the federal government and private parties acting by or for the government to use patents held by private parties without their consent.[22] This authority derives from a statute that limits the liability of the federal government and its contractors in suits for the use or infringement of patents to claims for reasonable and entire compensation that must be brought before a designated federal court of claims.[23] When the federal government or its contractor/supplier makes use of a patent without the authorization or consent of the holder it may not be enjoined from such use, but it must pay full compensation.

The European Communities, among other WTO members, have noted that this statutory authorization does not require the U.S. government to notify a party whose patent may be used without authorization.[24] The Commission states:

> Under U.S. law (28 US Code Section 1498) a patent owner may not enjoin or recover damages on the basis of his patents for infringements due to the manufacture or use of goods by or for the US Government Authorities. This practice is particularly frequent in the activities of the DoD but is also extremely widespread in practically all government departments. For obvious reasons this practice is particularly detrimental to foreign right-holders because they will generally not be able to detect such governmental use and are thus very likely to miss the opportunity to initiate the administrative claims procedure.
>
> Article 31 of the TRIPS Agreement introduces a requirement to inform promptly a right holder about the government use of his patent, but no action has been taken so far to bring [United States] legislation into conformity with this provision.[25]

The first paragraph of the Commission's objection demands careful reading. It is true, as the Commission says, that civil court damages actions and injunctions are not permitted, but on the other hand an effective claims court mechanism is established in which fair value compensation may be recovered. The decisions of the Claims Court may be appealed to the Court of Appeals for the Federal Circuit which ordinarily hears civil patent claims appeals.[26] As a practical matter, there would appear only modest inconvenience to European holders of U.S. patents in this procedure.

It is correct, on the other hand, that the U.S. government is not required by statute to give notice to parties whose patents might be used or infringed. This is at least partly inconsistent with the TRIPS Agreement on its face. Note, however, that the notice requirement of the TRIPS Agreement is limited. In cases involving "public non-commercial use", as to which the requirement of prior negotiation for a license may be waived, notification is only required where the government or private contractor does *not* make a patent search.[27]

Perhaps the drafters of Article 31(b) intended only to convey that governments are *not required* to conduct patent searches prior to using patented technology without notice. If so, the drafting is rather inelegant, since the express terms certainly imply that when a government *does* make a patent search, and *knows* it may infringe, it need *not* notify in cases of *public non-commercial use*. It is not abundantly clear why TRIPS Article 31(b) is so constructed. It may, however, limit the situations in which U.S. government measures and actions might be inconsistent with the TRIPS Agreement.

Two additional points. One's sympathy for the plight of the European patent holder in the United States could be muted by the fact that most such patents are applied for and held by European-based multinational enterprises that have very active intelligence arms. The cases in which the poor European garage inventor's rights are being abridged are likely to be only a small portion of non-notification cases. Second, documentation supporting the Commission's statement regarding the extent to which its enterprises are suffering losses might be interesting to study. Though U.S. private enterprises have long been subject to the same use without notice statute as European enterprises, there has not, to this writer's knowledge, been widespread objection from U.S. industry.[28]

State Enterprises

In the United States, there are few entities that might qualify as "state enterprises" from the standpoint of the GATT and GATS. Government use of private party patents for commercial purposes is extremely limited, at most.

The facts may be significantly different in other countries. The obvious candidates for state enterprise use of private party patents are in the countries in transition from socialist to market economies, or the remaining socialist market economies.

With respect to state enterprises in such economies, it is of considerable interest to note that TRIPS Agreement Article 31 does not impose any "purpose"-oriented limitation on the grant of compulsory licenses. There is some debate concerning whether the Agreement permits the grant of a compulsory license on the grounds of non-work.[29] Putting this question to the side, the obligations on a government granting a compulsory license to its state enterprise are those set out earlier; most notably, good faith *ex ante* license negotiations, reasonable compensation, and manufacture primarily for the domestic market.

Is there a "free market/morality constraint" somehow influencing the TRIPS Agreement compulsory licensing provision? If a government elects to pursue an active program of industrial development through the liberal use of compulsory licensing (within the express limitations of the TRIPS Agreement) in favor either of its state enterprises or local private enterprises, is it contravening the letter or spirit of the WTO Agreement? Where do the restrictions begin and end?[30]

On the one hand, the preamble to the TRIPS Agreement says that IPRs are "private rights"; on the other hand, the preamble says that developing countries will have "maximum flexibility" to create a sound technology base.

Article 8 emphasizes the public interest dimension of technology for the benefit of developing countries.

Article 30 permits limited exceptions to patent rights, provided that these do not interfere with the "normal exploitation of the patent".[31] What is normal exploitation in the context of a socialist or developing economy? Moreover, Article 31 refers specifically to "other use", suggesting that governments might act more favorably under Article 30 than would be the case under the conditions established by Article 31.

The governments that are members of the OECD negotiated the terms of the TRIPS Agreement so as to achieve a high level of IPRs protection on behalf of their enterprises.[32] Liberal compulsory licensing in favor of state or private enterprises would be inconsistent with demands for maximum protection. But whether it would be inconsistent with the terms of the TRIPS Agreement is not so clear.

The implications for WTO-based trade relations of liberal use, for example, by Chinese state enterprises of U.S.-owned patents in China would be considerable. Trade dispute would be inevitable; U.S. trade sanctions would be likely. Might the case be made in favor of liberal Chinese use of U.S.-owned patents? Perhaps a Chinese scholar or government official will choose to make this case.

IPRs and Competition

IPRs are by their nature "state chartered monopolies". The holder of an IPR is entitled to exclude competitors from its market. The scope of the market exclusion may be quite wide, as in the case of a patent on a basic invention, or it may be quite narrow, as in the case of a copyright on a poem. As a state-chartered monopolist, the IPRs holder is subject to restraints on abuse of its position or power. The relationship between IPRs and competition rules is considered by this writer and other contributors to this book *in extenso* elsewhere.[33] Jacques Bourgeois has, however, called particular attention to the potential analogy between EC competition rules relating to state monopolies, and competition law principles that may inform IPRs-related activities.[34] Just as with regard to a state monopolist in the EC, an IPR holder generally will not be considered as violating competition rules because of the mere existence of a monopoly — a monopoly position is precisely foreseen by the grant of the IPR. But if the IPR holder restricts access to an essential facility (as a state monopolist might), similar results might be foreseen from a competition law standpoint.

2. State-Mandated Local Content, Civil Offset, and Technology Transfer Requirements in WTO Law

Governments seeking to enhance the technology intensive industrial sectors of their economies may demand in trade and investment relations with foreign private enterprises that technology and capital be transferred into their local economies and enterprises. Demands for technology transfer often (and perhaps usually) are accompanied by demands that foreign enterprises purchase some quantity of the production of locally established technology transferees, or that they in fact establish (or aid in the establishment of) local enterprises. For this reason, this chapter analyzes WTO rules affecting not only mandated technology transfers *per se*, but also the rules affecting the closely related areas of local content requirements and civil offsets.

The practices of some governments and government contractors to pressure or require suppliers of goods, in particular suppliers of civil aircraft and aircraft components, to purchase locally produced parts, establish local production facilities, and/or transfer technology, as a condition of awarding a purchase contract may distort trade by reducing the quantity of exports that would be made in the absence of such practices, and thereby also adversely affect labor markets in exporting countries. From the standpoint of the governments making these demands, the practices may appear to be a necessary condition of industrial development and the establishment of a globally competitive national economy. While these demands are most prevalently a developing country phenomenon, they are not limited to developing country governments, especially in the military procurement context.[35]

Some countries whose governments engage in the subject practices are members of the WTO, and parties to the relevant Plurilateral Agreements, and some such countries are not members of the WTO and/or the relevant Plurilateral Agreements.

Local Content and Civil Offset Requirements in WTO Law

Local content and civil offset requirements are directly and indirectly addressed under various WTO agreements in respect to "foreign government" and "foreign government contractor" practices. The following discussion is directed at provisions that may concern these entities. Unless other-wise expressly stated, "foreign government contractors" will be considered subject to the same rules as "foreign governments" for the purposes of WTO law. Article III:8 of the GATT 1994 establishing an exception from the national treatment principle for government procurement (not for resale) (see discussion *infra*) does not specifically address the relationship between governments and contractors that may be acting on their behalf. However, the Plurilateral Agreements on Trade in Civil Aircraft (CAA) and Government Procurement (GPA) both include provisions that governments direct or impose contracting requirements on as falling within their scope.[36] The rules discussed in this chapter as applying to governments also apply to government contractors.

State enterprises are to be distinguished from governments and from government contractors in the procurement context. One of the central questions of the conference was how such distinctions are to be drawn. The "national airline" might be a good example of a state enterprise serving in the commercial marketplace under post-Uruguay Round assumptions regarding the role of the government in the economy. In an historical milieu of the not so distant past, a national airline might have been considered a public entity acting in the non-commercial context, particularly if such an airline provided state-subsidized fares to passengers.

Generally speaking, we might expect that state enterprises would be subject to rules relating to private sector enterprises regarding mandated transfers of technology. State enterprises would be entitled to demand and make use of foreign private enterprise technology to the extent authorized by public legislation. WTO members would be entitled to mandate transfers from foreign private enterprises to local state enterprises to the same extent they would be entitled to mandate such transfers to local private enterprises.

However, because of the close connection between states and state enterprises at the political level, the pressures exerted on foreign private contractors may be greater when dealing with state enterprises than with private enterprises. An operational distinction in the WTO legal context, as discussed below, might exist.

Local Content Requirements
"Local content" requirements refer to practices by which governments favor local producers by requiring that some amount of locally-produced goods be included within or alongside imported goods when sold in the local market. Local content requirements are generally prohibited by GATT Article III:1, 4, and 5.

GATT Article III:1 states that "requirements" concerning the use of domestic and imported products in specified amounts should not be applied "so as to afford protection to domestic products". Article III:4 states the general rule that with respect to laws and "requirements" imported products shall be given treatment no less favorable than domestic products for purposes of internal sale. GATT Article III:5 prohibits internal quantitative regulations regarding the "mixture, processing or use of products" requiring that a certain amount or proportion of products be supplied from domestic sources.

The WTO Agreement on Trade-Related Investment Measures (TRIMS Agreement) prohibits members from imposing on investors of other members measures requiring trade-related practices that would be inconsistent with GATT 1994 obligations. TRIMS Agreement Article 2:1 prohibits members (subject to other rights and obligations under GATT 1994) from applying any TRIM that is inconsistent with GATT Article III:4. TRIMS Agreement Article 2:2 incorporates an Annex illustrating TRIMS prohibited by Article III. These include:

. . . those which are mandatory or enforceable under domestic law or administrative rules, or compliance with which is necessary to obtain an advantage, and which require:

(a) the purchase or use by an enterprise of products of domestic origin or from any domestic source, whether specified in terms of particular domestic products, in terms of volume or value of products, or in terms of a proportion of volume or value of its local production; . . .

That local content requirements are generally prohibited by GATT Article III can be confirmed by reference to the substantial body of GATT panel decisions that interpret Article III to prohibit members from applying measures that effectively provide an advantage to domestic products. For example, United States - Taxes on Automobiles[37], European Community - Banana Regulations[38], United States - Section 337[39], Thailand - Cigarettes[40], Canada - Foreign Investment Review Act[41], Italian Tractors[42], and so forth. The proposition that GATT Article III generally precludes the application by members of local content requirements is not controversial. Local content requirements provide a clear advantage to domestic products over imported products in a manner that is generally inconsistent with GATT Article III.

However, since the creation of the GATT in 1947, an exception to the national treatment principle of Article III has existed with respect to government procurement. Article III:8(a) provides that:

The provisions of this Article shall not apply to laws, regulations or requirements governing the procurement by governmental agencies of products purchased for governmental purposes and not with a view to commercial resale or with a view to use in the production of goods for commercial sale.

The Article III:8 exception recognized the importance which government procurement played, and continues to play, in many economies as a tool for stimulating and maintaining domestic employment. The exception is not unlimited. It does not apply to goods purchased for the purposes of resale. However, goods used for income-generating purposes, such as telephone equipment used in the operation of a government telephone company, have not been considered "resale" goods, and discriminatory purchases of such products were at least initially tolerated under GATT Article III:8.

Under the exception of GATT Article III:8, a Member government *may* require that a foreign supplier of a good to the government include a certain proportion of local content in that good, even though this requirement will discriminate in favor of domestic products. The Plurilateral Agreement on Trade in Civil Aircraft (initially agreed to in the Tokyo Round), the Tokyo Round Government Procurement Code, and the more recent WTO Plurilateral Agreement on Government Procurement (GPA) that succeeded it, were and are intended to at least partially bring discriminatory government procurement practices such as local content requirements under the national treatment/non-discrimination standard.

Civil Offset Requirements under the GATT 1994
Governments sometimes require foreign producers to undertake activities with respect to the local economy as a condition of purchasing imported products . The required activities may include the construction of a local manufacturing facility or related infrastructure; the acceptance of locally produced products directly or indirectly in payment for imports (i.e. countertrade); the transfer of technology to governments or private enterprises, and; the purchase of locally produced products to incorporate in imported products (i.e. local content requirements as discussed in Section 2 above). Such conditions or requirements are customarily referred to as "offsets" or "civil offsets".[43]

Civil offsets other than local content requirements may have a different character under GATT 1994 and WTO law than do local content requirements.

GATT 1994 Article III

GATT Article III prohibits government regulations or requirements that discriminate in favor of locally produced goods. Local content requirements clearly discriminate in favor of locally produced goods because they mandate the purchase of such goods. However, civil offset requirements may be at least facially non-discriminatory. The government of a WTO Member may adopt a regulation or engage in a practice that requires *all* parties seeking to make a sale to that Member to engage in certain activities with respect to the local economy. Thus the Member might say that any winning bidder on a contract to supply construction equipment will be required to build a training center for local construction workers as a precondition of payment under the contract. Similarly, a Member government might require that *all* bidders on a contract to supply construction equipment provide the purchaser with the technology used to manufacture the equipment and a license to use that technology.

Civil offset conditions that apply in an equivalent manner to suppliers of domestically-produced and imported goods *may* in some contexts be *consistent* with the GATT Article III non-discrimination principle. Such conditions may operate to *favor* foreign suppliers because local suppliers may not possess the relevant technology, etc. to permit them to provide the offset. GATT Article III does not prohibit favoring imported over locally-produced products. In some contexts, for example in the OECD Member context, a domestic producer may be as capable as a foreign producer of providing a government the benefits it is seeking through a civil offset.

On the other hand, civil offset conditions that are facially neutral with respect to domestic and foreign suppliers may be inconsistent with GATT Article III if their operational effect is to favor local products. The GATT panel in the United States - Section 337 case made clear that internal measures must be equivalent not only on their face, but in the context of how they are designed to work in practice.[44] Civil offset requirements may be imposed by developing countries on high technology producers when their own industries lack the relevant high technology. Such requirements are likely to have a disproportionate impact on foreign producers and therefore may be operationally discriminatory with respect to foreign suppliers. For example, if the operational effect of a measure is to mandate the creation of local manufacturing capabilities so that imported products are displaced by domestic products, the measure would discriminate by providing a competitive advantage to domestic production over foreign production. There is no GATT panel decision that has specifically addressed this situation, but panel reports addressing the general question of the application of Article III, including the operational effect of measures (e.g., U.S.- Sec. 337) would appear to lead to this result.[45] In other words, a *mandated* transfer of technology *may* constitute an Article III violation.

Conversely, as alluded to previously, a mandated or required civil offset might not favor domestic production over local production if discriminatory competitive effect is not present. The requirement that a school be constructed may not have a sufficiently direct effect on local production to constitute a violation. In many cases, civil offset requirements other that local content requirements will not constitute as clear a GATT violation as an express local content requirement.

It is also essential to recall that GATT Article III contains an express exemption for government procurement not for resale. Therefore, to the extent that a civil offset requirement is used only to establish sales preferences for local sellers in respect to government purchases, such preferences may not fall within the scope of GATT Article III. There may of course be offset cases in which the government would be unable to demonstrate that the transferred technology or manufacturing plant would only be used in connection with domestic sales to the government, and if sales would be made outside the government procurement context this would provide a legal opening for the general invocation of Article III.

Quotas and Measures with Equivalent Effect

GATT 1994 Article XI provides that:

No prohibitions or restrictions other that duties, taxes or other charges, whether made effective though quotas, import or export licenses or other measures, should be instituted or maintained by any Member on the importation of any product of the territory of any other Member. . . .

A civil offset requirement that effectively restricted the export opportunities of a foreign supplier/exporter of goods might be argued to constitute a measure with the effect of an import restriction. A basic principle of the GATT is that tariffs bound under Article II are the only accepted means of trade protection, and that quotas and equivalent measures are prohibited.[46]

Assume that a producer manufactures with proprietary technology that constitutes a substantial asset. If the government of an importing country requires a transfer of technology that will effectively reduce the value of a foreign producer=s proprietary technology asset, that requirement may have the effect of reducing the producer's export opportunities. As such the measure may be argued to constitute a prohibited restriction on imports.[47] The advantage of the GATT Article XI argument against offsets over the GATT Article III argument is that there is no "government procurement exception" under GATT Article XI.

In the Japan - Trade in Semi-Conductors panel decision[48], the panel examined *informal* Japanese government practices that operated to restrict the export of products and said that such practices may constitute impermissible export restraints under GATT Article XI. Similarly, pressure imposed on foreign suppliers to build factories or transfer technology may act as a formal or informal import barrier. The export restraints included the collection of data regarding actual and proposed export levels by the Japanese government from manufacturers, and the government= transmittal to manufacturers of recommendations concerning appropriate future levels of exports.

The counter-argument to the foregoing is that civil offsets are part of a package of "terms of purchase and sale". There is no GATT rule stating that an import buyer may not demand that an exporter "bundle together" goods and services as a condition of purchase. If part of what a foreign government is buying from a foreign supplier is its proprietary technology, it is not restricting imports, rather it is driving a hard bargain. Imports are not therefore restricted, but the terms of purchase are harsh.

There is no GATT/WTO panel decision that reconciles these competing perspectives on Article XI. As a general rule panels are not inclined to stretch to find GATT violations.

The Plurilateral Agreements on Trade in Civil Aircraft (CAA) and Government Procurement (GPA)

As with respect to other Tokyo Round and Uruguay Round Agreements, the Plurilateral CAA and GPA seek to clarify more general WTO rules, and to eliminate previously existing exceptions. As plurilateral agreements, both the CAA and GPA are exceptional within the new "single undertaking" framework of the WTO, in that they only apply between the parties that have accepted them.[49] The plurilateral agreements may not be invoked against non-parties that are otherwise members of the WTO.

The Relationship Between the CAA and the GPA

The business of designing and producing civil aircraft and components thereof is a major component of both U.S. and EU external trade. The civil aircraft sector has been vulnerable to foreign government imposition of civil offset requirements. Article I of the CAA provides[50]:

Product Coverage

1.1 This Agreement applies to the following products:

(a) all civil aircraft,

(b) all civil aircraft engines and their parts and components,

(c) all other parts, components, and sub-assemblies of civil aircraft,

(d) all ground flight simulators and their parts and components,

whether used as original or replacement equipment in the manufacture repair, maintenance, rebuilding, modification or conversion of civil aircraft.

1.2 For the purposes of this Agreement "civil aircraft" means (a) all aircraft other than military aircraft and (b) all other products set out in Article 1.1 above.

Furthermore, the CAA covers "government-directed procurement". Thus, for example, Article 4.2. provides that:

Signatories shall not require airlines, aircraft manufacturers, or other entities engaged in the purchase of civil aircraft, nor exert unreasonable pressure on them, to procure civil aircraft from any particular source, which would create discrimination against suppliers from any Signatory.

Article 6 is addressed to government participation in aircraft subsidy programs. Article 7 provides:

Regional and Local Governments

7.1 In addition to *their other obligations* under this Agreement, *Signatories agree* not to require or encourage, directly or indirectly, regional and local governments and authorities, non-governmental bodies, and other bodies to take action inconsistent with provisions of this Agreement [emphasis supplied.]

Based on the foregoing language, it is reasonable to conclude that the direct and indirect government purchases of civil aircraft (*e.g.* through national airlines) are within the scope of the CAA.

The GPA applies to the purchase of goods and services by listed government "entities", including non-central government entities that will purchase in accordance with the Agreement.[51] A review of the GPA Annexes has not revealed the listing of public/government airlines.[52] Though it is possible that some obligations imposed by the GPA will be imposed on some Parties with respect to the purchase of civil aircraft and components, for the present it appears that the CAA is intended to govern procurement in this particular sector.[53]

Partes to the CAA are not freed from other relevant WTO obligations (*see* Preamble to the CAA). Both the CAA and the GPA address local content requirements and offsets, and at least arguably in somewhat different ways.

CAA and Related European Community - United
States Agreement Concerning Its Application

The CAA was negotiated during the GATT Tokyo Round and entered into force on January 1, 1980.[54] It is incorporated in the WTO framework as a

Plurilateral Agreement.[55] There are currently twenty signatories to the CAA, including the United States, the EC, and Japan.[56]

As noted previously, the CAA covers all civil aircraft, parts, components and subassemblies (Article 1.1). The CAA Signatories have agreed to eliminate all tariffs and related charges on trade in covered products (Article 2.1.1); and have agreed that the disciplines of the Agreement on Technical Barriers to Trade will apply to trade in covered products (Article 3).[57] Of particular relevance to the question of local content requirements and civil offsets are Articles 4 and 5 of the CAA which read as follows:

Article 4

Government-Directed Procurement, Mandatory Sub-Contracts and Inducements
4.1 Purchasers of civil aircraft should be free to select suppliers on the basis of commercial and technological factors.

4.2 Signatories shall not require airlines, aircraft manufacturers, or other entities engaged in the purchase of civil aircraft, nor exert unreasonable pressure on them, to procure civil aircraft from any particular source, which would create discrimination against suppliers from any Signatory.

4.3 Signatories agree that the purchase of products covered by this Agreement should be made only on a competitive price, quality and delivery basis. In conjunction with the approval or awarding of procurement contracts for products covered by this Agreement a Signatory may, however, require that its qualified firms be provided with access to business opportunities on a competitive basis and on terms no less favourable than those available to the qualified firms of other Signatories. n1

n1 Use of the phrase "access to business opportunities . . . on terms no less favourable . . ." does not mean that the amount of contracts awarded to the qualified firms of one Signatory entitles the qualified firms of other Signatories to contracts of a similar amount.

4.4 Signatories agree to avoid attaching inducements of any kind to the sale or purchase of civil aircraft from any particular source which would create discrimination against suppliers from any Signatory.

Article 5

Trade Restrictions

5.1 Signatories shall not apply quantitative restrictions (import quotas) or import licensing requirements to restrict imports of civil aircraft in a manner inconsistent with applicable provisions of the GATT. This does not preclude import monitoring or licensing systems consistent with the GATT.

5.2 Signatories shall not apply quantitative restrictions or export licensing or other similar requirements to restrict, for commercial or competitive reasons, exports of civil aircraft to other Signatories in a manner inconsistent with applicable provisions of the GATT.

In July 1992, the EC and the United States entered into an Agreement Concerning the Application of the CAA to Trade in Large Aircraft.[58] In the Preamble, the parties affirm their intention to act without prejudice to rights and obligations under the GATT. Of particular interest to the question of local content and civil offset requirements, the EC and United States agree to act in conformity with an Interpretative Note set forth in an Annex, which reads in relevant part:

Article 4.3.

(Mandatory Subcontracts)

The first sentence states that "signatories agree that the purchase of products covered by the Agreement should be made only on a competitive price, quality and delivery basis". This means that signatories will not intervene to obtain favoured treatment for particular firms and that they will not interfere with the selection of vendors in a situation where vendors of different signatories are competing.

By emphasizing that the only factors which should be involved in purchase decisions are price, quality and delivery terms, the signatories agree that Article 4.3. does not permit Government-mandated offsets. Further, they will not require that other factors, such as subcontracting, be made a condition or consideration of sale. Specifically, a signatory may not require that a vendor must provide offset, specific types or volumes of business opportunities, or other types of industrial compensation.

Signatories shall not therefore impose conditions requiring subcontractors or suppliers to be of a particular national origin [emphasis supplied].[59]

The Agreement on Government Procurement
(GPA)

The WTO GPA generally operates to apply the non-discrimination provision of GATT Article III to the government procurement sector with respect to covered entities. The GPA, adopted subsequent to the CAA and 1992 EC-U.S. Agreement concerning Civil Aircraft, more precisely addresses the subject of offsets, and more directly addresses the subject of technology transfer. It provides:

Article XVI

Offsets

1.   Entities shall not, in the qualification and selection of suppliers, products or services, or in the evaluation of tenders and award of contracts, impose, seek or consider offsets. [n 7]

n. 7 Offsets in government procurement are measures used to encourage local development or improve the balance-of-payments accounts by means of domestic content, licensing of technology, investment requirements, counter-trade or similar requirements.

2.   Nevertheless, having regard to general policy considerations, including those relating to development, a developing country may at the time of accession negotiate conditions for the use of offsets, such as requirements for the incorporation of domestic content. Such requirements shall be used only for qualification to participate in the procurement process and not as criteria for awarding contracts. Conditions shall be objective, clearly defined and non-discriminatory. They shall be set forth in the country's Appendix I and may include precise limitations on the imposition of offsets in any contract subject to this Agreement. The existence of such conditions shall be notified to the Committee and included in the notice of intended procurement and other documentation.

As discussed above, the provisions of Article 4 of the CAA, and not Article XVI of the GPA, appear to govern civil aircraft and component products. It is worthwhile to note, however: (a) that the GPA is more precise on the technology transfer issue than even the EC-U.S. Agreement regarding the CAA and (b) the GPA leaves open the possibility that developing countries acceding to the agreement might be exempt from the prohibition on offsets under certain conditions. These conditions are that civil offset requirements may only be a condition for "qualification" and not for award of a contract, that the conditions must be non-discriminatory, and that they must be set forth in an appendix to the GPA.

It is not entirely clear how an offset would be used as a condition to qualify for bidding, but not as a condition of award — since any accepted bid would presumably include the offset. This type of ambiguity is somewhat typical of WTO agreements that are the product of negotiation and compromise. The U.S. government might insist that the PRC accede to the WTO as a developed Member. There is some risk that new developing country signatories to the CAA, such as the PRC and similarly situated potential signatories, would claim a right to derogate from its prohibition on offsets by analogizing to the GPA provision on offsets. As developed signatories, they could not colorably make such a claim.

The GPA also addresses local content requirements in its Article III, which provides general rules against discrimination in the government procurement sector (for covered entities). Since local content requirements clearly discriminate in favor of local producers, they would be prohibited under GPA Article III, even without specific reference in Article XVI:1.

Exceptions

With respect to the CAA, the agreement expressly excludes military aircraft. Article 1.2 of the CAA says:

> For the purposes of this Agreement "civil aircraft" means (a) all aircraft other than military aircraft . . . .

Otherwise, there is no specific exception provision in the CAA. It may be recalled that the EC-U.S. Agreement regarding the CAA applies only to trade in large civil aircraft.[60]

The GPA contains a safeguard provision that covers both defense procurement matters and other concerns. Article XXIII of the GPA provides:

Exceptions to the Agreement

> 1. Nothing in this Agreement shall be construed to prevent any Party from taking any action or not disclosing any information which it considers *necessary for the protection of its essential security interests relating to the procurement of arms, ammunition or war materials, or to procurement indispensable for national security or for national defence purposes* [emphasis supplied].

> 2. Subject to the requirement that such measures are not applied in a manner which would constitute a means of arbitrary or unjustifiable discrimination between countries where the same conditions prevail or a disguised restriction on international trade, nothing in this Agreement shall be construed to prevent any Party from imposing or enforcing

measures: necessary to protect public morals, order or safety, human, animal or plant life or health or intellectual property; or relating to the products or services of handicapped persons, of philanthropic institutions or of prison labour.

Pursuant to Article XXIII, a Party to the GPA would be entitled to impose local content requirements in the defense procurement sector, and might also impose offsets such as requiring the disclosure of technology used in the production process. Outside the defense context, Article XXIII should not be interpreted to permit local content requirements or offsets. Article XXIII:2 of the GPA is similar to Article XX of the GATT 1994 that establishes the general "safeguard" exceptions under the GATT. As with respect to Article XXIII:2 of the GPA, Article XX of the GATT does not provide an exception for local content requirements. Article XXI of the GATT 1994 providing the national security safeguard might permit the use of local content and offset requirements in the defense procurement context. However, there is already a general government procurement exception in Article III:8, so this would be a redundant exception. An Article XXI defense procurement exception might be interposed against a claim of a GATT Article XI violation (see discussion of Article XI *supra*) in a specific case involving defense procurement.

Finally with respect to the GPA and defense procurement, governments are entitled to specifically exempt specific categories of defense procurement even with respect to government entities whose purchases are otherwise subject to the agreement. A review of the GPA Annexes suggests that governments have taken advantage of this possibility, and so, for example, are not subjecting the procurement of military aircraft to GPA disciplines.[61]

The WTO Legal System and the Interests of the Developing Countries

Special and differential treatment for developing members was a notable feature of GATT law,[62] which now is carried forward in various WTO texts. This special and differential treatment is presently reflected in transitional arrangements in a variety of WTO agreements[63], and in more general contexts such as reduced expectations in the negotiation of reciprocal concessions[64]. As noted earlier, the TRIPS Agreement expressly provides that exceptions may be made to the protection of patent rights provided that normal exploitation is not subject to interference, and the Agreement more generally promotes the goal of technology capacity building in developing members.[65] A developing Member of the WTO might seek to justify a technology transfer-related civil offset requirement otherwise potentially inconsistent with WTO rules on the basis of statements of principle in the TRIPS Agreement and elsewhere regarding the encouragement of technology capacity building. Though it seems doubtful that a DSU panel or the Appellate Body would find that such statements of principle would relieve a clear violation of the WTO texts, they might aid developing members as a source of interpretative guidance in cases in which the applicable rules are not so clear.

Conclusions in Respect to Civil Offsets

Article III of the GATT 1994 generally prohibits local content requirements outside the government procurement context. However, in light of the government procurement exception established by Article III:8, separate agreements must be adopted to subject government procurement to this discipline. In the CAA, Article 4.3 operates to eliminate an exception for local content requirements in the government procurement of civil aircraft and parts context. Articles III and XVI of the GPA perform the same function in the general government procurement context, but government procurement issues regarding civil aircraft appear to be governed by the CAA (among its signatories).

Civil offset requirements that are not local content requirements may also be precluded by GATT Article III, provided that such requirements have the requisite discriminatory effect. A non-discriminatory civil offset requirement may not be prohibited by Article III. As with respect to local content requirements, the government procurement exception will apply with respect to civil offsets, and the disciplines of the CAA and GPA are required to eliminate the exception. Article XI of the GATT 1994 may be argued to preclude civil offsets under certain circumstances. However, there may be difficulty in distinguishing impermissible import restrictions and "hard bargaining". The CAA, especially as interpreted by the EC-U.S. Agreement concerning its application, appears to preclude local content requirements and civil offsets, including requirements of technology transfer (i.e. in the EC-U.S. Agreement by precluding requirements of "other industrial compensation"). It should be noted that the CAA is not entirely without ambiguity, at least in the absence of the EC-U.S. interpretive note. The GPA certainly precludes civil offset requirements (GPA Article XVI), though developing countries are permitted the use of an ambiguous exception.

Accession of Non-Members to the WTO

Accession to the WTO is governed by Article XII of the WTO Agreement.[66] Any state or autonomous customs territory may accede to the WTO Agreement "on terms to be agreed between it and the WTO". Ordinarily, the WTO will continue the customary GATT practice of decision by consensus, including with respect to the question of accession.[67] In the absence of consensus, an accession agreement must be approved by a two-thirds majority of the members.[68]

Accession to the Plurilateral Agreements is governed by the terms of the Plurilateral Agreements.[69] The CAA distinguishes between acceptance by governments that are contracting parties to the GATT, and other governments.[70] The wording with respect to the two categories of adherence is somewhat different. It is clear that accession by non-members of the GATT (now WTO) is subject to an agreement between the existing signatories and the acceding state.[71] It would also appear that accessions by members of the WTO requires an agreement with the existing signatories regarding the terms of accession, though the language is less clear. Article 9.1.2. of the CAA provides:

> This Agreement shall be open for acceptance by signature or otherwise by governments having provisionally acceded to the GATT [i.e. Members], *on terms* related to the effective application of rights and obligations under this Agreement, which take into account rights and obligations in the instruments providing for their provisional accession [emphasis supplied].

Though Article 9.1.2 does not directly refer to an "agreement", the words "on terms" would appear to import the necessity of an agreement. It is of course of interest to note that the CAA leaves open the possibility that a state may become a signatory without acceding to the WTO. The CAA does not include any specific provisions on decision-making.

In order to accede to the GPA a Party must be a member of the WTO and must agree with the existing Parties on the terms of accession.[72] A Decision on Accession to the Agreement on Government Procurement was adopted by Ministers in connection with the Marrakesh Ministerial in 1994. The Decision makes clear, *inter alia*, that accessions to the GPA are approved by consensus.[73]

There is no express limitation in the WTO Agreement or in the Plurilateral Agreements on the type of terms of accession that may be demanded by existing members/signatories/parties as a condition of accession.[74] As discussed, the GPA permits acceding developing Parties to specify certain exceptions to the rule otherwise prohibiting their use of local content and civil offset requirements.[75] No comparable provision permitting exceptions is contained in the CAA.

Demands on EC and U.S. enterprises in the civil aircraft sector for transfers of technology have characterized commercial relations with China, which is seeking admission to the WTO. It is foreseeable that EC and U.S.

trade negotiators will seek to clarify rules governing this area in the context of concluding China's Protocol of Accession.

3. Conclusion

The rules of the WTO with respect to technology and the state are in an early stage of evolution. Up until the Uruguay Round, intellectual property and technology were largely outside the GATT/WTO lexicon. The TRIPS Agreement reflects demands by highly industrialized WTO members that the value of technology be adequately accounted for in world trade. From the very incipiency of rules protecting IPRs, there has been a tension between the goal of protection of knowledge and the goal of diffusion of knowledge. Over time, and with the accession of important new developing members, the WTO perspective on the proper balancing of IPRs-related interests may shift. The WTO texts appear to allow some flexibility in accommodating a range of perspectives.

As observed at the outset of this chapter, states are involved in the creation and dissemination of knowledge in many ways. A full appreciation and accounting for this role of the state requires a far more elaborate analysis than is provided for in this brief chapter, and would include reference to research and development subsidies, tax policy, education policy, and so forth. As the future unfolds, WTO rules relating to technology may further evolve to address this complex of subject matters.

NOTES

1. This conference is directed to the subject matter of state enterprises in the WTO system. State enterprises are expressly governed by Article XVII GATT (1994) and, in a somewhat more diffuse way, by Articles VIII and IX GATS. A considerable amount of the expertise among conference participants will be directed at defining the scope of Article XVII: what is a "state enterprise" and which of its activities are regulated in what way? The idea of devoting a conference to the subject of state enterprise presumably arises at least in part from the lack of clarity in Article XVII. Difficulties in distinguishing between "government" and "public activity" on the one hand, and "state trading" and "the commercial activity" on the other, have plagued legislatures and courts with respect to the notion of restrictive sovereign immunity in international law for a number of decades. Distinguishing between "government procurement" and "state trading" for the purposes of WTO law seems likely to prove difficult for WTO legal experts.

In his contribution to this book, William Davey notes that the 1994 Understanding on the Interpretation of Article XVII includes a refined working definition of "state trading enterprise", as follows:

> Governmental and non-governmental enterprises, including marketing boards, which have been granted exclusive or special rights or privileges, including

statutory or constitutional powers, in the exercise of which they influence through their purchases or sales the level or direction of imports or exports. See William J. Davey, Article XVII GATT: An Overview. In this volume.

2. Paris Convention, Article 4ter.

3. See, e.g., Articles 1–4, id.

4. See 35 U.S.C.A. ϶϶111(a), 115.

5. Though there is some ambiguity in the U.S. statutory scheme with respect to whether the federal government might apply for and be granted a patent in its own right, see 35 U.S.C.A. ϶ 207(a)(1), this writer has confirmed with the U.S. Patent and Trademark Office (PTO) that U.S. government patents are applied for by natural persons and assigned to the government.

6. Article 58 of the EPC provides that "[a] European patent application may be filed by any natural or legal person, or any body equivalent to a legal person by virtue of the law governing it".

7. See, e.g., 35 U.S.C.A. ϶ 209.

8. There is no apparent indication that the conditions of such licensing discriminate against non-U.S.-owned enterprises. If a government restricted access to its patented technology to nationally-owned enterprises, this might affect the competitive balance in trade and constitute, for example, an export subsidy, which under certain conditions might be prohibited by the Agreement on Subsidies.

The U.S. Patent Act does provide that:

> A Federal agency shall normally grant the right to use or sell any federally owned invention in the United States only to a licensee that agrees that any products embodying the invention or produced through the invention will be manufactured in the United States. 35 U.S.C.A. ϶ 209(b).

The foregoing provision does not limit the sale of resulting products to particular markets or purchasers, and does not appear to discriminate on the basis of the nationality of licensees.

9. See, e.g., TRIPS Agreement Articles 1:3, 39, and 42, note 11, for references to "nationals", "natural and legal persons", and "right holder", respectively. None of these provisions suggest that governments or state enterprises might not be capable of acting as patent right holders in the TRIPS context.

10. "*Recognizing* that intellectual property rights are private rights." TRIPS Agreement, preamble.

11. According to a senior member of the WTO Secretariat who participated in the TRIPS Agreement negotiations, the reference to "private rights" was included at the insistence of the Hong Kong delegation, which wanted clarification that the enforcement of IPRs is the responsibility of private rights holders, and not of governments. Assuming that this accurately reflects the genesis of the relevant language, other delegations may have attached different significance to the "private rights" language.

12. See Frederick M. Abbott, WTO Dispute Settlement and the Agreement on Trade-Related Aspects of Intellectual Property Rights, in: E.-U. Petersmann, ed.,

International Trade Law and the GATT/WTO Dispute Settlement System 415 (1997).

13. TRIPS Agreement, Article 2:1.

14. TRIPS Agreement, Article 2:2.

15. The TRIPS Agreement expressly contemplates that governments may use patent rights of private parties without authorization. This does not resolve an apparent ambiguity regarding the status of governments as owners of rights. Governments would not become rights "owners" under TRIPS Article 31, only "users".

16. Paris Convention, Article 5(2), (4).

17. Id. at 5(4).

18. TRIPS Agreement, Article 31, chapeau.

19. Id. at 31(b).

20. Id.

21. Conditions are also placed on authorizations to overcome patent dependence.

22. See generally, Donald Chisum, Patents, ∋16.06 (Lexis/Nexis 1997).

23. 28 U.S.C. ∋1498(a).

24. See European Commission, Report on United States Barriers to Trade and In-vestment 1997, at 6.1.

25. Id.

26. Chisum, op. cit. note 22, at 16.06[3].

27. See TRIPS Agreement, Article 31(b), supra.

28. This writer understands the Commission=s premise that foreign enterprises are more affected than domestic enterprises. While this argument may have at least limited validity, as noted in the text above, competition among large R&D-based multinational enterprises is not too terribly subject to differential playing fields in the United States and Europe.

29. Article 27:1 of the TRIPS Agreement provides that: "patent rights [shall be] enjoyable without discrimination as to . . . whether products are imported or locally produced". This suggests that importation should satisfy working requirements. However, TRIPS Agreement Article 2:1 provides that members will comply, *inter alia*, with Paris Convention Article 5 which permits the grant of compulsory licenses for non-working. This is a tension between the two Agreements which remains to be resolved. In any event, failure to supply a market either through importation or working should justify the grant of a compulsory license.

30. The question whether the WTO Agreement somehow demands that members adhere to an American-style market economy is also posed in John Jackson, The Institutional Ramifications of China=s Accession to the WTO, in Frederick M. Abbott, ed., China in the World Trading System: Defining the Principles of Engagement 75, 80 (1998).

31. TRIPS Agreement, Article 30, provides:

Exceptions to Rights Conferred: Members may provide limited exceptions to the exclusive rights conferred by a patent, provided that such exceptions do not unreasonably conflict with a normal exploitation of the patent and do not unreasonably prejudice the legitimate interests of the patent owner, taking account of the legitimate interests of third parties.

32. See Frederick M. Abbott, Protecting First World Assets in the Third World: Intellectual Property Negotiations in the GATT Multilateral Framework, 22 Vand. J. Transnat=l L. 689 (1989).

33. See Frederick M. Abbott and David J. Gerber, eds., Public Policy and Global Technological Integration (1997), including contributions from Thomas Cottier and Diane Wood who also participate in this volume.

34. Comments in Gerzenzee proceedings. On EC competition rules relating to state monopolies, see Jacques H.J. Bourgeois, "EC Rules on State Monopolies and Public Undertakings: Lesson for the WTO." In this volume.

35. See, e.g., discussion of offset arrangement involving Swiss government and McDonnell Douglas, Toni Wicki, Switzerland's Chief of Armament, Defense News, April 15, 1996 (Lexis/Nexis).

36. Regarding the CAA, see infra discussion text at notes 49–76. Article I:3 of the Plurilateral Government Procurement Agreement ("GPA") expressly provides that "enterprises" not covered under the Agreement which are required by covered "entities" to "award contracts in accordance with particular requirements" will be subject to the non-discrimination provisions (Article III) of the GPA.

37. United States - Taxes Affecting Imported Automobiles, DS31/R, Oct. 11, 1994 (not adopted) (concerning EC allegations that U.S. luxury tax on automobiles, U.S. gas guzzler tax, and U.S. legislation governing automobile fleet fuel economy, discriminated against automobiles imported into the United States from the EC).

38. EEC- Import Regime for Bananas, GATT report, Jan. 18, 1994 (not adopted), 34 I.L.M. 177 (1995) (concerning allegations by Central and Latin American banana producers that EC mechanism for allocating tariff-rate quotas discriminated in favor of particular importers in violation, inter alia, of GATT Articles I and III).

39. United States - Section 337 of the Tariff Act of 1930, report adopted Nov. 7, 1989, BISD 36S/345 (determining that U.S. Section 337 violated GATT Article III through discrimination against imported products by facilitation of prosecution for U.S. patent violations).

40. Thailand - Restrictions and Internal Taxes on Cigarettes, report adopted Nov. 7, 1990, BISD 37S/200 (determining that Thai restrictions on importation of cigarettes and related tax laws were not justified by health concerns since such restrictions discriminatorily affected imported cigarettes).

41. Canada - Administration of Foreign Investment Review Act, report adopted Feb 7, 1984, BISD 30S/140, para. 5.10 (determining that provisions of Canadian foreign investment legislation that had the effect of requiring investors to commit to the purchase locally produced products as a condition of investment approval violated GATT Article III:4).

42. Italian Discrimination Against Imported Agricultural Machinery, report adopted Oct. 23, 1958, BISD 7S/60 (determining that Italian legislation offering favorable financing to purchasers of locally produced farm equipment violated GATT Article III).

43. The use of the term Acivil≅ in connection with the term Aoffset≅ was presumably initiated in the defense procurement context and distinguished Acivil offsets≅ in the public sector from Amilitary≅ or Adefense≅ offsets.

44. United States - Section 337 of the Tariff Act of 1930, report adopted Nov. 7, 1989, BISD 36S/345, para. 5.13.

45. The factor that distinguishes this situation for those considered in prior GATT panel decisions on the general subject matter is that in this situation the creation of the domestic industry to produce goods that are favored over imported goods may be a "latent" effect.

46. See, e.g., Olivier Long, Law and Its Limitations in the GATT Multilateral Trading System (1985).

47. An argument might also be made that such transfer of technology requirements constitute a nullification or impairment of private rights which are protected under the TRIPS Agreements. However, for the time being the TRIPS Agreement prohibits members from bringing nullification or impairment claims. TRIPS Agreement, Article 64:2.

48. Report adopted May 4, 1988, BISD 35S/116, paras. 106–117.

49. WTO Agreement, Article II:3.

50. See also discussion of EC-U.S. Understanding infra.

51. GPA, Article 1, footnote, and ref. Annex 3.

52. This does not exclude the possibility that some government airline might be incorporated within the structure of a transport ministry, though it would seem that in most cases a government airline would stand alone as a public corporation.

53. The author has confirmed this in an informal discussion with a WTO Secretariat officer whose responsibilities include legal oversight of the CAA and GPA. This conclusion is implicitly confirmed by the URAA Statement of Administrative Action and the subsequent Report of the ACTPN regarding Trade in Civil Aircraft. The ACTPN is the public advisory group that consults with the USTR regarding the WTO and the implementation of the Uruguay Round Agreements. See ACTPN, WTO Implementation Report, Trade in Civil Aircraft, Internet http://www.ustr.gov/reports/ wto/civil_aircraft.html (07/04/96 03:24:56). For example, the Statement of Administrative Action states:

> The United States will also seek to ensure that all WTO Members, as well as countries applying for WTO membership, that are involved in the development, production, and integration of aerospace products undertake the obligations of the Agreement on Trade in Civil Aircraft (URAA Statement at B.1.o).

The ACTPN refers to the necessity of assuring that acceding members of the WTO such as the People=s Republic of China (PRC) sign and comply with the CAA, and says:

> The Agreement has eliminated imports duties on trade in aircraft, engines and other related assemblies and parts. It also prohibits certain non-tariff barriers such as requiring offsets (which require vendors to place procurement subcontracts in the local country), stipulating that national carriers purchase from na-

tional suppliers, and employing standards to discriminate against imported products. (ACTPN Report, at Introduction)

54. GATT BISD 26S/162 (1980), 31 UST 619.

55. Agreement Establishing the World Trade Organization, Article II:3 and Annex 4.

56. ACTPN Report, op. cit. note 53. According to the ACTPN Report, all major WTO members producing covered products (except Brazil and Indonesia) are Signatories.

57. This reference should now be understood to refer to the successor agreement, the WTO Agreement on Technical Barriers to Trade.

58. European Community - United States: Agreement Concerning the Application of the GATT Agreement on Trade in Civil Aircraft on Trade in Large Civil Aircraft, 1993 BDIEL AD LEXIS 60, done at Washington and Brussels, July 17, 1992.

59. Compare this provision to footnote 7 of Article XVI of the GPA which defines "offsets":

> Offsets in government procurement are measures used to encourage local development or improve the balance-of-payments accounts by means of domestic content, licensing of technology, investment requirements, counter-trade or similar requirements.

Certain passages from the ACTPN Report regarding the CAA are relevant to the foregoing texts. The Report states:

> It also prohibits certain non-tariff barriers such as requiring offsets (which require vendors to place procurement subcontracts in the local country), stipulating that national carriers purchase from national suppliers, and employing standards to discriminate against imported products.
>
> ***
>
> The Agreement has been effective in eliminating duties on trade in civil aircraft and related products, but has not proven capable of limiting foreign government involvement in the aerospace sector in the form of government inducements, offsets, and other influence.

Regarding Article 4 of the CAA as interpreted by the EC-U.S. Agreement, the ACTPN Report recommends:

> Adoption of the *non-controversial amendments to Article 4* are desirable, but only if it can be done in without otherwise altering the rights and obligations of the Agreement [emphasis supplied].

The text of Article 4.3 of the CAA does not expressly refer to "offsets", though there is a strong argument that the limitation of decision-making factors to "price, quality and delivery" has the effect of precluding offsets. The text is ambiguous with respect to transfers of technology, which might be considered part of a package of goods that is being purchased on the basis of quality and price. This ambiguity is reduced somewhat in the EC-U.S. interpretative Annex which prohibits the requirement of "other industrial compensation". This term may be considered to cover technology transfer.

The ACTPN Report refers to non-controversial "amendments" to Article 4 as being a desirable addition to the CAA. To the extent that adding an interpretation is considered an "amendment" to an international agreement, this terminology is reasonable. However, from a U.S. perspective, this interpretation should not "amend" Article 4, it rather should state more clearly what the signatories already intended. This distinction should be kept clear.

60. The EC-U.S. Agreement defines "large civil aircraft" to include their parts and components, as follows:

> 1. "large civil aircraft": with respect to such aircraft produced in the US by existing manufacturers of large civil aircraft and in the European Community by the Airbus consortium, or their successor entities, all aircraft, as defined in Article 1 of the GATT Agreement on Trade in Civil Aircraft, except engines as defined in Article 1.1(b) thereof, that are designed for passenger or cargo transportation and have one hundred or more passenger seats or its equivalent in cargo configuration.

61. See, e.g., GPA Annexes of the governments of Canada (Annex I regarding coverage of Department of National Defense) and Germany (European Communities, Annex I, Germany, note 13 and related provisions).

62. See, e.g., Long, supra note 46.

63. See, e.g., Agreement on Agriculture, Article 15; Agreement on Subsidies, Article 27; Agreement on TRIMS, Article 5; Agreement on TRIPS, Article 65.

64. See, e.g., GATT 1994, Part IV, Article XXXVI:8 and GATS Article IV:3.

65. See generally, Frederick M. Abbott, The WTO TRIPS Agreement and Global Economic Development, in Public Policy and Global Technological Integration xx (Frederick M. Abbott and David J. Gerber eds. 1997). Article 7, Objectives, provides:

> The protection and enforcement of intellectual property rights should contribute to the promotion of technological innovation and to the transfer and dissemination of technology, to the mutual advantage of producers and users of technological knowledge and in a manner conducive to social and economic welfare, and to a balance of rights and obligations.

Article 66, Least-Developed Country Members, provides:

> 2. Developed country Members shall provide incentives to enterprises and institutions in their territories for the purpose of promoting and encouraging technology transfer to least-developed country Members in order to enable them to create a sound and viable technological base.

66. The rules and procedures for accession to the WTO are addressed in detail in China in the World Trading System: Defining the Principles of Engagement. op. cit., note 30.

67. WTO Agreement, Article IX:1.

68. WTO Agreement, Article XII:2.

69. WTO Agreement, Article XII:3.

70. CAA, Article 9.

71. CAA Article 9.1.3 provides:

> This Agreement shall be open to accession by any other government on terms, related to the effective application of rights and obligations under this Agreement, *to be agreed between that government and the Signatories,* by the deposit with the Director-General to the CONTRACTING PARTIES to the GATT of an instrument of accession which states the terms so agreed [emphasis supplied].

72. GPA, Article XXIV:2.

73. Decision on Accession to the GPA, at para. 2.

74. See generally Stefan A. Riesenfeld and Frederick M. Abbott, eds., Parliamentary Participation in the Making and Operation of Treaties: A Comparative Study (1995) (discussion of the various ways in which constitutional systems treat the question of self-executing or direct effect of treaties).

75. Supra, text at note 61.

CHAPTER 7

Comments

Werner Zdouc

The first World Trade Forum's subject of *Trade Liberalization and Property Ownership: State Trading in the 21st Century* is a very topical choice for a couple of reasons. First, the legal framework conditions for state trading in the agricultural sector has changed due to the fact that stricter rules have been introduced in this sector as a result of the Uruguay Round. Second, many economies in transition are seeking WTO membership, presupposing the reorganisation of state trading enterprises on an unprecedented scale. The examples of Bulgaria and Mongolia and the pending cases of China and the ex-Soviet republics show how substantial the social cost of phasing-out state trading operations can be, given the tremendous need to catch up with privatization and demonopolization in these countries. There seems to be a general consensus among participants that the approaches taken in the accession process of Poland, Hungary, and Romania are outdated because they have largely failed to yield the expected results in practice.

William Davey's *Overview of Article XVII* explains why GATT needs special rules on state trading. GATT's legal system presupposes a market economy and may be circumvented in a situation where governments intervene systematically in the market place. State trading may undermine basic GATT concepts, e.g., the national treatment principle, the prohibition of quantitative restrictions, or the respect of tariff bindings, or render rules on antidumping or countervailing duties difficult to apply. State trading in a variety of agricultural products, energy, minerals, alcohol, salt, etc., was originally introduced in pursuance of regulatory objectives. The special or exclusive rights which are conferred upon state trading enterprises in order to tackle market structure problems may cause market conduct problems when such enterprises abuse these privileges by engaging in restrictive business practices.

An apparent lack of transparency in pricing and operational activities is typical of state trading monopolies and marketing boards as well as of sole import agencies. It remains to be seen whether the insufficient notification practice of GATT contracting parties is going to improve under the new WTO Understanding on Article XVII. One reason for the modest degree of compliance with the notification requirements might be that the relevant state trading questionnaire stems from a 1960 decision. Much will depend on whether the process of updating and clarifying the questionnaire as foreseen by the 1994 Understanding on Article XVII can be completed according to schedule. Also, the review procedure of received notifications in the state trading committee needs to be reinvigorated. If these problems are not solved in the short-run, it will be quite difficult to expect more informative notification practices from newly acceding countries than from original WTO Members. The possibility of cross-notifications by other WTO Members is probably the most significant innovation of the new Understanding on Article XVII because it might become a very potent tool for the enforcement of the notification requirements.

From a more general perspective, the possibility to abuse monopoly or monopsony power highlights the need for additional rules against the abuse of market power regardless of whether it is carried out by private or public monopolies or oligopolies. In the longer term, a more fundamental problem needs to be tackled. The question is whether it is possible to achieve regulatory objectives that historically caused governments to introduce state trading more efficiently through alternative means of regulation. In addressing this issue, drawing from Article 37 of the EC Treaty on the adjustment of state monopolies of a commercial character can only be a starting point for further reflection. More importantly, legislators should consider whether existing state trading entities reflect a philosophy about the role of the state and the function of governmental intervention that might be outdated in the globalized economy of the closing years of this century.

Ernst-Ulrich Petersmann's contribution, *Article XVII GATT on State Trading Enterprises: Critical Evaluation and Proposals for Reform*, first discusses the legalistic approach to defining state trading operations as reflected in the relevant GATT provisions. The language of Article XVII is imprecise in a couple of respects. Its scope covers state enterprises as well as (other) enterprises granted exclusive or special privileges. The benefit of this imprecision is the potentially wide field of application for GATT's state trading rules. It seems as if the increased clarity of the "working definition" of the 1994 Understanding on Article XVII could only be won by narrowing the potential scope of the broad state trading concept as embodied in Article XVII itself. This holds true in particular for the newly introduced requirement to show that state trading enterprises in the exercise of their exclusive or special rights or privileges actually *influence* through their purchases or sales the level or direction of imports or exports. It was certainly an unobjectionable intention of the Uruguay Round negotiators if it was their overriding rationale to concentrate attention on the functions state trading enterprises fulfil rather than on their form or ownership. However, the solution chosen amounts to a requirement to prove adverse trade effects, an element which panels have wisely refused to consider in the interpretation of other GATT principles, e.g., Article III. As one can learn from the experience in GATT dispute settlement with claims under the national treatment clause, the decision how to allocate the initial burden of proof in this regard essentially predetermines the outcome of the case.

It is striking how reticent panels have been in addressing claims under Article XVII. Whenever they saw an alternative route to resolving a case under more basic rules such as Articles I, II, III, or XI, they avoided dealing with a provision whose wording is one of the most ambiguous of the GATT treaty language. Those panels that have dealt with Article XVII have not taken advantage of the ambiguous phrasing of this article by developing expansive interpretations as they did with other rather general GATT provisions. Article XVII:1(a)'s obligation for state trading enterprises to act consistently with "general principles of non-discrimination" is a diluted compromise phrase. It has been used by panels as a leeway to read only a most-favoured nation treatment obligation into Article XVII:1(a). However, references to purported consistent practice of past panel do not make up for the failure of any such panel report to clearly address the issue why such "general principles" (sic!) do not comprise the additional requirement to respect the national treatment principle. At any rate, no panel to date has rebutted with a persuasive legal reasoning the U.S. argumentation in the F.I.R.A. case on this point (as explained in detail in the chapter by Horlick/Mowry).

The framers of the GATT were apparently aware that in drafting Article XVII:1(a) they had not a achieved a model of clarity. However, the attempt to define "general principles of non-discrimination" further by obliging state trading enterprises in Article XVII:1(b) to make purchases or sales solely in accordance with "commercial considerations" compounds these difficulties. To complicate things even more, the latter subparagraph further pursues this wrong track by stipulating that "state trading enterprises shall afford enterprises of other Members adequate opportunity, in accordance with customary business practice, to compete for participation in such purchases or sales". Whatever these phrases may mean, in any case, it is difficult to understand why panels found themselves not in a position to go beyond a mere MFN-treatment obligation and to develop an interpretation along the lines of Articles III and XI.

Hardly any GATT provision highlights as clearly as Article XVII does the gap left by the failure of the GATT contracting parties to complement the GATT of 1947 with Chapter V of the Havana Charter on rules against restrictive business practices. This assessment is reinforced by the fact that governments are the primary addressees of the obligations embodied in Article XVII:1, and that it is up to them to ensure that the enterprises at issue observe them. Complementary provisions to Article XVII, such as Article

II:4 and the Note Ad Articles XI, XII, XIII, XIV and XVII, might be well-suited to ensuring the respect of tariff bindings and the prohibitions of import and export restrictions by state trading enterprises, but are far from redressing the incomplete and vague phrasing of Article XVII.

The introductory part of Aaditya Mattoo's chapter, *Dealing with Monopolies and State Enterprises: WTO Rules for Goods and Services*, presents a thorough analysis of the differences and similarities between Article XVII of GATT and Article VIII of GATS. The state trading definition of GATT follows a rather legalistic, ownership-based concept, whereas the GATS' description of service monopolies and exclusive service providers reflects a more economic, market-based approach. Accordingly, monopoly service suppliers are those providers that are formally or *in effect* the sole suppliers of a given service. While this functional approach of Article VIII GATS has the merit of practicability, the potential scope of state trading operations and enterprises covered by Article XVII of GATT is clearly more comprehensive.

Article VIII's focus on monopolies and non-competing oligopolies reflects the primary concern of GATS negotiators of containing potential abuse of market power. Such abuse may occur in relation to downstream customers of the monopoly service or upstream suppliers of input services or goods. Monopoly suppliers are considered to be particularly prone to abusing their position where they also provide services or goods outside the scope of their service monopoly in competition with other service suppliers, since they may opt to cross-subsidize their economic activities in markets that operate under competitive conditions with rents generated in the service market they monopolize.

Among others, the atomized negotiating structure of the Uruguay Round and the lack of coordination between negotiating groups might be reasons for the gaps that continue to exist in the coverage of economic activities by Articles XVII of GATT and VIII of GATS. For example, in the area of government procurement, "goods" subject to Article XVII do not appear to include purchases of service inputs used for the production of goods or services sold by such state enterprises. Likewise, Article VIII does not seem to cover intermediate goods used as inputs in the production of monopoly services or the sale of goods produced with the use of monopoly service inputs.

While it is not clear whether Article VIII of GATS covers natural monopolies which emerge absent any facilitating governmental intervention, the disciplines do apply once a natural monopoly is reinforced or entrenched by legislation. Until recently, public service utilities were widely perceived to constitute *per se* natural monopolies. However, changing paradigms in economic theory have triggered a process of rethinking the classic natural monopoly concept. Moreover, technological innovation in many service sectors has substantially reduced the optimal scale of service production.

These days, full-fledged service monopolies and non-competing oligopolies, the primary targets of Article VIII, are rare, while significant gaps continue to exist in the coverage of other service suppliers that are endowed with special or exclusive rights. This raises the question of whether the conceptual approach underlying Article VIII GATS is sufficiently flexible to correspond to the ever-changing state-of-the-art of technological development. This holds true especially where the soundness of economic, technological, or regulatory reasons for protecting "natural" monopolies has vanished and liberalization, privatization, or complete phasing-out of exclusive monopoly has become the order of the day. To put it differently, it is proof enough that a monopoly is not (any more) a truly *natural* one in the economic sense where it needs legal protection against market entry by competitors.

With respect to substantive obligations, Article VIII GATS obliges monopoly service suppliers to honour the most-favoured nation treatment clause as well as commitments on national treatment and market access. However, the scope of the latter are, at any rate, limited to those sectors and modes of supply that a Member chose to bind in its country-specific schedule of GATS commitments. It remains to be seen whether panels deciding claims under Article XVII of GATT will be inspired to develop an interpretation of the state trading disciplines that mirrors the corresponding GATS obligations.

The case of accounting rates in international telecommunications is most illustrative of the limits of the classic non-discrimination concepts. A strict reading of the unconditional MFN treatment principle would arguably prevent price discrimination between different countries and induce providers of telecommunications services to charge uniform but inflated monopoly prices. In other words, the application of the MFN treatment standard in telecommunications markets would help entrench monopolies instead of fostering liberalization and deregulation. One has to recall that most basic GATT principles presuppose a functioning market economy and may cause quite unexpected, counterproductive results in non-competitive markets. This paradoxical result is probably an inescapable corollary to the overriding but short-sighted concern of Uruguay Round negotiators to come up with GATS rules that are as neutral as possible with regard to the ownership of utilities and the market structure in various service sectors. The examples of the maritime and air transport service sectors also underscore that general GATS disciplines are bound to remain rather ineffective unless anticompetitive national and international framework rules that entrench monopolization and cartelization are abolished.

The sectoral annex on telecommunications and the reference paper for scheduling additional commitments have been geared more towards adapting GATS rules to the specific problems arising in the interface between competitive and monopolized market segments. However, it has to be conceded that so far sectoral approaches to redressing these problems have worked well only where market forces and technological innovation have created an appropriate environment for changes in market and ownership structures. To date the WTO has been mostly reacting to market developments rather than being an active force in pursuing progressive sectoral deregulation in services. Nonetheless, sectoral approaches to introducing competition in closed services markets are more promising courses of action than general rules on private restrictive business practices (e.g., the "positive comity" rule embodied in Article IX of GATS). In the end, on a sectoral basis it is easier to ensure that operators from closed markets enter and benefit from liberalized markets only on the condition that equivalent market access is granted *vice versa*.

Gary Horlick's and Kristin Heim Mowry's chapter on *The Treatment of Activities of State Trading Enterprises under the WTO Subsidies Rules* explores a number of very interesting, novel issues. Little research has been done so far on questions concerning the interface between, on the one hand, WTO rules on state trading and, on the other hand, the rules on export and domestic support for agricultural products, or those on subsidies and countervailing duties with respect to industrial products.

For example, state trading standards such as "general principles of nondiscriminatory treatment" and "commercial considerations" as the sole reference point for purchases or sales, or the permission of export price discrimination, have not in so many words been taken into account in the categorization of prohibited, actionable, and non-actionable subsidies, nor in the drafting of criteria for the imposition of countervailing duties, e.g., the calculation of adequate remuneration. Likewise, it is evident that a benefit may be conferred by a government through a state trading enterprise serving as an intermediary, e.g., the provision of export subsidies by a statutory export marketing board for agricultural products which are subject to export subsidy reduction commitments.

However, there is no conflict in the real sense between the above-mentioned state trading rules and stricter disciplines on subsidization given that these different sets of rules do not appear to stipulate mutually exclusive or contradictory obligations. In other words, it is possible for governments and state trading enterprises (or monopoly service suppliers) to observe all these rules on a cumulative basis because the GATT 1994 does not mandate conduct which is contrary to and prohibited by the Agreements on Subsidies or Agriculture. Essentially, the issue is rather that the range of permissible state trading operations and practices which seemed perfectly compatible with Article XVII of GATT (or Article VIII of GATS), will become in fact much more limited due to potential inconsistencies with the tightened disciplines of the WTO Agreements on Agriculture or on Subsidies and Countervailing Measures. Thus, he who criticizes the 1994 Understanding on Article XVII of GATT and the relevant GATS provisions as weak and incomplete should acknowledge that an overall assessment of all Uruguay Round results that have a direct or indirect bearing on state trading leads to a different conclusion. State trading operations that are lawful under GATT (and GATS) will over time be narrowed down — indirectly, but not less effectively — to a considerable extent once the transitional periods for the phase-in of the specific multilateral agreements on trade in goods have lapsed. Whether this result was explicitly intended by Uruguay Round negotiators, or is due to a lack of coordination between negotiating groups on GATT articles, subsidies, and agriculture is not entirely clear. At any rate, for the economies in transition among the countries seeking WTO accession, this is an important factor to consider in their decisions whether to restructure or maintain state trading enterprises or operations on a large scale.

On the other hand, one should also not exaggerate the real impact of the obligations embodied in the various WTO agreements. Many state trading operations are carried out by regulatory marketing boards, where the potential for inconsistencies with the Subsidies or Agriculture Agreements is probably negligible. That is so because usually such marketing boards do not trade directly in the products which are subject to their regulation. Accordingly, "regulatory" subsidies do not really confer a financial contribution, and arguably they are often not specific enough to be actionable under the rules on countervailing measures. In the end, governments might decide to do not much more than to restructure state trading enterprises or operations without, however, being forced to completely abolish them.

David Palmeter's contribution on *The WTO Antidumping Agreement and the Economies in Transition* is a thorough analysis of the repercussions of the new Antidumping Agreement on the legal framework for state trading. One could summarize his conclusions as twofold. In the first place, economies in transition from state planning to market economy should not expect to find in the Antidumping Agreement exemptions especially tailored to their concerns that could serve as justifications for activities by state enterprises which are actionable under general antidumping rules, or which are otherwise not in line with general GATT standards for state trading. For example, it is unclear whether economies in transition which have not explicitly claimed developing country status may invoke the "special regard" rule of Article 15 of the Antidumping Agreement. This rule favours in the case of developing countries' price undertakings in preference to the imposition of antidumping duties. To the contrary, given that in economies in transition domestic prices are often not determined under market conditions, third country, surrogate country, or constructed value methodologies will even more likely be used for the determination of the normal value in transition economies than with respect to market economies.

Another point made is that, notwithstanding the difficulties with choosing the method for the normal value determination, the WTO antidumping rules are unlikely to have a similarly limiting impact on the existing parameters for state trading as the Agreements on Subsidies and Agriculture just dealt with above.

Part III: Regional Experience

CHAPTER 8

EC Rules on State Monopolies and Public Undertakings: Any Relevance for the WTO?

Jacques H.J. Bourgeois

1. Introductory Remarks

The rules of the Treaty establishing the European Community (ECT), previ-ously the Treaty establishing the European Economic Community, on the "adjustment" of state monopolies of a commercial character (Article 37 ECT) and those on the duties of European Community (EC) Member States regarding public undertakings and undertakings to which Member States grant special or exclusive rights (Article 90 ECT) have been extensively commented upon in the literature, have been applied in decisions of the European Commission (the Commission) and have been interpreted by the Court of Justice of the European Communities (ECJ).

The purpose of the present chapter is to examine some of the issues to which these rules have given rise and which could conceivably be of some relevance in a World Trade Organization (WTO) context.

The overview offered in Section 2 is thus selective. Section 3 seeks to identify some of the factors which account for the relatively successful op-eration of these ECT rules. Section 4 deals briefly with the question of whether rules comparable to Article 90 ECT could be of some relevance in a WTO context.

2. An Overview

Article 37 ECT and State Trading Monopolies

For various reasons State trading bodies are not an unknown phenomenon in the market economies of the Member States of the European Community, and certainly were not at the time of the drafting of the Treaty establishing the European Economic Community. Article 37 was thus inserted in order to regulate such state monopolies of a commercial character in the context of

*Advocaat, partner Akin Gump, Strauss, Hauer and Feld (Brussels); Professor at the College of Europe (Bruges). This chapter could not have been written without the collaboration of Maria Winther LL.M. (University of Aarhus), LL.M. (College of Europe, Bruges).

the free movement of goods. The drafters of this Treaty drew obviously inspiration from Article XVII GATT.

As indicated by Article 37(1) itself[1], the notion of a state monopoly must be interpreted broadly as covering any body through which a Member State can influence intra-Community trade, but in contrast to the *Dassonville* doctrine under Article 30 ECT a mere potential influence on this trade is not sufficient.[2]

State monopolies of a commercial character are monopolies in transactions in goods which affect intra-Community trade. Monopolies in services[3] or production[4] on the contrary fall outside the scope of the provision.[5] Furthermore only activities intrinsically connected with the specific function of the monopoly, i.e. its exclusive right, fail to be considered under Article 37 as opposed to general measures regulating the marketing and production of a product.[6] These are instead regulated by Articles 30 to 36 ECT.

"Progressive Adjustment"

The precise scope of the prescribed progressive adjustment to ensure that no discrimination takes place as regards the conditions for the procurement and marketing of goods, is not all too clear, and was not further clarified until the Court of Justice of the European Communities gave judgment in the *Manghera*[7] case concerning the Italian state monopoly on tobacco. In *Manghera*, it was disputed whether the "adjustment" required by Article 37 was to be understood as the total abolition of the exclusive right of importation. This would not seem to follow from a literal interpretation of the text which does not mention elimination, in contrast to a more contextual approach according to which the abolition would be necessary in order to fulfill the requirement of ensuring that no discrimination exists after the expiry of the transitional period. The ECJ opted for the abolition of the exclusive right of importation from other EC Member States considering such a right in itself as discriminatory. The application of Article 37 is thus tied to the notion of discrimination and non-discriminatory restrictions flowing from state monopoly rights can therefore be maintained under Article 37.

Remaining Issues

Two important questions remain unanswered. One is whether Article 37 requires the adjustment of exclusive rights of *exportation*. In this connection it is interesting to note that the ECJ has given the prohibition on exports in Article 34 ECT a more narrow scope than the parallel prohibition relating to imports in that under *Groenveld*[8] Article 34 ECT applies only to discriminatory measures. On this basis one might expect the ECJ to take the same more restrictive approach under Article 37 and find no violation as long as the prerogatives of the monopoly make no distinction between domestic products according to whether they are exported or marketed on the home market. However, it could be argued that in the Article 37 context there is no particular reason why an exclusive right of exportation should not — just as well as the exclusive right of importation — be considered as discriminatory as such and therefore be subject to the same obligation of adjustment.[9]

The same applies arguably for another unanswered question, namely the exclusive rights of wholesale marketing of imported products. Quite obviously the required abolition of the exclusive right of importation would be deprived of its practical relevance if independent importers could not themselves sell what they import. As regards marketing monopolies at the retail level these are, where non-discriminatory, compatible with Article 37.[10] They therefore cannot go hand-in-hand with a concurrent production monopoly under the same body as the conflict of interest in such a situation is difficult to avoid.[11] On the other hand, a state monopoly which merely appoints retail outlets falls completely outside the scope of application of Article 37 when it has no possibility of influencing the procurement choices of the retailers.[12]

The adjustment of state monopolies of a commercial character in order to further the free movement of goods was primarily undertaken between the 1970s and 1980. It does to some extent still continue, not least in connection with the newly entered Member States.[13] The possibilities offered by Article 37 are limited in two ways. Firstly, services monopolies are not included in spite of the importance of this sector. Secondly, the obligation of adjustment is restricted to the elimination of discrimination. A more comprehensive adjustment of the Member States' public and privileged bodies has thus taken place pursuant to Article 90 ECT under a wider framework than the free movement of goods.

Article 90: Public Undertakings and Undertakings Granted Special or Exclusive Rights

For the purposes of comparing the ECT rules with rules in other jurisdictions and with WTO rules it should be noted at the outset that Article 90 ECT deals not only with public undertakings which are monopolies but also with undertakings, be they public or private, to which the state grants special and exclusive rights. Such special and exclusive rights within the meaning of Article 90 ECT may take the form of antitrust immunities.

Up to then mainly of academic interest, Article 90 ECT[14] was taken up by the Commission in the mid-1980s and has since come to play a central role in the regulation of the legal monopolies created by the Member States which still divided the internal market along the national borders (see European Commission, *XXIIned Competition Report* 1992: item 24). Tackling the monopolies covering vital areas such as telecommunications, energy, transport, and other services became unavoidable if the internal market project was to have a truly comprehensive impact.

Article 90(1) ECT can be seen as prohibiting the Member States[15] from breaching the obligations of the EC Treaty, including those which are otherwise not directly addressed to the Member States, by proxy. As such, the provision is therefore arguably merely a specific application of general principles which are binding on the Member States,[16] *viz.* in particular Article 5(2) ECT, in that it concerns breaches committed through public undertakings and undertakings granted special or exclusive rights and for whose actions, in the words of the ECJ, the Member States must take special responsibility by reason of the influence which they may exert over these.[17]

Public Undertakings
The application of Article 90 ECT is generally restricted to those situations where the state is specifically intervening on the market through undertakings as opposed to its exercise of official authority. In this respect a functional Community criteria has been laid down in the case law[18], and thus any entity which carries out economic activity (no matter its financing or whether it is carried out by the administration or as a separate legal body[19]) qualifies as an undertaking. In other words, the legal forms chosen by Member States are not relevant.

A logical prerequisite for classifying an undertaking as public is that the state exercises some degree of control over it. The ECJ has not attempted to define the concept exhaustively but has stated that the special influence which a Member States is able to exert over the commercial decisions of public undertakings can be exerted on the basis of financial participation or rules governing the management of those undertakings.[20] It held that the Commission had not exceeded the limits of Article 90 ECT in qualifying any undertaking over which the public authorities directly or indirectly exercise a dominant influence as public undertakings in the context of the first Transparency Directive (Commission Directive 80/723 O.J. 1980 L 197/35). It assumed this to be the case where such authorities hold the majority of the share capital or of the votes or have the right to appoint the majority of the seats in the executive organ.

Special or Exclusive Rights
By granting special or exclusive market privileges[21] to public or private undertakings the state will almost inevitably gain a certain control over their commercial decisions, as these undertakings will become wholly or partly dependent on the continued goodwill of the state. Thus a special state-

enterprise link triggering a particular responsibility for the state also comes into play in these cases.

Article 90(2): Services of a General Economic Interest[22]

In addition to the exceptions to specific provisions of the EC Treaty such as Article 85(3), Article 90(2) provides a general public mission exception from the rules of the Treaty to the extent that their application would otherwise obstruct the performance of that special task and intra-Community trade is not affected by the non-application to an extent contrary to the interests of the Community. In the *Teleterminal* case[23] the ECJ stated that the purpose of this provision is to reconcile the Member States' interest in using certain undertakings, in particular in the public sector, as an instrument of economic or fiscal policy with the Community's interest in ensuring compliance with the rules on competition and the preservation of the unity of the common market. The Treaty can thus be said to recognize that bodies entrusted with certain public tasks[24], such as public utilities, cannot always play by the rules of the free market and therefore need a backdoor from the obligations of the Treaty.

A Limited Derogation
In spite of the "generic" wording of the provision, *viz.* "to the rules contained in this Treaty" the ECJ has rejected it as a valid exception from the rules on free movement.[25] As regards state aids it has recently been held by the Court of First Instance of the European Communities that state aids may be exempted under Article 90(2), provided that the aid in question does not exceed what is necessary to compensate for the extra costs arising from the fulfillment of the particular public service obligations imposed on the recipient undertaking, and the grant of aids is necessary for that undertaking to be able to fulfill its obligations in conditions of economic stability.[26]

Apart from these limitations, the specific conditions of applicability of Article 90(2) being a derogation from the general rule of Article 90(1), are interpreted restrictively by the ECJ. The concept of "services of a general economic interest" has been given a Community definition by the ECJ. Surely many of the activities carried out by those undertakings concerned are Article 90(1) activities but such public, special or exclusive activities are not necessarily of that special nature which characterizes Article 90(2) services. Under the case law there must be an economic activity[27] which benefits all its end users on equal terms which can only vary according to objective criteria valid for all. The group of end users must furthermore be of a certain general character for the activity to classify as being of a "general" interest[28], and so the main part of the cases where Article 90(2) has been successfully invoked have concerned bodies which by an act of official authority have been granted[29] a task involving an obligation of universal supply, no matter the profitability, such as basic mail services, electricity supply, basic placement services, and basic telecommunication services. On the contrary, value-added, dissociable services which correspond to more specific needs of certain clients (as, for instance, collection from the senders' address) are not exemptable.[30]

In addition to these requirements[31] comes the proportionality test of Article 90(2) ECT, according to which it must be demonstrated that the task granted would be impossible and not merely more difficult to carry out if the Treaty applied.[32] Under present case law, this test is first and foremost an economic test: it must be assessed whether the full application of the rules of the Treaty would endanger the financial equilibrium of the undertaking in question. This could then even justify the reservation of profitable activities to an Article 90(2) undertaking which is obliged to deliver its basic services at equal conditions and tariffs no matter the economic profitability of each individual operation and therefore has to be able to cross-subsidize from profitable sectors to loss-making ones[33] if it is to maintain a financial equilibrium.

Should Article 90 Be Amended?
In the negotiations which led to the latest batch of amendments to the EC Treaty contained in the Amsterdam Treaty proposals were put forward with respect to Article 90 ECT. In the end this article remained unchanged.

Services of General Economic Interest

However, the Amsterdam Treaty inserted Article 7d, which mandates the EC and the Member States to take care that services of general economic interest "operate on the basis of principles and conditions which enable them to fulfill their mission". How far this new provision can be seen as effectively amending Article 90(1) and (2) ECT is unclear.

One of the declarations adopted by the IGC relating to the EC Treaty states that

> The provisions of Article 7d of the Treaty establishing the European Community on public services shall be implemented with full respect for the jurisprudence of the Court of Justice *inter alia* as regards the principles of equality of treatment, quality and continuity of such services.

This declaration indicates at the very least that, by adopting Article 7d, the High Contracting Parties did not intend to reverse the Court's case law. Not much weight should be attributed to the fact that the declaration singles out certain elements of the case law. This is introduced by the term "inter alia", which points to the need to give some political satisfaction to those Member States that had difficulty in accepting the "full respect for the jurisprudence of the Court of Justice". Article 7d can thus not be seen as introducing the "absolute sovereignty" approach[34] (advocated by France in the *Telecoms Terminal Equipment* case[35]) according to which the grant of special and exclusive rights cannot in itself constitute a measure subject to EC control within the meaning of Article 90.

The question arises, however, whether Article 7d, together with the corresponding Declaration, is a *monitum* addressed to the ECJ and the Commission with respect to issues that have not been definitively settled and to the concrete application in the future of the existing case law. This may be the case for cross-subsidization by a public service undertakings. Cross-subsidization may result in distortions of competition and in an infringement of Article 86 ECT where a public service undertaking subsidizes activities for which it competes on the market by its returns from activities for which it has special or exclusive rights.

Public Credit Institutions

The Declaration of the IGC on Public Credit Institutions in Germany should be mentioned in this connection. This declaration notes the Commission's opinion, according to which the EC competition rules take account in full of facilities granted to public credit institutions in Germany to compensate for the costs connected with services of general economic interest which they provide. The declaration states that the way in which this is done is a matter "for the organization of Germany", but recalls that "such facilities may not adversely affect the conditions of competition to an extent beyond that required in order to perform these particular tasks and which is contrary to the interests of the Community".

Austria and Luxembourg added their own declaration saying that the Declaration on Public Credit Institutions in Germany also applies to their credit institutions with a comparable organizational structure.

Again, even leaving aside that they take the form of "declarations", these texts do not change the existing rules. They as well are at best a *monitum* addressed to the Court and the Commission when applying Article 90 ECT to public credit institutions.

Enforcement of Article 90 ECT

In the system of the EC Treaty, only infringements of the Treaty for which there can be said to be a causal link to the Member States can be brought to an end through Article 90 ECT. Autonomous conduct on the part of public or privileged enterprises must be sanctioned through other provisions addressed to them and then only through a procedure aimed at the undertakings themselves. This was clearly shown when the ECJ struck down a provision in the Teleterminal and in the Teleservices Directives issued pursuant to Article 90(3) ECT in which the Commission addressed autonomous conduct by the undertakings.[36]

Article 90(3) ECT gives the Commission an additional instrument of enforcement pursuant to which it can issue both decisions and directives in appropriate cases. When the Commission started using this provision, this was initially fiercely challenged by Member States before the ECJ. The ECJ has, however, appeared willing to broadly interpret the powers of the Commission under Article 90(3)[37] *inter alia* by holding that the supervisory power conferred on the Commission includes the possibility of specifying, pursuant to Article 90(3), obligations arising under the Treaty. Thus the Commission can issue decisions to address the breach of a particular obligation under the Treaty instead of having to issue a reasoned opinion under Article 169. It can furthermore adopt preventive regulatory measures that specify obligations on Article 90(1) and (2) undertakings[38] flowing from the Treaty in general terms. This in fact means that the Commission has on its own the power to compel Member States to liberalize. This power as "regulator and supervisor of the public sector"[39] has not been fully exploited by the Commission, which in the energy sector has chosen to base its proposals on Article 100A, thereby involving the Council and the Parliament. To liberalize sectors dominated by public and privileged undertakings is no doubt a legitimacy-demanding task. However, the risk that the Commission may act on its own has proven to be a significant factor in unblocking the decision making process in the Council.

Enforcement furthermore takes place before national courts through the doctrine of direct effect, either of the relevant Treaty provisions or of a directive or a decision containing a clear and precise obligation. Indeed many of the milestone cases in this area have been brought before the ECJ in the course of a national case where the monopoly was challenged by a customer[40] or by a competitor who is charged in public proceedings for breaching the rights of the monopolist.[41]

Article 90 and "the Rules Contained in This Treaty"

Article 90 and the Free Movement Provisions
Article 90 can be said to add little to the EC Treaty provisions on free movement apart from reminding the Member States that the obligations imposed on them by these provisions also apply when they act through public and privileged undertakings. In addition, as mentioned above, the ECJ

has not allowed the derogation in Article 90(2) to be applied in the case of Article 30 *et seq.*, and any derogation would therefore have to be based on the non-economic justifications of Articles 36 and 56 and mandatory requirements/objectives in the general interest.[42] Thus the only substantial difference seems to be the one arising from the possibility for the Commission to apply the Article 90(3) procedure instead of Article 169 to address a breach of the free movement provisions.

It is a fairly simple exercise to imagine how an exclusive or special right in a Member State can hinder the actual or potential free movement of goods, services, labor, or establishment from other Member States where the ECJ has interpreted those provisions more widely than as merely prohibiting discrimination with the result that any restriction of trade must be justifiable on the basis of objective reasons of a non-economic nature. It has already been seen how import monopolies[43] are contrary to Article 37, but other forms of special or exclusive rights concerning production and services fall outside the scope of this article. It has, however, been confirmed by the ECJ that such special or exclusive rights can be challenged under the other free movement provisions.

Thus, in the *Teleterminal* case[44] the Commission's use of Article 30 ECT as a legal basis to challenge prohibiting rights of importation and marketing was confirmed by the ECJ applying its normal *Dassonville* doctrine supported by the finding that Article 30 *et seq.* must be interpreted in the light of the competition aspect of Article 3f.[45] Thus in line with the approach taken in *Manghera*, the very existence of an exclusive right is threatened when such a right amounts to a restriction of trade in goods with effects equivalent to those of quantitative restrictions.

Services monopolies have been found by the ECJ to infringe Article 59. Initially under the condition of discrimination[46] but later in the *Dutch Television* cases[47], it was held that Article 59 precludes measures which, although non-discriminatory, effectively restrict the freedom of provision of services by impeding its enjoyment without any objective justification. It is more doubtful whether the freedom of establishment will be infringed by a legal monopoly in the Member State of establishment. This was rejected in *Costa v. ENEL.*[48] That case concerned the nationalization of the Italian electricity sector on the ground that there was no discrimination since when Italian nationals and nationals from other Member States were equally excluded from the national market. Article 59 ECT still seems to apply to discriminatory measures only.[49]

Competition Rules Over the Free Movement Rules ?
As mentioned, Articles 30 and 59 ECT can prohibit the very existence of special or exclusive rights which directly or indirectly, actually or poten-

tially, affect intra-Community trade without being justified by objective reasons of a non-economic nature or Articles 36 and 56 ECT if there is discrimination. Hence, in situations which are not confined to the territory of a single Member State, grants of such rights which even indirectly or potentially affect inter-state trade can be challenged without the more detailed market analysis required under the competition rules. This raises the question of when one set of rules should be applied over the other to control legal monopolies. There seems to be a certain preference in the case law for coupling Article 90 with the competition rules. For instance in the *Merci* case[50] the ECJ did not consider the contested monopoly of providing dock services under Article 59 ECT although the ship was indeed itself equipped to carry out the unloading but the shipping company was prevented from doing so as a result the monopoly of the Italian dock workers. A preference for the competition rules might be the more consistent approach since the free movement rules do not apply in situations with no cross-border aspect[51] and therefore different legal solutions might result depending on which set of rules is applied (Edward and Hoskins 1995:175). Furthermore, the use of the free movement rules to control legal monopolies might therefore better be restricted to cases where monopolies are first and foremost of a protectionist nature and thus constitute a genuine barrier to trade rather than a restriction on the number of providers of a specific economic activity in a Member State.[52]

Article 90 Coupled with the Competition Rules
A combination of Article 90 and the prohibition on abuse of dominant position has turned out to be instrumental in the ongoing liberalization of the public and privileged legal monopolies. The obligation on the Member States flowing from Article 90 under this interpretation is, according to the ECJ, a duty not to take or maintain any measure which could deprive Article 86 of its effectiveness.[53] Since the *RTT* judgment[54] this is the case where the state places the undertaking in a situation that it could not have attained by its own conduct without abusing its dominant position.

However, when exactly this is the case does not follow all too clearly from the case law. Although since *Sacchi*[55] the ECJ explicitly insists on a distinction between the existence and the exercise of Article 90 ECT rights, the question remains whether Community law as it stands limits itself to the control of the restraints on competition resulting from the exercise of Article 90 ECT rights or whether it has actually crossed that boundary by prohibiting the existence of such rights. This move would arguably collide with the interest of the Member States in organizing the degree of public intervention in their economies, in support of which Article 222 ECT[56] has been invoked by Member States when challenging Commission measures of liberalization perceived as going too far.

In some cases the distinction is blurred and the ECJ arrives at a result which *de facto* puts the right itself into question (e.g., where the mere exercise of the right granted to the undertaking is in itself an abuse, the so-called inevitable abuse cases). In *Höfner*[57], Germany had granted a monopoly to its federal employment office. This agency was incapable of satisfying the demandfor employment services, creating a situation of permanent undersupply.[58] The ECJ thus considered that the Bundesanstalt für Arbeit was induced to abuse its dominance. Likewise, in *Merci*[59], the monopolist could charge exorbitant prices and refuse to introduce modern technology. But one cannot say that this abuse was an *inevitable* consequence of the state having granted the monopoly, and therefore it rather seems that the ECJ is challenging the market structure created by the grant itself. The grant makes this conduct on the market possible by protecting the monopolist from competition.

Another situation in which the existence itself was contested is *ERT*[60], where a proof of actual abusive behavior on the part of the privileged undertaking was not even required. Greece was found to have breached Article 90 ECT in combination with Article 86 ECT by granting the national broadcast company an additional exclusive right to broadcast imported programs which could induce it to discriminate in favor of its own programs. By circular argument, the abuse is the enabling of the beneficiary to prevent effective competition which is the very definition offered by the ECJ of a dominant position.[61]

Finally, Article 90 ECT in combination with Article 86 ECT applies the "essential facility" doctrine in that the abuse consists of restricting actual and potential competition by refusing to grant access to an essential facility held by the Article 90 ECT undertaking and without which the competitor cannot compete on the market for ancillary activities. In EC law this doctrine can be seen as the follow-up of Article 90 ECT as the special or exclusive right of such undertakings very often concern the control over "essential facilities" such as physical infrastructures (including networks).[62]

As has been pointed out in the literature there has been ebb and flow in the case law and high-water marks are not the final position.

In conclusion Article 90 ECT has, particularly in combination with Article 86 ECT, over a relatively short period of time played a considerable role in the ongoing liberalization of many formerly heavily regulated sectors of the EC. This process was triggered by the Commission and helped by a liberal interpretation of the ECJ, all outside the forum of the legislator. It should be pointed out that nowadays the EC "legislator", i.e., the Council and the European Parliament, has stepped in not only to lay down the main elements of an EC-wide regulatory framework in several sectors in which state monopolies are active, but also to assess the complex economic, political, and social factors involved in the (further) phasing out of special and exclusive rights.

3. Profile of a Regional Experience

Can conclusions be drawn from the relatively successful EC experience of the European Community of curbing the degree of state intervention on the market taking place through public and privileged undertakings? Surely one should not ignore the inherent limitations that lie in the fact that it is nothing more than a regional experience. The relatively high degree of homogeneity that characterizes the group of EC Member States does admittedly detract from the value of a transposition of their common experience. Nevertheless, there are certain characteristics whose applicability deserve to be examined.

Institutional Characteristics

Firstly, the impetus behind turning a dormant provision into a strong weapon for bringing state intervention through public and privileged undertakings in line with the basic scheme of the EC Treaty came from a supranational body supported by a supreme adjudicator. These two institutions had early on perceived that the political winds were shifting from economic dirigism and that proponents of more liberalized economies were getting the wind in their sails. This shift was eventually also felt within the Council, where for the first time agreement on liberalization of national statutory monopolies in a number of sectors could be reached. This consensus was undoubtedly furthered by an awareness of the fact that the Commission could otherwise have proceeded on its own by virtue of the extensive powers given to it under Article 90(3).

This leads to a related issue, namely the fact that the guardian of the Treaty is a supranational body. Therefore, no matter how contentious the issue, the case and its outcome need not trigger recriminations or otherwise affect the working climate among the Member States. That this form of enforcement is preferred by all parties is furthermore shown by the fact that Article 170 ECT, which gives the Member States a possibility to bring actions against each other before the ECJ, has hardly ever been used.

Secondly, as mentioned in the previous section, the enforcement powers of the Commission are supplemented by private actions before the national courts made possible by the doctrine of direct effect. This legal remedy obviously ensures enforcement of the Community rules in a number of cases which would otherwise never have been taken up, and the creativity of legal advisers seems no smaller than usual. Public and privileged undertakings are challenged in a variety of situations, for instance by the customer of a customer of a monopoly (dock) service[63], competitors[64], or a client of a competitor trying to demonstrate in a contractual dispute that he should not pay for a service which has been carried out in violation of the rights of the monopoly and therefore claimed to be unlawful[65]. It can be added in parenthesis that in every one of these three important cases the Member State in question was held to infringe Article 90 in conjunction with another Treaty provision.

Thirdly, the interpretation of the obligations of the Member States under Article 90 in conjunction with the competition rules is generally in line with the case law pertaining to Member States' measures which could deprive the competition rules of the Treaty of their effectiveness.[66] More precisely, from a combination of Articles 3(f) now (g), 5, 85, and 86 ECT, the ECJ has derived an obligation on the Member States not to impose, encourage, or reinforce behavior which would contravene the competition rules.[67] This is consistent because Community law hereby requires the Member States to loyally respect the effectiveness of the competition rules, otherwise addressed to undertakings, regardless of whether they affect the market through public and privileged undertakings or through legislative measures.

4. Could the EC Experience Be Relevant For the WTO?

When examining whether the EC experience could be relevant for the WTO, one should from the start bear in mind that the relevant EC Treaty provisions and the current GATT clauses differ in several respect.

First, while Article 37 ECT concerns only export and import monopolies, Article 90 ECT covers in addition public enterprises and enterprises to which Member State grant special or exclusive rights. To that extent, the EC rules and Article XVII GATT overlap. However, GATT regulates only trade in goods, whereas Article 90 ECT applies to public enterprises and enterprises to which Member States grant special and exclusive rights in relation to trade in goods and free movement of persons, trade in services, establishment, and free movement of capital.

Second, in the EC public enterprises and enterprises to which Member States grant special and exclusive rights are subject to the EC rules on competition insofar as the application of such rules does not obstruct the performance of services of general economic interest (the operation of which may have been entrusted to such enterprises). This is not the case under the GATT, which does not cover restrictive business practices.

The GATS Article VIII clause on Monopolies and Exclusive Service Suppliers goes a step further in that it provides that a monopoly supplier may not act in a manner inconsistent with a member's MFN obligations and specific commitments, not only in the supply of the monopoly service but also where it competes with other service suppliers outside the scope of its monopoly rights. The substantive scope of this competition clause is however limited: it depends *inter alia* on the scope of the specific commitments.[68]

A further limitation could result from an interpretation based on the purpose of this competition clause, i.e., protecting market access rights resulting from the specific commitments, which is only part of the anti-competitive aspect of state trading enterprises. It should be noted that another clause addressing business practices of service suppliers other than monopolies and exclusive service suppliers is worded more broadly ("restrain competition and thereby restrict trade in services"), but provides only for a soft consultation clause.

More interesting are the Fourth Protocol to the GATS and the Reference Paper setting forth a number of principles designed to ensure that the advantages of the former monopoly telecommunications operator are not used to the detriment of new entrants on the telecommunications market.[69]

The institutional framework of the EC Treaty has been seminal for the development of a politically very contentious issue. Interpretation, compliance, and legislative action came about through a strong enforcement (made possible by the existence of a supranational organ as watchdog) and an authoritative interpreter, complemented by enforcement through private litigants in EC Member States' courts. Therefore, the attention is inevitably focused on the dispute settlement of the WTO as set out in the Understanding on Rules and Procedures Governing the Settlement of Disputes (DSU).

Provisions similar to Article 90 ECT could not be expected to have quite the same impact in a WTO context as the law stands today. Enforcement of specific provisions in the WTO agreements is fundamentally by way of disputes between two or more members. Private parties depend on their governments to be willing to take up their case. Consequently, the enforcement of the rules would not be as fine-meshed, as only the very large cases would probably be taken up among the members. This would of course still be a step forward in the right direction, furthered by the significant improvement of the dispute settlement system and perhaps furthermore by the political *Zeitgeist* of liberalization. Thus, introducing EC standards in the WTO would not as such effectively bring about a comparable degree of liberalization on the global level. Nevertheless, they could serve as a model for future initiatives.

Whether more integrationist features such as direct effect or supranational enforcement will ever be introduced into the WTO framework appears doubtful to say the least. In addition, direct effect would probably require the possibility of some kind of referral from the national courts to a supreme interpreter in order to ensure authoritative answers to unprecedented questions and uniform application of WTO law. An alternative, less far-reaching, solution could be a standing surveillance body with powers of investigating cases of its own motion or at the request of private undertakings. In a mild version of Article 90(3) ECT, a report would have to be adopted by the WTO to have a legal effect along the lines of the present DSU. Obviously it remains to be seen whether members of the WTO would be willing to relax their insistence on sovereignty and introduce institutional arrangements of this kind.

NOTES

1. (1) Member States shall progressively adjust any State monopolies of a commercial character so as to ensure that when the transitional period has ended no discrimination regarding the conditions under which goods are procured and marketed exists between nationals of Member States.

The provisions of this Article shall apply to any body through which a Member State, in law or in fact, either directly or indirectly supervises, determines or appreciably influences imports or exports between Member States. These provisions shall likewise apply to monopolies delegated by the State to others.

(2) Member States shall refrain from introducing any new measure which is contrary to the principles laid down in paragraph 1 or which restricts the scope of the Article dealing with the abolition of customs duties and quantitative restrictions between Member States.

(3) The timetable for the measures referred to in paragraph 1 shall be harmonized with the abolition of quantitative restrictions on the same products provided for in Articles 30 to 34.

If a product is subject to a State monopoly of a commerical character in only one or some Member States, the Commission may authorize the other Member States to apply protective measures until the adjustment provided for in paragraph 1 has been effected; the Commission shall determine the conditions and details of such measures.

(4) If a State monopoly of a commercial character has rules which are designed to make it easier to dispose of agricultural products or obtain for them the best return, steps should be taken in applying the rules contained in this Article to ensure equivalent safeguards for the employment and standard of living of the producers concerned, account being taken of the adjustments that will be possible and the specialization that will be needed with the passage of time.

(5) The obligations on Member States shall be binding only in so far as they are compatible with existing international agreements.

(6) With effect from the first stage the Commission shall make recommendations as to the manner in which and the timetable according to which the adjustment provided for in this Article shall be carried out.

2. I.F. Hochbaum, Groeben, Thiesing, and Ehlermann 1991:573 (Nomos: Baden-Baden, 1991).

3. Services monopolies will only be caught where they have an indirect influence on intra-Community trade in goods, particularly where this influence results in discrimination between imported and domestic products. See Bodson v. Pompes Funèbres [1988] ECR 2479.

4. Production monopolies are instead covered by Article 222. As a consequence of the fact that such monopolies fall outside Article 37, an ancillary exclusive right of importation of a raw material necessary for the state-monopolised production in question can be compatible with Article 37 if it so to speak adds nothing new to the situation. See Commission v. Greece, [1990] ECR 4749 (exclusive importation of crude oil was ancillary to a monopoly on the oil refining and was held not to fall within the scope of Article 37).

5. See respectively Sacchi [1974] ECR 409 and Costa v. ENEL, [1964] ECR 1150.

6. Cassis de Dijon [1979] ECR 649.

7. [1976] ECR 91.

8. [1979] ECR 3409.

9. Hochbaum, op. cit., 587.

10. See, e.g., the Swedish and Finnish alcohol monopolies in connection with which the Commission in contrast to the discontinued exclusive rights of importation, exportation, wholesale distribution and production considers the exclusive right of retail sales to be compatible with Article 37 "taking account of the objectives pursued, provided that there is no discrimination between national products and products imported from other Member States". European Commission, XXVIth Competition Report at 48 (1996).

11. Hochbaum, op. cit., 588.

12. Banchero [1995] ECR I 4663

13. European Commission XXVIth Competition Report at 47.

14. (1) In the case of public undertakings and undertakings to which Member States grant special or exclusive rights, Member States shall neither enact nor maintain in force any measure contrary to the rules contained in this Treaty, in particular to those rules provided for in Article 6 and Articles 85 to 94.

(2) Undertakings entrusted with the operation of services of general economic interest or having the character of a revenue-producing monopoly shall be subject to the rules contained in this Treaty, in particular to the rules on competition, in so far as the application of such rules does not obstruct the performance, in law or in fact, of the particular tasks assigned to them. The development of trade must not be affected to such an extent as would be contrary to the interests of the Community.

(3) The Commission shall ensure the application of the provisions of this Article and shall, where necessary, address appropriate directives or decisions to Member States.

15. Including their regional and municipal authorities. Bodson v. Pompes Funèbres [1988] ECR 2479.

16. Inno v. ATAB [1977] ECR 2115.

17. France and others v. Commission [1982] ECR 2545.

18. C.-D. Ehlermann, "Managing Monopolies: The Role of the State in Controlling Market Dominance in the European Community," 14 ECLR 61 (1993).

19. Höfner [1991] ECR I-1981.

20. France and others v. Commission [1982] ECR 2545, at § 26.

21. If all undertakings which fulfil certain objective criteria in principle can obtain the grant of a market privilege it is not a special right in the sense of Article 90 (Inno v. ATAB [1977] ECR 2115) — and surely even less an exclusive right.

22. There is so far no case law on the notion of revenue producing monopolies. It should probably be understood as monopolies on a given activity with the aim of producing revenues to the state (such as alcohol or tobacco monopolies). Their importance in the Member States is declining and will typically be state trading monopolies in the sense of Article 37.

23. [1991] ECR I-1223, at § 12.

24. It should be stressed that it is not the undertaking as such but only its specific activity of a general economic interest that is exemptable.

25. Campus Oil [1984] ECR 2742, at § 19.

26. Fédération Francaise des Sociétés d'Assurances v. Commission, judgment of 27 February 1997 n.y.r.

27. As opposed to, e.g., social, health, or cultural activities. The purpose of the activity however need not be an economic one.

28. Hochbaum, op. cit., 2568.

29. A requirement of such a formal act has been upheld by both the Commission and the ECJ (BRT/SABAM [1974] ECR 313). It is thus not sufficient that a public authority subsequently authorises or recognises the activity. In some cases the insistence on this formality can seem arbitrary. (Waelbroeck 1996:5).

30. Corbeau [1993] ECR I-2533, at § 19.

31. The tailpiece concerning the requirement of a non-adverse development of intra-Community trade has so far been developed neither in the decisional practice of the Commssion nor in the case law. The interest of the Community is taken to be understood as the fundamental objectives of the Community (Waelbroeck 1996:7) taking account of the objectives of general economic policy pursued by the Member States. Port of Mertert [1971] ECR 723.

32. Hochbaum, op. cit., 2573.

33. Cross-subsidization from reserved areas to areas exposed to competition, on the contrary, is banned. To this end separate and transparent accounting is necessary.

34. The terminology is used by D. Edward and M. Hoskins, "Article 90: Deregulation and EC Law, Reflections arising from the XVI FIDE Conference," 32 CML Rev 157 (1995).

35. [1991] ECR I-1223.

36. Cases [1991] ECR I-1223 and [1992] ECR I-5833.

37. M. Kerf, "The Policy of the Commission of the Commission of the EEC towards National Monopolies," 16 World Competition 73, 80 (1993).

38. But it cannot through directives address specific situations in a Member States and thereby infringements of the Treaty. [1991] ECR I 1223.

39. M. van der Woude, "Article 90: Competing for Competence," 16 ELR 60, 70 (1991).

40. Merci [1991] ECR I-5889.

41. Corbeau [1993] ECR I-2533.

42. However, arguably the considerations of a general economic interest of Article 90(2) and mandatory requirements are very much alike.

43. And, as it will be remembered, arguably also monopolies of exportation to Community countries and of wholesale marketing of imported products.

44. France v. Commission [1991] ECR I-1223.

45. This last finding is not the same as saying that the free movement provisions cannot be infringed independently of whether there is an abuse of the dominant position following from the special or exclusive right. See L. Gyselen, "Case Note," 29 Common Market L. Rev. 1229, 1231 (1992).

46. Elliniki Radiophonia Tileorassi [1991] ECR I-2925.

47. Gouda [1991] ECR I-4009 and Commission v. Netherlands [1991] ECR I-4072.

48. [1964] ECR 585.

49. Van der Woude op. cit., 72; M. Kerf, "The Impact of EC Law on Public Service Concessions," 18 World Competition 85, 101 (1995); Edward and Hoskins op. cit., 174.

50. [1991] ECR I-5889. The right to provide dock services at the port of Genoa was reserved to a number of Italian companies which were to employ Italian nationals only. Due to strikes, these companies did not unload a German ship and the owner of the cargo carried by the ship therefore sued them for damages incurred by this delay. The national referring court did not explicitly ask if this exclusive right infringed Article 58, but referred to Article 7 on the basis of which the ECJ proceeded to find an infringement of Article 48 as the specific application of the principle of non-discrimination and then went on to consider Article 86.

51. Such as *Höfner* ([1991] ECR I-1979), where the monopoly of the German employment service was challenged in a dispute between two German companies over a bill for the recruitment of German nationals.

52. Edward and Hoskins op. cit., 176.

53. Inno v. Atab [1977] ECR 2115.

54. [1991] ECR I- 5941.

55. [1974] ECR 409.

56. Which reads "[t]his Treaty shall in no way prejudice the rules in the Member States governing the system of property ownership".

57. [1991] ECR I-1979.

58. A situation envisaged by Article 86b.

59. [1991] ECR I-5889.

60. [1991] ECR I-2925.

61. United Brands [1978] ECR 207 (the fact that an undertaking enjoys a position of economic strength enables it to prevent effective competition being maintained on the relevant market by affording it the power to behave to an appreciable extent independently of its competitors, customers and ultimately of its consumers).

62. J. Temple Lang, "Defining Legitimate Competition: Companies' Duties to Supply Competitors, and Access to Essential Facilities," in: B. Hawk, ed., 1994 Annual Proceedings of the Fordham Corporate Law Institute 245, 281 (Kluwer: The Hague, 1995).

63. Merci [1991] ECR II-5889.

64. Corbeau [1993] ECR I-2533.

65. Höfner [1991] ECR I-1981.

66. Inno v. ATAB, op.cit.

67. E.g., Vlaamse Reisbureaus [1987] ECR 3801.

68. For further reading see A. Mattoo, "Dealing with Monopolies and State Enterprises: WTO Rules for Goods and Services," in this volume.

69. For a comprehensive analysis see M.C.E.J. Bronckers and P. Larouche, "Telecomunications Services and the World Trade Organization" 31:3 J. World Trade 5 (1997).

REFERENCES

"Editorial Comments." 1996. Common Market L. Rev. 33: 395–400.

Edward, David and Mark Hoskins. 1995. "Article 90: Deregulation and EC Law: Reflection Arising from the XVI FIDE Conference." Common Market L. Rev. 32:157–186.

Ehlermann, Claus-Dieter. 1993. "Managing Monopolies: The Role of the State in Controlling Market Dominance in the European Community." European Competition L. Rev. 14:61–69.

European Commission. 1996. *XXIIth Competition Report* (OPOCE: Luxembourg).

European Commission. 1992. *XXVIIth Competition Report* (OPOCE: Luxembourg).

Gyselen, Luc. 1992. "Case Note." *Common Market Law Review* 29: 1229–1245.

Kerf, Michel. "The Policy of the Commission of the E.E.C. toward National Monopolies." World Competition 17:73–111.

Kerf, Michel 1995. "The Impact of EC Law on Public Service Concessions." World Competition 18:85–130.

Lang Temple, John. 1994. "Defining Legitimate Competition: Companies' Duties to Supply Competitors, and Access to Essential Facilities." *Annual Proceedings of the Fordham Corporate Law Institute* 245–311.

Thiesing, Groeben and C.-D. Ehlermann. 1991. *Kommentar zum EWG Vertrag* 4th ed. Nomos: Baden Baden.

Van der Woude, Marc. 1991. "Article 90: Competing for Competence." European Law Review Competition Checklist 12:60.
Waelbroeck, Denis. 1996. "Les conditions d'applicabilité de l'artile 90 paragraphe 2b du Traité CE." In Robert Kovar and Denis Simon, eds. *Colloque cedece*. Irene: Strasbourg.

CHAPTER 9

State Trading Enterprises and Multilateral Trade Rules: The Canadian Experience

*Robert Howse**

1. Introduction

Public enterprises (Crown Corporations) and regulated private monopolies are a long-standing characteristic of the Canadian political economy.[1] Canada has certainly not been exempt from the global trend towards privatization and regulatory reform[2]; nevertheless, Crown Corporations remain for many a symbol of national unity and strength, as well as something that is seen as differentiating us from the United States[3]. Thus, the ideological agenda of privatization advanced in the 1980s by the Conservative Mulroney government met with considerable public resistance. In the end, a grab-bag of Crown Corporations were privatized, but as of the early 1990s these enterprises still accounted for 15.7 percent of corporate assets and 11 percent of GNP.[4] More recently, the pragmatic, rather than the ideological, approach to privatization of the Liberal government has resulted in some national symbols, such as the Canadian National Railroad Company (CN) being sold off with extraordinarily little public outcry — the Liberals have handled labour relations issues sensitively, and have deftly managed as well the deployment of alternative policies to deal with, for instance, rural development concerns. Increasingly, Canadian privatizations have been accompanied by an open approach to foreign investment — in the CN case no restrictions were placed on the purchase of shares by foreigners, and in the petroleum sector, the nationalization of which was a major trade irritant during a certain period of Canada-United States relations, foreign capital and participation is now welcomed and PetroCanada has been privatized. In justifying privatizations, the Chretien government has emphasized the unsustainability of subsidization to loss-making enterprises and a changing regulatory and global trade

*Faculty of Law, University of Toronto; Email: robert.howse@utoronto.ca. An earlier version of this chapter was presented at the World Trade Forum, Gerzensee, Switzerland, 12–13 September 1997. I am grateful to participants in the Forum for helpful comments and criticisms, especially Jacques Bourgeois, Garly Horlick, David Palmeter, and Diane Wood. Michael Trebilcock also provided useful advice on a previous draft. Daniel Markel, 1L Harvard provided excellent research assistance. All shortcomings are my responsibility.

environment, rather than the Thatcherite ideology that made the Mulroney program unpopular.

With respect to regulated monopolies (whether public or private) and regulated industries where enterprises are granted special privileges, change has been either slow or has come in a piecemeal fashion, without much thought to the competition or other regulatory issues to be resolved in a shift to a competitive market. In telecommunications, the monopoly in long-distance voice traffic was ended by a regulatory decision in 1992 without a prior public debate or any legislative action. The regulatory authority has been making up rules of the game for a competitive market as it goes along, at the same time as foreign competition continues to be limited by ownership restrictions, as will be discussed in detail in a later section of the chapter. Not even the ultra-right-wing Harris government in Ontario has dared to risk unpopularity by dismantling the liquor or the electric power monopolies.[5] The one government that moved towards liquor demonopolization, Alberta, nevertheless retained a monopoly on importation and wholesale trade. And cultural industries also remain sacred cows, where a host of protective measures including Canadian control, ownership, and content requirements remains broadly popular — to the point that in the *Sports Illustrated* dispute, where Canada lost both at the WTO panel and Appellate Body level, there may be some pressure for the government to remain in non-compliance with the GATT, even if this entails paying compensation or opening up Canada to retaliatory action. At the same time, a kind of faction is emerging in government policy circles in favour of using trade pressures as a beginning point for a re-thinking of a wide range of instruments of cultural protectionism. The political risks of doing so remain high.

This chapter is intended to provide a *tour d'horizon* of the interaction of state trading practices in Canada with the world trading system, past, present, and emerging. Because the focus of this conference is on the trading system, I have certainly not attempted to present an overview of public enterprise, privatization, and related regulatory reform in Canada — instead I have selected areas where I believe there have been significant issues of trade policy and law intertwined with domestic regulation and deregulation of such enterprises.

In defining the scope of this undertaking, it is important to recognize that the expression "state trading enterprises", as it appears in Article XVII of the GATT includes not only state-*owned* and/or -*controlled* enterprises engaged in trade, but any enterprise that has been granted by the state "exclusive or special privileges". This includes, in my view, privately-owned and -controlled enterprises in Canada in sectors like broadcasting, telecommunications, and financial services, where entities must be licensed and conform to a variety of regulatory requirements in order to participate in the sector concerned (particularly where there is a discretionary element in the granting of a license, such as broadcasting or where, at least in the past, monopoly rights have been granted, such as telecommunications). Also, Article XVII applies to marketing boards, which application is confirmed in an Interpretive Note to Article XVII. Moreover, while the GATT applies only to goods, I have taken a broad view of my mandate and examined the trade issues in these service sectors as a major part of the chapter, if only because so many of the important trade issues now focus on the involvement of STEs in the services sector. In any case, even Article XVII itself arguably applies to these enterprises in as much as they are *purchasers* of goods.

2. Liquor

In almost all of Canada, provincial governments continue to operate mono-polies on the importation, distribution, and sale of alcoholic beverages. As mentioned in the introduction, the main exception is the province of Alberta, which privatized its retail operations in 1993 while retaining a public mo-nopoly on importation and wholesale trade.[6] In some other provinces, there are also very limited elements of private retailing, ranging from sales in grocery stores of certain items in Quebec to the privately-owned retail distri-bution system for beer in Ontario — a system, which, however, due to its ownership by the two dominant Canadian beer manufacturers and its special rights under the provincial regulatory regime, poses its own issues with respect to state trading enterprises.

It is no exaggeration to say that trade complaints about these provincial liquor monopolies have been the context for a very significant part of the GATT jurisprudence with respect to the application of multilateral trading norms to public monopolies. The practices of the provincial liquor boards have been the subject of two major GATT panels, and several agreements or understandings between either the United States and Canada or the Euro-pean Communities and Canada. The federalism dimension in these disputes has not been unimportant. Exclusive provincial jurisdiction over liquor was established early on in the evolution of Canadian constitutional jurispru-dence and the constitution does not contain an explicit federal treaty imple-mentation power.[7] Nevertheless, the real problem is not so much constitu-tional, since the federal government has powers, including over general trade and international and interprovincial trade and commerce, which, where legitimately exercised, would be paramount over provincial jurisdic-tion with respect to liquor; indeed, provincial importation monopolies have been enabled explicitly by federal legislation.[8] Most of the disputes peaked during the Mulroney Government's tenure in office in the late 1980s and early 1990s and this Government was more deferential to provincial prerogatives than almost any other in recent Canadian history. Thus compliance problems have been endemic and on-going with regard to these disputes. But, as we shall see, this is far from the only complexity with respect to compliance — the internal practices of public monopolies, and their often less than transparent relationship with explicit government regulation, make protectionism something of a moving target. Apparently minor and byzantine changes in pricing, stocking, and distribution practices can easily create a protectionist impact equivalent to that of a measure impugned by a trade panel.

The first GATT panel to consider the practices of a provincial liquor monopoly was provoked by a complaint of the European Communities (EC). In response to EC concerns raised during the Tokyo Round negotiations, governments in Canada issued a "Provincial Statement of Intentions with respect to Sales of Alcoholic Beverages by Provincial Marketing Agencies in Canada" on April 5, 1979. This Statement, while not constituting a formal agreement between the EC and the Canadian authorities, addressed two particular practices of the liquor boards. The first was discriminatory markups as between domestic and imported products; the second was discrimination with respect to access to retail marketing, i.e., listing in provincial liquor stores.

In the case of the discriminatory mark-ups, the provinces agreed to eliminate these with respect to distilled spirits, while merely agreeing not to increase the existing margin of discrimination with respect to wines, where (at least at that time) the Europeans arguably had a greater competitive advantage over Canadian producers than in the case of spirits. (Any remaining differentials would have to be based on the greater costs that might be associated with the handling of imported products, such as customs clearance, transportation, etc.). With respect to listing, it was agreed that these decisions would be made on the basis of commercial criteria, such as quality, price, and historical demand, and without discrimination as between domestic and foreign products. It is not surprising that the EC turned out to be unable to live with this arrangement. First of all, as noted, not all discriminatory mark-ups were eliminated; secondly, by using historical demand as a criterion for listing, liquor boards were in a certain sense perpetuating the sins of the past, since historical demand was related to what could be listed, and hence demanded, by provincial consumers when overt and egregious discrimination was being practiced against foreign brands; thirdly, with the announcement of negotiations with the United States on a comprehensive bilateral free trade agreement, the EC faced the prospect of substantial trade diversion assuming that provincial liquor board practices would be on the table in those talks.

The Fate of Article XVII in the *Liquor Board* Decisions

In 1985, the EC filed a formal GATT complaint with respect to both the mark-up and the listing practices. The resultant panel decision held that Canada was, in both respects, in violation of its GATT obligations.[9] However, as with the subsequent ruling on a U.S. complaint, the panel decided to deal with the issues by the application of various general GATT provisions to the dispute, rather than breathing life into Article XXVII, the state trading enterprises provision, despite the panel members' apparent view that, in principle, the liquor monopolies were state trading enterprises for purposes of Article XVII.

Article II:4 GATT and the Pricing Practices of Monopolies

In the case of discriminatory mark-ups, the panel choose to consider these as affording protection in excess of tariff bindings, and therefore a violation of Article II:4. Article II:4 provides:

> If any contracting party establishes, maintains or authorizes, formally or in effect, a monopoly of the importation of any product described in the appropriate Schedule annexed to this Agreement, such monopoly shall not, except as provided for in that Schedule or as otherwise agreed between the parties which initially negotiated the concession, operate so as to afford protection on the average in excess of the amount provided for in that Schedule.

Does Article XVII Limit the Applicability of Other GATT Provisions to STEs?

Canada's invocation of Article XVII was for purposes of *limiting* its obligations under II:4, arguing that Article XVII(b), in effect, exempts state trading enterprises (STEs) from other GATT strictures provided that they make purchases and sales "in accordance with commercial considerations, including price, quality, availability, marketability, transportation and other conditions of purchase and sale" and afford other contracting parties "adequate opportunity . . . to compete for participation in such purchases and sales". This represented one particular view of Article XVII, namely that it is intended to provide a comprehensive GATT code for STEs, rendering other provisions of the General Agreement inapplicable to them, or at most applicable only by reference in Article XVII itself.

Such a perspective on Article XVII is, I believe, fundamentally flawed; if one looks at the Article as a whole it is clear that its thrust is to ensure that state trading enterprises are not used as a vehicle for escaping or undermining other GATT obligations, i.e., to the need to subject such enterprises to special scrutiny, not to a less demanding set of trade strictures than that found in the GATT as a whole. Thus, Article XVII:3(b) states that "contracting parties recognize that [State Trading Enterprises] might be operated so as to create serious obstacles to trade" and in fact contemplates further negotiations on a reciprocity basis to deal with these obstacles. Moreover, almost all of the provisions of Article XVII are drafted as obligations on such enterprises, none as carve-outs on the obligations of governments themselves. In sum, Article XVII imposes on certain enterprises, which may or may not be state-owned or -managed, obligations in addition to the obligations of governments themselves, by virtue of the capacity of these enterprises to create serious obstacles to trade (and indeed the very language of this Article shows that even the architecture of the original 1947 GATT did not embody a strict public/private distinction, imposing strictures on formally governmental entities alone).

Despite these considerations, the view of Article XVII as a kind of separate code for STEs seemed to be given a lease on life by an earlier panel, also involving Canada, in which certain practices of the Canadian Foreign Investment Review Agency were found to violate provisions of the General Agreement. In that decision, the panel suggested, in *dicta* as it were, that it "saw great force in Canada's argument that only the most-favoured nation and not the national treatment obligations fall within the scope of the general principles [of non-discrimination] referred to in Article XVII:1".[10] In this case, the United States challenged local sourcing undertakings that foreign companies had made to the Canadian foreign investment authorities — undertakings not required in the first instance under any law or regulation, but binding in law once made, and believed to be an implicit condition for approval of investments by the FIRA. It should be born in mind, however, that the panel decided the matter by finding that these undertakings violated the national treatment obligation in Article III:4; it simply did not see the fact that the practices in question were those of firms and not governments, or that the undertakings were not in the first instance governmentally-imposed as barriers to the application of national treatment, given the context of an overarching governmental scheme for screening foreign investment. This left open the question of when *only* Article XVII, with its possibly truncated non-discrimination requirement limited to MFN, would apply and not the national treatment and other provisions of the GATT.

In the EC-Canada liquor ruling, the panel had to consider the Canadian position that provisions other than Article XVII applied to state trading enterprises only by specific reference because, although the mark-ups could be found to violate an article that referred explicitly to state monopolies, the listing requirements were argued primarily on the basis of Articles XI and III:4 which do not specifically refer to monopolies or other state trading enterprises. In finding that Article XI applied to a state trading enterprise in this situation, viewing the discriminatory listing requirements as analogous to quotas or quantitative restrictions on imports, the panel in effect rejected the view that Article XVII is a self-contained code of trade rules governing such enterprises with other GATT provisions incorporated only by reference, making truly irrelevant the issue raised by the FIRA panel as to whether only Article I, or Article III as well was incorporated into Article XVII. If we put together the FIRA and EC Liquor panels, then we get the result that: 1) Article XVII is not needed to pierce the public/private distinction and render GATT norms applicable even where, formally, the actual trade-limiting conduct is not that of government (FIRA); and (2) Article XVII is not a self-contained code for state trading enterprises. Given these propositions, it becomes very difficult to puzzle out what Article XVII actually is.

One answer is that Article XVII is intended to catch protectionist conduct not easily impugned under other provisions of the General Agreement, given the avenues that state trading enterprises have for building protectionism into their day-to-day business decisions. On this understanding, Article XVII would go beyond even national treatment and actually impose on STEs a kind of competition law-like requirement that they not engage in conduct whereby they exploit their market power to distort trade between contracting parties. On this view, the language of Article XVII concerning "adequate opportunity . . . to compete" could be interpreted as more not-less-than-equal opportunities in the sense of national treatment, and extending to a broader notion of contestability.

In the second panel ruling on liquor boards, a wider range of measures was claimed, this time by the United States, to have violated various provisions of the GATT, including Article XVII. At the same time, the United States asserted that almost all provinces in Canada were cheating on their commitment to implement the earlier EC panel ruling by using methodologies for calculating differentials in mark-ups based on marketing costs in such a way as to reintroduce protectionism, i.e., a greater differential than justified on the basis of real additional costs of sale. This last claim particularly would seem to have been likely to drive the panel to consider Article XVII because in effect it invited the panel to penetrate the internal business decisions of an STE and determine whether particular decisions, as opposed to general policies, were being made in accord with commercial considerations (in this case, the actual additional cost of bringing to market imported products). As well, the United States complained about at least two kinds of measures or practices that seemed on their face to be non-discriminatory, thereby inviting analysis in light of a broader contestability concept arguably implicit in Article XVII:1(b). One such measure was a minimum price requirement for retail sales. While applicable both to domestic and imported products equally, this was said to disadvantage foreign producers in as much as it prevented them from competing on the basis of a cost advantage they possessed over Canadian producers with respect to beer, the minimum price being set in relation to the wholesale price of domestic product. Another measure related to a purportedly environmental tax on all beer containers not part of a deposit/return system; American brewers did not have access to the existing system, run by a consortium of domestic brewers in the case of Ontario, and setting up their own parallel system would be, it was claimed, prohibitively expensive.

Perhaps surprisingly, given the extent to which these claims were about real market access as opposed to formal equality of treatment, the panel nevertheless chose to resolve them without considering Article XVII, despite the Article's invocation, among other GATT provisions, by the complainant the United States. In the case of the methodologies for calculating the cost-of-service charges, the Panel simply found that the charges, or differential mark-ups, included costs not "necessarily associated with imported beer" and thus conferred additional protection in violation of Article II:4.[11] In order for Canada to prove the contrary, it would have to adopt some kind of independent auditing, or reference to an independent expert, who — familiarized with the applicable law of the GATT — would examine in detail the accounts of provincial liquor monopolies.

With respect to minimum price requirements, the Panel found that there was a *de facto* violation of Article III:4, with equal competitive opportunities not being provided to imported beer, given that the minimum price was based on the wholesale price of the domestic product. This, in my view, stretched Article III:4 to, if not beyond, the limit. In fact, the minimum price requirement actually limited the competitive opportunities of any particular *domestic* brewer who sought to undercut the going domestic market price, in effect determined largely by the brewers with the greatest market share. In other words, this was a form of government-sanctioned price cartelization that affected domestic as well as international competition. It might have been better handled in terms of the Article XVII:1(b) concept of *adequate* opportunity to compete for purchases and sales, as opposed to the national treatment concept of *equality* of competitive opportunities. With respect to the container taxes, the Panel found that these in themselves did not violate the GATT — the violation was the denial of equal access to the domestic deposit/return system, which contravened Article III:4.

After Canada itself won a GATT complaint against discriminatory taxation practices that afforded protection to U.S. brewers[12], negotiations ensued between the two parties on implementation of GATT rulings, which culminated in a Memorandum of Understanding, signed on August 5, 1993. The Memorandum included an agreement on a method of calculating minimum prices, and where applicable gave American brewers a right of access to the retail distribution system, including the Brewer's Retail Inc. (BRI) stores in Ontario.

Brewer's Retail Inc. is a private chain ninety percent owned by Canada's two largest brewers, Labatt and Molson's. It is noteworthy that under the Memorandum, the provincial government is to *mandate* that BRI itself provide equal terms of access to foreign brewers, i.e., the provincial government does not merely commit not to influence BRI in order to afford protection to domestic producers but to ensure that it does not use its own market power, albeit derived from the general privilege conferred by the government as the exclusive non-governmental seller of beer, for protectionist purposes.

General Lessons for WTO Jurisprudence

What more general lessons can one draw from this dispute for the treatment in GATT/WTO jurisprudence of state trading enterprises? First of all, the panels have not found it necessary to utilize Article XVII in order to overcome a formalistic private/public distinction and reach protectionist behaviour indirectly rather than directly linked to mandatory governmental laws, policies, and regulations — this is a consistent theme through the *FIRA*, and both the EU and U.S. *Alcoholic Beverage* panels. The same approach can also be discerned in the *Japanese Semi-Conductor* ruling, where the panel considered export restraints nominally undertaken on a voluntary basis by private firms.[13]

Secondly, at least one panel, the U.S. *Alcoholic Beverage* panel, found it possible to characterize anticompetitive conduct of public monopolies, which on its face was not explicitly discriminatory, as a violation of Article III:4, thereby once again obviating resort to the "commercial considerations" and "adequate opportunity to compete" benchmarks in Article XVII:1(b).

Thirdly, apart from a single reference in the *FIRA* panel to the possibility that that national treatment was not incorporated into Article XVII (which would only matter if Article III did not apply directly to STEs), there has been a consistent rejection of the view that the thrust of Article XVII is to insulate STEs from more general GATT obligations.

How is one to explain the apparent failure to operationalize Article XVII? A simple explanation is that panels (and domestic courts are often no different) prefer if they can decide a case by the application of a provision that has been frequently the subject of prior interpretations, rather than one that requires that novel interpretive issues be addressed. An additional and not unrelated explanation is that panels are less comfortable with criteria such as those in Article XVII:1(b) that require that conduct be judged against some kind of notion of market contestability, or a model of normal commercial behaviour, than with rules, such as national treatment, that permit an analysis of the equality of competitive opportunities against common sense notions of discrimination and disadvantage, and which have rarely been seen by panels to involve the necessity of technical economic analysis.

Perhaps most fundamentally, inasmuch as Article XVII has the promise of catching protectionism embedded in the on-going, day-to-day business decisions of STEs in ways difficult to do through general rules such as national treatment or the prohibition on quantitative restrictions, this promise is difficult to realize through sporadic panel dispute settlement, and would seem to imply continuous surveillance of something like a global competition body. To illustrate this I advert to some purely anecdotal evidence from Liquor Board outlets in Ontario — whatever may have been done to address discriminatory listing requirements, one tends to notice, for example, that the selection of chilled wines is heavily tilted towards domestic products or poor quality imports, often the less popular brands mixed with a few more popular ones. Or take the practice of frequently changing the location of foreign product in the store, particularly common in those outlets frequented by busy workers buying a bottle of wine in their rush home — one week a wine might appear under the heading "Old World", the next in the section described as "Southern Europe", and then finally on some hybrid shelf, labelled perhaps "South African and East European". Similarly, those outlets selected for experimental opening on Sundays or holidays seem to be the ones that have fewer popular or high-quality foreign brands in comparison to domestic products. It is, of course, impossible to prove that this is protectionism and the point is that we are dealing with a moving target, hard to make amenable to panel dispute settlement.

Finally, it is worth noting that contracting parties took the trouble in the Uruguay Round negotiations to negotiate the "Understanding on the Interpretation of Article XVII of the General Agreement on Tariffs and Trade" (the Understanding). The Understanding is largely focused on creating a meaningful process of reporting on and analysis of the practices of STEs, including facilitation of the development of an "illustrative list showing kinds of activities, engaged in by these enterprises, which may be relevant for purposes of Article XVII" (para. 5). This appears to reflect some kind of recognition that, if it is to be brought to life, the interpretation of Article XVII in dispute settlement may require special analytic and institutional support. However, the measures themselves contemplated in the Understanding appear weak and hardly up to the task — they are not much more emphatic than the transparency requirements in Article XVII itself, and the "illustrative list" idea certainly falls into conventional old-style GATT thinking, a substitute for bringing the economics of competition policy to bear on these problems.

3. Electric Power

Trade in electric power across the Canada-U.S. border has existed since the early twentieth century, including during the long period in which the industry was dominated on both sides of the border by State, provincial, or regional monopolies, vertically integrated with respect to generation, transmission, and wholesale and retail distribution.[14] Gradually, monopoly has been chipped away on both sides of the border, but with vastly differing degrees of liberalization across different State and provincial jurisdictions.[15] In the case of Canada, Alberta has already moved to full-blown competition in generation, whereby generators compete to supply a power pool that in turn provides supply to retail monopolies through a regulated transmission system. Other provinces have made lesser reforms, such as allowing limited competition in the direct supply of power to wholesale customers, with Ontario being the major player that has opened up its system the least (allowing only for small purchases by the erstwhile monopolist, Ontario Hydro, of power produced by independent generators).

In the United States, the Federal Energy Regulation Commission (FERC) has moved to promote competition in the wholesale provision of power by generators through a regulation that conditions approval for the export, or "wheeling", of power across State boundaries upon the exporter either operating in a genuinely competitive home market or mitigating its market power if it is a private or public monopoly.[16] Mitigation normally entails the provision of access to the transmission system on transparent, non-discriminatory, market-based terms to out-of-State generators wishing to compete in the wholesale market, in accordance with FERC regulatory approaches.

In two early decisions with respect to access of Canadian exporters to the U.S. market, the FERC appeared to apply the same criteria to Canadian exporters in question as it applied to domestic U.S. utilities seeking to wheel power across *State* lines.[17] Perhaps concerned that this was beginning to appear like extraterritorial regulation of foreign entities, possibly beyond the legal jurisdiction of the FERC, the FERC has now begun to apply a somewhat different approach to foreign imports of electricity, approving such imports if the jurisdiction of the exporting utility permits reciprocal market access for U.S. exporters. Thus, a Canadian utility need not conform to a given U.S. regulatory approach to competition in order to be permitted to wheel power into the United States — a variety of approaches is acceptable provided the effect is reciprocal market access.[18]

In reality this amounts to the application of the mitigation of power principle, with a somewhat broader view of the kinds of measures able to fulfill it, so as to guarantee reciprocal market access.[19] The reciprocal market access approach for foreign utilities is incorporated in FERC Order 888 and especially 888A, which explicitly applies to foreign exporters of electricity.[20]

In addition to seeking a court review of the reciprocity and related provisions of Orders 888 and 888A on administrative law grounds, Ontario Hydro has been claiming that the reciprocity requirement violates the national treatment provisions of GATT and NAFTA.[21] The FERC has responded that this reading of national treatment

> would place transmission-owning Canadian entities (or their corporate affiliates) in a better position than any domestic entity . . . they would be able to use the open access tariffs we have mandated without providing any reciprocal service.[22]

The question is whether the trade law issue here is one of national treatment at all. As interpreted by the panels in *Tuna/Dolphin I* and *Tuna/Dolphin II*[23], national treatment is relevant only where the measure in question relates to the traded product as product. Clearly, the reciprocal market access requirement does not affect electricity as a product, or even for that matter the physical process by which it is produced, but rather the regulatory environment of the exporting jurisdiction.

This means that Ontario Hydro's argument should be based, perhaps, on Article XI, i.e., that the reciprocal market access condition represents a restriction on trade other than a duty, tax, or other charge, namely in this case an import license. Here, the FERC's argument that domestic and foreign entities are being treated the same would be irrelevant to GATT consistency.

Ontario Hydro's own near-monopoly over the generation and transmission of power may, by contrast, be GATT-legal. Given that Ontario Hydro does not act, except in marginal cases, as a purchaser of power on the market, the issue of national treatment of foreign providers does not really arise, nor that of adequate opportunity to compete for purchases and sales within the meaning of Article XVII. Once, however, a vertically integrated monopoly is unbundled, and the transmission and distribution systems remain as separate monopoly operations, then access to those systems for foreign producers would have to be consistent with Article III:4, Article XI, and Article XVII. This means that it is virtually impossible to shift towards competition domestically without entertaining foreign competition. And indeed, it seems that what sparked to some extent pro-competitive reform in Alberta and, more modestly, Quebec was a recognition of the inevitability of *foreign* competition, i.e., that continued access to the U.S. market would depend upon opening up the intra-provincial market to competition — and in both cases, the FERC has accepted the changes as sufficient to meet its requirement of reciprocal market access, although the mitigation of market power issue has not been definitively resolved with respect to Quebec.

This being said, from a GATT/WTO perspective, some of the thornier issues may well be raised where a jurisdiction adopts what could crudely be described as "half-way" reforms, as was proposed for Ontario by the Advisory Committee on Competition in Ontario's Electricity System in its May 1996 Report.[24] The Report recommended retaining nuclear plants and a huge hydroelectric facility in public hands (about seventy percent of existing generation capacity) while privatizing the remaining generation facilities. Public enterprises and profit-maximizing private enterprises would then compete to sell power to a power pool, based on lowest marginal cost in a given time period. This raises significant level playing field concerns, especially given the possible advantages, including "soft" capital market constraints, that the public enterprises might have over competitors, both domestic and foreign. This also bears on the so-called "stranded assets" problem and how it is handled. In the case where the public enterprises, particularly nuclear generators, were not assigned the burden of the full capital costs of building the generation facilities, they might be able to outbid most other generators, given the relatively low marginal cost of nuclear energy in Ontario. Yet this might in effect hobble real competition before it got started, and from a dynamic perspective act as a major disincentive to investments in new more efficient generating facilities. Might Article XVII:1(b) apply to require that a publicly-owned generator make its decisions on the price at which it offered power to the pool on the basis of commercial considerations including its own fully allocated costs of generation (including fixed costs)? This would imply that, for purposes of competition in the pool, the Government cannot simply make these costs disappear, for instance through a tax aimed at paying off the debt incurred to build the generation facilities with general revenues.

4. State Trading Enterprises and Trade in Services

With the exception of an important public sector in broadcasting, most (although not all) of these entities in Canada have traditionally been privately-owned. They have also, however, been granted monopoly or other privileges and been subject to extensive regulatory demands as a condition of receiving these privileges (e.g., licenses).

All these sectors have been subject to considerable market-oriented regulatory reform, with the exception of broadcasting, where cultural autonomy concerns have resulted in the continuation of a system of strictly controlled licensing, conditioned on Canadian content requirements and related measures.[25] However, in all these sectors, *foreign* competition has been limited, to a greater or lesser degree, by the continuation of foreign ownership restrictions or related restrictions on the manner in which foreign entities can establish a presence or enter the market.[26] Indeed, as regulatory rents have tended to dry up, industry interests have defended ever more vociferously ownership restrictions, trying to get some shelter from foreign competition. Moreover, limiting foreign competition in some sectors has been a means of resisting the shift to competition altogether — this has been the case in telecommunications, where it has been difficult to marshal the capital and technology needed to challenge the dominant position of the former monopolist without foreign investment. At the same time, the federal government, which regulates most of these sectors or large parts of them[27], has signalled that some of the restrictions may need to be rethought, perhaps in connection with the Multilateral Agreement on Investment (MAI) negotiations.[28]

Telecommunications and Broadcasting

Telecommunications is generally considered a key economic sector in Canada. According to industry estimates, as of 1995 it employed about 154,000 people and represented a total market for equipment and services (1993 estimate) of $21.5 billion CDN.[29] With the exception of SaskTel (a state enterprise), most telecommunications services in Canada were traditionally provided by federally-regulated, private provincial or regional telecommunications monopolies, most of which are owned by Bell Canada Enterprises (BCE). In June 1992 the regulator, the Canadian Radio-Television and Telecommunications Commission, opened up the long-distance voice market to competition in its *Telecom Decision 92-12*.[30] Much more recently, the Commission decided to allow competition in local service as well. The beginnings of long-distance competition have been plagued by issues surrounding the effects of the market dominance of the former monopolist and the terms of access to the common carrier elements of the system. In addition, its status as continuing monopolist with respect to local service gave Bell/Stentor extraordinary access to potential long-distance customers, leading to complaints of unfair practices by competitors (for instance, competing long-distance service companies would hardly be prominently be featured in the Bell "Phone Stores" where customers sign up for basic local service, added services, and equipment purchase or rental.

As already mentioned, one of the reasons that competition got off to a rocky start was the limits on foreign ownership in the industry. Thus in order to operate as a facilities-based telecommunications carrier in Canada (as opposed to a mere long-distance reseller) a company must have at least eighty percent of its shares owned by Canadians.[31] However, given the need for foreign capital, this has been watered-down through regulations that allow for 33.3 percent foreign ownership of a carrier's holding company.[32] The net result is a total limit on direct and indirect foreign investment combined of 46.7 percent.[33]

In the WTO negotiations on basic telecoms, Canada refused to lift or liberalize these restrictions, although commitments have been made in Canada's schedule to remove a host of other protectionist measures.[34] This reflects strenuous lobbying by Stentor, and perhaps as well the status of BCE as a corporate giant deeply intertwined with the Canadian political and business establishment (competition, it should be underlined, was not introduced by legislative reforms but through a decision of a commission purportedly independent, or largely independent, of the legislature and cabinet). Stentor claimed, *inter alia*, that but for ownership restrictions, Canadian carriers would be bought up at "fire sale" prices by foreign multinationals.[35] This is highly implausible, given that one is dealing with publicly-traded, privately-owned companies and a relatively efficient equity market. More worthy of attention is the claim that other parties to the WTO negotiations, while offering to commit to removal of ownership restrictions, would still not have markets genuinely open to foreign competition, due for instance to non-transparent licensing practices (here the U.S. and EU are cited).[36] There are also the usual "strategic investment policy" arguments about capturing rents and the internalization to the domestic economy of externalities from research and development (R&D), etc.[37] Concerns about the lack of investment in domestic R&D on the part of "branch plant" operations have an historical basis in the record of BCTel, the one long-standing foreign-owned telecommunications firm, whose largest shareholder is GTE, grandfathered under the existing ownership restrictions. Apparently, BCTel's decisions about technological innovation were skewed by its vertical integration through GTE with a leading U.S. manufacturer of telecommunications technology.[38] Perhaps the real point here is that genuine competition policy issues *will* arise with greater participation of multinationals in the telecommunications industry in Canada. But even for the sake of *domestic* competition, guidance from competition policy for this sector is sorely needed.[39] Unfortunately, in this respect the WTO Reference Paper that contains regulatory principles applicable to liberalized trade in basic telecommunications goes very little distance even towards acknowledging the need for common competition principles, merely stating that "appropriate measures shall be maintained" to prevent three kinds of anticompetitive practices, including anticompetitive cross-subsidization.[40]

The foreign ownership rules are relatively straightforward, once one understands the holding company twist; however, the relevant statutes also state that a licensed telecommunications carrier must also be Canadian-controlled, and this conception of control as something other than majority share ownership raises serious transparency issues. This was put to the test when AT&T, along with a consortium of creditor banks, sought to rescue Unitel, the main Canadian long-distance competitor to the former monopolist, from collapse. Had Unitel simply disappeared, the shift to competition would have looked like something of a farce, perhaps a predictable result of the absence of adequate regulation to address the market dominance of the former monopolist and the anticompetitive impact on long-distance markets of its continuing monopoly on local service. Both the former monopolist, Stentor, and another competitor, Call-Net, sought to challenge the AT&T-Unitel deal on grounds that it would result in effective foreign control of the resulting entity, in violation of the foreign investment restrictions. The regulator chose to hear this matter entirely *in camera*. This meant literally excluding any participation from affected parties, such as competitors.[41] A detailed analysis of the resultant decision, which approved the transaction despite evidence of control by AT&T on the basis of most of the criteria employed by the regulator itself, has argued that possibly "the Commission simply closed its eyes to the truth"[42], having come to the view that, without the rescue, long-distance competition in Canada would largely disappear. Whatever the validity of this analysis, the combination of vague criteria (such as the "strength" of the Canadian company's Board of Directors) with a secret or private process suggests a very serious shortfall of transparency: it should be noted that one of Canada's commitments in its schedule to the WTO basic telecoms agreement is to maintain its "existing transparent regulatory regime", and one wonders if there was not something rather disingenuous in such a commitment, i.e., in fact entrenching a regime that is far from adequate in transparency through the fiction that it is already transparent.

In broadcasting, unlike in telecommunications, public and private entities are both very active, with the government-owned Canadian Broadcasting Corporation a major presence in the market even today, despite substantial reductions in subsidies; public educational broadcasting also exists at the provincial level, and one important state enterprise of this kind, TVOntario, may soon be put up for sale by the right-wing provincial government in that province. Restrictions on foreign ownership of broadcasters are considerably more draconian than in the case of the telecommunications sector; the limit on foreign ownership is twenty percent. Further, the ownership limits should be seen as part and parcel of a wide range of regulatory requirements related to the cultural autonomy objectives of Canadian broadcasting policy, the most extraordinary being that of Canadian content: these requirements are imposed on both public and private broadcasters as a condition of licensing.

At first blush, the requirement that Canadian broadcasters air a minimum quota of "Canadian" programs, which in television amounts to sixty percent of airtime, would appear to be a flagrant violation of national treatment.[43] However, Canadian content is defined in terms of the participation of Canadian *citizens* in various ways in the production of the material.[44] Thus, a distinction is not drawn between Canadian and imported *products* — in many cases, a program from any country in the world could qualify provided enough Canadian citizens were involved in making it. Perhaps it could be argued that foreign producers face disproportionate costs in employing Canadian citizens, for instance transboundary search and relocation costs might be higher than intra-Canadian ones.[45] Nevertheless, there is a great deal of personal mobility in these businesses, and Canada imposes no restrictions on the export of entertainment personnel. In this respect, it should be noted that the Illustrative List in the Trade-Related Investment Measures (TRIMs) Agreement, in specifying which domestic purchasing requirements may be violations of Article III:4 is framed in terms of the "domestic" origin or source of products, "in terms of volume or value of products, or in terms of a proportion of volume or value of its local production", and makes no mention of requirements that relate to the nationality or citizenship of personnel.[46]

Despite this rather formal national treatment analysis, it seems intuitively compelling that citizenship-based content requirements are a barrier to global contestability of the Canadian market; and perhaps here we may have the elusive example of the kind of measure, not covered by other provisions, that Article XVII might catch with its requirement that purchases and sales be made on the basis of commercial criteria, and that there be an "adequate opportunity" to compete for such purchases and sales.[47]

United States trade officials like to make belligerent noises about getting tough on Canadian cultural protectionism, and Canada's recent loss of a panel and Appellate Body ruling on the tax treatment of split-run publications, the *Sports Illustrated* case, has raised fears that a wider range of so-called cultural policies will be subject to trade scrutiny, with implications for Canadian content requirements in broadcasting. In fact, there is still political capital to be made in Canada by standing up to American "bullying", and the American position is often expressed in the crude proposition that culture is a business like any other, and that the reasons for protecting it are simply bogus. If there are pressures for liberalization they may come from within more than without: a sense that in practice the policies have been manipulable by rent-seekers producing cheap Canadian versions of U.S. police shows etc., a recognition that Canada itself is now a successful exporter of many cultural products, and also a growing awareness of the technological reality that a free society, in the long run, cannot effectively control what its people pick up over the airwaves, or more on point, off a satellite in space.[48]

Finally, to return briefly to issue of ownership restrictions in both telecoms and broadcasting, new pressures on these restrictions are occurring by virtue of the federal government's pursuit of a policy of convergence, which allows — in theory — telecommunications carriers and broadcasters to compete in each others' markets.[49] The government has stated that it does not seek to harmonize ownership restrictions for the two sectors. What it has done is to allow, through a regulatory change, a telecommunications firm that has more than 20 percent foreign ownership (obviously, up to the telecom limit of 46.7 percent) to set up a separate broadcasting entity which must observe all broadcasting regulatory requirements, including with respect to Canadian control and Canadian content.[50]

This, however, falls considerably short of achieving competitive equality under conditions of convergence, because a *broadcasting* entity cannot compete in the telecom market by acting through a telecom entity that takes advantage of the more liberal limits on foreign ownership, without the risk of losing its broadcast license. Thus, telecommunications companies have options for capitalizing their participation in an integrated telephony/cable market that broadcasters do not. Arguably through convergence, a purportedly *pro*-competitive policy direction, the government has actually managed to *increase* the discriminatory impact of the foreign investment restrictions in the broadcasting sector.

Financial Services[51]

The financial services sector is currently undergoing transformation in Canada. The recently established Task Force on the Future of the Canadian Financial Service Sector has invited nation-wide submissions on a number of issues, including the reform of ownership rules that would apply to both domestic and foreign financial institutions. The Task Force report will, however, be delayed due to the resignation of the Chair, Jim Baillie, in consequence of a conflict of interest.

The Canadian financial services sector has been constantly evolving over the last thirty years, in response to both international and global pressures.[52] Regulation in this industry has responded to the need for prudential supervision in an increasingly complex and globalized financial services environment. Regulation has also provided the financial services industry with guidance in order to preserve its strength, to promote national champions, and for distributive purposes.[53] Ownership and other restrictions have been reduced. At the same time, there has been a blurring of the separate pillars of financial institutions, beginning in 1986 when the Ontario government permitted banks to own securities firms.

Many of the restrictions on access of foreign providers to the Canadian market apply to both domestic and foreign firms (for instance the requirement that banks be widely-held). However, the original *intent* of such legislation was to prevent foreign firms from obtaining control of Canadian banks. In particular, this prevented the Chase Manhattan Bank of New York from obtaining control of the Toronto Dominion Bank in 1976 when the legislation was passed.[54] In addition to the restrictions on the direct ownership of financial institutions, there are further restrictions on what banks can own.[55] The Bank Act continues to prevent foreign banks from engaging in what is called "direct branching" — entering the wholesale banking market in Canada through a branch of the foreign bank itself rather than as a bank subsidiary subject to regulatory requirements, including capital requirements, appropriate to a bank that takes deposits and is part of the payments system.

The federal government recently tabled legislation in response to the White Paper review of financial services regulation[56], which considered a number of changes to financial services legislation in Canada. The proposed legislation will introduce a new "branching regime" in order to allow foreign banks to branch directly into Canada.[57] Specifically, the legislation no longer requires regulated foreign banks which own a Schedule II bank to own other financial institution subsidiaries through the Schedule II bank. Near banks, entities which provide a banking service but do not take deposits and are not regulated as banks in their home jurisdiction, will be subject to lesser regulatory burdens provided that their unregulated activity does not include taking deposits. Thus, it would lift the requirement that a variety of institutions who enter the Canadian market with one or more financial products (for instance, credit cards with distinctive features, or no-red-tape loans for small businesses) do so as bank subsidiaries, where the foreign institution itself is regulated as a bank in its home country or engages in the banking business there. At the same time, these institutions do not play a role in the Canadian market that would invoke the kinds of prudential regulatory concerns that underlie the rationale for regulation as a bank.[58] Secondly, even where not regulated as a bank in its home jurisdiction, the foreign institution might be deemed a "near bank" and prohibited from raising funding for it operations with securities in denominations of less than $100,0000. As the Standing Senate Committee on Banking, Trade and Finance notes, "the White Paper Proposal leads to firms in the same business in Canada being treated markedly differently solely on the basis of their parentage".[59] This policy debate reveals a number of important insights about the challenge posed by restricting foreign ownership in the current economic environment. In a regulated industry, as the range of activities that domestic entities can engage in changes, the question arises of how the treatment of foreign participants must also evolve. This can lead to considerable controversy over the meaning of "level playing field". Canadian banks view foreign institutions that do banking abroad but enter the Canadian market simply to sell a particular kind of financial product as "cherry-pickers" avoiding the regulatory burden that would be associated with operating as a bank in Canada.[60] The current proposed legislation does not address this issue.

The foreign institutions themselves argue, as a senior officer of GE Capital Corporation puts it, that

> our major competitors in Canada are not banks but other asset-based lenders . . . not subject to any bank oversight in Canada. . . . In our view the notion of national treatment under NAFTA and the WTO suggests that foreign banks such as GE Capital should be entitled to treatment similar to that received by domestic asset-based lenders with which we compete.[61]

From a trade law standpoint, this interpretation of the national treatment standard seems correct — the government is required to treat a foreign provider as favourably as a similarly-situated domestic provider. How a provider is regulated in its home country is irrelevant to application of this standard. Furthermore, "cherry-picking" is not an offense under any international trade agreement.

The broader point is, however, that even if Canada is able to reserve its current restrictions under an MAI, the changing market — as well as regulatory approaches to that market — will lead to adjustments or new interpretations with respect to the restrictions, or will alter their effects, thereby potentially provoking new trade complaints or arguments that the regime has become more restrictive than that which was initially reserved. These rules reflect an historic attitude in Canada that bank charters should be granted only sparingly.[62]

An additional dimension is the pressure that may come from regulatory and market structure changes abroad that raise new concerns about reciprocity of access. The recent announcement of proposed reforms in the regulation of the financial sector in the United States, entailing the dismantling of strict separation of different financial activities into different business entities required by the Glass-Steagall legislation, evokes the possibility that review of access to commercial banking markets as between Canada and the

United States will be triggered in accordance with NAFTA Article 1404.4 (which requires NAFTA members to consult on the liberalization of cross-border trade in financial services). While in theory such a review would likely facilitate greater access for Canadian institutions to the U.S. market, in practice it is unlikely that the United States would not attempt to impose some additional concession in terms of the liberalization of access to the Canadian market.[63]

As is envisaged in the draft MAI, free trade in financial services, given the prudential issues involved, would probably entail some form of mutual recognition of home country regulation. This would allow a foreign institution to enter the Canadian market and engage in the full range of banking activities without establishing itself as a banking subsidiary subject to prudential regulation by Canadian authorities — in effect, the bank would be regulated by its home country regulators. Obviously, such a solution entails regulatory co-operation, and perhaps some minimum standards that are accepted by all regulators as a condition of mutual recognition. As well, since regulation is related to deposit insurance provided by the Canadian government on personal deposits in financial institutions, under home country regulation, it might be reasonable to require that the home country also assume responsibility for the costs and risks entailed in providing deposit insurance.

5. Agricultural Marketing Boards

Although an active member of the Cairns Group of countries pushing for liberalization of agricultural trade, particularly towards the end of the Uruguay Round, Canada expended enormous efforts to preserve the right to impose quotas on agricultural exports as a means of sustaining the system of domestic controls on production and marketing of agricultural commodities such as chicken and eggs.[64] In the end these efforts failed, and to sustain these domestic market-rigging schemes, the Canadian government made full use of the tariffication provisions of the Agreement on Agriculture, converting quotas into tariff equivalents sometimes in the range of several hundred percent. The United States made a dramatic gambit to bring down the Canadian system by arguing that Canada's right to tariffy under the Agreement on Agriculture was limited by its commitments under the NAFTA to eliminate tariffs, including on agricultural products not the subject of negotiated market access quotas. The matter was taken to a NAFTA dispute settlement panel, producing a carefully crafted ruling that will undoubtedly have significance in future disputes about the meaning of the tariffication provisions in the WTO Agreement on Agriculture.[65]

A central issue before the panel was the meaning of Article 710 of the Agriculture Chapter of the Canada-U.S. Free Trade Agreement, incorporated by reference into the NAFTA. Article 710 stated that

> unless otherwise specifically provided in this Chapter, the Parties retain their rights and obligations with respect to agricultural, food, beverage and certain related goods under the . . . GATT . . . and agreements negotiated under the GATT, including their rights and obligations under Art. XI.

In addition to rather more arcane and implausible arguments, the United States claimed that the word "retain" here suggested that this Article could not apply prospectively (to any new agreements negotiated under the GATT), but only to rights and obligations already existing at the time of the FTA or at the time of entry into force of NAFTA. The United States also argued that while the Agreement on Agriculture did discuss tariffication, this was stated in the Agreement neither as a right nor an obligation.

On the first argument, the panel sensibly concluded that the most reasonable interpretation was that Article 710 applied to the GATT as an "evolving system of law" and not a static set of rights and obligations frozen at a given point in time — as the panel noted, the contrary interpretation would have the bizarre result that, as between Canada and the United States, Article XI:2(c) would still apply[66], permitting quantitative restrictions, while the trade of each country with the rest of the world would be governed by the tariffication approach in the Agreement on Agriculture, surely a highly anomolous result of the interaction between NAFTA and the WTO Agreements.

The second argument concerning the absence of a "right" or "obligation" to tariffy in the Agreement on Agriculture exposed some drafting flaws in the Agreement. While explicitly providing for the removal of the right to impose quantitative restrictions in connection with domestic supply management systems, the Uruguay Round text did not contain a self-standing provision unambiguously stating that there is a right or obligation to convert QRs to tariff equivalents. Article 4.2 of the Agreement on Agriculture thus states:

> Members shall not maintain, resort to, or revert to any measures of the kind which have been required to be converted into ordinary customs duties, except as otherwise provided for in Article 5 and Annex 5.

But while the expression "have been required" clearly suggested an antecedent provision creating such an obligation, no such provision exists. Indeed, as the panel observed, the Agreement could hardly require that these measures be tariffied, since that would imply that Members could not exercise the first-best liberalizing option of simply eliminating QRs and related domestic policies without resort to alternative means of protection. Ably using the *travaux* of the Agreement on Agriculture and the interpretative principles of the Vienna Convention, the panel came to the finding that the textual provisions in question were merely an imprecise way of stating what was understood to be the basic deal in the Agreement on Agriculture:

> The essence of tariffication was that states were required to eliminate their agricultural non-tariff barriers and were *permitted* to establish tariff-rate quotas in their place.[67]

The panel thus established tariffication as a right under the Agreement on Agriculture.

A final, not unimportant dimension of the panel ruling is to be found in its response to the further U.S. claim that, in fact, some of the tariffs in question did not constitute replacements of non-tariff barriers. On this argument, tariffs created and bound under the Uruguay Round agricultural trade liberalization process would be open to scrutiny on the basis of whether or not they actually were replacing non-tariff barriers, and by the same logic whether they were merely providing an equivalent level of protection, or perhaps in fact increasing it. The panel came to the conclusion that the tariffs created through tariffication were part of a "package" that could not now be challenged; here the panel referred to a part of the *travaux* called the Modalities Document, which stated that "negotiating modalities shall not be used as a basis for dispute settlement proceedings . . .". This suggested to the panel an intent that Members not be able to open up, after the fact, the package agreed to on the grounds that a Member had not followed the appropriate methodology in converting non-tariff barriers to tariffs, or on grounds of a lack of equivalency between prior non-tariff barriers and tariff equivalents.

The result is that the protective measures that now sustain Canadian marketing boards are largely beyond challenge under existing trade law. While there are some domestic pressures to liberalize supply management (including a constitutional challenge to aspects of the Egg Marketing Act on mobility rights grounds) and although discontent with the export monopoly of the Wheat Board is growing among some Canadian farmers, governments remain in terror of protectionist agricultural constituencies. Even a purported comprehensive political accord on free trade within Canada between the provinces and the federal government contained virtually no hard obligations to liberalize *internal* agricultural trade.[68]

6. Conclusion: Does Article XVII have a Future?

This review of the entanglement of Canadian state trading with the world trading system evokes the considerable range of trade rules and issue areas implicated by the practices of state trading enterprises. Thereby if nothing else, this dramatizes the very limited, if not negligible retrospective and arguably prospective impact of Article XVII. Article XVII appears like an untenable half-way house between the national treatment obligation on the one hand and a kind of comprehensive code to ensure market contestability where state trading enterprises are present in the market on the other. But the idea of evolving Article XVII into such a code seems overtaken by the multiple initiatives to clarify and develop the rules of the game where state trading enterprises are part of the picture, and often a large part (e.g., sectoral accords, whether in telecoms or financial services or agriculture; the general trade and competition agenda; the evolution of domestic and transnational rules on subsidies and countervailing duties; and multilateral investment negotiations). As well, as illustrated by the approach of GATT panels in the liquor cases, general GATT norms will continue to provide important disciplines on the protectionist potential of state trading. Finally, regulatory reform and privatization do not make these issues go away, but can complicate them and make them more important — a little competition is a dangerous thing and often, as the electricity and telecoms examples illustrate, more is at stake for the trading system than where competition is absent altogether.

NOTES

1. See J. Robert S. Prichard, ed., *Crown Corporations in Canada: The Calculus of Instrument Choice* (Toronto: Butterworth's, 1983) for an overview of the origins and rationales of public ownership in Canada.

2. On the meaning of this trend generally as well as in the Canadian context, see R. Howse, J.R.S. Prichard, and M.J. Trebilcock, "Smaller or Smarter Government?" 40:3 Univ. Toronto L.J. 498 (1990).

3. See J. Laux and M. Molot, *State Capitalism: Public Enterprise in Canada* (Ithaca: Cornell University Press, 1988); see also, R. Howse and M. Chandler, "Industrial Policy in Canada and the United States," in: K. Banting, G. Hoberg, and R. Simeon, eds., *Degrees of Freedom: Canada and the United States in a Changing World* 238–240 (Montreal and Kingston: McGill-Queen's, 1997). On the virtual lack of State Trading in the United States, see the contribution to this volume by Diane Wood.

4. D.W. Taylor, *Business and Government Relations: Partners in the 1990s* 97 (Toronto: Gage, 1991).

5. Although public sentiment on electricity may be affected by recent revelations of Ontario Hydro's gross and reckless mismanagement of nuclear facilities.

6. An excellent description and analysis of the privatization can be found in D. West, "Case Study: Alberta's Liquor Stores," 10 Can. Invest. Rev. 22, 33–34 (1997).

7. The argument that such a power was implicit in provisions of the Constitution was rejected by the Privy Council in A.-G. Can. v. A.-G. Ont., [1937] A.C. 326, 1 D.L.R. 673 (P.C.).

8. See R. Howse, "The Labour Conventions Doctrine in an Era of Global Interdependence: Rethinking the Constitutional Dimensions of Canada's External Economic Relations," 16 Can. Bus. L.J. 160 (1990); ibid., "NAFTA and the Constitution: Does *Labour Conventions* Really Matter Any More?" 3 Const. Forum 54 (1994).

9. Canada - Import, Distribution and Sale of Alcoholic Drinks by Canadian Provincial Marketing Agencies, BISD 35S/37 (1987–88).

10. Canada - Administration of the Foreign Investment Review Act, BISD 30S/140, para. 5.16 (1984).

11. Id. at para. 5.21.

12. United States - Measures Affecting Alcoholic and Malt Beverages, BISD 39S/206 (1992).

13. Japan - Trade in Semi-Conductors, BISD 38S/116 (1987–88).

14. For an overview, see R. Howse and G. Heckman, "The Regulation of Trade in Electricity: A Canadian Perspective," in: R.J. Daniels, ed., *Ontario Hydro at the Millenium: Has Monopoly's Moment Passed?* 104–155 (Kingston and Montreal: McGill-Queen's, 1996).

15. For an overview of the characteristics of the shift to competition in the United States, see R.J. Pierce Jr., "The State of the Transition to Competitive Markets in Natural Gas and Electricity," Energy L.J. 323 (1994).

16. Promoting Wholesale Competition Through Open Access Non-Discriminatory Transmission Services by Public Utilities and Recovery of Stranded Costs by Public Utilities and Transmitting Utilities, Order No. 888, 61 Fed. Reg. 21,540 (May 10, 1996), FERC Stats. & Regs. 31,036.

17. Energy Alliance Partnership, 73 FERC 61,019 (1995); TransAlta Enterprises Corporation, 75 FERC 61,268 (1996).

18. For a comprehensive and rigorous survey of the different approaches possible for introducing competition in the electric power industry, see S. Hunt and G. Shuttleworth, *Competition and Choice in Electricity* (Chichester: Wiley, 1996).

19. See Ontario Hydro Interconnected Markets Inc., 78 FERC 61,369 (1997) (denying access to Ontario Hydro); H.Q. Energy Services (U.S.) Inc., 79 FERC 61,152 (1997) (provisionally granting access to Hydro-Quebec pending a thorough mitigation of power analysis).

20. 62 Fed. Reg 12,274 (March 14, 1997), FERC Stats. & Regs. 31,048.

21. Independent Power Producers Society of Ontario, "Integrated Monopoly Costs Hydro a Sale in Ohio," 11 Fin. & Tech. Bull. (July 1997) at 10–11.

22. Ibid. at 111.

23. United States - Restrictions on Imports of Tuna, BISD 39S/155 (1991) (unadopted); United States - Restrictions on Imports of Tuna, DS29/R (1994) (unadopted).

24. Ministry of Environment and Energy, "A Framework for Competition: The Report of the Advisory Committee on Competition in Ontario's Electricity System to the Ontario Minister of Environment and Energy" (May 1996). I acted as adviser to the Committee on trade law issues entailed in the shift to competition and the following draws from this work: R. Howse, "Trade Law Implications of Competition in Electrical Energy," Research study, Advisory Commitee on Competition in Ontario's Electricity System, April 29, 1996.

25. See D. Schwanen, "A Matter of Choice: Toward a More Creative Canadian Policy on Culture," C.D. Howe Institute Commentary (April 1997).

26. For a survey and critique, see R. Howse and J. Solway, "Rethinking Foreign Ownership Restrictions as a Tool of Canadian Public Policy," Centre for the Study of State and Market Working Paper (August 1997). The restrictions are usefully summarized in Canada, Department of Foreign Affairs and International Trade, "Canada's International Investment Policy," (1997); see also, OECD, "Canada: Reservations to the Code of Liberalisation of Capital Movements," at http://www.oecd.org.

27. Certain elements of the financial services business are regulated provincially including insurance and trust companies.

28. See the remarks of Industry Minister Manley earlier this year, "Foreign Investment Rules May Be Re-examined," Foreign Investment in Canada News, Report Bulletin IC133, (1 February 1997) at IC133-6.

29. Stentor, "Comments in Response to Review of Canadian Telecommunications Policy in the Context of Global Trade Development," Canada Gazette, Part I, Notice No. DGTP-008-96 (August 24, 1996) at 3.

30. CRTC, "Competition in the Provision of Public Long-Distance Voice Telephone Services and Related Resale and Sharing Decisions," Telecom Decision 92-12 (June 12, 1992).

31. Telecommunications Act, s. 16(3).

32. Telecommunications Common Carrier Ownership and Control Regulations, SOR/94-667; P.C. 1994-1772, October 25, 1994.

33. The rules are discussed in detail in A. Henriquez, "Canada's Foreign Ownership Policy in an Era of Globalizing Telecommunications," LL.M. thesis, Faculty of Law, University of Toronto (1997).

34. These commitments include an end to Teleglobe Canada's monopoly on the handling of overseas traffic on October 1, 1998; the removal of Teleglobe's own specific ownership restrictions; 100 percent foreign ownership and control in the resale sector and international submarine cable landings in Canada, as of October 1, 1998; removal of all restriction on the use of foreign-owned and -controlled global mobile satellites effective October 1, 1998; and removal of the Telesat monopoly on fixed satellite service effective March 1, 2000. See Government of Canada, News Release, February 15, 1997, http://xinfo.ic.gc.ca/ic-ta/anno...releases/1997/english/-e_02_15.html.

35. Stentor, "Comments in Response to Review of Canadian Telecommunications Policy in the Context of Global Trade Development," op. cit., 3.

36. Ibid., at 9–10.

37. For a powerful critique of these arguments in the telecommunications context, see S. Globerman, "Foreign Ownership in Telecommunications: A Policy Perspective," 19 Telecommunications Policy 21 (1995).

38. H. Janisch, "Emerging Issues in Foreign Investment in Telecommunications," in: W.F. Averyt and A.C. Averyt, eds., *Managing Global Telecommunications: North American Perspectives* 151–152 (Burlington: University of Vermont, 1990).

39. See H.N. Janisch, "From Monopoly Towards Competition in Telecommunications: What Role for Competition Law?" 23 Can. Bus. L.J. 239 (1994); cf. W.T. Stanbury, "Competition Policy and the Regulation of Telecommunications in Canada," in: ibid., ed., *Perspectives on the New Economics and Regulation of Telecommunications* 103–162 (Montreal: Institute for Research on Public Policy, 1996).

40. WTO Group on Basic Telecommunications, "Reference Paper," 1.1, 1.2.

41. CRTC Letter Decision, Re: Call-Net's Application to Review and Vary the Commission's Decision in the Matter of Call-Net's Right to Participate in the Investigation of Unitel's Ownership and Control.

42. A. Henriquez, "Canada's Foreign Ownership Policy in an Era of Globalizing Telecommunications," op. cit., 51.

43. In the FTA there was a rather odd "exception" for Canadian cultural policies — odd because the United States reserved the right to retaliate against the "reserved" measures.

44. See S. Globerman, H.N. Janisch, and W.T. Stanbury, "Convergence, Competition and Canadian Content," in: W.T. Stanbury, ed., *Perspectives on the New Economics and Regulation of Telecommunications*, op. cit., 217ff.

45. I do not wish to suggest, however, that formal Canadian content requirements are the only kind of protectionism at issue — when a license is being sought for a new broadcasting entity, whether a radio station or cable speciality channel, it is typical for the entity to make various kinds of commitments or undertakings as to the contribution to Canadian culture. Ultimately, the regulator has the discretion to grant or not the license, and various kinds of protectionist promises may well influence it.

46. There is actually no reason why these kinds of requirements would be any more or less a violation of Article III:4 when imposed on a domestic as opposed to a foreign enterprise — the discrimination that impugns the measures under III:4 is not discrimination as between foreign and domestic investors, but between foreign and domestic *products* that are purchased by enterprises, the latter being favoured by the purchasing requirements. And see the *FIRA* panel, op. cit. Of course, there may be an *additional* element of discrimination in the imposition of the requirements on a foreign enterprise where it is unable to take advantage of established networks of supply in its home country or other countries of operation.

47. Given the approach taken by the Panel and Appellate Body in the recent *Sports Illustrated* case towards the respective scope of the GATT and the GATS, it is unlikely that characterizing the citizenship requirements as going to the nationality of service providers would remove the issue of the criteria for the purchase of the outputs produced with those services from the GATT.

48. See the excellent analysis of Schwanen, op. cit.

49. The general policy is set out in Public Works and Government Services Canada, "Competition and Culture on Canada's Information Highway: Managing the Realities of Transition" (19 May 1995); Industry Canada, "Convergence Policy Statement" (August 1996).

50. See Direction to the CRTC (Ineligibility to Hold Broadcasting Licenses), SOR/97-192, 8th April 1997, Canada Gazette, Part II, vol. 131, No. 9, 1222–1228.

51. The following draws on Howse and Soloway, "Rethinking Foreign Ownership Restrictions as a Tool of Canadian Public Policy," op. cit.

52. S. Harris, "International and Domestic Influences on the Evolution of Financial Services Regulation in Canada: a Retrospective View," Paper Delivered at a Conference on Canadian Regulatory Institutions: Globalization, Choices and Change (May 22–23, 1996).

53. Ibid. at 6.

54. Interview with Canadian Bankers Association, August 11, 1997.

55. See Task Force on The Future of the Canadian Financial Services Sector, "Discussion Paper," (June 1997).

56. Canada Department of Finance, *1997 Review of Financial Sector Legislation: Proposals for Changes* (Ottawa: 1996).

57. Canada Department of Finance, "Government Introduces New Legislation for Financial Institutions and Announces Decisions to Allow Foreign Bank Branching," News Release (February 14, 1997).

58. See Standing Senate Committee on Banking, Trade and Commerce, *1997 Financial Institution Reform: Lowering the Barriers to Foreign Banks* (Ottawa: October 1996).

59. Id. at 14.

60. See the testimony of various representatives of the Canadian banking industry before the Senate Standing Committee, 1–3 October 1996.

61. Testimony of Michael Davies, Vice-President and General Counsel, General Electric Capital Canada Inc., Senate Standing Committee on Banking, Trade and Commerce, 11-9 (March 10, 1996).

62. Task Force on the Future of the Canadian Financial Services Sector, "Discussion Paper," op. cit., at 22.

63. See B. McKenna, "U.S. Banking Reforms Pressure Canada," Globe and Mail Report on Business, 26 May 1997, pp. B1–4.

64. On the negotiations see M.J. Trebilcock and R. Howse, "Trade in Agriculture," in: ibid., *The Regulation of International Trade: Legal Order and Political Economy*, ch. 8 (London and New York: Routledge, 1995).

65. North American Free Trade Agreement, Arbitral Panel Established Pursuant to Article 2008, In the Matter of Tariffs Applied by Canada to Certain U.S.-Origin Agricultural Products, Final Report of the Panel, December 2, 1996, Secretariat File No. CDA-95-2008-01.

66. Ibid., paras. 158–165.

67. Ibid., para. 174.

68. "Agreement on Internal Trade" (July 1994). For an overview of the agreement, see D. Schwanen and M.J. Trebilcock, eds., *Getting There: An Assessment of the Agreement on Internal Trade* (Toronto: C.D. Howe, 1995).

CHAPTER 10

State Trading in the United States

*Diane P. Wood**

While state trading is not entirely unknown to the United States economy, its role at both the federal and State government levels is, for most sectors, negligible. Depending on how strictly one applies the definition of a state trading enterprise from Article XVII of the General Agreement on Tariffs and Trade (GATT 1994), there is either one such entity in the United States or perhaps as many as a dozen. This does not reflect the full presence of the government in the U.S. economy, however, because there are other government-owned or -operated enterprises that compete alongside private companies, which for one reason or another do not fall within the Article XVII definition. After taking a brief look at the list of possible state trading entities, this chapter therefore goes on to look more broadly at government corporations and the ways in which their activities are regulated. In the end, while it is possible to identify market distortions caused by this kind of government corporation as well as by a state trading enterprise, the United States — apart from the important area of agricultural markets — engages in very little state-sponsored trade that affects international markets.

1. The Concept of State Trading

By way of very brief introduction, the working definition of the term "state trading enterprise" that has been adopted by the Members of the World Trade Organization (WTO) reads as follows:

> Governmental and non-governmental enterprises, including marketing boards, which have been granted exclusive or special rights or privileges, including statutory or constitutional powers, in the exercise of which they influence through their purchases or sales the level or direction of imports or exports.[1]

Article XVII itself requires each contracting party (or WTO Member), insofar as it has established or maintained a state enterprise, or it has granted exclusive or special privileges to any other enterprise, to ensure that

---

*Circuit Judge, United States Court of Appeals for the Seventh Circuit, Chicago, Illinois, and Senior Lecturer, The University of Chicago Law School. The views expressed in this chapter are entirely personal and should not be attributed to any part of the United States Government.

the enterprise, in its import or export transactions, acts "in a manner consistent with the general principles of non-discriminatory treatment" prescribed for governmental measures affecting imports or exports by private behavior. This in turn means that those enterprises should act "solely in accordance with commercial considerations".[2] Without this constraint, a state enterprise or a private enterprise with special privileges would be disruptive to the general system of market-based international trade upon which the GATT was built, because normal constraints of cost, efficiency, and profit operate quite differently when the government is the commercial actor.

In a comprehensive study of the subject conducted approximately fifteen years ago, M.M. Kostecki suggested that state trading could be approached from a number of different perspectives, including (1) state control of the essential terms on which exports and imports must take place, (2) public property, (3) public management, (4) public grant of exclusive rights, or (5) a catalog of the typical functions for which state trading has been maintained (without looking for further consistency).[3] He argued that the most useful perspective from the standpoint of a study looking at market distortions caused by state trading was the first — government control — and contrasted state trading with private trading as follows:

> Under private trading, imports and exports take place on terms defined by private exporters and importers. The state authorities who collect duties[,] impose quantitative restrictions, etc., are distinct from the traders themselves. More or less competitive private traders compare domestic with foreign prices, and either refrain from or engage in foreign-trade activities. Governments interfere with these activities basically through instruments of trade control which either affect price relations (tariffs, subsidies) or impose direct limits on quantities traded (quotas, licences). Within that framework, the private traders determine the baskets of traded goods, their prices, direction of trade and the logistic terms of transactions. A trader's freedom to choose, guided by the profit motive, is either limited or non-existent under state trading.[4]

The idea here, therefore, is government control of an entire sphere of trade, not just government control of the particular enterprise. One government-owned company, amidst ten or twenty privately-owned companies competing in the same relevant market, would have no ability to "define" the terms of trade.[5]

Another approach to this question is reflected in the Treaty Establishing the European Community, usually known as the Treaty of Rome. Tucked at the end of Title I to Part Three of the Treaty, most of which is concerned with dismantling traditional state-imposed obstacles to the free movement of goods, is Article 37, which provides in pertinent part:

1. Member States shall progressively adjust any State monopolies of a commercial character so as to ensure that when the transitional period has ended no discrimination regarding the conditions under which goods are procured and marketed exists between nationals of Member States.

The provisions of this Article shall apply to any body through which a Member State, in law or in fact, either directly or indirectly supervises, determines, or appreciably influences imports or exports between Member States. These provisions shall likewise apply to monopolies delegated by the State to others.

As always, there are special rules for agricultural trade, found in Article 37(4). Article 90 of the Treaty adds important qualifications to the rules in Article 37, as it clarifies the extent to which these types of enterprise must comply with the competition rules the Treaty lays down for all "undertakings". Article 90 requires that:

1. In the case of public undertakings and undertakings to which Member States grant special or exclusive rights, Member States shall neither enact nor maintain in force any measure contrary to the rules contained in this Treaty, in particular to those rules provided for in Art. 7 [prohibiting discrimination on the basis of nationality] and Arts. 85–94 [the competition rules].

2. Undertakings entrusted with the operation of services of general economic interest or having the character of a revenue-producing monopoly shall be subject to the rules contained in this Treaty, in particular to the rules on competition, in so far as the application of such rules does not obstruct the performance, in law or in fact, of the particular tasks assigned to them. The development of trade must not be affected to such an extent as would be contrary to the interests of the Community.[6]

In a sense, one could say that Articles 37 and 90 also address the concept of state trading, but they do so in a different way from GATT Art. XVII, through their more direct focus on competition law concepts.

Both the GATT and the Treaty of Rome have attempted to bring within their regulatory regime the activities of state traders, public enterprises, or private enterprises with special privileges, when those activities operate as the functional equivalent of, or as a substitute for, government regulation of trading. Direct government actions are already covered by both agreements, and they comprehensively forbid tariffs, quantitative restrictions, or other nontariff barriers inconsistent with their terms. It is plain enough that states should not be able to evade these restrictions by the simple expedient of creating a state-owned enterprise, or of conferring special privileges on a nominally private enterprise. As we look at the entities and programs that may qualify as "state traders" in the United States, therefore, it is this ultimate purpose that should govern their characterization.

2. State Trading Enterprises in the United States

1995 WTO Notification

The best starting point for an overview of state trading in the United States, in the Article XVII sense, is the 1995 notification made by the United States to the WTO, pursuant to Article XVII:4(a) of the GATT 1994 and Paragraph I of the Understanding on the Interpretation of Article XVII. In that document, the Office of the United States Trade Representative identified nine programs or enterprises that at least potentially fell within the scope of Article XVII:

1. The Commodity Credit Corporation;

2. The Federal Helium Program;

3. The Isotope Production and Distribution Program;

4. United States Enrichment Corporation;

5. Naval Petroleum and Oil Shale Reserves;

6. Strategic Petroleum Reserves;

7. The Alaska, Bonneville, Southeastern, Southwestern, and Western Area Power Marketing Administrations;

8. Tennessee Valley Authority; and

9. National Stockpile of Strategic and Critical Materials.

With the exception of the Commodity Credit Corporation (CCC) and the United States Enrichment Corporation, all of these programs or enterprises operate side-by-side with private actors in the market in question. They have few, if any, special privileges that stem from their governmental connections. Nonetheless, a brief look at what all nine do will set the stage for a consideration of the legal constraints provided by U.S. law on these enterprises and activities.[7]

The Commodity Credit Corporation is now a federal corporation within the U.S. Department of Agriculture (USDA), established under the authority of the Commodity Credit Corporation Charter Act of 1948.[8] Under its Charter Act, the CCC may support prices of agricultural commodities through loans, purchases, payments, and similar actions. It may sell agricultural commodities to other government agencies and to foreign governments, and it may make food donations to domestic, foreign, or international relief agencies. Finally, the CCC has a marketing function whereby it seeks to develop new domestic and foreign markets for U.S. agricultural commodities. The CCC is an integral part of the overall system whereby the U.S. regulates agricultural commodities, supports production, stabilizes supplies, and assures certain returns for farmers. It can even act as the financing agent for export credit guarantee programs and certain export subsidy programs, through the Export Enhancement Program and the Dairy Export Incentive Program. Its activities fit into the broader web of regulations administered by the USDA, all of which combine to make agricultural markets one of the most heavily controlled in the world. Not only prices for export, but also baseline domestic prices, are profoundly influenced by the activities of the CCC and the related USDA entities and regulations.

The Federal Helium Program (FHP) as it currently exists began in 1960 with the passage of the Helium Act.[9] Under the FHP, the Secretary of the Interior (who for this purpose acts through the U.S. Bureau of Mines) is authorized to "acquire, store, transport, sell, and conserve helium-bearing natural gas", to explore and produce helium, and to engage in helium-related research, among other things. The FHP operates alongside an active private sector: for example, the Bureau of Mines operated only one of eighteen helium production plants in 1994, while the other seventeen plants were operated by private companies that had no connection to the FHP. There is therefore nothing exclusive or special about its operations, as those terms are used in Article XVII, nor is it a state-owned monopoly. In fact, the United States Trade Representative (USTR) reported in 1995 that it was a program for which privatization had been recommended, and pursuant to the Helium Privatization Act of 1996[10], the Secretary is required to cease "producing, refining, and marketing refined helium" and to cease all other activities relating to helium under the former law no later than April 9, 1998.

The Isotope Production and Distribution Program is housed within the Department of Energy (DOE). It covers the production and sale of radioactive and stable isotopes, byproducts, surplus materials, and related isotope services, such as irradiation, target preparing and processing, source encapsulation, shipping, and processing returned isotopes. The DOE sells the isotopes worldwide to a variety of purchasers, both domestic and foreign. Importantly, it produces isotopes only where there is no U.S. private sector capability to do so.

The United States Enrichment Corporation (USEC) was created by the Energy Policy Act of 1992.[11] It began operations in the middle of 1993 when the DOE transferred its uranium enrichment responsibilities to USEC. At that time, USEC was a wholly-owned government corporation. It had a lease arrangement for the two gaseous diffusion uranium enrichment facilities owned by the DOE, and it was the exclusive marketing agent for the United States government for contracts for enriched uranium, as well as uranium enrichment and related services. USEC sells enriched uranium to both foreign and domestic firms. The enabling legislation contemplated that privatization would occur when certain criteria were met.[12] This in fact occurred in April 1996. The privatization legislation stipulates that the Secretary of Energy "shall not lease to the private corporation any facilities necessary for the production of highly enriched uranium".[13] In general, the privatized USEC has assumed the contracts and liabilities of the former government-owned entity, but on the whole it no longer appears to belong in the list of state trading entities. Interestingly, the former law[14] had a specific provision requiring the corporation to "conduct its activities in a manner consistent with the policies expressed in" the Sherman Act[15], the Clayton Act[16], and the Wilson Tariff Act[17]. As a privatized entity, there is no need for special legislation to make the corporation accountable under the antitrust laws.

Although in light of the volume of world trade in oil the next program is practically infinitesimal, the U.S. Naval Petroleum and Oil Shale Reserve program, also under the control of the DOE, is also included in the U.S. Government's list for the WTO.[18] These reserves were established by Executive Order in the early 1900s to provide an emergency source of fuel for the Navy's fleet, as it converted from coal to oil power. The only oil shale reserves that are currently developed are those in California, for which the oil is produced under lease to private companies. By law, both production and sale must occur competitively on the open market, with all receipts from sales going to the U.S. Treasury. The provision governing the disposition of products once again specifically states that "[n]othing in this chapter shall be deemed to confer on any person immunity from civil or criminal liability, or to create defenses to action, under the antitrust laws"[19], which is the best assurance available under U.S. law that commercial considerations will prevail. At the time of the 1995 USTR report, all oil produced was being sold to the private sector, as were all natural gas and natural gas liquids not required for field operations. As is the case with the helium program described above, the petroleum and oil shale reserve program is slated for full privatization, although that does not appear to have occurred yet.

The Strategic Petroleum Reserve, also under the DOE, is a crude oil stockpile created under the Energy Policy and Conservation Act of 1995[20], both to reduce the impact of disruptions in supplies of petroleum products (for which the U.S. for many years has been a net importer) and to carry out the obligations of the United States under the International Energy Programme. The DOE owns and operates five Strategic Petroleum Reserve storage facilities for the underground storage of crude oil, with a combined capacity of 750 million barrels. In recent years, acquisition and fill activities have been quite limited, and there have been some drawdowns; the decreased level of activity is partly because Congress has decided not to fund this program. Oil is acquired for the Reserve both from the Naval Petroleum Reserve just described and through a competitive bidding process from private firms.

The next two items on the U.S. Government's list both relate to electric power generation and its sale. Several power administrations were created under the Flood Control Act of 1944[21]: the Southwestern Power Administration; the Southeastern Power Administration; and the Alaska Power Administration. The Bonneville Dam Act of 1937 created the Bonneville Power Administration within the Department of the Interior (later transferred to the DOE), and the Western Area Power Administration operates under authority from the federal reclamation laws, particularly the Reclamation Act of 1939, § 9(c). Last, Congress created the Tennessee Valley Authority (TVA) in 1933 for a variety of purposes, including national defense, agricultural and industrial development of the region, and the improvement of navigation and flood control along the Tennessee and Mississippi Rivers.[22] As a side-line (though eventually a very important one), the TVA was authorized to sell "surplus" electric power. It now supplies power to approximately 110 municipal and 50 cooperative electric systems, for distribution to over 3.3 million customers.

Some of the Administrations own their own generating facilities (e.g., Alaska), and others simply market and transmit power produced by federal dams (e.g., Bonneville, Southeastern, and Southwestern). The power is typically sold wholesale to public bodies, cooperatives, and other buyers. None of them participates in either import or export transactions. The TVA, for example, is limited by law to operating within its "power service region".

The last program mentioned in the U.S. Government filing is the National Stockpile of Strategic and Critical Materials, operated by the Department of Defense (DOD) under the authority of the Strategic and Critical Materials Stock Piling Act.[23] The Stockpile Manager purchases new materials for the stockpile through open bidding, without discrimination between foreign and domestic suppliers; payment is made in cash. The Manager also may upgrade materials in the stockpile, which is often done by bartering the new materials for excess stockpile materials authorized for disposal. The government has no exclusive rights over either the purchase or sale of these products in a more general sense: most purchases for the stockpile are made from foreign sources, and disposals from the stockpile are open to both domestic and foreign enterprises on a non-discriminatory basis.

U.S. Government-Owned Corporations

Another way of looking at public sector corporations in the United States — many of which, once again, do not appear to fall within the definition used for Article XVII — is to consult the Government Corporation Control Act.[24] That statute defines a "government corporation" as a "mixed-ownership Government corporation and a wholly owned Government corporation", and it provides a list of the particular entities that qualify as each.[25] At present, the mixed-ownership Government corporations include:

(A) Amtrak;

(B) the Central Bank for Cooperatives;

(C) the Federal Deposit Insurance Corporation;

(D) the Federal Home Loan Banks;

(E) the Federal Intermediate Credit Banks;

(F) the Federal Land Banks;

(G) the National Credit Union Administration Central Liquidation Facility;

(H) the Regional Banks for Cooperatives;

(I) the Rural Telephone Bank when the ownership, control, and operation of the Bank are converted under section 410(a) of the Rural Electrification Act of 1936 (7 U.S.C. 950(a));

(J) the Financing Corporation;

(K) the Resolution Trust Corporation[26]; and

(L) the Resolution Funding Corporation.

31 U.S.C. § 9101(2). The list of wholly-owned government corporations is as follows:

(A) the Commodity Credit Corporation;

(B) the Community Development Financial Institutions Fund;

(C) the Export-Import Bank of the United States;

(D) the Federal Crop Insurance Corporation;

(E) Federal Prison Industries, Incorporated;

(F) the Corporation for National and Community Service;

(G) the Government National Mortgage Association;

(H) the Overseas Private Investment Corporation;

(I) the Pennsylvania Avenue Development Corporation;

(J) the Pension Benefit Guaranty Corporation;

(K) the Rural Telephone Bank until the ownership, control, and operation of the Bank are converted under section 410(a) of the Rural Electrification Act of 1936 (7 U.S.C. 950(a));

(L) the Saint Lawrence Seaway Development Corporation;

(M) the Secretary of Housing and Urban Development when carrying out duties and powers related to the Federal Housing Administration Fund;

(N) the Tennessee Valley Authority;

(O) the Uranium Enrichment Corporation;

(P) the Panama Canal Commission; and

(Q) the Alternative Agricultural Research and Commercialization Corporation.[27]

The United States Postal Service has its own title of the U.S. Code, Title 39, which spells out its structure and responsibilities. In 1970, through the Postal Reorganization Act[28], the Post Office Department was abolished as a Cabinet-level Department, and in its place Congress created an independent establishment within the Executive Branch of government to own and operate the postal system.[29]

Almost all of the entities on the "mixed-ownership" list operate in the banking and insurance industries, where they provide financial support or insurance of last resort to borrowers in various sectors of the economy (private homeowners, farmers, credit unions, etc.). Federal Deposit Insurance protects small savings accounts (up to $100,000) in all federal- and State-chartered banks. When the savings and loan crisis hit the United States in the late 1980s, the Resolution Trust Corporation was created in order to facilitate the transfer of assets from failing banks to healthy institutions. None of these functions, however, is reserved exclusively to the government in the sense of either Article XVII or even Treaty of Rome Article 37 or 90. Indeed, the government would have been happy if private insurers had stepped forward to protect depositors or to save the savings and loan associations. The effect of the government's intervention was to preserve some institutions that might have failed, not to control terms of trade or to keep others out of these markets.[30]

Most of the corporations on the "wholly-owned" list are the same, such as the Community Development Financial Institutions Fund, the Federal

Crop Insurance Corporation, the Pension Benefit Guaranty Corporation, the Housing Administration Fund, and the Government National Mortgage Corporation. Since the Commodity Credit Corporation, the TVA, and the Uranium Enrichment Corporation have already been described in connection with the U.S. Government's WTO list, we turn to the remaining entities on the Title 31 list: Amtrak; the Export-Import Bank; Federal Prison Industries; the Overseas Private Investment Corporation; the Pennsylvania Avenue Development Corporation; the Saint Lawrence Seaway Development Corporation; and the Panama Canal Commission. The Pennsylvania Avenue Development Corporation and the Saint Lawrence Seaway Development Corporation are dedicated to the particular areas suggested by their names, but they certainly do not have the kinds of effect on trade in goods or services described by our "state trading" definitions. (For purposes of international trade regimes, they are or could be subject to constraints from agreements pertaining to government procurement or other nondiscrimination obligations, but they do not present state trading problems.) The same is true of Amtrak, the struggling national passenger railroad company. The existing private companies were on the verge of bankruptcy at the time Amtrak was created; through the government partial take-over, rail service was preserved in some parts of the United States (although in many areas it is nonexistent — it is principally an East Coast phenomenon, with some residual service in the rest of the country).

The Export-Import Bank can have an indirect effect on international trade, to the extent that its intervention permits transactions that would otherwise be unsuccessful in finding private financing. It is not, however, something that persons wishing either to export or import from the United States must use; it has no monopoly over export terms, nor does it have "special privileges" apart from the fact that its losses are, in part, guaranteed by the Treasury.[31] This fact sets the Export-Import Bank apart from many of the other institutions discussed here, such as the TVA and the former government-owned USEC, for which the enabling legislation specifically states that their obligations are not obligations of the United States. Notwithstanding those statements, even that kind of government corporation appears to have some psychological advantage in markets, perhaps because it is seen to be too important to fail.[32]

The kinds of advantages that may go along with government association may be illustrated by a recent case before the U.S. Court of Appeals for the Seventh Circuit involving the United States Postal Service, *Baker v. Runyon*.[33] The case was brought by Mitzi Baker, who believed that she had suffered from sexual harassment in violation of federal law while she was employed by the Postal Service. The district court concluded that the Postal Service had to pay punitive damages, on the ground that it did not qualify as a "government, government agency, or political subdivision" for purposes of 42 U.S.C. § 1981a(b)(1) (part of the anti-discrimination law). The Seventh Circuit disagreed. It first noted that federal agencies, while subject to the general rules regarding nondiscrimination on the basis of race, sex, national origin, and religion, are exempt from the statute's punitive damage rules. Even though the Postal Service must be run in a manner similar to a private commercial entity, it remains a governmental agency for most purposes. For example, it is still part of the Executive Branch of government, and it possesses certain unique governmental powers, such as the power of eminent domain. Furthermore, the fact that the Postal Service can be sued (and thus has waived its sovereign immunity for these purposes) does not mean that it is non-governmental; the waiver is necessary precisely because it is part of the government.

The Supreme Court went even further in *Lebron v. National Railroad Passenger Corp.*[34] in which it was asked to decide whether Amtrak was subject to the constraints of the First Amendment to the United States Constitution (which would only have been true if it was part of the "government"; the First Amendment does not apply to private entities). The specific question was whether Amtrak could censor political advertising that had been tendered for display in Penn Station in New York City. The Court decided that despite the fact that Amtrak (which, as it noted, had been established "in order to avert the threatened extinction of passenger trains in the United States") was created under an authorizing statute that expressly declared that it would "not be an agency or establishment of the United States Government"[35], it was still "the government" for purposes of the First Amendment[36]. Although Congress undoubtedly had the power to deprive Amtrak of attributes that were within Congress's power to give or withdraw (such as sovereign immunity, obligations under the Administrative Procedures Act, and the like), Congress had no power to make a final determination of Amtrak's status for constitutional purposes.

In a sense, *Lebron* and *Baker* illustrate how different matters in the United States are from those in many other countries. The oddity, in U.S. law, is the corporation with some government ownership or control. If such a corporation is before the court, it may have special responsibilities (as was the case in *Lebron*, which held that Amtrak could not censor advertisements for their content), and it may enjoy some special exemptions (such as the *Baker* exemption from liability for punitive damages). Amtrak, while it may be a monopolist of passenger rail services, is so only because the advent of ubiquitous and cheap air travel in the United States practically killed off the trains. The Postal Service is a somewhat more complicated case, both because it competes with large private sector firms like United Parcel Service, Federal Express, and DHL for many types of delivery (not to mention electronic mail — an increasing substitute for the old-fashioned letter), but also because it is protected from competition in some other respects (only the Postal Service may use private mailboxes, for example). It certainly has no monopoly over either overnight delivery, small package delivery, or any other type of service one could name; competition has become the name of the game, and it advertises just as aggressively as any other company.

The United States therefore has some small number of corporations with partial or full state ownership, and its executive departments run some number of programs that have an effect on certain private markets. However, with the exception of the Commodity Credit Corporation and possibly USEC, Kostecki's statement about the United States' interest in state trading in agriculture remains true:

> State trading lost its battle in the United States during the 1920s. The commitment of the US Congress to the philosophy of economic liberalism resulted in a refusal of the so-called McNarry-Haugen bills (1924– 8) which provided, among other things, for the establishment of a government export corporation.[37]

Debate over state trading in the United States regularly focuses on its incidence elsewhere and whether this is something that a country that has largely opted out of this system of economic organization should be worried about. For example, when the U.S. General Accounting Office (GAO) (an arm of Congress) prepared a report in August 1995 on "State Trading Enterprises: Compliance with the General Agreement on Tariffs and Trade", it highlighted the potential future importance of this issue as countries like the People's Republic of China, Russia, and Ukraine seek to become further integrated into the world's trading system, and it stressed the need for better monitoring of state trading activities both within the WTO and in the United States. It did not, however, identify any state trading activities in the United States that were of concern.

The GAO Report noted that reporting under Article XVII has been spotty at best. Even so, it was able to glean some information from the notifications that had been turned in. They showed the following:

> With respect to purpose, some member countries have reported using STEs to help agricultural producers "achieve their full potential in overseas markets," to ensure "protection of the domestic agricultural production against low-priced imports," and to ensure a "stable and adequate supply" of certain agricultural commodities as part of "national defense preparedness." Regarding operations, member countries have reported that STEs acted as sole agents for production, imports, and/or exports in the sectors covered. Additionally, the STEs assessed levies on production and/or imports, issued export licenses, and received govern-

ment guarantees on borrowed funds. Other state trading practices reported included government-guaranteed minimum prices and subsidized exports.[38]

Again, taking these purposes and operations and looking back to the U.S. entities that could conceivably qualify as state traders, it appears fairly clear that most do not even come close to these kinds of activities. Only the Commodity Credit Corporation, which has consistently been on the lists provided by the United States, has performed enough of these (as part of the far wider web of regulations pertaining to U.S. agriculture) that it logically belongs in this category.

"State Trading" in the U.S. States

The last point to make about state trading in the United States is that vestiges of it exist at the State level, as opposed to the federal level, in a few industries. Although data is hard to find, it appears from statistics collected by the U.S. Department of Commerce that the most important of these are the utilities (electric, water, and gas), local or regional transit systems, and alcoholic beverages. In 1993, for example, the State and local governments collectively obtained revenues of $65,081,000,000 from these four areas, which apparently reflect both ownership and franchise fees. In the same year, the Statistical Abstract of the United States reported that, in the aggregate, State and local governments took in $48.8 billion from government enterprise, out of a total of $507.8 billion in gross domestic product altogether. (Unfortunately, the term "government enterprise" is not defined in the charts, which makes it exceedingly difficult to tell what is covered by these numbers.) Breaking it down further, the Census reported that in 1995, all States took in $3.85 billion in utility revenue and $3.07 billion in liquor store revenues.

Although States and local governments do not tend to own production facilities for electric power, gas, and water, municipally-owned distribution facilities are not uncommon. State participation in the liquor industry is a vestige of the Prohibition Era in the United States. From 1919 until 1933, the Constitution prohibited the manufacture, sale, or transportation of intoxicating liquors within the United States, as well as its importation and exportation. (Had there been a GATT at the time, this would undoubtedly have been defended as a health and safety measure; it was unquestionably even-handed in its application — and just as unquestionably a miserable failure.) When the Eighteenth Amendment to the Constitution was repealed in 1933 by the Twenty-First Amendment, the Twenty-First Amendment preserved an unusual degree of State power in this area: it continued to prohibit that transportation or importation of intoxicating liquors into any State *in violation of the laws of that State.* Ordinarily, the Commerce Clause of Article I of the Constitution prohibits States from impeding or discriminating in any way against goods that originate in other States; the Twenty-First Amendment is a unique exception for liquors. Some States, accordingly, have remained "dry," and have continued to prohibit alcoholic beverages; other States have left the matter of alcohol regulation to their counties or cities, and thus have "dry" counties and "wet" counties; still others have chosen to regulate alcohol by retaining a monopoly over its sale. In some States, both State-owned liquor stores and private liquor stores operate side-by-side.

It is possible that someone seeking access to a State's market, who found his goods severely restricted or blocked at the border by the State alcohol control board, might be able to argue successfully that the State was imposing a barrier on trade for reasons other than commercial ones. It is doubtful, however, that such a complainant would be able to show any discrimination against goods of foreign origin. It is also doubtful that a complaining party would be able to show that the State operated its store in any way inconsistent with commercial considerations, which is all that is required under Article XVII. But the existence of these odd commercial monopolies is worth noting in any overall consideration of state trading in the United States, even if they are vestiges of the era remembered more for its speakeasies and its powerful gangsters than for its abstemiousness.

3. Domestic Regulation of Government Enterprises

To the extent that government corporations are exercising powers conferred in their enabling legislation, standard principles of legislative interpretation require courts in the United States first to seek to construe that legislation consistently with other Acts of Congress (especially, in this context, the antitrust laws), and second, to resolve irreconcilable conflicts by looking to the enactment that is later in time. In a sense, this is the counterpart doctrine to Article 90 of the Treaty of Rome: require the antitrust laws, and therefore competition, to take place except insofar as it is flatly inconsistent with the alternative regime at issue.

If the corporation in question is chartered by a State (as in the case of the liquor stores just discussed), the question is somewhat more complex. The Commerce Clause of the U.S. Constitution has both an explicit and a "dormant" dimension. The explicit dimension is clear: when Congress passes legislation using its powers under the Commerce Clause, then under the Supremacy Clause the States are not entitled to retain any conflicting rules. For historical reasons, the 21st Amendment to the U.S. Constitution shifts this presumption for liquor control measures, and in so doing it permits States or localities that wish to be liquor-free or to monopolize the sale of liquor to do so. It is also interesting to note that the Sherman Act[39], the principal U.S. antitrust law, has been construed as not reaching State economic regulations that purport to displace competition. In this way, the potential conflict between the federal mandate for free competition and the economic policy of the individual States has been avoided through a restrictive interpretation of the federal antitrust statute.

The "Dormant" Commerce Clause becomes important when Congress has not spoken about a matter. It would have been theoretically possible to argue that the States are free to have whatever legislation they want, free of the constraints of the Supremacy Clause, unless or until Congress enacts a law. That, however, is not the way that the Supreme Court has interpreted the Constitution. Instead, by reading the Commerce Clause as a general charter for a free internal trade system, the Supreme Court decided very early that the Clause implicitly forbade the States from enacting any legislation that either discriminated against interstate commerce or that placed an undue burden on interstate commerce.[40] Thus, the State of Texas may not decide that its schoolchildren will drink only milk produced within Texas, when milk meeting all relevant health and nutrition standards can be purchased just as easily from Oklahoma or Louisiana. Nor can the State of Iowa decide that all trucks using its roads must be only sixty feet long, if most of the other States permit sixty-five-foot trucks (even though the rule is nondiscriminatory). One would think, based on this theory, that a State would also be forbidden to use a State-owned company to hamper interstate commerce.

There is, however, a "market participant" exception to the Dormant Commerce Clause that the Court has applied when the State was acting not as a regulator of the market, but rather as a participant.[41] Congress, of course, could always control the State even when it was a market participant, through positive legislation, but the Dormant Commerce Clause alone was not thought to be enough to restrain the State from preferring its own citizens in these kinds of transactions. In *Reeves v. Stake*, the Court made explicit the analogy it was drawing between the freedom of the State as a trader to decide with whom it would do business, and the freedom ordinary commercial traders enjoy to do the same.[42] In *South-Central Timber,* a plurality of the Court made it clear that it did not intend to make this a wide exception to the limitations that would otherwise exist on State powers:

> The limit of the market-participant doctrine must be that it allows a State to impose burdens on commerce within the market in which it is a participant, but allows it to go no further. The State may not impose conditions, whether by statute, regulation, or contract, that have a substantial regulatory effect outside of that particular market. Unless the

"market" is relatively narrowly defined, the doctrine has the potential of swallowing up the rule that States may not impose substantial burdens on interstate commerce even if they act with the permissible state purpose of fostering local industry.

Using that rule, the Court struck down an Alaska law that required buyers of timber from the State partially to process the timber in Alaska before it was shipped out of the State. This means, in essence, that the Supreme Court will allow States to behave as market participants in their direct sales, to the extent necessary to treat them *equally* with private market participants, but it will not allow them to escape Commerce Clause scrutiny for anything that goes beyond what a private party could do. In addition, the Supreme Court has also made it clear that subdivisions of the States, including municipalities and presumably other State-created corporations, are not entitled to the State's own immunity from the antitrust laws.[43] These doctrines therefore enshrine within U.S. constitutional law a set of principles that are compatible with the obligations required in the GATT.

4. Conclusion

Although it is possible to identify entities in the United States, both at the federal and State levels of government, that have some attributes of state traders in the broadest sense of the term, the issue of state trading as it is debated within the WTO hardly arises in the U.S. economy. Those programs that exist are normally not exclusive; corporations do not have monopoly power or notable special privileges; and activities have little effect on international trade flows. A simple antitrust-style market analysis would reveal which companies or entities were even capable of threatening the harms against which Article XVII GATT was directed. As for those companies, measures to ensure behavior consistent with commercial considerations is necessary for the WTO, but it is also necessary under the constitutional jurisprudence of the Supreme Court.

The interest in state trading in the United States therefore continues to manifest itself in a more defensive posture. Private traders fear that state trading practices elsewhere will put them at a disadvantage, because they might not be able to gain access to an import monopoly, or they might find their efforts to export to a third country stymied by low-cost competition from a state trading corporation. These are real fears, and they help to explain why Article XVII was included in the agreement to begin with. In spite of the events of the early 1990s, during which some people wondered if state ownership would go the way of the dodo, it now appears that we will be facing mixed ownership patterns in many countries, and we must find ways to integrate countries with state trading systems more fully into the international trading regime. Stronger measures than those that have been used thus far will be necessary before private traders around the world will be confident that they are operating on their "level playing field", and the United States is likely to take a strong interest in their development.

NOTES

1. Understanding on the Interpretation of Article XVII of the General Agreement on Tariffs and Trade 1994 ("Article XVII Understanding"), para. 1.

2. GATT 1994, Art. XVII:1(a), (b).

3. M. M. Kostecki, "State Trading by the Advanced and Developing Countries: The Background," in: ibid., ed., *State Trading in International Markets: Theory and Practice of Industrialized and Developing Countries* 7–8 (New York: St. Martin's Press, 1982).

4. Id. at 6.

5. In this connection, it is useful to compare the concept of market power outlined in the 1992 U.S. Department of Justice and Federal Trade Commission Guidelines for Horizontal Mergers, as amended. The Guidelines attempt to define markets in which the merging firms would be able to have a significant (negative) effect on competition. See §§ 1.1 (product market), 1.2 (geographic market). If a firm is the only operator with respect to a particular product, and it would be able to force price up by cutting back on the quantities it makes available (because customers have no acceptable substitutes to which they can turn), that firm has "market power", and the antitrust laws normally require some corrective action. Here, if the state trader has that kind of "market power", it can influence the terms and direction of trade, both within the country concerned and externally.

6. Subsection 3, which relates to the Commission's enforcement powers, is omitted.

7. The descriptions that follow are taken principally from the U.S. Government's Notification to the WTO dated September 12, 1995. I have both summarized where that seemed appropriate and added additional information where that seemed necessary.

8. 15 U.S.C. § 714. That statute reads as follows:

> For the purpose of stabilizing, supporting, and protecting farm income and prices, of assisting in the maintenance of balanced and adequate supplies of agricultural commodities, products thereof, foods, feeds, and fibers (hereinafter collectively referred to as 'agricultural commodities'), and of facilitating the orderly distribution of agricultural commodities, there is created a body corporate to be known as Commodity Credit Corporation . . . , which shall be an agency and instrumentality of the United States, within the Department of Agriculture, subject to the general supervision and direction of the Secretary of Agriculture . . . .

9. 74 Stat. 918, Pub. L. No. 86-777. Amusingly enough, it appears that the program had its inception in the 1920s, when the federal government had the idea that it

needed a large helium reserve for the purpose of fielding a fleet of blimps in time of war. To my knowledge, no one has suggested that this justification retained much force in more recent times.

10. 50 U.S.C. § 167a *et seq.*

11. 42 U.S.C. §§ 2297-2297e-7 (repealed by Pub. L. No. 104-134, April 26, 1996, 110 Stat. 1321-349, which transferred 100 percent of the ownership of the USEC to private investors).

12. See 42 U.S.C. § 2297d (repealed by Pub. L. No. 104-134).

13. 42 U.S.C. § 2297h-5(c).

14. 42 U.S.C. § 2297b-11(a) (repealed by Pub. L. No. 104-134).

15. 15 U.S.C. §§ 1–7.

16. 15 U.S.C. §§ 12–27.

17. 15 U.S.C. §§ 8–9.

18. See Naval Petroleum Reserves Production Act of 1976, Pub. L. No. 94-258; Pub. L. No. 95-91 (transferring responsibilities from the Navy to the Dept. of Energy).

19. 10 U.S.C. § 7430(h).

20. Pub. L. No. 94-163.

21. 16 U.S.C. § 825s.

22. See 16 U.S.C. § 831 *et seq.*

23. 50 U.S.C. § 98 *et seq.*

24. 31 U.S.C. §§ 9101–9110.

25. 31 U.S.C. § 9101(1).

26. Although the statute continues to list the Resolution Trust Corporation (RTC), the RTC has actually been folded back into the Federal Deposit Insurance Corporation (FDIC) as of December 31, 1995, in accordance with a sunset provision that was written into the law creating RTC. See 12 U.S.C. § 1441a(b), (m). As of this writing, therefore, the RTC has formally ceased its functions.

27. 31 U.S.C. § 9101(3).

28. Pub. L. No. 91-375.

29. See 39 U.S.C. § 201-08.

30. The most that one might say is that the presence of these governmentally sponsored entities in the credit and insurance markets may have an effect on the rates that other market participants can charge, because the risks borne by the mixed governmental entities and the cost of funds for them are lower than those that commercial counterparts might bear. *Cf.* A. Michael Froomkin, "Reinventing the Government Corporation," 1995 U. Ill. L. Rev. 543 (1995); Carrie Stradley Lavargna, "Government-Sponsored Enterprise Are 'Too Big To Fail': Balancing Public and Private Interests," 44 Hastings L. J. 991 (1993).

31. 12 U.S.C. § 635k, 635*l*.

32. See Lavargna, *supra* note 30.

33. 114 F.3d 668 (7th Cir. 1997).

34. 115 S.Ct. 961 (1995).

35. 84 Stat. at 1330.

36. The opinion contains a useful summary of the history of government corporations in the United States, at 115 S.Ct. 968–971.

37. Kostecki, *supra* note 3 at 28.

38. GAO Report, at 7–8.

39. 15 U.S.C. §§ 1–7.

40. See generally Laurence H. Tribe, *American Constitutional Law* chapter 6 (2d ed. Westbury, NY: Foundation Press, 1988); Ronald D. Rotunda & John E. Nowak, 2 *Treatise on Constitutional Law: Substance and Procedure* chapter 11 (2d ed. St. Paul: West Publishing, 1992).

41. See Hughes v. Alexandria Scrap Corp., 426 U.S. 794 (1976); Reeves v. Stake, 447 U.S. 429 (1980); White v. Massachusetts Council of Construction Workers, 460 U.S. 204 (1983); South-Central Timber Development, Inc. v. Wunnicke, 467 U.S. 82 (1984).

42. Compare United States v. Colgate, 250 U.S. 300 (1919), the leading antitrust case establishing this proposition.

43. See City of Lafayette, Louisiana v. Louisiana Power & Light Co., 435 U.S. 389, 403, 406–408 (1978).

CHAPTER 11

The Role of Articles 37 and 90 ECT in the Integration of EC Markets: The Case of Utilities

André Sapir[*]

1. Introduction

The European Community (EC) was established in 1958 under the Treaty of Rome (ECT, or the Treaty) to promote economic well-being throughout the area. The key for achieving this objective is the *common market*, implying the abolition of obstacles to freedom of movement for goods, services, persons, and capital between Member States. The Treaty considers that the abolition of such obstacles is a necessary, but not sufficient, condition for the creation of a truly single market.[1] The Treaty recognises that obstacles to free circulation could be replaced by anticompetitive behaviour on the part of firms and/or states, and therefore calls for a system ensuring that competition in the common market is not distorted.

The Treaty does not address explicitly the issue of a common market in the area of utilities, but contains two important provisions on the role of the state in regulated industries. The first, Article 37, belongs to the part of the Treaty dealing with free movement of goods. The second, Article 90, falls under rules on competition.

The purpose of this chapter is to analyse the role performed by these two articles in the creation of a single European market in utilities. It can be viewed as a complement to the chapter by Bourgeois, also published in this volume, which argues that "the possibilities offered by Article 37 [to achieve a single market in regulated industries] can . . . be said to be limited". By contrast, this same author argues that:

Article 90 has . . . played a momentous role in the ongoing liberalisation of many formerly heavily regulated sectors in the Community. This process was triggered off by the Commission helped by a pro-liberalisation interpretation by the [European Court of Justice].

[*]ECARE, Université Libre de Bruxelles, European Commission and CEPR. Views expressed here are the author's alone and should not be attributed to the European Commission. The author is grateful to conference participants and to Michel Waelbroeck for helpful comments.

The present chapter contends that the actions of the Commission and the ECJ in the area of utilities may be less far-reaching and more short-lived than assumed by Bourgeois. It is organised as follows: Section 2 reviews the actions of the Commission and the Court of Justice based on Articles 37 and 90 aimed at establishing a single market in utilities; and Section 3 concludes.

2. Articles 37 and 90 ECT as Tools for Achieving a Single Market in Utilities

Article 37 ECT calls on Member States to ensure that *state monopolies of a commercial nature* apply no discrimination, between nationals of Member States, in the procurement and marketing of goods by the end of the transitional period.

Article 90(1) ECT requires that Member States apply, in the case of *public undertakings and undertakings to which Member States grant special or exclusive rights*, no measure contrary to the rules contained in the Treaty, in particular those on competition policy. Article 90(2) ECT specifies that *undertakings entrusted with the operation of services of general economic interest* are subject to such rules only insofar as their application does not obstruct the performance of the particular tasks assigned to them. Article 90(3) ECT grants considerable power to the Commission in the application of these provisions, which includes addressing directives or decisions to Member States.

There is a clear relationship between Articles 37 and 90 illustrated in the context of utilities:

- Article 90(1) applies to all utilities, since they all enjoy special or exclusive rights;

- Article 37 only applies to the subset of utilities dealing with goods, namely energy (gas and electricity[2]) and water. Since, by definition, state monopolies of a commercial nature always constitute undertakings to which Member States grant special or exclusive rights, Article 90(3) also pertains to situations covered by Article 37; and

- Article 90(2) covers all utilities insofar as they provide services of general economic interest.

The close connection between Articles 37 and 90 ECT is such that the two are often analysed together. This practice is followed, *inter alia*, by the European Commission's Annual Report on Competition, which includes a section entitled "State Monopolies and Monopoly Rights: Articles 37 and 90 of the EC Treaty".[3]

A preliminary appraisal of the efforts by Community institutions to establish a single market based on Articles 37 and 90 can be obtained with the help of table 1, which shows the number of liberalisation judgements by the European Court of Justice (ECJ or the Court) during the period 1958–97.[4,5] Table 1 reveals that the liberalisation activity of the Court was almost non-existent until the mid-1980s, and seems to have peaked out in 1993–94. As a result, two-thirds of all liberalisation judgements occurred during the decade from 1985 to 1994. The impetus for this activity was, clearly, provided by the Single Market Programme, as set out in the Commission White Paper of 1985.

The remainder of the section reviews the activity of the Commission and the Court of Justice in seeking to achieve a single market by means of Articles 37 and 90, with a particular focus on utilities.

Table 1. Liberalisation Judgements by the European Court of Justice, 1958–97 (number of judgements)

Year	Number	Year	Number	Year	Number	Year	Number
1958	0	1968	0	1978	0	1988	8
1959	0	1969	0	1979	5	1989	1
1960	0	1970	1	1980	0	1990	1
1961	0	1971	1	1981	2	1991	11
1962	0	1972	0	1982	2	1992	7
1963	0	1973	0	1983	2	1993	13
1964	1	1974	1	1984	2	1994	13
1965	1	1975	0	1985	4	1995	5
1966	0	1976	2	1986	2	1996	4
1967	0	1977	2	1987	2	1997	1
1958–67	2	1968–77	7	1978–87	21	1988–97	64

Community Actions On State Monopolies (Article 37)

Article 37 does not require the total abolition of state monopolies having a commercial character, but simply that they should be adjusted so as to ensure that no discrimination regarding the conditions under which goods are procured and marketed exists between nationals of Member States.

The aim of Article 37 is to guarantee the free movement of goods and to ensure normal conditions of competition between Member States in products which are subject to a national monopoly of a commercial character in one or more of those states. Hence, by the end of the transitional period, a state monopoly may not maintain exclusive rights to import, and producers from other Member States must be free to sell their products directly in the Member State where the national monopoly subsists. Equally, all quantitative measures of equivalent effect must be abolished.[6]

Article 37 has direct effect and therefore can be used by parties before national courts. It can also be enforced by the Commission by proceedings under Article 169 of the Treaty[7], or by a directive or a decision under Article 90(3).

Bodies which have fallen within the scope of Article 37 include: state alcohol monopolies in France, Germany, Portugal, and Sweden; state tobacco monopolies in France, Italy, and Spain; the state monopoly in potash fertiliser in France; various monopolies regarding the import and sale of natural gas and electricity in Belgium, Denmark, France, Greece, Ireland, Italy, the Netherlands, Spain, and the United Kingdom; petroleum monopolies in Greece, Portugal, and Spain; and the monopoly of the German Bundespost in the supply of telecommunications equipment.

What has been the role of private parties and the Commission in these cases? During the period 1958–97, roughly thirty-five cases involving Article 37 were judged by the ECJ, of which only nine were brought by the Commission in the context of Article 169: against Italy's tobacco monopoly (78/82); against France's tobacco monopoly (90/82); against Greece's petroleum monopoly (C-347/88); against Portugal's alcohol monopoly (C-361/91); against electricity monopolies in the Netherlands, Italy, France, and Spain (Cases 157-160/94); and against Sweden's alcohol monopoly (C-189/95). The Commission was fully successful only against France's tobacco monopoly and Greece's petroleum monopoly, and partly successful in the case against Sweden's alcohol monopoly. It must be stressed, however, that in many instances the Commission was successful in imposing changes on Member States through Article 169 proceedings without bringing actions before the Court.[8]

During the period 1958–97, the Commission only issued one directive based on Articles 37 and 90(3). During the 1980s, the Commission had taken actions against several Member States (Belgium, Germany, and Italy) following complaints about the impact of state monopolies on the free circulation of telecommunications equipment.[9] In order to avoid dealing with individual complaints, the Commission addressed Directive 88/301/EEC of 16 May 1988 on competition in the markets in telecommunications terminal equipment (in particular, telephone sets, modems and telex terminals) to all Member States. The directive states:

> In all the Member States, telecommunications are either wholly or partly, a State monopoly generally granted in the form of special or exclusive rights to one or more bodies responsible for providing and operating the network infrastructure and related services. Those rights, however, often go beyond the provision of network utilization services and extend to the supply of user terminal equipment for connection to the network. . . . The special and exclusive rights relating to terminal equipment enjoyed by national telecommunications monopolies are exercised in such a way as, in practice, to disadvantage equipment from other Member States, notably by preventing users from freely choosing the equipment that best suits their needs in terms of price and quality, regardless of its origin. The exercise of these rights is therefore not compatible with Article 37.

The directive declares that:

> Member States which have granted special or exclusive rights . . . [related to terminal equipment] ensure that those rights are withdrawn [and] ensure that economic operators have the right to import, market, connect, bring into service and maintain terminal equipment.

When this Commission directive was adopted, there were thirty-five exclusive rights on terminal equipment in the Community. Its success in establishing the conditions for free circulation in telecommunications equipment can be measured by the fact that at the beginning of 1991 only three Member States (Belgium, Italy, and Spain) had not yet withdrawn the exclusive rights covered by the directive which they had granted to public telecommunications organisations.[10]

By contrast to telecommunications equipment, Article 37 has played little role in establishing the conditions for a common market in gas and electricity, the only utilities (besides water) falling within its scope.

The effort to set up a single energy market was initiated by the Commission in 1988.[11] Thereafter the Commission has followed a two-pronged approach. Firstly, the Commission noted in 1991 that several Member States maintain legislation providing for exclusive rights to import or export gas and/or electricity which are clearly contrary to Article 37.[12] Accordingly, it initiated infringement proceedings under Article 169 against the nine Member States granting such exclusive rights: Belgium; Denmark; France; Greece; Ireland; Italy; the Netherlands; Spain; and the United Kingdom. In

1994, the Commission decided to refer the continuing existence of exclusive rights to import and export of gas and electricity contrary to Article 37 in France, Italy, the Netherlands, and Spain to the Court.[13] The Commission's action was dismissed in October 1997.

The ground for the dismissal differs among Member States. In the Spanish case, the Court found that the Commission had not demonstrated the existence of any legislative provision granting exclusive import and export rights to the state electricity monopoly. By contrast, the Court admitted the evidence provided by the Commission regarding the existence of such legislative provision contrary to Article 37 in France, Italy, and the Netherlands. These three Member States argued, however, that such exclusive rights are granted to gas and electricity undertakings entrusted with the operation of services of general economic interest. They are thus exonerated, by virtue of Article 90(2), of their obligations to abolish exclusive import and export rights provided under Article 37. The Court accepted their reasoning and found that the Commission had failed to demonstrate that the abolition of such rights is not necessary for the performance of the services of general economic interest entrusted to these undertakings.

The position of the Court is interesting in two respects. *Primo*, it seems to be the first instance where the Court has accepted Article 90(2) as a basis for maintaining exclusive rights incompatible with Article 37. *Secundo*, it appears that the Court has reverted to its earlier view according to which the burden of proof for exemptions under Article 90(2) falls on the Commission rather than on the Member States.[14]

The second approach the Commission has taken is that noted by it in 1991. It stated that, besides import and export rights, there are other exclusive rights which prevent the establishment of a single market in gas and electricity, such as transmission, distribution, and production rights.[15] In January 1992, the Commission acted to put an end to exclusive rights of this kind. However, instead of issuing a directive under Article 90(3), the Commission chose to merely put forward proposals to the Council under Article 100a (introduced in 1987 by the Single European Act) which provides the legal basis for adopting by qualified majority measures for the approximation of national provisions relating to the single market. The Commission, therefore, chose not to fully exploit its powers, but rather to directly involve the Council and the Parliament given the political sensitivity of liberalisation in gas and electricity markets. Progress along this road has been quite slow. A disappointed Commission noted that:

[I]t has been impossible in 1995 to make any substantial progress with the liberalization of the Community's electricity and natural gas markets, which, with a few exceptions, are still dominated by exclusive rights or monopolies.[16]

A breakthrough occurred in December 1996 with Directive 96/92/EC of the European Parliament and the Council concerning common rules for the internal market in electricity. The directive provides for a gradual opening of the electricity market over six years, starting no later than January 1999. However, its ultimate impact in achieving a single market in electricity remains unclear given its many loose provisions, including one relating to the protection of public service obligations. A similar directive of the European Parliament and the Council for the internal market in gas is expected to be adopted in 1998.

Community Actions On Public Undertakings (Article 90)

Article 90(1) ECT prohibits a Member State from enacting or maintaining in force any measure contrary to the rules of the Treaty relating to a public undertaking or an undertaking with special or exclusive rights. It is addressed not to undertakings but to Member States. Article 90(1) is infringed only in conjunction with another provision. The most common provisions which measures falling within this article can infringe are Article 30 (free movement of goods), Article 59 (free movement of services), Articles 52 and 53 (right of establishment), and the competition provisions in Articles 85 and 86.[17]

The obligation in Article 90(1) has direct effect, but only insofar as it concerns those Treaty provisions that themselves have direct effect. Like Article 37, Article 90(1) can also be enforced by the Commission acting under Article 169 ECT or Article 90(3) ECT.

Article 90(2) provides a limited exemption from the rules of the Treaty, including Article 90(1). In contrast to Article 90(1), Article 90(2) is addressed to undertakings. To benefit from the exemption, an undertaking must show that application of the Treaty rules would obstruct the performance of the operation of services of general economic interest assigned to it. When applicable, the exemption only operates to the benefit of the undertaking in question. Member States remain fully exposed to any liability they might incur under Article 90(1).[18]

The Treaty provides no definition of "general economic interest". Accordingly, Member States enjoy a large degree of freedom, with the proviso specified in Article 90(2) that the development of trade must not be affected to such an extent as would be contrary to the interests of the Community. Activities which have been considered by the Court as serving the general economic interest include: telecommunication services; postal services; water; electricity; and employment services.[19]

Until the mid-1980s, the Commission remained totally inactive with respect to Articles 90(1) and 90(2).[20] Its first effort under Article 90(3) to challenge legislation of the type prohibited by Article 90(1) is Decision 85/276/EEC of 24 April 1985 concerning the insurance in Greece of public property and loans granted by Greek state-owned banks.[21] This related to a legislation requiring all public property in Greece to be insured with a Greek state-owned insurance company, and also compelling state banks to recommend customers seeking a loan to take out insurance with a state-owned company. The legislation therefore was a restriction on freedom of establishment, contravening Article 90(1). Greece's compliance with the Commission decision was a long and difficult process. Failure to comply led the Commission to an infringement proceeding under Article 169, and eventually an action before the Court. Although the Court ruled in favour of the Commission (judgement of 30 June 1988 in Case 226/87), Greece only modified the incriminated legislation in February 1990, after the Commission had brought against it a new infringement procedure under Article 169. The Commission was more successful in its second action against a legislation contrary to Article 90(1). Commission Decision 87/359/EEC of 22 June 1987, concerning reductions in air and sea transport fares available only to Spanish nationals resident in the Canary Islands and the Balearic Islands, was immediately followed by a change in Spanish legislation effective January 1988.

The Commission only turned to utilities in 1990. In its twentieth Competition Report, the Commission stated its new policy in this area:

> Regulated sectors and those in companies enjoy exclusive rights will have to be subject to the rules of competition if the internal market is to function properly. Whilst the Commission recognises that account must be taken of the need to supply services of a general economic interest, this must be done in the manner least restrictive to competition. With the aim of opening up the possibility for competition the Commission will apply the rule of proportionality in deciding whether these services of a general economic interest can be effectively provided by any other way than by granting exclusive rights to particular suppliers. Such services of a general economic interest are usually found for basic utilities (e.g. gas, water, electricity, telecommunications, etc.). Exclusive rights given to a company which are necessary to provide these services of a general economic interest should not be allowed to extend into other areas which are not essential to the provision of the services in question and for which competition is possible.[22]

This new policy was immediately implemented by the Commission with a directive and two decisions pursuant to Article 90(3).

Commission Directive 90/388/EEC of 28 June 1990 on competition in the markets for telecommunications services was the first step toward a single market in telecommunications services. It was later amended by four other Commission directives: Directive 94/46/EC on satellite communications;[23] Directive 95/51/EC on the abolition of restrictions on the use of cable television networks for the provision of already liberalised telecommunications services; Directive 96/2/EC on mobile and personal communications; and Directive 96/19/EC on the implementation of full competition in the telecommunications markets. Altogether, these five directives prepared the ground for the full liberalisation of telecommunications services, which became effective on 1 January 1998.

The five telecommunications services directives constitute the largest of the three groups of directives based on Article 90(3), which comprise a total of nine directives. The second group consists of three directives (80/723/EEC,[24] 85/413/EEC, and 93/84/EC) on the transparency on financial relations between Member States and public undertakings. The transparency directives require that Member States supply certain financial data on public undertakings to the Commission, so as to allow it to ascertain the absence of state aids. The last group contains two directives on telecommunications equipment (88/301/EEC and 94/46/EC, the latter covering also telecommunications services). The striking element is that, leaving aside the transparency directives which are not sector-specific,[25] all Commission directives based on Article 90(3) concern the telecommunications area.

Another remarkable feature relates to the fact that all three groups of directives pursuant to Article 90(3) have been challenged by Member States. In Cases 188-190/80, *France, Italy and United Kingdom v. Commission*, the Court was called upon to examine the competence of the Commission to issue Directive 80/723/EEC (on transparency) on the grounds that it establishes general rules defining obligations imposed on Member States. In Case C-202/88, *France v. Commission*, France (supported by Belgium, Germany, Greece, and Italy) challenged the competence of the Commission to issue Directive 88/301/EEC (on telecommunications equipment). France based its case on the argument that the Directive constitutes a normative act which requires Council action. Furthermore, in Cases C-271, C-281 and C-289/90, *Spain, Belgium and Italy v. Commission*, the Court was asked to rule on the competence of the Commission to issue Directive 90/388/EC (on telecommunications services) on the grounds that it amounts to a repressive act which requires the use of an Article 169 procedure. In all these cases, the Court rejected the challenge of the Member States, supporting the Commission's view that Article 90(3) empowers it to establish general rules defining obligations already imposed on Member States by the Treaty, and that such rules are neither normative nor repressive.

Besides the first telecommunications services directive, the Commission also issued two decisions on postal services in 1990, both concerning the provision of express delivery (in the Netherlands) or courier services (in Spain). These actions marked the beginning of a series of Commission decisions against Member States for breach of Article 90(1) together with Article 86, i.e., for measures resulting in the abuse of dominant power by a public undertaking. They also marked a radical change in the attitude of the Commission with regard to Article 90(2). Until then, the Commission's interpretation of this article had clearly been biased in favour of granting monopoly rights to undertakings entrusted with the operation of services of general economic interest, since it did not require Member States to provide proof that the exemption from competition rules was necessary for the performance of the particular tasks assigned to such undertakings. This interpretation was changed in the Commission's decision on express-delivery services in the Netherlands.[26]

The next public undertaking decision pursuant to Article 90(3) was issued by the Commission in 1994. Two more were issued in 1995, and eight in 1997. Altogether, therefore, 16 such decisions have been put out by the Commission during the period 1958–97.[27] Seven of these relate to telecommunications services, of which only two concern the distortion of competition (the other five, all issued in 1997, grant additional implementation periods to Greece, Ireland, Luxembourg, Portugal, and Spain for the execution of the full competition directive beyond the 1 January 1998 deadline); five decisions relate to (fluvial, sea, or air) ports; two to postal services; one to insurance; and one to television. With the exception of the two decisions issued before 1990 and the five telecommunications decisions granting time extensions, all the other nine public undertaking decisions issued by the Commission pursuant to Article 90(3) are based on Articles 90(1) and 86.

As already indicated, the Member States have continuously challenged the application of Article 90(3) by the Commission as a basis for issuing directives. Equally, incriminated public undertakings and their governments have contested Commission decisions based on Articles 90(1) and 86 on the grounds that these decisions fail to take sufficient account of the general economic interest nature of the services provided by such undertakings. Member States have also resented the attitude of the Court of Justice which has generally supported the Commission's views with respect to Article 90.

The opportunity to modify Article 90 arose with the 1996 Intergovernmental Conference (IGC) concluded at the Amsterdam European Summit in June 1997. This occasion was especially seized by Belgium and France, championing the cause of services of general economic interest.

The Commission pleaded in favour of the *status quo*, arguing that:

Liberalization of the traditionally monopolized sectors is a crucial step in the establishment of a real single market for the benefit of European consumers. Nevertheless, the Commission is aware that the particular way these sectors are organized very often reflects legitimate concerns to ensure social cohesion; in its liberalization strategies it therefore seeks to keep in view objectives of public service whilst ensuring that the means by which they are achieved entail the minimum possible restrictions for competition and trade. . . . The Commission is of the view that the objectives of liberalization and of public service can be kept fully compatible under the existing Community rules. It has therefore opposed the proposals to amend Article 90. . . .[28]

The Commission also defended its power under Article 90(3) to adopt decisions or directives that are binding on the Member States. It argued that this power is limited and has always been used with caution, seeking a broad dialogue with the other Union institutions (Council, Parliament, Economic and Social Committee, Committee of the Regions), Member States, and interested parties.[29]

The Commission's view prevailed in Amsterdam, leaving Article 90 ECT untouched.[30]

3. Conclusion

The picture that emerges regarding the success of Community actions based on Articles 37 and 90 ECT in bringing about a single market in utilities is a mixed one. In telecommunications services, the Commission has issued five directives and two decisions pursuant to Article 90(3) during the period 1990–97 which have led to the full liberalisation of ten national markets since 1 January 1998. Nevertheless, the establishment of a real single market in telecommunications services must still await Community legislation on open network provisions designed to ensure that new applicants can obtain leased lines from and interconnection with existing providers. The Commission has chosen to introduce such legislation by proposing Article 100a directives of the European Parliament and the Council.

In other utilities sectors, the outcome of the liberalisation policy based on Articles 37 and 90, launched nearly a decade ago, is more disappointing. In postal services, the Commission has not followed its several infringement proceedings under Article 169 and its two decisions under Article 90(3) on express courier by a more sweeping directive based on 90(3). It has drafted a proposal for an Article 100a directive of the European Parliament and the

Council on common rules for the development of postal services, which still waits for the approval of these institutions. In energy, Article 100a directives of the European Parliament and the Council on common rules for the internal market in electricity and gas have been, or are in the process of being, adopted. But none of these three Article 100a directives has a clear impact in terms of furthering the internal market. Finally, in transportation, Article 90(3) until now has only been used in marginal cases, as indicated by the Commission with respect to the airline industry.[31]

In conclusion, it turns out that the success in telecommunications is an exception rather than a forerunner of future developments towards the integration of other EC utilities markets. This pessimistic view rests on two observations. First, the telecommunications sector is characterised by a feature shared at the moment by no other utilities. Undoubtedly, much of the telecommunications liberalisation has occurred as a response to rapid technological progress, which renders obsolete the previous monopoly organisation of the sector.[32] In other words, it is probably fair to argue that the emerging single market in telecommunications owes less to Community actions based on Articles 37 and 90 than these actions owe to technological progress. Second, the Commission and the Court of Justice are far from enjoying the political support of other Community institutions which is required to ensure sufficient legitimacy in pursuing the liberalisation of politically-sensitive utilities sectors. This is plainly demonstrated by the actions of the Commission and its declarations before and after the 1996 IGC, and by the marked decrease in the liberalisation activity of the Court after the 1993–94 peak.

NOTES

1. The expressions "common market", "single market", and "internal market" are used interchangeably throughout the chapter.

2. The Court of Justice confirmed that gas and electricity are to be treated as goods in Case 6/64, Costa v ENEL.

3. See also Bellamy & Child [Rose (1993)], chapter 13.

4. It should be borne in mind that liberalisation judgements (based *inter alia* on Articles 37 and 90) embrace other regulated activities besides utilities.

5. Table 1 is based on the information provided by the Directorate General for Competition (DG IV) on *Europa*, the Commission's web server at http://www.cc.cec:8080/en/comm/dg04/dg4home.htm.

6. See, for instance, Bellamy & Child [Rose (1993)], § 13-005.

7. "If the Commission considers that a Member State has failed to fulfil an obligation under this Treaty, it shall deliver a reasoned opinion on the matter after giving the State concerned the opportunity to submit its observations. If the State does not comply with the opinion within the period laid down by the Commission, the latter may bring the matter before the Court of Justice."

8. Megret (Séché et al. (1990), para. 355) notes that, given the sensitive political nature of activities affected by Article 37, the Commission tends to prefer political negotiations with Member States to actions before the Court.

9. See European Commission (1995), para. 215.

10. See European Commission (1992), para. 323.

11. See European Commission (1988).

12. See European Commission (1992), para. 328.

13. See European Commission (1995), para. 228.

14. See Section 2.2.

15. See European Commission (1992), para. 329.

16. See European Commission (1996), para. 113.

17. See Rose (1993), § 13-018.

18. See Wyatt and Dashwood (1993), 560.

19. See, for instance, Waelbroeck and Frignani (1997), para. 289.

20. Nonetheless, the Court judged a number of cases dealing with these articles brought by private parties.

21. This Commission decision is the first ever under Article 90(3).

22. European Commission (1991), 12.

23. This directive also amends Directive 88/301/EEC on telecommunications market equipment.

24. This Commission directive is the first ever under Article 90(3).

25. The first transparency directive did not apply to public undertakings operating in water and energy, post and telecommunications, transport, and public credit. Its scope was extended by the second directive to cover these, mostly utilities, undertakings from 1 January 1986. See Rose (1993), § 13-032.

26. The Commission stated that "[u]nder . . . Article [90(2)], the rules of . . . competition apply to postal services unless their application obstructs the performance . . . of the particular tasks assigned to such services. It is for the Member States to prove that the application of the rules would have such an effect". (OJ L 10, 12.01.1990, p. 51; emphasis supplied). See Sapir, Buigues, and Jacquemin (1993).

27. In addition, the Commission has brought a number of infringement proceedings against Member States under Article 169 for failing to fulfil their obligations under Article 90(1). Several actions have resulted in changes in Member States legislation without the need to bring the matters before the Court.

28. See European Commission (1997), paras 113–4.

29. Commission notice of 11 September 1996 on services of general economic interest in Europe, OJ C 281, 26.09.1996, p. 3.
30. However, the new treaty incorporates a new article on services of general economic interest.
31. See European Commission (1995), para. 226.
32. See, e.g., CEPS (1996) and Institut d'Economie Industrielle (1997).

REFERENCES

Bourgeois, J.H.J. .1997. "EC Rules on State Monopolies and Public Undertakings: Lesson for the WTO." In this volume.
CEPS. 1996. "Towards A Single Market in Utilities, Working Party Report No. 14." Brussels: CEPS.
European Commission. 1988. *Energy in Europe*. Brussels.
European Commission. 1991. *XXth Report on Competition Policy–1990*. Brussels.
European Commission. 1992. *XXIst Report on Competition Policy–1991*. Brussels.
European Commission. 1995. *XXIVth Report on Competition Policy–1994*. Brussels.
European Commission. 1996. *XXVth Report on Competition Policy–1995*. Brussels.
European Commission. 1997. *XXVIth Report on Competition Policy–1996*. Brussels.
Institut d'Economie Industrielle. 1997. "Network Industries and Public Service." Report prepared for the Directorate-General for Economic and Financial Matters of the European Commission, Université des Sciences Sociales de Toulouse. Mimeo.
Sapir, A., P. Buigues and A. Jacquemin. 1993. "European Competition Policy in Manufacturing and Services: A Two-Speed Approach?" Oxford Review of Economic Policy 9/2: 113–132.
Séché, J.C., S. Van Raepenbusch, J.V. Louis, *et al.* 1990. 3 *Commentaire J. Megret (Le Droit de la CE): Libre Circulation des Personnes, des Services et des Capitaux. Transports*. 2nd edn. Brussels: Editions de l'Université de Bruxelles.
Rose, V., ed. 1993. *Bellamy & Child, Common Market Law of Competition*, 4th edition. London: Sweet & Maxwell.
Waelbroeck, M. and A. Frignani. 1997. 4 *Commentaire J. Megret (Le Droit de la CE): Concurrence*. 2nd ed. Brussels: Editions de l'Université de Bruxelles.
Wyatt, D. and A. Dashwood. 1993. *Wyatt & Dashwood's European Competition Law*, 3rd edn. London: Sweet & Maxwell.

CHAPTER 12

State Trading in Japan

Mitsuo Matsushita[*]

1. Introduction

In Japan today, "deregulation" is one of the most important economic policy objectives. Deregulation is called for in order to promote business activities based on private initiatives, particularly in view of the pessimistic sentiments that are prevailing over the future of the Japanese economy. The Japanese economy is still suffering from a long process of depression after the collapse of the "bubble" economy. The Japanese economy is losing competitiveness and viability in manufacturing due to rising costs, the aging population, the growing expenses for social security, and a variety of other factors. Views have been expressed that the Japanese economy has been over-regulated by laws and regulations and that it is an "absolute must" to lessen governmental regulations and to release potentials of private initiatives.[1] Various proposals have been made to carry out deregulation with more or less degrees of success.[2]

The system of state trading enterprises is a kind of economic regulation. Their activities limit the scope of private initiative in international trade, and in the context of the policy for deregulation, the necessity for the system of state trading enterprises has been critically reviewed. The general direction of policy today is toward reducing the number of state trading enterprises and their scope of activities. As we will see later in more detail, some state trading agencies have been privatized and other have been abolished.

This chapter is structured as follows: before discussing the state of the existing state trading enterprises in Japan, a brief overview of the constitutional framework for state trading enterprises (STEs) in Japan is given; after reviewing the state-of-play of the Japanese STEs, we turn to two cases involving such enterprises, one international and the other domestic, to illustrate some of the unique characteristics of the Japanese state trading enterprises.

[*]Professor of Law, Seikei University; Member of the Appellate Body, World Trade Organization (WTO). The views expressed are personal and should not in any way be attributed to the WTO or the Appellate Body. I would like to thank Ichiro Araki, Legal Affairs Division of the WTO, for his invaluable assistance in preparing and editing the draft.

2. Constitutional Framework for State Trading Enterprises in Japan

The Freedom of Trade

Article 22(1) of the Japanese Constitution provides for the principle of free-dom of choosing an occupation, which has been interpreted to include the freedom of business activities such as exporting and importing.[3] Under this constitutional commandment, private enterprises in Japan are in principle free to engage in export, import, foreign investment, and other economic activities. Article 22(1), however, also states that the freedom of occupation (trade) may be restricted for the purpose of promoting the public welfare. Generally, under laws, state trading enterprises have a monopoly over ex-porting/importing of products and some related activities, and private enter-prises are excluded from such activities. In the constitutional context as touched upon above, the existence of STEs and the exclusion of private enterprises from activities assigned to state enterprises are allowed only if it serves the purpose of promoting the public welfare.

The Interpretation of Public Welfare

Although there are only a handful of Supreme Court decisions which deal with the meaning of the public welfare as enshrined in Article 22, they shed some light on this subject matter. Therefore, a brief review of those decisions follows.

There have emerged several interpretational doctrines with regard to the concept of the public welfare. First, the restriction of the freedom of trade to promote the public interest must be based on legislation. In other words, the nature of the public interest and the necessity of restricting the freedom of trade must be explicitly declared in law.

In the *COCOM* case[4], the issue was an export ban imposed by the Ministry of International Trade and Industry (MITI) on the exportation of electronic items to the Peoples' Republic of China under the Foreign Exchange and Foreign Trade Control Law (the Control Law) and the Export Control Order, the implementing Cabinet ordinance for this law. A person who wanted to exhibit certain electronic items in a trade fair held in the Peoples' Republic of China requested MITI to issue an export licence as required by the Control Law. The licence was denied for the reason that the items were treated as contraband by an agreement of the Coordinating Committee for Export Controls (COCOM). On the basis of Article 22(1) of the Constitution, the plaintiff sought an injunction to restrain MITI from denying a licence.

The Tokyo District Court held that the imposition was unconstitutional since Article 1 of the Control Law stated that the objective of the law was to "maintain the balance of payment and the stability of the currency as well as to contribute to the healthy development of the national economy", which were economic objectives and the control of export for the purpose of achieving political and strategic goals as incorporated in the COCOM Agreement fell outside the scope of the legislation.

Secondly, in the *Public Bathhouse* case[5] and the *Pharmaceutical Affairs Law* case[6], the Supreme Court announced that the permissible scope of restriction of private activities under Article 22 should be construed narrowly if the legislation in question is a "police power" type. If the objective of the legislation in question is the preservation of the public order, the public moral, the health of the people, the safety of products, etc., courts are authorized to scrutinize the legislation to see if its scope is not unduly wide. The notion behind this doctrine is that the police power regulation is not based on specific political, economic, or social policies, that the legislature is under the obligation to enact laws and regulations within the limit of the constitutional constraint, and that therefore the legislative discretion in this area is not as wide as it would be if the legislation dealt with a policy matter such as the protection of farmers, small enterprises, and so forth. This doctrine may be called the "judicial activity" doctrine.

Thirdly, in the *Retail Market* case[7] and the *Kyoto Necktie* case[8], the Supreme Court developed a doctrine which holds that courts should refrain from scrutinizing the wisdom of legislation if the law in question relates to a political, economic, or social policy such as the protection of agriculture, small enterprises, consumers, the regulation of business for the purpose of preventing "excessive competition", or the phasing out of sunset industries, and so on. The rationale behind this doctrine is that a decision with regard to policy matters is in the realm of legislative discretion and courts should not lightly interfere with this discretion unless the measure in question is manifestly unreasonable or the method of achieving the policy purpose is excessively restrictive. This doctrine may be called the "judicial passivity" doctrine.

The dichotomy of judicial passivity versus judicial activity in Supreme Court decisions may be criticized for the reason that a law that restricts the freedom of trade is treated more strictly under the Constitution if its purpose is to promote the interest of the public in general, whereas it is dealt with more leniently if it is based on a political, economic, or social policy which is often the product of activities of a special interest group and is nothing but the protection of that particular group. Although this criticism may be justified, it is also true that under the separation of powers, the legislature has discretion in deciding which policy to adopt, even if the policy adopted is unwise from another policy perspective. Undue interference by courts in this legislative discretion would upset the balance of powers between the legislature and the judiciary.

Especially significant for our purpose is the *Kyoto Necktie* case. The details of this case will be discussed later. In short, the case dealt with whether or not a law which established a state trading enterprise was contrary to Article 22(1) of the Constitution. The law in question was the Cocoon and Silk Price Stabilization Law, designed to protect domestic silk farmers from imports of low-priced foreign silk. Under this law, the Japan Raw Silk and Sugar Price Stabilization Agency (the Silk Agency)[9] was given the exclusive authority for importing silk from abroad, excluding thereby private enterprises producing neckties from importing low-priced silk from abroad. The Supreme Court upheld the validity of this law, stating (and citing previous cases) that the issue was whether protecting silk farmers was an economic policy matter in which the legislature was generally free to exercise discretion. The Supreme Court further stated that courts should refrain from passing judgment on the wisdom of this legislation.

As explained in the following section, there are several types of state trading enterprises in Japan: some are designed to accomplish a politico-economic policy (such as the Livestock Industry Promotion Corporation (LIPC)[10] and the Silk Agency) and others are based, at least partly, on public order considerations (such as the Ministry of Health and Welfare, which is authorized to export/import opium). The extent to which monopoly of trade by a state trading agency is subject to constitutional constraint depends on to which type the state trading agency in question belongs.

3. State Trade Agencies in Japan

General Observation

State trading enterprises are closely linked with domestic policies of one kind or another. Important among such policies is the promotion and protection of agricultural sectors as exemplified in the areas of rice, milk products, and raw silk. Often activities of state trading agencies are linked with domestic price stabilization programmes and stockpile policies. Sometimes state trading enterprises stockpile agricultural products such as is the case with rice. In those areas, state trading enterprises are instruments to carry out policies for balancing demand and supply and maintaining prices of agricultural products.

A brief overview of the existing state trading enterprises in Japan is given below.

Leaf Tobacco[11]

In this area, Japan Tobacco Inc. (JTI) is the state trading agency. The predecessor of JTI was Japan Tobacco and Salt Public Corporation, a public corporation which was closely linked with the government. This was privatized in 1985 and JTI was created. At the same time, the importation of leaf tobacco and manufactured tobacco was liberalized.

JTI still retains a monopoly over the domestic production of tobacco under Article 8 of the Tobacco Business Law. This monopoly is established for the purposes of securing revenue from tobacco tax and of protecting domestic farmers producing leaf tobacco. Even though private enterprises can import leaf tobacco, if fact, they have no choice but to sell it to JTI since no entity other than JTI can produce tobacco and all the importation of leaf tobacco depends on subsequent purchase of the imported leaf tobacco by JTI.

Therefore, JTI is the primary agency to import leaf tobacco from abroad. JTI imports leaf tobacco on the basis of commercial considerations and, in purchasing, it takes into consideration demand and supply of manufactured tobacco as well as quality, market prices, and other relevant features of the product. Prior to the purchase of domestic leaf tobacco, JTI annually enters into contracts with domestic tobacco cultivators concerning the acreage of cultivation for each kind of leaf tobacco and price thereof.

Salt

The production, reproduction, purchase, import, and processing of salt were monopolized by JTI under the Salt Monopoly Law.[12] However, in April 1997, the monopoly was abolished, and the liberalization took place.[13]

Opium[14]

Under Article 2 of the Opium Law, opium trade is carried out exclusively by the Ministry of Health and Welfare (MHW), although this authority can be delegated to private persons. MHW not only imports opium exclusively, it also purchases all the opium produced in Japan. The objective of this exclusive authority given to MHW is to regulate the supply of opium for medical and scientific purposes and, at the same time, to exercise necessary control over the cultivation of opium poppy and over the transfer, obtainment, and possession of opium and poppy straw. Use of opium other than in the ways designated by the government is prohibited and, in this sense, the monopoly of opium trade by the government is primarily for the purpose of keeping public order. The Opium Law is an instrument to implement the Single Convention on Narcotic Drugs of 1961.[15]

The Ministry of Health and Welfare determines quantity of opium to be imported to Japan based on demand and supply of opium. MHW, in consultation with the Ministry of Finance, determines the purchase prices for opium offered by domestic planters based on production conditions of opium poppy planters, import prices of opium, and other economic conditions. MHW imports opium at market prices.

Alcohol[16]

Under Article 4 of the Alcohol Monopoly Law, MITI holds a monopoly over trade of alcohol with a strength of ninety percent by volume or higher. The purpose of this monopoly is to separate the distribution of industrial alcohol from that of liquor and to regulate the production and sale of industrial alcohol.

MITI (or agents entrusted by MITI) imports alcohol at market prices on the basis of demand and supply situations. All imported alcohol is redistilled by the New Energy and Industrial Technology Development Organization (NEDO) or private factories commissioned by MITI.

Alcohol is produced by NEDO and private factories entrusted by MITI. The amount of production is determined by MITI on the basis of demand and supply situations. MITI purchases all the alcohol domestically, and fixes prices on the basis of production costs and other economic conditions.

Rice, Wheat, and Barley[17]

This is undoubtedly the most important area of state trading that exists in Japan today. The Food Agency, part of the Japanese government, has exclusive authority to import rice, wheat, and barley. Private enterprises can import these items if they obtain licences from the government.

The Food Agency is in charge of stabilizing domestic demand and supply situations with regard to rice, wheat, and barley. It is also responsible for stabilizing prices for staple foods including rice, wheat, and barley. Among the three items, rice is the most important because it is the basic staple food for the Japanese. Therefore, our discussion focuses on rice.[18]

The system of control is rather complicated. The law in point is the Law for Stabilization of Supply-Demand and Price of Staple Food (the Staple Food Law), promulgated in December 1994. This law authorizes the government (the Ministry of Agriculture, Forestry and Fisheries) to promulgate "the basic plan" for each year in which it formulates the forecast of demand and supply, the target production amount, and related matters with respect to production adjustment and the amount of purchase by the government. Secondly, the law obligates the government to keep a stockpile of rice for emergencies and the imported rice is generally used for this purpose.

The government carries out the policy of production control. Although the government does not exert legal control over production of rice, producers are encouraged to observe the production line established by the government. Only those producers who comply with the production line established by the government can sell rice to the government.

Rice is categorized into "rice in the planned distribution" and "rice outside the planned distribution", and the former is subdivided into "government rice" and "privately distributed rice". Government rice is that owned by the government. The government sells the rice to registered distributors, who in turn sell it to registered retailers, and consumers purchase the rice from them. In privately distributed rice, private enterprises are basically the instruments for distribution. However, distribution is carried out through registered distributors and retailers. Therefore, in this category, producers sell the rice to registered distributors, who in turn sell it to registered retailers, and consumers purchase the rice from them. With regard to rice outside the planned distribution, producers sell rice to consumers through whatever channels they prefer, although producers and sellers must file reports with the government.

As part of its measures to stabilize demand and supply as well as price, the Food Agency imports and exports rice exclusively, although private enterprises can import rice upon being granted licences by the government. The relevant legal provisions are Articles 60, 62, 63, 67, and 69 of the Staple Food Law. The Food Agency imports rice under the minimum access opportunities provided in the WTO Agreement on Agriculture.

The government sales prices for imported rice are determined on the basis of such factors as import prices, administrative costs, consumer prices of milled rice and other economic conditions. The government sales prices for imported rice should not be above the sum of the respective government purchase prices.

Milk Products[19]

The Agriculture and Livestock Industries Corporation (ALIC)[20] is authorized to import designated dairy products for general use (skimmed milk powder, skimmed milk solids, milk powder and other solids, condensed milk, buttermilk powder and other solids, whey and modified whey, butter, and butter oil). Pursuant to the provisions of the Manufacturing Milk Producers Compensation Temporary Law, ALIC is empowered to take measures to stabilize supply and demand situations of milk products and prices thereof. As part of such measures, under Article 13 of the above-mentioned law, ALIC imports designated dairy products to ensure the smooth operation of the supply-demand and price stabilization system for milk products.

The ALIC deals with in-quota imports of designated dairy products established in Japan's Uruguay Round tariff schedule (Schedule XXXVIII). However, ALIC is not engaged in the marketing or distribution of over-quota imports of designated dairy products, except to collect part of the over-quota tariffs and to inspect the quantity, quality, and safety of such imports. Private enterprises can freely import designated dairy products subject to over-quota tariffs established in Schedule XXXVIII, which will be reduced by fifteen percent over the six-year period between 1995 and 2000. ALIC imports designated dairy products under the current access opportunities established in Schedule XXXVIII.

Domestic sales prices for designated products are determined on the basis of such factors as import prices, administrative costs, domestic prices for dairy products, and other economic conditions. Domestic sales prices for designated dairy products should not be above the sum of the respective ALIC purchase prices and the mark-ups bound in Schedule XXXVIII.

Raw Silk[21]

ALIC also controls the supply and demand, as well as the prices, of raw silk.[22] ALIC is authorized to take measures to stabilize supply and demand situations of raw silk and silk-worm cocoons and the prices thereof under Article 12-6 of the Cocoon and Raw Silk Price Stabilization Law. As part of such measures, ALIC is authorized to import raw silk exclusively to ensure a smooth operation of the supply-demand and price stabilization system for raw silk.

ALIC exclusively imports raw silk within the tariff-rate quota established in Schedule XXXVIII. However, ALIC is not engaged in the marketing or distribution of over-quota imports of raw silk, except to collect part of over-quota tariffs and to inspect the quantity, quality, and safety of such imports. Private enterprises can import raw silk subject to over-quota tariffs established in Schedule XXXVIII. ALIC imports raw silk under the current access opportunities established in that Schedule.

Domestic sales prices for imported raw silk are determined on the basis of factors such as import prices, administrative costs, domestic prices for raw silk, and other economic conditions.

Future of State Trading Agencies in Japan

As observed above, the majority of state trading agencies in Japan operate in the agricultural sector. As mentioned earlier, deregulation is an important aspect of the economic reforms envisaged in Japan and the agricultural sector lags behind other sectors in the progress of deregulation. However, a criticism has been raised against "over-protection" in the agricultural sector, arguing that it has caused high price levels in this sector. Price stabilization programmes exercised in some areas, as above mentioned, will be gradually phased out and, in the long run, state trading agencies in this sector will also be phased out.

4. The GATT and State Trading in Agriculture: *Twelve Agricultural Items* Case

Outline of the Case

Article XI:1 of the General Agreement on Tariffs and Trade (GATT) provides that contracting parties shall not impose quantitative restrictions on imports with an exception in Article XI:2(c) that allows the imposition of quantitative restrictions under certain conditions. In 1986, the United States filed a complaint with the GATT claiming that the restrictions imposed on twelve agricultural items by the Japanese government were contrary to the provisions of the GATT.[23] The items in question were as follows:

(i) milk and cream, preserved, concentrated, or sweetened;

(ii) processed cheese;

(iii) dried leguminous vegetables;

(iv) starch and insulin;

(v) groundnuts;

(vi) meat of bovine animals, prepared or preserved in airtight containers;

(vii) other sugars and syrups not containing added flavouring or colouring;

(viii) fruit puree and pastes;

(ix) fruit pulp and pineapple, prepared or preserved;

(x) fruit and vegetable juices, excluding certain juices;

(xi) tomato ketchup and sauce; and

(xii) food preparations not elsewhere specified (excluding preparations of rice and seaweed).

Import quotas were set with respect to these items under Article 52 of the Foreign Exchange and Foreign Trade Control Law and the Import Control Order and the Import Control Regulations which implemented this law. Import quota levels varied from item to item, and on some items the quota level was set at zero.

The GATT established a panel to examine the question as to whether or not those restrictions were contrary to the relevant provisions of the GATT as claimed by the United States.[24] The Panel came to the conclusion that most of such restrictions were contrary to the provisions of the GATT.[25]

Among the above items, dairy products and beef products were state trading items. The Japanese government claimed that import restrictions exercised through state trading agencies were outside the scope of Article XI of the GATT. The Panel ruled on this issue that such restrictions were banned under Article XI. In the following pages, legal issues with regard to these items will be taken up.

Dairy Products[26]

State trading of dairy products was closely related to the domestic price support programme of the products. The Law concerning Temporary Measures on Deficiency Payments for Manufacturing Milk Products (1965) provided for a "deficiency payment" to eligible producers of manufacturing milk. The Ministry of Agriculture, Forestry and Fisheries (MAFF) provided the funds for the deficiency payment to LIPC[27], which made the payment through the prefectural designated milk producers' organizations to individual farmers based on the use for which the raw milk was sold. The amount of deficiency payment was equal to that between the "guaranteed price" and the "standard trading price" of the milk used for manufacturing the specified milk products (butter, skimmed milk powder, sweetened condensed whole milk, sweetened condensed skimmed milk, whole milk powder, sweetened milk powder, evaporated milk, and skimmed milk for calf feed).

Both "guaranteed price" and the "standard trading practice" were set by MAFF to guarantee a certain level of income to farmers producing the above products.

The "designated products" (butter, sweetened condensed whole milk, sweetened condensed skimmed milk, and skimmed milk powder) were subject to a price stabilization programme. LIPC conducted the buying and selling operations of these products in order to ensure stable prices at the "stabilization indicative price levels" established by MAFF. When the prices of these products exceeded or were likely to exceed the set levels, LIPC had the exclusive right to import and sell these products and others (whole milk powder, whey powder, buttermilk powder) under state trading procedures. However, imports of skimmed milk powder for stockfeed or school lunch programmes, as well as whey powder for feed use, could be imported by traders other than LIPC within the import quota system.

Beef Products[28]

The Law concerning Price Stabilization of Livestock Products provided for a price stabilization scheme for beef. The price stabilization system with regard to beef was operated by LIPC, which purchased domestic beef at central wholesale markets whenever the price of beef fell or was likely to fall below the minimum stabilization price and sold domestic and imported beef whenever the price exceeded the minimum stabilization price. LIPC also sold beef to the market when the price of beef was within the stabilization range.

LIPC maintained monopoly rights, based on the Livestock Products Price Stabilization Law, to import beef although some categories of beef and beef products could have been imported by users and traders.

The Relevant GATT Provisions

Some of the major GATT provisions relevant to this case are as follows:

Note Ad Articles XI, XII, XIII, XIV and XVIII

Throughout Articles XI, XII, XIII, XIV and XVIII, the terms "import restrictions" or "export restrictions" include restrictions made effective through state-trading operations.

Article II

4. If any contracting party establishes, maintains or authorizes, formally or in effect, a monopoly of the importation of any product described in the appropriate Schedule annexed to this Agreement, such monopoly shall not, except as provided for in that Schedule or as otherwise agreed between the parties which initially negotiated the concession, operate so as to afford protection on the average in excess of the amount of protection provided for in that Schedule. . . .

Article XX

Subject to the requirement that such measures are not applied in a manner which would constitute a means of arbitrary or unjustifiable discrimination between countries where the same conditions prevail, or a disguised restriction on international trade, nothing in this Agreement shall be construed to prevent the adoption or enforcement by any contracting party of measures: . . . ;

(d) necessary to secure compliance with laws or regulations which are not inconsistent with the provisions of this Agreement, including those relating to customs enforcement, the enforcement of monopolies operated under paragraph 4 of Article II and Article XVII. . . .

The Panel Report

On 22 March 1988, the Contracting Parties to the GATT adopted the panel report on the above case. We will touch on the aspects of the panel report which deal with state trading issues.

Japan argued before the panel that Article XI:1 of the GATT did not apply to import restrictions made effective through an import monopoly for the reason that the drafters of the Havana Charter intended to deal with the issue of trade restrictions by import monopolies through a provision under which a monopoly of the importation of any product for which a concession had been negotiated would have "to import and offer for sale such quantities of the product as will be sufficient to satisfy the full domestic demand for the imported product" (Article 31:5 of the Havana Charter). That the provision was not incorporated into the GATT, and that quantitative restrictions made effective through import monopolies, could therefore not be considered to be covered by Article XI:1 of the GATT.[29]

The panel stated that Article XI:1 covered restrictions on the importation of any product, "whether made effective through quotas, import . . . licences or other measures". The wording of this provision was comprehensive, thus comprising restrictions made effective through an import monopoly. According to the panel, this was confirmed by the Note to Articles XI, XII, XIII, XIV and XVIII, according to which the term "import restrictions" throughout these articles covers restrictions made effective through state trading operations. The basic purpose of this note is to extend to state trading the rules of the GATT governing private trade and to ensure that the contracting parties cannot escape their obligations with respect to private trade by establishing state trading operations. This purpose would be frustrated if import restrictions were considered to be consistent with Article XI:1 simply because they were made effective through import monopolies.[30]

The panel also mentioned that the Note to Article II:4 of the GATT specified that that provision "will be applied in the light of the provisions of Article 31 of the Havana Charter". It stated that the obligation of a monopoly importing a product for which a concession had been granted "to import and offer for sale such quantities of the product as will be sufficient to satisfy the full domestic demand for the imported product" was thus part of the GATT. For these reasons, the panel found that the import restrictions applied by Japan fell under Article XI regardless of whether they were made effective through quotas or through import monopoly operations.[31]

Another argument raised by Japan was that import restrictions made effective through state trading operations could be justified under Article XX(d) of the GATT. The panel noted that Article XX(d) permits measures necessary to the enforcement of monopolies. Article XX(d) therefore permits measures necessary to enforce the exclusive possession of the trade by the monopoly, such as measures limiting private imports that would undermine the control of the trade by the monopoly. However, Article XX(d) permits only measures necessary to secure compliance with those laws and regulations which are not inconsistent with the provisions of the GATT. Article XX(d) does not permit contracting parties to operate monopolies inconsistently with the other provisions of the GATT. The GATT contains detailed rules designed to preclude protective and discriminatory practices by import monopolies (cf. in particular Article II:4, the Note to Articles XI, XII, XIII, XIV and XVIII, and Article XVIII). These rules would become meaningless if Article XX(d) were interpreted to exempt from the obligations under the General Agreement protective or discriminatory trading practices by such monopolies. The Panel found that the enforcement of laws or regulations providing for an import restriction made effective through an import monopoly inconsistent with Article XI:1 was not covered by Article XX(d).[32]

Comments On the Case

This panel report is significant for the reason that it recognized that the prohibition on import restrictions under Article XI:1 covers import restrictions made effective through state trading agencies. The panel report drew this conclusion largely from the textual analysis. It is to be noted that the achievement of free trade through the prohibition of import restrictions under Article XI:1 would be easily circumvented if activities of state trading agencies were exempted from the ban on import restrictions under Article XI:1. Although operations of state trading agencies are permitted under the GATT/WTO system, they inevitably involve some restrictions of trade, and their operations should be made as close to those of private enterprises as possible and their distorting effect should be kept to a minimum.

5. The GATT/WTO and State Trading Operations in Japanese Constitutional Law – the *Kyoto Necktie* Case

The *Kyoto Necktie* Decision[33] handed down in 1990 is the only Supreme Court decision which deals with the relationship between the GATT and domestic laws which come into conflict with it. Also involved in this case is the status of a state trading agency when the law on which it is based is held to be contrary to the GATT. Although the conclusion drawn by decisions of courts in this case is somewhat inconclusive, there are some findings that shed some light on this issue. An analysis of this case follows.

The Issues Involved

There are three decisions with regard to the *Kyoto Necktie* case: the decision of the Kyoto District Court[34]; that of the Osaka High Court[35]; and that of the Supreme Court. Parts of this case dealing with the freedom of trade has been already touched upon.[36]

Once Japan was the major producer and exporter of raw silk. However, in recent decades, Japanese farmers who produce raw silk have lost their international competitiveness due to their rising costs of production vis-à-vis producers in neighbouring countries, especially Korea and the Peoples' Republic of China.

To deal with this difficulty, the National Diet enacted a law entitled the Cocoon and Silk Price Stabilization Law which established the price stabilization programme. Under this law and the relevant regulations, the government was authorized to set up the price range with upper and lower price limits within which the domestic price of raw silk should stay. When the market price went above the upper limit, the Silk Agency[37] sold raw silk from the stockpile it held and made it come down within this price range. If the price of raw silk went below the lower limit, the Agency purchased raw silk to make the price go up above the lower limit. In this way, the price was manipulated to stay within this price range.

As stated above, under the stabilization programme, the government was authorized to engage in either selling operations or buying operations, depending on the situation. In reality, however, the problem with which silk growers in Japan were faced was that of over-production and a falling price. Therefore, the main function of the Agency was to engage in purchase of raw silk to support the market price in Japan.

In the above situation, if low-priced foreign silk had been allowed to enter the Japanese market freely, then the price stabilization programme under the Cocoon and Silk Price Stabilization Law would have been disrupted, since the low-priced foreign silk would have pushed down the domestic price below the lower limit even though the agency bought up domestically produced raw silk.

An amendment was made to the Cocoon and Silk Price Stabilization Law in which the Silk Agency was given the exclusive authority to import raw silk from abroad. Under the Law, the Agency imported raw silk from abroad, but was prohibited from selling it in the domestic market when the domestic price was below the price range described above. When it sold imported silk in the domestic market, it had to sell it at the price within the price band determined by the Minister of Agriculture, Forestry and Fisheries.

Due to this price stabilization programme, the exclusive importing of foreign-produced silk by the Agency, and also the restricted price at which imported silk was sold, the price of raw silk in Japan was much higher than the international price of this product. Japanese producers of neckties in the Kyoto area had to use fabrics made of this high-priced silk. In Europe there was no protective measure for raw silk production, and imports of raw silk were freely accepted. Thus the price of raw silk in Europe was much lower than that in Japan. Producers in Korea and the Mainland China exported raw silk to the European countries. European necktie producers produced ties using fabrics made of inexpensive raw silk and they exported ties to Japan. Even though a seventeen percent *ad valorem* duty was imposed on imported ties in Japan, due to the differences in costs, Japanese tie producers had difficulty in competing with imported ties from Europe.

The producers in the Kyoto area brought a legal action in the Kyoto District Court against the government claiming that their interests were adversely affected by the restriction of imports and the high price of raw silk. They maintained that this government measure protected silk growers but sacrificed tie producers, unreasonably restricted the right of tie producers to import silk freely from abroad, and violated Article 22(1) of the Constitution. This aspect has been touched upon already.

The plaintiffs also alleged that the measure was in violation of Article II:4 of the GATT, which stipulated that whenever a tariff concession under the GATT had been made of a commodity which was an object of state trading, a contracting party shall not sell the commodity in the domestic market at a price which was above the actual import price plus the import duty, i.e., charge a price in excess of costs plus a reasonable margin of profit. They also alleged a violation of Article XVII of the GATT, which required that state trading agencies operate solely in accordance with commercial considerations including price, quality, and availability.[38] Their argument was that the Silk Agency was required by law to sell imported raw silk at a price which was artificially determined by the government and this was contrary to the cited provisions of the GATT and, since the GATT had been ratified by the National Diet as a treaty[39], it should override a conflicting law under Article 98(2) of the Constitution[40].

The Decisions of the Kyoto District Court and the Osaka High Court

The Kyoto District Court held that the tariff imposed on imported ties protected the domestic producers of ties, that the government could invoke Article XIX of the GATT and take safeguard measures if the condition of Japanese tie producers has seriously deteriorated, and that therefore, the plaintiff had not been disproportionately disadvantaged by the governmental protection of silk growers.

With regard to the compatibility of the exclusive import system under the amended Cocoon and Silk Price Stabilization Law with the GATT, the court rejected the arguments by the plaintiffs and upheld the validity of the law and the measure. The court stated that the exclusive importership and the price stabilization system in this case were designed to protect raw silk producers from the pressure of imports for a while, and that this had the same effect as the emergency measures permitted under Article XIX of the GATT. Thus, the court said, although there should be a limit to the duration period for the exclusive importership (based on the nature of an emergency measure), such a limit should be determined flexibly, depending on the situation. Since this duration period should be decided in relation to the duration of the pressure from the imports, the provisions of the law for the exclusive importership could not be regarded as unreasonable.

As above, the court argued that the exclusive importership was not incompatible with the GATT as an emergency measure which would be permitted under Article XIX of the GATT. As long as the exclusive importership was lawful under the GATT, it was not necessary for the court to decide the effectiveness of the Cocoon and Silk Price Stabilization Law and the exclusive importership of raw silk as under domestic law. However, the court went on to state its position on this matter in the form of *obiter dicta*.

The court stated that a violation of a provision of the GATT had the impact on the violating country in the way that it would pressure the country to rectify the violation by being confronted with a request from another member country for consultation and retaliatory measures to be taken. However, it further stated that it would have no more effect than that. Therefore, it would not necessarily follow that the legislation in question was invalid as a domestic law simply because it was contrary to the GATT.

The case was appealed to the Osaka High Court, which handed down a decision on 25 November 1986. With regard to the issue of whether the exclusive importership in question was contrary to the freedom of business activities as guaranteed under Article 22(1) of the Constitution, the court upheld its compatibility simply by reiterating the doctrine pronounced by the Supreme Court in the previous cases. As to the issue of compatibility of the exclusive importership with the GATT and the validity of the Cocoon and Silk Price Stabilization Law, the Osaka High Court distorted the issue. It stated that the appellants argued that the sales price of imported raw silk was contrary to Articles II:4 and XVII of the GATT and that the sales price was determined by the Silk Agency on the basis of the standard price established by the Minister of Agriculture. The court held that the argument of the appellants was nothing but using the action of the Silk Agency as the basis for the illegality of legislation and, therefore, was wrong.

The Decision of the Supreme Court

An appeal was taken by the petitioners to the Supreme Court. The petitioners presented a detailed petition. As its contents are relevant to our discussion, an account of the part of the petition which deals with the relationship between the Cocoon and Silk Price Stabilization Law and the GATT is made here.

a. Under Article II:4 of the GATT, the petitioners argued, a state trading agency should not sell imported products in the domestic market at a price above the import price plus the amount of duty and other expenses and a reasonable margin of profit when the imported product is subject to tariff concession under the GATT. Also, under Article XVII:1 of the GATT, each contracting party promises to engage its state trading agencies to operate solely in accordance with commercial considerations. The exclusive importership is established under Articles 12-13-2 and 12-13-3 of the Cocoon and Silk Price Stabilization Law. These provisions of the law are contrary to Articles II:4 and XVII:1 of the GATT and the enactment of those provisions are illegal in that the Diet passed provisions of law which violate the GATT. The petitioners argue that damage has been caused by this illegal legislation and do not argue that the actions of the Silk Agency are contrary to the GATT.

b. The Osaka High Court, however, was mistaken in understanding this legal issue and decided the matter on a wrong basis. If the arguments of the petitioners in the Kyoto District Court had been unclear, then the Osaka High Court should have used its power for requesting an explanation of the meaning and should have come up with a correct understanding of the issue.

c. The Osaka High Court did not touch upon the question of whether the exclusive importership and the price stabilization programme violated Articles II:4 and XVII:1 of the GATT or whether the measures taken pursuant to the relevant provisions of the Cocoon and Silk Price Stabilization Law amounted to a safeguard measure as permitted under Article XIX of the GATT. Article XIX permits a safeguard measure when there is an increase of imports as a result of unforeseen developments. However, in this case, an increase in the imports of raw silk from abroad had long been anticipated and, therefore, the measures do not satisfy the requirements of Article XIX.

d. Article XIX permits a safeguard measure to the extent and for such time as may be necessary to prevent or remedy serious injury to domestic producers. However, the exclusive importership provides for excessive protection to domestic growers of raw silk and a permanent system for import control. Therefore, such measures cannot be permitted under Article XIX of the GATT.

e. The decision of the Kyoto District Court states that the effect of a violation of a GATT provision is simply that the violating country would be faced with a request for consultation under Article XXIII of the GATT or with a retaliatory measure and there is no more legal effect than this. However, in the view of the petitioners, the existence of measures designed to guarantee the effectiveness of treaty observance is an entirely separate issue from the validity of a domestic stature in violation of the GATT and, therefore, cannot provide the ground for holding that a domestic law in violation of the GATT is valid.

The Supreme Court handed down a decision in this case on 6 February 1990. The decision consisted of only twenty-five lines and said very little. The Supreme Court briefly touched on the constitutionality of the exclusive importership under the Cocoon and Silk Price Stabilization Law, cited the relevant previous decisions by the Supreme Court and noted that, in view of the precedents, the judgment as to whether domestic silk growers should be protected belonged to the realm of legislative discretion, which should not be lightly interfered with by courts. The Court then said that the decision by the National Diet to protect domestic silk growers by means of the price stabilization programme and the exclusive importership could not be legally challenged unless the law provided protection to one group and an undue detriment to other members of the society, or the means for achieving the legislative objective was unreasonable. For this reason, the Supreme Court upheld the decisions of the lower courts.

With regard to the issue of whether or not the exclusive importership and the price stabilization programme violated the articles of the GATT and, for this reason, was invalid, the Supreme Court merely stated:

In light of the reasoning given by the original court, the judgment of the original court can be approved. Therefore, there is no illegality in the decision as claimed by the petitioners.

An Evaluation of the *Kyoto Necktie* Case

There is a wide gap between the legal doctrine with regard to the superiority of treaties over conflicting domestic laws propounded by commentators and some court decisions on the one hand and the consequences for the decisions which dealt with this relationship on the other.[41] In brief, treaties are given a very high status in the Japanese legal order, but courts have never actually nullified domestic laws on account of their incompatibility with treaties.

The only court case in which this issue was squarely dealt with is the *Kyoto Necktie* Case. In this case, the Kyoto District Court recognized that there was a possibility for conflict between the treaty obligation under the GATT and the domestic regulation incorporated in the Cocoon and Silk Price Stabilization Law. After examining issues, the court held that there was no conflict between the articles of the GATT and the provisions of the law. One of the reasonings given by the court for holding that the exclusive importership and the price stabilization programme did not violate Articles II:4 and XVII:1 of the GATT was that the import measures in question could be justified under Article XIX of the GATT, which recognizes the right of contracting parties to use import quotas and other measures temporarily and with compensations to other contracting parties when an increase of imports is causing serious injury to the domestic industry producing like or directly competitive products.

The reasoning of the Kyoto District Court in this regard is hardly persuasive. Whereas Article XIX of the GATT requires that there be a serious injury to the domestic industry, that relief measures be temporary, and that compensation be granted to other contracting parties, the measures provided in the Cocoon and Silk Price Stabilization Law neither requires serious injury to be found nor contains any procedures for determining serious injury. The exclusive importership under the Cocoon and Silk Price Stabilization Law is to last "for a while" under the terms of the law but, in actuality, it has lasted since its enactment (seventeen years) and there is no prospect that it will be lifted.[42] This would hardly satisfy the requirement that the relief be temporary. Furthermore, there is no provision for compensation. The Supreme Court could have taken a close look at this issue and could have stated its legal position with regard to this issue.

The Kyoto District Court further stated that the provisions in the Cocoon and Silk Price Stabilization Law for the exclusive importership and the price stabilization programme would not be denied the validity as domestic law for the reason that they were incompatible with the provisions of the GATT had that been the case. The reasons given by the Kyoto District Court are that the GATT provided in Article XXIII for actions to be taken against violations of its provisions, that the violating party would be confronted with the possibility of consultation or retaliation, and that these remedial measures available in the GATT should have been sought by recourse to its dispute settlement mechanism.

As argued by the petitioners, however, the simple fact that the GATT provides for the dispute settlement process does not mean that there should be no remedy in the domestic legal order if a domestic law is in violation of the GATT and a party is suffering from the violation. Private parties cannot have recourse to the dispute settlement process as provided in Article XXIII of the GATT — it is only the government of a contracting party that can make use of this process. Viewed in this way, the rationale used by the Kyoto District Court for denying the relief to the plaintiffs (i.e., that the remedy provided in Article XXIII of the GATT for violations of GATT provisions precludes other relief in domestic law) is hardly persuasive since the plaintiffs, who are private parties, could not have utilized the procedure under Article XXIII of the GATT. Also, in this case, it was the Japanese government which imposed the restrictions on imports which were allegedly in violation of the GATT and, therefore, the plaintiffs could not have petitioned the Japanese government to invoke the dispute settlement procedure under Article XXIII of the GATT. In any event, the Japanese government is not obligated to bring a claim under Article XXIII of the GATT even if private parties had petitioned the government to that effect.

As stated earlier, Article 98(2) of the Constitution provides for the supremacy of treaties over domestic laws. Also, as some commentators argue, it follows logically that the National Diet is obligated not to pass laws that contravene treaties and that if the National Diet did enact a law which violates a treaty, the domestic law should be overridden by the treaty.[43]

It may be observed that this high constitutional status of treaties may have had the paradoxical effect of inhibiting courts from closely examining the relationship between treaties and domestic laws when they come into conflict and declaring the domestic laws as invalid. To do so may have serious political consequences. For example, if the Supreme Court decided that a law setting up import quotas on certain agricultural products (for instance, rice) was in violation of Article XI of the GATT and, for this reason null and void, then all the laws and regulations which establish similar quotas or restrictions might have to be held invalid as a matter of domestic law in Japan. Even though this may be a desirable consequence in the long-run, the political impacts of such a decision are far-reaching and will produce strong reactions from interest groups at least in the short-run. Yet the Supreme Court and lower courts might have no choice but to hold that a domestic law in violation of the GATT or other international trade agreements was null and void under Article 98(2) of the Constitution. The only alternative then is to avoid the issue.

As noted earlier, there are some court decisions which affirmed the supremacy of treaties over domestic laws in Japan, but those statements were made as *dicta* and in situations in which the courts did not have to strike down the domestic laws in question. The Kyoto District Court did squarely face the question of whether or not a domestic law was in violation of the GATT and, if so, whether the domestic law should be held invalid. The Kyoto District Court decided negatively to those questions, but with dubious reasonings. As we saw, the Osaka High Court distorted the issue and, in effect, avoided facing the above stated questions. The Supreme Court simply did not take up the question.

As we have seen, the petitioners in the *Kyoto Necktie* Case brought forth detailed arguments as to the relationship between the GATT and the exclusive importership and the price stabilization programme under the Cocoon and Silk Price Stabilization Law and distinguished the legal points they wished to bring up from the decision of the Osaka High Court. From just reading the briefs of the petitioners, it seems clear that the petitioners clarified their positions with regard to this issue. In light of this, it is quite strange that the Supreme Court dismissed the argument of the petitioners simply by declaring that there was no fault in the decision of the Osaka High Court. A possible interpretation concerning this attitude of the Supreme Court is that the Supreme Court did not wish to take up this issue and wished to avoid answering the questions as to whether the provisions of the Cocoon and Silk Price Stabilization Law were in violation of the GATT and, if so, what domestic law effects such provisions might have.

6. Conclusion

As stated earlier, the state trading system in Japan is under review in the context of deregulation of the economy. Although it is difficult to predict the future role of state trading agencies in Japan, it is foreseeable that their role will be decreased. This will be true especially in agriculture, with its inefficiency and high prices. It is true also that, in view of a food crisis which may come in some decades, the viability of this system may resurface.

NOTES

1. See, for instance, Economic Planning Agency, "Economy-wide Effects of Structural Reforms in Japan: FY1998–2003" (5 June 1997) (http://www.epa.go.jp).

2. Prime Minister Hashimoto has repeatedly stressed that he will devote himself to the Six Reforms (Administrative Reform; Fiscal Structural Reform; Reform of the Social Security System; Economic Structural Reform; Financial System Reform; and Educational Reform). See various speeches and statements at the Prime Minister's Official Home Page (http://www.kantei.go.jp). See also World Trade Organization, *Trade Policy Review Japan Report by the Secretariat* 85 (Geneva: WTO, 1998). Opposition parties have even bolder proposals for economic reform.

3. The text of Article 22(1) of the Constitution states "Every person shall have freedom to choose and change his residence and to choose his occupation to the extent that it does not interfere with the public welfare".

4. Judgment of 8 July 1969, Tokyo District Court, 20 Gyosai Reishu 842.

5. Judgment of 20 January 1989, Supreme Court, 43 Keishu 1.

6. Judgment of 30 April 1975, Supreme Court (Grand Bench), 29 Minshu 572.

7. Judgment of 22 November 1972, Supreme Court (Grand Bench), 26 Keishu 586.

8. Judgment of 6 February 1990, Supreme Court, 36 Shomu Geppo 2242.

9. See footnote 21, *infra*.

10. Id.

11. WTO document G/STR/N/1/JPN, 22 August 1995, Section A.

12. Id. Section B.

13. WTO document G/STR/N/3/JPN, 13 November 1997.

14. G/STR/N/1/JPN, op. cit., Section C.

15. 520 UNTS 151.

16. G/STR/N/1/JPN, op. cit., Section D.

17. Id., Section E.

18. For general discussion of the rice issue in Japan today, see the Trade Policy Review Report (1988), op. cit., 99–102.

19. G/STR/N/1/JPN, op. cit., Section F.

20. Formerly the Livestock Industry Promotion Corporation (LIPC). The LIPC and the Japan Raw Silk and Sugar Price Stabilization Agency (the Silk Agency) were merged into one organization called the Agricultural and Livestock Industry Corporation as of 1 October 1996. WTO document G/STR/N/2/JPN, 30 October 1996.

21. G/STR/N/1/JPN, op. cit., Section G. See also Section 5 *infra*.

22. See footnote 20 *supra*.

23. GATT document L/6037.

24. Panel established on 27 October 1986 (C/M/202).

25. Japan - Restrictions on Imports of Certain Agricultural Products, BISD 35S/163 (1988).

26. Id., paras. 2.2.1 to 2.2.4.

27. See footnote 20, *supra*.

28. Panel Report on Twelve Agricultural Items, op. cit., paras. 2.6.1–2.6.2.

29. Id., para. 3.3.3.

30. Id., para. 5.2.2.2.

31. Id.

32. Id., para. 5.2.2.3.

33. See footnote 9, *supra*.

34. Judgment of 29 June 1984, Kyoto District Court, 31 Shomu Geppo 207.

35. Judgment of 25 November 1986, Osaka High Court, 634 Hanta 186.

36. Section 2, *supra*.

37. See footnote 20, *supra*.

38. See generally William J. Davey, "Article XVII GATT: An Overview," in this volume.

39. To be exact, only the Protocol of Terms of Accession of Japan to the General Agreement on Tariffs and Trade was approved by the Diet. It was promulgated on 10 September 1955 as Treaty No. 13 of 1955.

40. The text of Article 98(2) of the Constitution reads as follows:

> The treaties concluded by Japan and established laws of nations shall be faithfully observed.

41. See generally Yuji Iwasawa, "Constitutional Problems Involved in Implementing the Uruguay Round in Japan" in: J. Jackson & A. Sykes, eds., *Implementing the Uruguay Round* (Oxford: Clarendon Press, 1997).

42. The law was amended in 1994 to implement Japan's Uruguay Round commitments on tariff rate quotas. However, as noted above, the exclusive importership is retained for the in-quota trade. See Section 3, *supra*.

43. See, e.g., literature cited in Iwasawa "Constitutional Problems," op. cit., 157.

CHAPTER 13

Privatisation in the OECD Area: The Main Issues and Lessons

*Stilpon Nestor**

1. The General Context

During the last fifteen years, a major process of redefining the role of the state has been under way in many countries, among them major economies that are members of the Organisation of Economic Cooperation and Development (OECD). Privatisation is the central component of this process; deregulation of markets is another. As a result, the state's role as supplier of goods and (especially) services in the economy has been consistently diminishing and competition among private agents has been increasing.

During the 1990s, the divestiture of state assets has gathered considerable pace in OECD economies (see chart 1 in Annex). In 1996, $68 billion were raised in OECD countries alone — out of a global figure of $88 billion. This record-breaking figure could be matched in 1997.

Privatisation in the twenty-nine OECD member countries is underpinned by a highly developed legal framework and sophisticated financial markets. This environment plays a major role in the selection of privatisation methods, procedures, and in general, the design of policies and privatisation programmes. In contrast, in transition economies of post-communist Europe and the former Soviet Union, privatisation is the backbone of a revolution taking place in a legal and structural vacuum. Hence the difficulty in directly applying lessons and experiences from developed capitalist economies to the transition context (Lieberman 1997:1).

The present paper will focus on certain elements that are of essence to making a success out of a privatisation programme. They are drawn from the experience of several OECD member countries and also of some developing market economies (like Chile and Argentina) that have long-running programmes. In fact, privatisation in these countries has been one of the major contributors to recent economic growth and financial market maturity.

---

*Head of Unit, Privatisation and Enterprise Reform, OECD. The opinions expressed in this note are the author's own and should not be attributed to the OECD.

2. The Objectives of Privatisation

Privatisation policies have multiple and often conflicting objectives (Nestor and Nigon 1996:10):

1. to change the corporate governance environment of state-owned enterprises (SOEs) by introducing incentives based on private ownership rather than on bureaucratic oversight;

2. to improve competitiveness in products and services markets and to enhance financial discipline by removing the implicit guarantee of the state (or "soft budget constraint"[1]);

3. to create a wide share-owning class and boost the role of equity markets as a means of channelling savings in the economy;

4. to create a windfall for the state budget, and to improve certain macroeconomic indicators, notably the public sector borrowing requirement.

From an efficiency perspective, the rigor of a private owner (or the capital markets, in large companies with diffused shareholdings) is far superior to a state bureaucracies. In most countries, the latter are heavily politicised and tend to exercise their governance functions towards state-owned enterprises so that they can fulfil overall political goals. This creates costs for both the companies under the tutelle and society at large; it may result in a substantial misallocation of resources within the economy. Given the fact that SOEs are often large, important, and influential companies in the economy, politicisation of their governance structures also has a negative impact on the business environment and culture of countries (Boycko et al. 1996:309): cronyism and other practices that border on (or include) corruption become the norm and a healthy and efficient market for managers does not easily emerge.

But even where the state is a benign owner, state bureaucracies have an inherent disadvantage over private owners: they are born with an "original sin". They can be correctly described as "agents without principals".[2] From the point of view of an institutional economist, state ownership is an interminable series of agents (the state appointed member of the board, the bureaucrat who oversees him/her, the minister overseeing the latter, the prime minister, the parliament who is the agent of "the people") — the residual owners vote every four years and usually pay little attention to SOE performance track record.

Contrary to small shareholders of large companies, "the people" cannot vote with their feet, i.e., sell their shares and thus influence the price of a company; they are bound to it and its costs, in their capacity as taxpayers. In this respect, corporate governance should be the primary concern of every privatisation policy. Schemes that aim to raise capital for the budget without change in governance incentives and structures in companies (for example, through the retention of substantial golden shares/majority rights or the creation of cross-shareholding and "stable cores") do not bring most of the long-term benefits of privatisation to the companies or the economy as a whole.

The goal of creating competitive markets and enhancing financial discipline suggests a break-up of huge monopolies and the establishment of a rigorous regulatory framework in natural monopoly sectors before privatisation. The U.K. has chosen this path, which is admittedly time-consuming and demanding both in resources and regulatory capacity (Beesley and Littlechild 1986:35). France, Germany, and Italy are following similar paths; they are very often urged down that road by deregulation efforts at an EU-wide level. Such is the case with the electricity and telecom markets.

On the other hand, selling public monopolies as such would certainly fetch a better price for the treasury and is thus tempting, especially in situations of budgetary contraction. Buyers are willing to pay a premium for future monopoly rents. Hungary rushed to sell a part of its electricity generation to foreign investors without a carefully, *ex ante*-established regulatory framework; Argentina did the same thing with a number of other utilities in the early 1990s. Experience has shown what economic theory had postulated, namely that this approach is very short-sighted. Efficiency gains from better governance and performance are pocketed exclusively by shareholders and do not contribute substantially to increased consumer welfare (Vickers and Yarrow 1988:35). The resulting problems of credibility towards the electorate might have a negative impact on the future of reforms. The investors are unhappy to have to face a change in the initial agreement and might even pull out or significantly alter their investment plans. In general, the costs of *ex post* remedies are often higher than the short-term rents paid to the government.

There is another concern with privatising big monopolies as such. Such companies will be "too big/important to fail". The state might thus become (or continue to be) the victim of a moral hazard situation and the political pressure that comes with it. It explicitly or implicitly guarantees the solvency of a private company, thus creating a lopsided playing field for investors and giving the wrong incentives to company managers with regard to risk. The result is a continuing misallocation of financial and productive resources and a low level of financial discipline.

Improving public finances is the most obvious privatisation objective these days. Its direct budgetary impact is rather minor since it replaces assets with cash — an operation which in principle should add little to the asset side of the state budget. It might, however, have significant indirect effects on the budget, all of them welcome in a period of macroeconomic belt-tightening. On one hand, it lowers the public sector borrowing requirement. On the other, it increases the state's tax revenues in the medium term. Some of the enterprises were previously exempt from tax or had a favourable tax regime. But even where this was not the case, the tax returns will be greater in the medium term, assuming that the enterprises will become more efficient. Finally, enterprises are freed from public sector constraints on investment. They can tap the unlimited supply of the capital markets without any impact on the state budget (Ridley 1996:151).

Chart 1. **Global amount raised from privatisation**
(US$ billion)

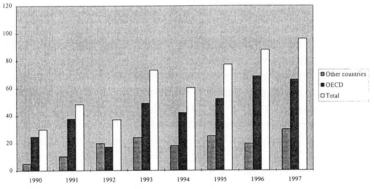

Source: OECD, Financial Market Trends, No. 66, March 1997.

3. Legal Issues

Privatisation, just like the nationalisation that preceded it in the last fifty years, is bound to alter the role of the state in the economy fundamentally. It is therefore natural that it should require the adoption of new legislation and, in certain cases, an amendment to the constitution (Graham and Prosser 1991:34).

In most market economies, the constitution does not contain precise rules for delimiting the public and private sectors. Nevertheless, certain areas of the economy might be reserved for state activity. In Germany the Basic Law had to be amended in order to allow for the privatisation of tele-communications. Mexico had to go through several constitutional amendments in the 1980s to allow for the privatisation of certain "sensitive" sectors of the economy. More importantly, the Portuguese constitution had to be changed in 1989, to allow for the privatisation of more than forty-nine percent of all nationalised firms (Nestor and Nigon 1996:12).

Privatisation has sometimes, albeit not very often, been the victim of a poor assessment of the constitutional and legislative framework by eager governments. The Turkish constitutional court has halted the process many times by overturning regulatory and legislative measures as unconstitutional. The French Conseil Constitutionel inferred general rules on enterprise valuation to be followed in privatisation from the general constitutional clause on the protection of property[3] (Carreau 1996:124).

In several countries, such as the U.K. and Portugal, transaction-specific legislation had to pass through Parliament. This can be useful for privatising a few large utilities and it also helps the cause of a proper *ex ante* regulatory framework mentioned above (Guislain 1995:127). Where, however, a large number of enterprises in the competitive/tradable goods sectors of the economy are earmarked for privatisation, a general, "framework" law might be a more flexible instrument; this was the approach in France. Such legislation usually prescribes the institutional set-up of privatisation and allows for a large degree of flexibility in the choice of methods and techniques. It will usually ensure a minimum of accountability over the process. For example, in France, the privatisation law empowers the privatisation commission to set a minimum price for the state assets to be sold (Durand 1996:99). In most countries, the state audit office has the power to review *ex post* all privatisation transactions.

Finally, various aspects of the privatisation policy might be contrary to certain supranational rules of the game, especially in the investment area. Any discriminatory provisions favouring nationals of an EC member country might fall foul of the non-discrimination clauses of the Treaty of Rome; the same might be true in the case of NAFTA (where, for example, Canada has reserved its right to discriminate in the context of the privatisation process). These problems have arisen a few times, mainly in three areas of privatisation:

1. incentives given to domestic small investors to participate in privatisation in the context of public offerings in the capital markets; most

countries have by-passed this problem by allowing incentives to all "residents", i.e., subjects of a country's capital market regulations;

2. the selection process for strategic partners in an enterprise in the context of a trade sale. This selection might favour domestic investors simply by being non-transparent to outsiders. More importantly, the creation of "stable cores" of shareholders, a method adopted by French and, as of late, Italian privatisation authorities, might indeed result in indirect discrimination by favouring local industrial and financial champions as core shareholders over foreigners. In order to address such considerations, French privatisation of the early 1990s made a point of including other (non-French) European industrial groups in the constitution of the "noyaux durs" (Graham and Prosser 1991:154); and

3. special share arrangements or "golden shares", that allow the state to maintain some control over the ownership structure, strategy, and direction of the privatised company. While in principle golden shares do not have a discriminatory character, the exercise of such rights might result in *de facto* discrimination by denying the acquisition or exercise of control in a company by foreign investors, on the basis of their nationality (Rideau 1989:226).

Neither the Treaty of Rome nor the NAFTA treaty contain specific provisions on privatisation. It is assumed that they fall under the broad obligations of national treatment and non-discrimination that are at the core of single market arrangements.[4] On the contrary, the Multilateral Agreement on Investment (MAI), currently being negotiated by the twenty-nine member countries of the OECD, envisages a special chapter to this effect. The purpose of this chapter would be to make clear that the general rules on non-discrimination and national treatment do apply in the area of privatisation; to address directly some of the thorny issues mentioned, mainly by raising transparency; and to provide some degree of flexibility by allowing discrimination in certain forms of "transitional" privatisation (such as voucher schemes) in the first stage of their implementation. It is felt that international investors might benefit from such an explicit approach by getting a better understanding of their rights in the area of privatisation.

4. Institutional Issues

The constitution of a privatisation team for every transaction from the line or sectoral ministry and/or the treasury, which will simply supervise the work of private syndicates of bankers/advisors, is an effective way to proceed where:

1. the companies to be privatised are few, large, and highly specific;

2. the public administration has developed sophisticated and efficient mechanisms of horizontal co-operation; and

3. the financial markets and financial intermediaries are well-developed.

In the absence of the above pre-conditions, i.e., where a large number of small or large enterprises in the tradable sector are envisaged for privatisation, the creation of privatisation-specific institutions might be advisable (Nestor 1997:19). These institutions can be independent agencies or government ministries with a special, clear mandate to privatise. Once privatisation of a company has been engaged, they should have the power to override other interested parties such as line ministries or the company management.

Privatisation is more than anything a political decision that might face enormous opposition by vested interests[5]: lower-level bureaucrats that want to retain their spheres of influence; public sector trade unions that want to maintain their comfortable employment conditions; SOE managers that may like the lack of competitive pressure and tight oversight of their performance. All these interests are compact and highly vocal; on the other side are the interests of the average consumer and taxpayer — not much of an organised lobby. In order for privatisation to proceed smoothly, it needs the highest level of political coverage at every stage.

Because privatisation is so political, transparency of the process is essential (Nellis 1994:1). Prizing government flexibility over transparency is a fallacious proposition that has caused the demise of many privatisation efforts. One has only to look at the recent debacle over the Thompson privatisation in France to be convinced. In striving to make a quick decision, the government disregarded due process and thus marred its credibility with important potential investors and the markets in general. A process based on closed negotiations with hand-picked investors might suit the government's direct objectives, but might also prove to be extremely vulnerable to political accusations of favouritism. Wherever possible, open tendering should be the preferred solution by governments.

Similarly, giving too much power to enterprise insiders during the process might result in reduced social welfare gains — and increased political "heat" for the government. Very often, enterprise managers might push for privatisation methods that favour a reduced corporate governance potential by the new investors to their own — but no one else's — benefit. Recent examples of such attempts to reduce the corporate governance edge of privatisation can be found in Czech bank privatisation as well as in certain Greek privatisation transactions.

5. The Main Privatisation Methods

There are a number of different privatisation methods:

1. initial public offerings (IPOs) in the capital markets;

2. trade sales to strategic investors;

3. management/employee buy-outs; and

4. asset sales, often following the liquidation of the SOE.

In OECD countries the predominant method has been that of IPOs (see chart 2 in Annex). The choice of public offerings can be easily explained (Ridley 1996:160). The main requirements for an effective use of this method are in principle met in most OECD economies: namely, deep capital markets; a few large privatisation candidates; and a sophisticated financial and legal infrastructure that facilitates such transactions.

Initial public offerings are important for additional reasons: they are the most transparent method of privatisation and they help boost equity ownership in the economy. In the U.K., share ownership more than doubled due to privatisation (U.K. Treasury 1995:14). The down-side is that IPOs are expensive and require considerable pre-privatisation restructuring of companies (both financial and operational). Nevertheless, the development of second tier stock exchanges in many OECD regions and the rapid expansion of an equity culture among savers and investors bodes well for the lowering of costs of IPOs, making them attractive for smaller privatisation candidates as well.

Initially, governments feared that IPOs might flood equity markets, i.e., that the latter would not be in a position to absorb these large amounts of fresh equity capital (OECD 1995:13). Such discussions dominated the early stages of the Deutsche Telekom privatisation. (It is one of the reasons that the initial offering was not more ambitious in size.) These fears have largely proven excessive. Capital markets have shown an impressive capacity to adapt to increased supply. In certain countries (a non-OECD country, Chile, is here the best example), privatisation has provided the basic impetus for a rapid development of collective savings and investment institutions, such as pension and insurance funds (Saez 1996:171). In countries that already had sophisticated systems of financial intermediation, privatisation has helped to shift the structure of the latter from the bank to the non-bank sectors (the process of disintermediation).

Trade sales to individual investors are more suitable where an important infusion of technical and managerial know-how is sought. Transparency, however, is more difficult to ensure in trade sales. Where companies on sale are fairly small, trade sales are the cheapest and most transparent way to privatise. In bigger companies, however, political, social, or other considerations might make a more complex tender arrangement necessary. Future investment and employment levels, an obligation to continue certain activities or specialised know-how and industrial logic requirements might render the selection process more complicated and opaque. A clear set of tendering rules is in this case very important, as is a full justification of the final choice.

Regulators (in the case of large utilities) may not like trade sales for two additional reasons: they might represent a lowering of actual or potential competition since usually the buyer is another company from the relevant industry; and the functioning of a subsidiary is usually much less transparent than that of an autonomous, widely-held, publicly-quoted company. The upside of this is that an effective owner is probably the most effective corporate governance agent and therefore, the best solution for a rapid and effective restructuring of a company. These benefits, however, should not be overestimated. Very often the buyer will simply import its own monitoring and control problems and fail to adapt in the very different (and usually not restructured) environment of the former SOE. This type of problem might be even more acute when the buyer is itself an SOE. A failure to turn around companies such as CSA and MALEV by, respectively, Air France and ALITALIA testifies to this effect.[6]

Chart 2. **Privatisations in OECD countries by type of transaction**
(US$ billion)

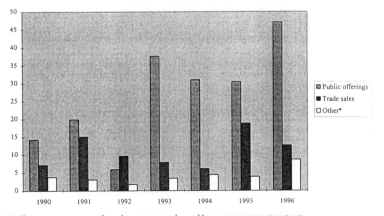

* Including management or employee buy-out, asset sales, and lease or management contracts.
Source: OECD, Financial Market Trends, No. 66, March 1997.

Management and employee buy-outs are well suited for smaller companies with low capital intensity and high human resource specificity (Wright and Robbie 1994:57). Overall, however, employee ownership and control of companies has not proven to be an efficient way of privatisation; it creates significant conflicts of interest and hence might be not conducive to restructuring in privatised companies, at least in the short- and medium-term. Moreover, employees do not seem to regard share ownership as a serious means of co-determination. While some bonus shares in the context of privatisation might be an effective way for the company to swallow the restructuring and streamlining that will come with the private owners, a controlling stake will do little to enhance competitiveness or attract further investment (Gates and Saghir 1995:7).

In many cases the sale of assets is the only way to privatise, since many SOEs have a negative present value as a going concern. In Hungary, more than 500 SOEs went through bankruptcy proceedings and in the majority of cases were liquidated. This was due to an especially tough bankruptcy law that was implemented from 1992 to 1994.[7] In reality, it was an alternate way of rapidly privatising a large part of the economy. In Poland and in Greece, special liquidation procedures were enacted, aiming to preserve some going concern value and employment; hundreds of smaller SOEs went through them in both countries.

6. Issues on the Supply Side of Privatisation

The core of any privatisation programme consists of the list of enterprises to be privatised. It is very important that these firms be identified early on and enter the privatisation "pipeline". A clear list and timetable of privatisation and its consistent implementation builds confidence in the market and therefore contributes substantially to the success of future offerings.

Creating a track record for the companies in the pipeline is the next important task of privatisers. This will usually start with the corporatisation of the enterprise, i.e., the creation of a commercial company with the state as a sole shareholder. In New Zealand, corporatisation was viewed as a very important part of the privatisation process as the enterprises (and their owner, the state) were made aware of their real cash flow and operational costs for the first time; they very often discovered that previous "profits and losses" or other yearly results were very far removed from commercial reality and that, correspondingly, their value was very different than what was previously assumed (Franks 1993:84).

During this preparatory process, the company will in some cases be broken up to create a number of independent firms. This might be the consequence of either a policy to enhance competition in the sector or simply the need to create "saleable" units. Governments have in the past lumped together firms for strategic, political, or even bureaucratic reasons, with little consideration for the efficiency results of such conglomeration. At this early stage, another important task would be to eventually separate the regulatory from commercial functions and the social assets and services from active commercial assets. The U.K. was the pioneer of this competitive restructuring process.[8] Before privatisation, a single company was the regulator, producer, and distributor of a product or service (as well as of all the ancillary services that go with it). Where it was felt that barriers to entry were high and thus, the competitive pressures very low, these sectors were broken up into smaller units with the logic that even benchmark competition between several local natural monopolies is better than a single nation-wide one, at least in terms of effective regulatory oversight. The privatisation of British Rail, for example resulted in the creation of more than thirty independent companies (or franchises) (OPRAF 1996:32).

Pre-privatisation restructuring is of paramount importance for companies that are scheduled to be floated. It is a rather lengthy process which usually starts with the appointment of a new management team with the explicit mandate to prepare the government for privatisation. The new team undertakes the operational restructuring of the company, a painful exercise that sometimes involves a considerable amount of lay-offs. It has to review and revamp the financial structure of the company, which can be expensive for the government and may raise questions of state aids (in the EC context). It also has to prepare the introduction of the company to the market with the use of advisors.

In contrast, companies slated for a trade are not usually subject to substantive pre-privatisation restructuring. The new owners are better placed to deal with making the company fit. Moreover, experience has shown that it is very difficult for the state to recuperate the full value of pre-privatisation restructuring in a trade sale (Kikeri et al. 1992:60).

In the case of floatations, most of the corporate governance gains that privatisation brings are accomplished at the pre-privatisation stage.[9] It is, therefore, extremely important that the government follows through with privatisation immediately after restructuring has produced results and the company has established a satisfactory track record. If not, the gains might prove to be temporary and the signals sent to other SOE managers are conflicting and counter-productive. The same might be true where the government, after floating an initial minority tranche, shies away from further privatisation.

Contrary to some arguments voiced by reluctant government officials, companies in good shape should be the first on the list (Galal, Jones et al. 1992:CD:1). This approach creates a positive momentum in the markets, makes the process easier for privatisation officials by allowing a smoother learning curve (i.e., mistakes are more likely to happen in tough cases), and provides for some time to prepare companies in the pipeline that are in worst shape.

7. Pricing and Demand Side Issues

As an asset class, privatisation issues do not outperform relative indices. According to a recent study (Morgan Stanley 1996), since 1984, fifty percent of all European privatisations actually underperformed the index. Governments should therefore be aware that there is no perceived inherent advantage in IPOs by the state, and should formulate their offer and pricing strategy accordingly.

In general, governments should be more concerned about the total proceeds from their privatisation programme than individual proceeds from company sales. Offerings should be perceived by the public as being successful. This means that the price development should be satisfactory in the aftermarket, and that the demand from various subscribers, retail and institutional, domestic and foreign, be balanced. The importance of a strong retail component should be underlined; this is politically helpful and creates a strong small-investor culture; it has a deepening effect on the capital markets; and it signals to the markets/institutions a commitment by the government (OECD 1997:28).

The objective of broadening the retail base has to be balanced against the goal of revenue maximisation per share. Some governments, for example the Netherlands, perceive no advantage in underpricing shares or using other incentives to increase the number of shares sold. Other countries have made extensive use of incentives to make offerings attractive to the domestic investing public. U.K. privatisations included discounts to retail investors, as have the French privatisations. In Germany, the DT privatisation included discounts and loyalty bonuses, and has developed schemes to ensure investors against future downside risk. A similar approach has been used in Spain.

The participation of international investors in privatisation has been increasing since the early 1990s (see table 3). This is important both from the narrow perspective of a better bid price and for broader reasons of attracting foreign direct and portfolio investment in the country. The fact that international institutional investors seem to have a smaller share of the pie in recent years is probably explained by the positive impact of privatisation on the development of domestic equity markets and the increasing interest of retail investors. On the other hand, and contrary to the rule in developing and transition economies, domestic direct investors are the main buyers of state assets in trade sales. This indicates the relatively limited importance of know-how and technology imports in the OECD area as a whole.

Concerns about maximising revenues but also about the absorptive capacity of the markets suggest the organisation of large issues in tranches. Tranche sales translate into residual government ownership. Residual shareholdings may allow the government to participate in potential capital gains. Governments that have a good track record of respecting the private status of companies and that refrain from intervening in their affairs, do not have to pay a premium when holding residual shareholdings and/or golden shares. That has been the experience in both the Netherlands and, more recently, Spain. When such a positive track record does not exist, the government needs to make firm commitments on the future privatisation of its residual stakes as well as on a "hands-off" approach to their management for as long as they remain in the Treasury.[10]

8. Advisors

Using private advisors both at the policy and the transaction levels is a core characteristic of all OECD privatisation programmes. Without the help of market professionals, little could have been accomplished. However, it is important to develop some expertise in selecting advisors and controlling their performance (Guislain 1995:198). These types of skills are difficult to develop and therefore are very scarce in the public sector. It might be a better solution, especially in countries with a weak administrative/public management capacity, if these resources were concentrated in a single institution. This could be a part of the unitary privatisation institution; or could be an independent server, or different privatisation authorities, depending on the institutional approach adopted.

OECD countries have had different experiences in working with government advisors. In the Netherlands, advisors to the government are excluded from underwriting syndicates. A number of other countries have addressed the issue of a potential conflict of interest between advisory and sales functions. Some, like Italy, only allow advisors to have a junior role in underwriting syndicates. Others have adopted rotation between advisors and lead underwriters in order to receive objective advice. In the U.K., separate private agents were used for pre-privatisation restructuring and for conducting the primary transaction; however, a joint appointment was given to a global co-ordinator and advisor to counsel on and bring the secondary transaction to the market.

Chart 3. Privatisations in OECD countries by residence of buyer
(in per cent)

Public offerings

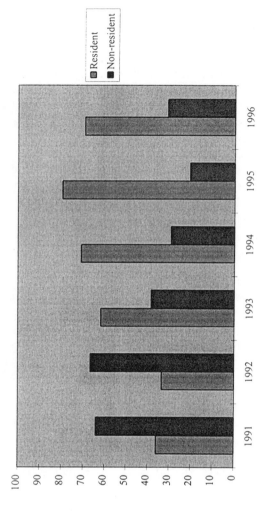

Trade sales

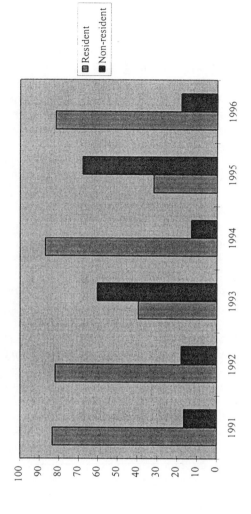

Source: OECD, Financial Market Trends, No. 66, March 1997.

9. Conclusions

The importance of unequivocal government support for the success of a privatisation programme cannot be underestimated. Without an active engagement at the centre of government, privatisation will not be successful. Where support for privatisation is ambiguous in different (especially senior) levels of the administration, the creation of a special privatisation unit in the centre of government, holding real powers, communicates commitment to the markets and helps push the process through.

Privatisation institutions are *sui generis*. On one hand, they have an evident public interest aspect like other parts of the state apparatus; they represent political authority not private profit-seekers. On the other, they are sellers of assets in the market — a merchant function that requires ample flexibility. The only way to address these often conflicting mandates is to couple flexibility with maximum transparency.

Privatisation should not be conducted on an *ad hoc* basis. Markets do not like to be surprised and the government could become easy prey to narrow sectoral interests if it had to fight each battle without a general plan. A strategy and a programme are important both from a political and return-maximisation perspective.

It is important to separate *ex ante* public policy and the protection of public interest from commercial operations in large natural monopolies about to be privatised by placing all regulatory functions firmly outside of the industry and minimising regulatory capture risks. The latter is often easier said than done. Again, the maintenance of high levels of transparency might help in achieving regulatory neutrality.

Finally, privatisation is often perceived as a cause of unemployment and social friction. There exists a number of case studies and analyses that indicate the contrary is true in the medium term; enhancing private incentives both in specific companies and the economy as a whole results in job creation, after an initial wave of restructuring. Nevertheless, it is important for governments to address the short-term labour issues of industrial restructuring in privatisation candidates, especially when the latter are large regional employers. Special social measures have been devised in a number of OECD countries along with employee participation in privatisation (Thellman et al. 1995). This is a price (and often a steep one) that the state must pay for achieving the long-term gains of a more efficient enterprise sector without endangering social cohesion.

NOTES

1. A term first coined by Kornai (1986:1).
2. This argument is expanded upon in Bos (1991:32).
3. Decision 86-217 D.C.
4. In the case of the EC Treaty Articles 221 and 52–58.
5. On the question of a political strategy and sequencing for privatisation see Douglas (1996:23).
6. Both countries have bought back the shares acquired by these airlines and have had (or are in the process) to re-privatise the companies.
7. For an extensive discussion of different types of insolvency proceedings in the context of transition see Nestor (1996:147).
8. For a thorough examination of different sectoral regulatory structures in post-privatisation U.K. see the papers (mostly written by the regulators themselves) published in Beesley (1995).
9. This is evident in the case of U.K. privatisation. See U.K. Treasury (1995:6).
10. Brom (1997) expands on these arguments in the context of transition economies but most of them hold as well for OECD members that retain residual stakes in privatised companies.

REFERENCES

Beesley, Michael and Stephen Littlechild. 1986. "Privatisation: Principles, Problems and Priorities." In John Kay, Colin Mayer, and David Thompson, eds. *Privatisation & Regulation: The U.K. Experience.* Oxford: Clarendon Press

Beesley, Michael, ed. 1995. *Utility Regulation: Challenge and Response.* London: IEA.

Bös, Dieter. 1991. *Privatisation: A Theoretical Treatment.* Oxford: Clarendon Press.

Boycko, Maxim, Andrei Shleifer, and Robert Vishny. 1996. "A Theory of Privatisation." *Economic Journal* 106:309–319.

Brom, Karla. 1997. "On the Management and Sale of Residual State Shareholdings." In Ira W.Lieberman, Stilpon S. Nestor, and Raj M. Desai. *Between State and Market.* Washington, D.C.: World Bank. pp 65–70.

Carreau, Dominique, 1996, "Legal and Institutional Aspects of Privatisation." In *Privatisation in Asia, Europe and Latin America.* Paris: OECD.

Douglas, Sir Roger. 1996. "The Role of Government in the Economy." In *Privatisation in Asia, Europe and Latin America.* Paris: OECD.

Durand, Patrice. 1996. "Privatisation in France." In *Privatisation in Asia, Europe and Latin America.* Paris: OECD.

Franks, Stephen. 1993. "Rigorous Privatisation: the New Zealand Experience." *Columbia Journal of International Business* 28/1:84.

Galal, Ahmed, Leroy Jones, Pankaj Tandon, and Ingo Vogelsang. 1992. *Welfare Consequenses of Selling Public Enterprises (Synthesis of Cases and Policy Summary).* Mimeo.

Gates, Jeffrey and Jamal Saghir. 1995. *E.S.O.P.s.* CFS Discussion Paper No. 12 Washington, D.C.: World Bank.

Graham, Cosmo and Tony Prosser. 1991. *Privatising Public Enterprises: Constitutions, the State and Regulation in Comparative Perspective.* Oxford: Clarendon Press.

Guislain, Pierre. 1995. *Les Privatisations: Un Défi Stratégique, Juridique et Institutionnel.* Bruxelles: De Boeck.

Her Majesty's Treasury. 1995. *Privatisation: Sharing the U.K. Experience.* London.

Kikeri, Sunita, John Nellis, and Mary Shirley. 1992. *Privatisation: Lessons of Experience.* Washington, D.C.: World Bank.

Kornai, Janos. 1986. "The Soft Budget Constraint." Kyklos 39:1.

Lieberman, Ira. 1997. "Mass Privatisation in Comparative Perspective." In Ira W.Lieberman, Stilpon S. Nestor, and Raj M. Desai, eds. *Between State and Market.* Washington, D.C.: World Bank.

Morgan Stanley. 1996. *Privatisation:the Second Tranche.* Euroletter. London: Morgan Stanley.

Nellis, John. 1994. "Is Privatisation Neccessary?" FPD Note 7. Washington, D.C.: World Bank.

Nestor, Stilpon and Marie Nigon. 1996. "Privatisation in Europe, Asia and Latin America: What Lessons Can Be Drawn?" In *Privatisation in Asia, Europe and Latin America.* Paris: OECD.

Nestor, Stilpon. 1996. "Insolvency Procedures in Transition Economies." In Joseph Norton and Mats Andenas, eds. *Emerging Financial Markets and the Role of International Financial Organizations.* The Hague: Kluwer Law International.

Nestor, Stilpon. 1997. "Institutional Aspects of Mass privatisation: A Comparative Overview." In Ira W.Lieberman, Stilpon S. Nestor, and Raj M. Desai. *Between State and Market.* Washigton D.C.: World Bank.

OECD. 1995. "Privatisation and Capital Markets in OECD Countries." Financial Market Trends 60:13–31.

OECD. 1997. "Privatisation: Recent Trends." Financial Market Trends 66:15–35.

Office of Passenger Railway Franchises. 1996. *Passenger Railway Industry Overview.* London: OPRAF.

Rideau, Jean. 1989. "Aperçu du Point de Vue Communautaire sur les Privatisations Dans les Etats Membres." In Charles Debbasch, ed. *Les Privatisations en Europe.* Paris.

Ridley, Sir Adam. 1996. "Financial Aspects of Privatisation." In *Privatisation in Asia, Europe and Latin America.* Paris: OECD.

Saez, Raul. 1996. "Financial Aspects of privatisation in Chile." In *Privatisation in Asia, Europe and Latin America.* Paris: OECD.

Thellman Beck, Brigitta, Erik Johansson, and David Fatwell. 1995. *Privatisation and Restructuring: Issues Related to Divesting Labor and Social Assets.* Mimeo.

Vickers, John and GeorgeYarrow. 1988. *Privatisation: An Economic Analysis.* Cambridge, MA: MIT Press.

Wright, Mike and Ken Robbie. 1994. "Management Buy-outs in OECD Countries." In *Trends and Policies in Privatisation.* 1:3:57 Paris: OECD.

CHAPTER 14

State Trading in China

William Martin[*] and Christian Bach[**]

Under the planning system operating prior to 1978, China's trade was conducted under a strict system of state trading where between ten and sixteen
foreign trade corporations held monopolies or near monopolies on a specified range of products. During the reform process, the system has changed
utterly, with the number of trading firms increasing to over 200,000.
Further, China is becoming enormously more important as a participant in
world trade. Its share of world trade has risen from one percent to three
percent over the last twenty-five years, and is projected to triple again, to
around ten percent by 2020 (World Bank 1992b:92), making it the world's
second largest trader.

The gradualist approach used to reform China's trade regime since 1978
has involved retaining many of the forms of the pre-reform trade regime,
although its operation has changed enormously. A number of the original
foreign trade corporations continue to operate, and some of them retain state
trading monopolies on particular products. Not surprisingly, there is considerable uncertainty and confusion about the nature of the resulting trade
regime. This uncertainty appears to have played a role in making the negotiations on China's admission to the World Trade Organization (WTO) more
difficult and protracted, with the lack of transparency associated with state
trading frequently raised as a concern in the context of the accession negotiations (see Dixit and Josling 1997).

The purpose of this chapter is to examine the role of state trading in
China's current trade regime, with a view to clarifying the nature of China's
current trade regime. The first section deals with the nature of state trading
under the WTO. The second deals with the pre-reform Chinese system. Then
the process of economic reform is discussed. The role of state trading in the
current system is examined in the third section. Finally, some options for
reform are considered.

[*]Development Research Group, World Bank. Thanks are due to John Croome, Bernard
Hoekman, Bart Kaminski, and Nicholas Lardy for very helpful comments. Responsibility for any
remaining errors is ours.
[**]Institute of Economics, University of Copenhagen.

1. State Trading

The concept of state trading outlined in Article XVII of the GATT, as interpreted under the Uruguay Round, deals with situations where enterprises are given exclusive or special trading rights. Such enterprises are seen as potentially creating serious obstacles to trade either by creating general impediments to trade, and hence nullifying and impairing liberalization commitments, or by creating discrimination between suppliers that contravenes the Most-Favoured Nation (MFN) principle of Article I of GATT 1994 (World Trade Organization 1994). As Hoekman and Kostecki (1995:110) emphasize, what matters under the GATT is not ownership, but the exclusivity that allows non-competitive behavior.[1] The GATT imposes no restrictions on the existence or creation of state trading enterprises, although such arrangements must be reported to the WTO's Council on Trade in Goods.

The emphasis on exclusivity is even stronger under the GATS, where Article VIII focuses entirely on monopolies and exclusive service providers, without even raising the issue of ownership. Any WTO member granting monopoly rights regarding the supply of a service already covered by a specific commitment under GATS must notify the Council on Trade in Services, and affected parties may seek compensation for the resulting loss of market access.

State trading, as defined under the WTO provisions, clearly raises two quite distinct concerns — one being the use of state enterprises as mechanisms for direct policy control of trade volumes, and the other the possible adverse consequences of monopoly power on the level and fairness of trade outcomes.

Direct policy control of trade might nullify or impair market access commitments provided under the WTO by bringing into play undeclared and unrestrained policy instruments. However, Article XVII of the GATT prohibits discrimination between suppliers from different countries, by including an MFN obligation (WTO 1994:509). GATT Article II:4 prohibits state trading enterprises from charging margins that exceed the tariff bindings provided for that commodity, and hence from violating the national treatment principle. This Article is to be read in conjunction with Chapter 31 of the Havana Charter (Petersmann 1998), which requires that importing state trading enterprises must import sufficient quantities of the product to meet domestic demand at its selling price (GATT 1995). These two requirements constrain the use of state trading enterprises to raise domestic prices of imports above world prices by more than the country's binding, and from using a *de facto* quantitative restriction to bring about the same result.

The market distortions created by state trading are, in principle, measurable in a market economy by measuring the markup charged by the state trading enterprise[2], as envisaged in paragraph 4(b) of GATT Article XVII.

The measurement of distortions resulting from state trading is much less clear-cut in a planned economy such as the pre-reform Chinese economy, where domestic market prices bore virtually no relationship either to world prices or to domestic scarcity values. Even if the planning system exactly replicated market quantities, there would be no guarantee that the state trading enterprises would earn the zero pure profits associated with a competitive equilibrium.

2. The Pre-Reform Chinese Trade Regime

The pre-reform Chinese trade regime was dominated by between ten and sixteen foreign trade corporations (FTCs) with effective monopolies in the import and export of their specified range of products (Lardy 1991). Planned import volumes were determined by the projected difference between domestic demand and supply for particular goods, with export levels being determined by the planners at levels necessary to finance the planned level of imports. The product ranges of the FTCs paralleled those of the industrial ministries responsible for production, and both were, in principle, under the overall control of the State Planning Commission and the State Economic Commission.

Clearly, this pure planning system had the ability to have the effects envisaged by the authors of Article XVII. If domestic costs are well above world prices, then the state trading system can create an effective nontariff barrier. Further, an FTC has the ability to discriminate between suppliers either in an attempt to exploit any market power it may have or in an attempt to achieve non-economic objectives.

Under the pre-reform Chinese system, commodity prices were set without regard to scarcity or cost, and were intended to serve only an accounting function. Further, the exchange rate was very substantially overvalued, creating a general disincentive to export and an artificial incentive to import. Thus, it was not possible to use estimates of commodity markups to determine whether FTCs were creating trade barriers. Many producer goods had low prices that would have made exports artificially profitable and that made imports of some needed goods unprofitable. An explicit objective of the foreign trade corporations was to create an air-lock between producers and foreign markets that would vitiate the artificial incentives created by the pricing system.[3]

An interesting feature of the pre-reform Chinese trade regime was the limited importance of conventional trade policy instruments such as tariffs, quotas, and licenses. Price-based measures such as tariffs were obviously unimportant since the planning system was based on quantity decisions rather than behavioral responses to prices. There was little need for quotas or licenses since the quantities to be imported could be controlled by the relevant monopoly trading corporations. As Lardy (1991) notes, the introduction of licensing actually reflected a liberalization of China's trade regime.

A major World Bank study (1988) of China's foreign trade regime highlighted the many disadvantages and costs of China's pre-reform trade regime, many of the features of which were still present in the mid-1980s. The air-lock between China and the world market created by the state trading monopolies was a particular focus of concern because it led to inefficiency in exporting, inappropriate export patterns, a lack of information about the needs of export markets, and a lack of competition from imports. The rigid foreign exchange system was another major cause for concern because it created a need for inefficient, bureaucratic allocation of foreign exchange. A final concern was the protection created by the use of trade planning, import pricing, licensing, and tariffs.

3. Reform of China's Trade Regime

Reform of China's trade regime had four major dimensions: increasing the number and type of enterprises eligible to trade in particular commodities; developing the indirect trade policy instruments that were absent or unimportant under the planning system; reducing and ultimately removing the exchange rate distortion; and reforming prices so that they could play a role in guiding resource allocation. These reforms of the trading system were inextricably linked with reform of the enterprise sector to allow indirect regulation through market-determined prices to replace direct regulation of enterprise output through the planning system. These reforms were undertaken incrementally, with feedback from each reform taken into account in designing the next stage of the reform — an approach colorfully described as "crossing the river by feeling the stones" — rather than proceeding according to a comprehensive overall plan for reform.

A central feature of the reforms was the decentralization of foreign trade rights beyond the handful of centrally controlled foreign trade corporations. This was not done according to the usual negative list approach (where any enterprise can trade in any good except those subject to restricted trading rights). Rather, a combination of a negative list for commodities and a positive list for trading firms was introduced. A negative list approach is used to reserve a list of commodities for trading by specified enterprises. Firms wishing to trade in other products are required to be on a positive list of firms with trading rights for those particular goods. The reform process gradually increased both the number of firms allowed to trade, and the number of different types of firms eligible for trading rights.

The number of FTCs with trading rights was progressively expanded, with trading rights provided to branches of the FTCs controlled by the central government, and to those controlled by regions and localities. Since 1984, these trading enterprises have been legally independent economic entities (Kueh 1987) and state-owned trading enterprises of this type now appear to operate very strongly along commercial lines (Rozelle et al. 1996). Joint ventures between domestic and foreign firms, and firms located in the special economic zones were also allowed the right to trade their own products relatively early during the reform process. At a later stage, large producing firms began to gain direct foreign trade rights. The process of decentralizing trade was gradual, but the trend was very consistent, with commodities removed from export and import planning progressively — these plans covered only a small share of products in 1992 (World Bank 1994; Yin 1996:103) and have since been abolished.

An important feature of the reforms was the introduction of special arrangements for processing trade. Imports of intermediate inputs for use in the production of exports were almost completely liberalized, as were capital goods inputs for use in joint ventures with foreign enterprises. These categories of imports came to represent a very large share of total imports, with intermediate inputs into exports accounting for almost half of total imports in 1996.

Import and export licensing measures were introduced in 1980 to replace the controls imposed under the previous trade monopoly (Lardy 1991). The coverage of licensing was initially small, but increased sharply as more and more trade was removed from the planning process. Lardy (1991:44) notes that licensing covered two-thirds of China's imports in 1988. The coverage of licensing has since fallen dramatically.

The primary transitional device used to reduce and ultimately remove the distortions in both commodity prices and exchange rates was the two- (or more-) tier pricing system. Under the two-tier pricing system for commodities, the plan price continued to operate for the quantity of the commodity that producers were contracted to supply. However, to stimulate output, producers were allowed to supply additional output at a secondary market price. Where plan prices are below market prices, this system can, in the short-run, allow revenue to be generated in a non-distorting manner (see Sicular 1988). The revenues raised were frequently redistributed to consumers within the same market. This was the case with revenues from grains, where consumers were supplied with fixed rations of grain at below-market prices. The two-tier system for foreign exchange involved an overvalued official exchange rate and a higher secondary-market rate, and did distort trade by discouraging both exports and imports (see Martin 1993, World Bank 1994). Over time, the retention rates were raised, lowering the gap between the rates received by exporters and paid by importers, reducing the extent of the distortion. The exchange rate was unified in 1994, removing this distortion.

The importance of market prices relative to plan prices increased very rapidly as the reforms progressed, as is evident from table 1. The share of retail commodities sold at state-fixed prices declined from ninety-seven percent in 1978 to only five percent in 1993. Even for agricultural goods, where state-pricing of some basic commodities such as grains remains important, only ten percent of total sales were at state-fixed prices. These figures to some degree overstate the importance of sales at state-fixed prices, since sales at fixed prices under a two-tier price regime may have no economic impact — such sales are inframarginal and it is the price prevailing at the margin that is most influential in determining economic behavior (Sicular 1988). Only a very small set of products was subject to state-pricing in 1993. In a significant reversal of the trend towards liberalization, the share of goods subject to state-pricing increased substantially between 1993 and 1995, although this share remained much lower than it had been prior to the early 1990s.[4]

Table 1. Share of Goods Sold at State Fixed Prices 1978–1993

Year	Retail commodities	Agricultural goods	Capital and industrial goods*
1978	97	94	100
1992	10	15	20
1993	5	10	15
1994	7	17	16
1995	9	17	16

*Capital goods up to 1993 and all industrial goods thereafter. The two were essentially the same in the only overlap year, 1993.
Source: Lardy (1995) up to 1993; Garbaccio (pers. comm.) from 1994.

4. State Trading and Related Measures

The positive-list system for allocating trading rights in China would potentially allow direct control of imports if the number of trading enterprises were small, and if these enterprises were subject to a single supervisory body. However, it is estimated that over 200,000 firms now have rights to engage in foreign trade (see East Asia Analytical Unit 1997). While not all of the enterprises with trading rights are active in any one year (ITC 1996), there is clearly a very large number of enterprises active in any year. Table 2 presents data collected by the Geneva-based International Trade Center on the number and type of importing and exporting firms active in 1994.

Table 2. Contribution of Different Firms to China's Trade, 1994

	Exporting		Importing	
	No. of firms	Share of exports	No. of firms	Share of imports
		%		%
Foreign trade corporations	9400	53	8700	44
State-owned enterprises	7800	17	3600	8
Joint ventures	30000	19	64800	34
Foreign-owned firms	9730	9	23239	12
Collective and private	1060	1	1828	1
Other	520	0.2	5378	1
Total	58500	100	107513	100

Note: Some numbers may not add because of rounding.
Source: ITC 1995: 22.

The firms in the first row of table 2 are the foreign trade corporations with trading rights for a range of commodities. The other enterprise types in the table typically have trading rights only for their own inputs and outputs. The enumeration of firms in table 2 is based on the enterprise identification codes on individual customs declarations. These numbers may differ substantially from the official numbers of firms officially granted trading rights. MOFTEC (personal communication) reports that only 8000 foreign trade corporations had trading rights in 1994 even though the ITC reported 9400 firms active in importing alone. It appears that the larger number of firms reported on the customs declarations results from the use by subsidiary firms of the trading rights granted to a parent firm. According to the MOFTEC data, the number of foreign trade corporations has increased dramatically since 1994. In October 1997, the number of them with trading rights had increased to 15,000.

Clearly, the very large numbers of enterprises involved in China's foreign trade in 1994 and the diversity of their ownership and control would make direct control — of the type envisaged in Article XVII — over the quantities traded an impractical form of trade policy except in cases where the number of firms that may trade a particular product is very tightly restricted. While the 8700 importing FTCs are all government-owned, they report to different levels of government ranging from the center to the locality and are typically accountable to their supervising entity for their financial performance.[5] Similarly, the 3600 importing state-owned enterprises with direct trading rights involve a wide range of types of enterprise in an economy where such enterprises frequently have a high degree of autonomy (Sicular 1995). Imposing direct controls on import volumes through the close to 90,000 foreign joint ventures and foreign-owned firms engaged in import trade would clearly be impossible without explicit trade policy measures such as quotas or licenses.

While trading enterprises are typically subject to restrictions on the range of products that they may trade, the constraints imposed on the business scope of most foreign trade corporations appear to be very liberal. While joint ventures and foreign-owned enterprises are subject to tighter restrictions on the scope of the products they trade, the sheer number of these enterprises means that a large number is likely to be active for most important product groups. As a consequence, consumers and producers wishing to purchase imports or sell exports will typically have a range of enterprises through which they can undertake these transactions.

Naughton (1996) notes that state-owned enterprises (SOEs) accounted for a relatively large share of the trade subject to ordinary customs duties (as distinct from preferential regimes such as imports for processing). In 1996, this trade accounted for only twenty-eight percent of imports (Economic Information and Agency 1997), and SOEs of one form or another accounted for seventy-nine percent of this trade. However, these SOEs include a very wide range of firm types, including the state trading monopolies, FTCs administered by the central government, FTCs administered by provinces and municipalities, producing SOEs with direct trading rights, and wholesale and retail trading firms. Except for those cases where there are restrictions on trading rights, the very large numbers of potential importers within and outside the ranks of the SOEs seem likely to create a relatively competitive trading environment.

A policy to allow the establishment of foreign joint venture trading companies has been introduced on an experimental basis (MOFTEC 1996). These are to be formed between sizable foreign firms and relatively large Chinese enterprises (over US$ 200 million per year in foreign trade) with direct trading rights. These joint ventures are to apply for trading rights within a particular business scope subject to procedures broadly similar to those for approval of FTCs. Initially, only a few such joint ventures are to be established, and only in Shanghai and Shenzhen.[6] However, if this experiment is judged a success, it could develop into a much more general liberalization of trading rights.

Since the positive list system of trading rights no longer provides a realistic means for exercising direct control over trade, there seems little reason to persist with this cumbersome approach to trade administration. While control of entry into foreign trade may have made sense in an era of unrealistic market prices and consequent arbitrage opportunities, it is neither needed nor effective in the highly competitive environment in which China's trading enterprises now operate. It is sometimes argued that registration of foreign trade enterprises is needed to ensure that they engage qualified staff, including staff with foreign language skills able to engage in trade with non-Chinese counterparts.[7] However, the discipline of the competitive market place is likely to be much more effective than the registration process in determining which enterprises are qualified, motivated, and ultimately effective in trading activities.

Despite the large number of trading firms overall, there are two broad groups of commodities for which the number of firms entitled to engage in trade is tightly restricted. One of these groups is subject to state trading, while the other is subject to designated trading. The state trading system applies to a relatively small number of commodities that are believed to be of particular importance for the peoples' livelihood and for the nation's economic development. The system of designated trading applies to a range of other important commodities. The seventy tariff lines subject to state trading on the import side are drawn from the commodity groups set out in table 3, as are the 115 tariff lines covered by state trading on the export side. The 229 tariff lines subject to designated trading are primarily importables.

Table 3. Products Covered by State Trading and Designated Trading

	Imports	Exports
State trading	Grain, vegetable oils, sugar, tobacco, refined oil, chemical fertilizer, cotton	Tea, maize, soybeans, tungsten, coal, crude oil, refined oil, silk, unbleached silk, cotton, antimony
Designated trading	Rubber, timber, plywood, wool, acrylics, steel and products	Rubber, timber, plywood, wool, acrylics, steel and products

Source: Government of China

The products subject to state trading are typically handled by one or a few foreign trade corporations, making direct control of the quantities imported and exported relatively practical. The system of coordination and control used for major state-traded commodities such as grains and fertilizer appears to follow the basic lines used under the traditional planning system. Estimates of the gap between supply and demand are made up to eighteen months in advance of the actual trade decision, and there appears to be considerable reluctance to adjust the quantity targets in response to developments such as unanticipated shocks to domestic supply or demand. Recent empirical research concludes that, rather than helping to stabilize domestic grain prices, this inflexible system contributes substantially to the volatility of domestic grain prices (World Bank 1997a).

The trading system for products subject to designated trading involves substantially more trading firms than for state trading, with 60 to 100 firms eligible to trade in most of these commodities. The case of steel products has been examined in detail by Dickson (1996). He finds that three national foreign trade corporations are permitted to import steel, together with fifty-five companies approved to undertake imports for particular localities. In addition, foreign joint ventures are allowed to import steel needed for their own operations, but not generally for resale. The relatively large numbers of firms make it difficult to exercise direct control over the total amount of the commodity imported. However, the geographic range within China of some traders may be restricted, creating the possibility that market power might be used against buyers or sellers within the domestic market.

Table 4. Non-Tariff Barriers Affecting China's Import Trade

	State	Desig.	Lond.	Licen.	Quota	Tend.	All
Rice	100	0	0	100	0	0	100
Wheat	100	0	0	100	0	0	100
Coarse grains	0	0	0	0	0	0	0
Nongrain crops	50	22.9	0	72.9	72.9	0	72.9
Livestock	0	72.7	0	72.7	72.7	0	72.7
Meat and milk	0	0	0	0	0	0	0
Other food products	37.2	0	0	32.9	31.7	0	38.4
Natural resources	46.6	12.8	0	0	0	0	59.5
Textiles	0.3	5.7	0	12.7	12.7	0	12.7
Wearing apparel	0	0	0	0	0	0	0
Light manufactures	0	9.3	0	0	0	0	9.3
Transport equipment	0	0	0	35.8	35.8	6.6	42.4
Machinery and equipment	0	0	0	9.2	9.2	20.4	26.8
Basic heavy manufactures	18.7	16.2	0.3	23.5	22.7	0	37.7
Services	0	0	0	0	0	0	0
TOTAL	11	7.3	0.1	18.5	16.3	7.4	32.5

The measures listed include state trading, designated trading, the London Convention, import licenses, import quotas, and price tendering.
Source: World Bank 1997c.

The coverage of state trading and designated trading is shown, together with other non-tariff barriers affecting China's import trade, in table 4. From the table it is clear that state trading and designated trading accounted for eleven and seven percent, respectively, of total imports, and made up over half of the total trade coverage of nontariff barriers in China. Clearly, the regime used for state trading and designated trading is an important special feature of the Chinese trade regime, but very much a minority part of the overall system, rather than the dominant part. The heavy reliance on state trading for major agricultural trade has, however, raised concerns about the transparency of China's agricultural trade regime (see Dixit and Josling 1997).

The average protective impact of the complete set of nontariff barriers presented in table 3 was estimated to be 9.3 percent (World Bank 1997c). This evaluation was undertaken using information on the tariff equivalents of these nontariff barriers obtained from the Unirule Institute study prepared for the Institute of International Economics (Unirule Institute 1996) and from price comparisons drawn from the International Comparisons Project. While the coverage of the information available was less than we would have liked, it did provide some initial basis for evaluation. Products imported under the state trading categories accounted for only 0.7 percentage points of this total protection. On this basis, it appears that state trading of imports has been a very minor restriction on trade in the past, although it could become a more serious distortion in the future, depending upon the manner in which state trading is undertaken.

5. Proposals and Options for Reform

In the context of the negotiations on China's accession to the WTO, China has offered to phase out the restrictions on entry into foreign trade (for both domestic and foreign firms) within three years of entry to the WTO for all commodities except those currently subject to state trading and designated trading. The restrictions on trading rights for goods subject to designated trading are to be phased out over periods of up to five years, with only state trading commodities left after this time. It is also reported that China has proposed allowing part of the imports covered by the minimum and current market access provisions of the agreement on agriculture to be imported by foreign enterprises. China's GATS offer of November 1997 allows for the formation of joint ventures in wholesaling and retailing, and for the removal of geographic and quantitative restrictions on joint venture retailers within five years. Taken together, these offers go a long way towards ensuring that importing and distribution will be competitive activities within five years of accession to the WTO.

WTO accession will automatically impose a number of disciplines on state enterprises. In particular, it will constrain the margin that can be charged by these enterprises to be less than or equal to the agreed tariff binding, require these enterprises to operate strictly according to commercial considerations, and require them to avoid discrimination (Carson 1997:87). The market access provisions of the agriculture agreement will require that market access be provided for agreed quantities at tariff rates substantially below the tariff bindings. Clearly, the market access provisions will require some changes in procedures to increase transparency, to constrain the tariff equivalents of importing margins, and to allow for the possibility of imports not subject to quantitative constraints at the bound tariff rate. The proposal to allow some of the imports covered by market access agreements under the Agreement on Agriculture to be handled by foreign enterprises would greatly increase the transparency of the state trading regime.

Modifying the current trade regime to take into account the requirements of a WTO accession agreement would result in a substantially improved trade regime. However, there will still be a need to evaluate carefully whether the resulting regime best meets the needs of China's dynamic economy. While state trading enterprises are allowed under the GATT, there is always a need to carefully evaluate their efficacy in achieving their objectives. Such trading enterprises are frequently not transparent in their operation, frequently create vested interests, and fail to achieve their objectives. These problems have caused governments in many developing countries and transition economies to disband parastatal trading agencies and to allow open competition between trading firms.

The objectives of state trading in the remaining commodities covered in China appear to involve assuring supplies and avoiding fluctuations in the prices of these commodities. However, it is far from clear that these institutions are the most effective means for achieving these objectives. An important problem with the current Chinese system of state trading is the long lags in the procurement processes for imports, and in the planning process for exports; these lags and the inflexibility of the system frequently result in imports being insufficient and exports being excessive. In fact, it appears that imports and exports of grains under current state trading policies have been quite sharply destabilizing (World Bank 1997a). Given the volatility of domestic production and consumption levels, this inflexibility generates instability in domestic commodity prices, and increases the average stock levels needed to achieve any given degree of price stability.

Over the longer term, serious consideration needs to be given to alternatives to state trading that might achieve its objectives without the costs and lack of transparency associated with state trading. If the objective is to raise and stabilize prices, for example, methods such as tariffs that vary in response to changes in a world market price indicator and, within the range allowed by tariff bindings, are widely used in Latin America (Valdés 1996) and other regions. Even better would be policies that focus directly on the problems of income instability and poverty to which the interventions in these markets are ultimately directed.

6. Conclusions

Prior to the economic reforms, China's trade regime was one of pure state trading, with imports and exports of all products essentially monopolized and the quantities of imports and exports determined through a planning process where prices played a purely accounting role. The reforms have changed this regime utterly, with the number of trading enterprises increased from around 12 to around 200,000.

The reforms have involved massive changes in the structure of policies, including the freeing up of prices for all but a handful of goods, introducing indirect trade policy instruments, making the exchange rate convertible on current account, and allowing a wide variety of firms to participate in trade. For most commodities, the volume of imports and exports is determined by the actions of a wide range of enterprises responding to market prices.

A small set of products, mainly agricultural products and oil, remains subject to state trading, where trade is restricted to only one or two importing firms. Another set, including rubber, timber and steel, is subject to designated trading, where 60 to 100 firms are given rights to trade in these products. The state trading arrangements allow the government to directly control imports. The designated trading arrangements do not allow such control, but probably create some local monopoly power, to the disadvantage of importers and exporters of these products.

Reforms proposed in the context of the WTO accession negotiations would phase out designated trading, leaving products that accounted for eleven percent of 1992 imports subject to state trading. Following WTO accession, the operation of these state trading agencies would be subject to disciplines on their behavior, including the access provisions under the agreement on agriculture, and tariff bindings that would limit their margins on imports. Even following these reforms, there would be a continuing need to examine whether these state trading monopolies were the most effective means to achieve the objectives to which they are directed.

NOTES

1. This focus on exclusivity has a long history in the trade policy literature. Irwin (1996:46) reports that the term "free trade" emerged in parliamentary debates at the

end of the sixteenth century as an antonym for trade managed through foreign trade monopolies.

2. Any such measurement assumes that the state trading enterprise meets market demand at its selling price, rather than merely selling a predetermined amount at a price not determined by internal market conditions.

3. Or, in the original conception, to insulate the economy from the harmful irrationalities of world market prices (World Bank 1988).

4. China's submission to the WTO accession negotiations lists products under the following categories as subject to state-pricing in 1996: grain; edible oil; cotton; tobacco; compressed tea; timber; crude oil; natural gas; gasoline; kerosene; diesel oil; heavy oil; urea; polyethylene sheeting; steel for locomotives and rolling stock; aircraft and aircraft engines; edible salt; pharmaceuticals; and silk cocoons.

5. Von Kirchbach (1996) estimates that 5700 of these firms report to regional administrations, while 3000 report to a range of central government bodies. The 3000 centrally administered firms account for twenty-seven percent of total imports, as against seventeen percent for the regional FTCs.

6. http://www.chinadaily.net/bw/history/b1-5firm.at12.html.

7. Proposals for the establishment of FTCs must be approved by MOFTEC at the national level. The criteria used for approval include the trade volume of the enterprise and the skills of its staff.

REFERENCES

Byrd, W. 1989. "The Impact of the Two-Tier Plan/Market System in Chinese Industry." Journal of Comparative Economics 11: 295–308.
Carson, C. 1997. "The Removal of Quantitative Restrictions, Tariffication and Minimum Access Provisions as They Affect Importables." In J. Cordeu, A. Valdés, and F. Silva, eds. Implementing the Uruguay Round Agreement in Latin America: the Case of Agriculture. Santiago: The World Bank and the FAO Regional Office for Latin America and the Caribbean.
Dickson, I. 1996. "China's Steel Imports: an Outline of Recent Trade Barriers." Chinese Economy Research Unit Working Paper No. 96/6.
Dixit, P. and T. Josling. 1997. "State Trading in Agriculture: a Background Paper." Seminar Paper presented at the Economic Research Service, U.S. Department of Agriculture.
East Asia Analytical Unit. 1997. China Embraces the Market. East Asia Analytical Unit. Canberra: Department of Foreign Affairs and Trade.
Economic Information and Agency. 1997. China's Customs Statistics Monthly, December 1996. Hong Kong: Economic Information and Agency.
GATT. 1995. Analytical Index: Guide to GATT Law and Practice, Sixth Edition. Geneva: World Trade Organization.
Hoekman, B. and M. Kostecki. 1995. The Political Economy of the World Trading System: from GATT to WTO. Oxford: Oxford University Press.
Irwin, D. 1996. Against the Tide: an Intellectual History of Free Trade. New Jersey: Princeton University Press.
ITC 1996. Survey of China's Foreign Trade. Geneva: International Trade Centre.

von Kirchbach, F. 1996. "Selling to China: Which Import Channels?" *International Trade Forum* 1.

Kueh, Y. 1987. "Economic Decentralization and Foreign Trade Expansion in China." In J. Chai and C.K. Leung, eds. *China's Economic Reforms.* Hong Kong: University of Hong Kong.

Lardy, N. 1991. *Foreign Trade and Economic Reform in China, 1978–1990.* Cambridge: Cambridge University Press.

Lardy, N. 1995. "The Role of Foreign Trade and Investment in China's Economic Transformation" The China Quarterly 144: 1065–1082.

Martin, W. 1993. "Modeling the Post-Reform Chinese Economy." Journal of Policy Modeling 15:5, 15:6: 545–579.

MOFTEC. 1996. "Provisional Measures on the Establishment of Sino-Foreign Joint Venture Trading Companies on a Pilot Basis." Decree No 3, 1996, Beijing: Ministry of Foreign Trade and Economic Cooperation.

Naughton, B. 1996. "China: From Export Promotion to an Open Economy?" San Diego: University of California at San Diego.

Petersmann, Ernst-Ulrich. 1998. "Article XVII GATT on State Trading Enterprises: Critical Evaluation and Proposals for Reform." In this volume.

Rozelle, S., A. Park, Jikun Huang, and Jin Hehui. 1996. "Bureaucrat to Entrepreneur: the Changing Role of the State in China's Transitional Commodity Economy." Mimeo.

Sicular, T. 1988. "Plan and Market in China's Agricultural Commerce." Journal of Political Economy 96/2: 383–387.

Sicular, T. 1995. "Redefining State, Plan and Market: China's Reforms in Agricultural Commerce." China Quarterly 144: 1020–1046.

Unirule Institute. 1996. "Measuring the Costs of Protection in China." Beijing: Report prepared for the Institute of International Economics by the Unirule Institute.

Valdés, A. 1996. *Surveillance of Agricultural Price and Trade Policy in Latin America During the Major Reforms.* World Bank Discussion Paper No. 349. Washington, D.C.: World Bank.

World Bank. 1988. *China: External Trade and Capital.* Washington, D.C.: World Bank.

World Bank. 1994. *China: Foreign Trade Reform.* Washington, D.C.: World Bank.

World Bank. 1997a. *China: Long-term Food Security.* Washington, D.C.: World Bank.

World Bank. 1997b. *China 2020: Long Term Issues and Options for the 21st Century.* Washington, D.C.: World Bank.

World Bank. 1997c. *China Engaged: Integration with the World Economy.* Washington, D.C.: World Bank.

World Trade Organization. 1994. *The Results of the Uruguay Round of Multilateral Trade Negotiations.* Geneva: World Trade Organization.

Yin, Xiagshuo. 1996. "China's Trade Policy Reforms and their Impact on Industry." In D. Wall, J. Boke, and Xiangshuo Yin, eds. *China's Opening Door.* London: The Royal Institute of International Affairs.

CHAPTER 15

State Trading in Russia

Vladimir Drebentsov and Constantine Michalopoulos[*]

1. Introduction

The rapid progress that countries in Central and Eastern Europe and the former Soviet Union (FSU) are making in introducing market reforms and in integrating into the international economic system has resulted in a fundamental change in the institutions used for the conduct of international trade. State trading organizations dominated international trade under central planning. Today, in Russia and most other economies in transition, trade is primarily conducted by private firms, and the role of state trading, in some respects the last vestige of central planning, has shrunk considerably.

Russia as well as many transition economies are also applying for accession to the World Trade Organization (WTO), which under Article XVII of the GATT requires countries to make notifications on the activities of state trading enterprises (STE).[1] The empirical question of how much state trading is actually still occurring has implications for several important policy issues: Russia and most previously centrally planned economies are applying for accession to the WTO without seeking any special consideration for state trading activities. If, nonetheless, state trading practices continue to be of importance, the question arises of what assurances Russia would need to provide the WTO in the context of its accession negotiations about the future role of state trading in its economy. More broadly, if state trading practices are significant in many transition economies seeking accession, the question arises of whether and how the disciplines of Article XVII of the GATT need to be modified to address issues to which accession of these new members could give rise. Finally, Russia and most FSU countries continue to be classified as "non-market economies" in the context of antidumping regulations

[*]Vladimir Drebentsov is Economist in the Moscow Resident Mission of the World Bank. Constantine Michalopoulos is Special Economic Advisor at the World Trade Organization but was Senior Advisor in the Europe and Central Asia Region of the World Bank when this paper was prepared. The findings, interpretations, and conclusions expressed in this paper are entirely those of the authors and should not be attributed in any manner to the WTO, the World Bank and its affiliated organizations, or to members of its Board of executive Directors or the countries they represent. The authors wish to thank Harry Broadman and David Tarr of the World Bank and Elizabeth Shaeffer of the WTO for helpful comments on an earlier draft of this paper.

of the EU and the United States, a classification which may result in discriminatory treatment that limits market access. If evidence shows that state trading practices in these countries are not significantly different from those of other countries, for example those that are already members of the WTO, this would pose questions as to whether these EU and U.S. classifications and regulations should be reconsidered.

This chapter examines the evolving role of state trading in Russia. First, there is a short discussion of the meaning of state trading. Next, we discuss the evolution of state trading in Russia until mid-1997. The fourth section analyses the implications of the findings for WTO accession and for Russia's designation as a "non-market economy". The final section presents conclusions and recommendations.

2. The Meaning of State Trading

Past experience with notifications of GATT members under Article XVII offers little clarification on the meaning of the term "state trading enterprise" (STE). Over the period 1980–1994 few countries bothered to notify the existence of such enterprises. For example, in 1993 (the last "full" reporting year under the GATT), only 11 of 105 members notified. Most notifications came from developed countries. Some members, for example, Hungary in 1984, notified that they had no state trading activities, although there is ample evidence of state trade organizations playing a major role in these countries' trade at the time (Tarr 1992). Most of the enterprises notified were involved in trade in agricultural commodities, and a few in alcohol and tobacco and petroleum products (GAO 1995).

In an effort to clarify what enterprises should be classified as an STE, a working definition was agreed upon during the negotiation of the "Understanding on the Interpretation of Article XVII" in the Uruguay Round:

> Governmental and non-governmental enterprises, including marketing boards, which have been granted exclusive or special rights or privileges, including statutory or constitutional powers, in the exercise of which they influence through their purchases or sales the level or direction of imports or exports (WTO 1996).

It is too soon to tell what kind of enterprises will fall under this definition. But the interest in some OECD countries such as the United States so far appears to focus, as in the past, on concerns regarding the activities of state trading in the agricultural sector of other developed countries, such as Canada, Australia, and New Zealand (GAO 1996).

The working party of the WTO established to address Article XVII issues has focused its attention on defining a suitable questionnaire and an illustrative list of enterprises that will permit the development of a better understanding of the extent and scope of state trading activities of enterprises in member countries. In the meantime, since 1995, notifications under the Article have increased, with forty-five members (including many developing countries and transition economies) providing new and full notifications and sixteen members providing updates (WTO 1996). But the Article was designed to deal not with centrally planned, non-market economies that controlled essentially all trade, but with the state trading activities of enterprises operating as exceptions to the overall, market-based environment of GATT members. While interest in the issue is rising, to date the Article has been used sparingly by WTO members as an instrument to address nullification or impairment of commitments through state trading.[2]

Throughout this period, GATT members, faced with all-encompassing state trading activities of centrally planned economies (most of which were not members of the GATT) classified these countries as "non-market economies" and applied special trading regimes to imports from them. For example, the EU and the United States adopted special procedures regarding antidumping measures taken against enterprises from these countries. A key element of these procedures is the use of a surrogate. A market economy's cost structure is used instead of the country's own in the determination of "normal" value for establishing whether dumping is occurring.

In antidumping, the focus in both the United States and the EU has been on the country rather than the enterprise.[3] The EU Commission annually determines a list of countries designated as non-market economies whose enterprises by definition would be considered as engaging in state trading activities. The current list includes Russia, China, and fifteen other countries (Hindley 1997).

It is interesting in this regard that the trade agreement signed between the EU and Russia in 1994 does not appear to change this treatment. The relevant paragraph has a somewhat vague reference:

> In respect of anti-dumping or subsidy investigations, each Party agrees to examine submissions by the other Party and to inform the interested parties concerned of the essential facts and considerations on the basis of which a final decision is to be made. Before definitive anti-dumping and countervailing duties are imposed, the Parties shall do their utmost to bring about a constructive solution to the problem. . . .

> ***

> The Parties agree that, without prejudice to their legislation and practice, when establishing normal value due account shall be taken overall,

in each case on its merits, when natural comparative advantages can be shown by the manufacturers involved to be held with regard to factors such as access to raw materials, production process, proximity of production to customers and special characteristics of the product.[4]

In the United States there is no list, but the determination is made on a case-by-case basis in light of whether a country meets a set of criteria embedded in the relevant legislation. The following criteria are used, and may be of interest in the discussion of state trading: (a) currency convertibility; (b) determination of wages through free bargaining between labor and management; (c) the extent to which foreign joint ventures are permitted; (d) the extent of government ownership or control of the means of production; (e) the extent of government control over the allocation of resources and the price and output decisions of enterprises; and (f) other factors the administering authority considers appropriate — usually related to the extent to which exporters are able to export goods on terms and conditions they fix without government interference (Ehrenhaft 1997).

As can readily be seen, these criteria are far broader than those suggested in the definition contained in the Understanding on Article XVII, but the last three criteria pertaining to ownership and government control over output and price contain elements also present in the definition of the Article.

Based on these procedures, a number of antidumping actions have been taken both by the EU and the United States in recent periods against Russia and several other FSU countries. A recent analysis of these procedures suggests that they probably made only a small additional difference to the fundamental protective effect of the antidumping actions taken. However, the procedures undoubtedly introduced the possibility for greater arbitrariness and biases extraneous to the economic circumstances of the enterprises affected (Michalopoulos and Winters 1997). No matter what the final judgement may be on the fairness of these procedures, it could be argued that if state trading is no more prevalent in Russia than in some other market economies, it should no longer be treated differently by the United States and EU in this or other respects.

Thus, how much state trading goes on in Russia today is of special importance, both with respect to Russia's accession to the WTO — and in particular regarding the enforcement of GATT Article XVII — as well as in the context of the treatment that Russian exporters receive in major international markets. It is possible that following Russia's accession to the WTO, governments will stop treating Russia as a non-market economy (and that it is only a matter of time until accession occurs). On the other hand, accession negotiations have often taken a long time, and it is important to deal with the issue of how much state trading occurs in Russia today, even on an interim basis.

3. The Evolving Role of State Trading in Russia

During its first months of independent existence, the Russian Federation formally abandoned the state monopoly on foreign trade that had been a key element of USSR planning. Yet, the country inherited a complex system of centralized exports and imports implemented through a number of specialized state trading firms, so-called foreign trade organizations (FTOs), which exercised a foreign trade monopoly for the state in the Soviet era.

Over time, privatization throughout the economy reduced the role of the FTOs. There are no detailed, comprehensive data that would demonstrate this, but there is strong evidence of a sharply declining trend: in 1992–1993 up to seventy percent of exports outside the FSU were controlled by trading companies designated as sole legal exporters of so-called "strategic commodities". This regime has been abolished for all intents and purposes (see below). Also there is evidence of a drastic decline in the role played by a subset of FTOs for which data are available over time. In 1996, turnover for these FTOs (see Annex) was only about one-third of its 1992 level.

Elements of state trading remain in three main areas: (a) companies that are either fully state-owned or state-controlled that exercise monopoly power in the export trade of their respective products (e.g., natural gas, diamonds, pipelines); (b) companies engaging in barter trade with other CIS or centrally planned economies; (c) other companies, whether FTOs or not, which do not have monopoly positions but may enjoy certain privileges or advantages in trade. A key concern in almost all cases is that the relationship between the government and the enterprises is not transparent and gives rise to ambiguities regarding the role of each.

Until 1995, the trade regime was characterized by an effort to restrain the main exports of energy and raw materials through first, quotas and licensing and subsequently, export taxes, while imports were relatively protection-free and for a time some categories were heavily subsidized through the federal budget. Protection to domestic manufacturers was provided by the relatively undervalued exchange rate and by the domestic prices of the main exportable inputs (such as energy and raw materials) being kept below international prices.[5]

State Needs and Other Privileges

Throughout this period, the government used the FTOs (and other companies, e.g., oil producers which had been privatized) to operate a system of centralized exports for so-called "state needs". This meant that the state would specify the exportation of certain quantities of a particular product to a particular customer at a predetermined price. In 1992–1994, these included a wide range of the country's commodity exports, such as petroleum and petroleum products, natural gas, electricity, aluminum, copper, nickel, some timber and cellulose, and weaponry. Even in 1995, when both the commodity coverage and volumes of established export quotas for state needs contracted significantly, centralized exports still accounted for fifteen percent of the total petroleum exports, and eleven percent of natural gas exports.

Beginning in 1996, exports for state needs involved only crude oil shipments. Yet the government's take during the year was increased from fifteen to twenty-five percent of total oil exports. The program was supposed to be terminated in the spring of 1997, when most of previous decrees for oil shipments under "state needs" were abolished. However, some elements in the government still have a notion of keeping the system of oil exports for state needs.

In 1992–1995, the main privilege granted to companies involved in state exports was the exemption from payment of export taxes. This privilege was terminated in July 1996 with the elimination of the last export taxes. Since then, the priority access to oil export pipelines with a constrained capacity granted to companies involved in state export contracts[6] has become the major privilege for oil exporters; but such a privilege does not necessarily imply that the activities of these privatized companies fall under the purview of GATT Article XVII.

Alongside centralized exports, several other types of privileges were extended to certain Russian companies in 1992–1995 which could be construed as making their activities "notifiable" under Article XVII. Most notable were the preferential provision of export quotas and licenses and the institution of special exporters — export trading companies registered by the Ministry of Foreign Economic Relations (MFER) as the sole legal exporters of the so-called "strategic commodities". Lists of such commodities have been periodically amended by the government, yet in the early years of reform (1992–1993) they covered up to seventy percent of Russia's total exports to non-FSU countries.

Being nominated a special exporter and getting a license to export within a quota set by the government was an important privilege which would have made such companies fit the state trading criteria of Article XVII, especially in the light of the discretion and non-transparent criteria used by the MFER in selecting special exporters and distributing export quotas. However, both export quotas/licenses and special exporter lists were abolished by the government in March 1995, and there have been no similar privileges granted to Russian companies since then.[7] Moreover, in April 1997, a Presidential decree established a competitive tender system for all procurement of state needs at all governmental levels and repealed all previous decrees on this issue.

The only exceptions that remain are: (a) the privileges granted to the companies Diamonds of Russia-Sakha (ALROSA) and Almazyuvelirexport, which have the exclusive right to sell Russia's raw natural diamonds and test lots of natural diamonds, respectively, on foreign markets; (b) the monopolies for the export of natural gas (Gazprom), and oil pipelines (Transneft) — as well as for coal and electricity which are not involved significantly in trade; and (c) state trading FTO in armaments (Rosvooruzhenie) — whose activities would not normally be covered by the provisions of state trading of Article XVII. At the same time there is still a number of FTOs, some still state-owned, others privatized (but with the state maintaining controlling interest) or in the process of being privatized, whose status regarding "privileges" in trade is unclear. However, the impression is that most of these companies actually do operate as commercial enterprises at present, in terms of decisions regarding pricing, output, and distribution.

On the imports side, the main focus of centralized purchases was for agricultural foodstuffs and raw materials and their trends have closely followed those for centralized exports. In 1992, imports financed directly from the federal budget accounted for 40 percent of total imports from outside the CIS ($14.8 billion); in 1993 their share decreased to 23.3 percent ($6.5 billion), in 1994, to 9.2 percent ($2.6 billion), and in 1995–1996 to 3 to 4 percent, shrinking basically to purchases for consumption in governmental use. Beginning in 1995, there have been no funds allocated in the federal budget for centralized imports of agricultural commodities and foodstuffs — imports which constituted the bulk of centralized purchases in previous years.

The government has employed state trading for imports of products that used to be in great shortage on the domestic market, on a clearly declining basis. With the emergence of private trading companies that successfully saturated the Russian consumer market, the government has gladly withdrawn itself from import activities. This has also put an end to import subsidies that the federal government used to grant prior to 1995. Since neither import quotas/licenses, nor the institution of special importers have ever existed in Russia, budget financing of centralized imports via FTOs was the sole privilege that could be construed as making these companies' activities fall under Article XVII. But with the end of this financing, the "privileges" also ended.[8]

Intergovernmental Agreements With CIS and Centrally Planned Economies

These agreements, which envisage mutual shipments of specified goods — the so-called "interstate barter" — are used by the Russian government in its relations with Commonwealth of Independent States (CIS) members and several former COMECON countries (Cuba and Mongolia).[9] The agreements also appear to entail elements of state trading, although the precise relationships between the government and the companies engaging in these transactions are opaque and difficult to pin down.

Following the break-up of the Soviet Union, in an effort to sustain trade relations in the face of a collapsing payments system, Russia and the other CIS countries established a series of barter agreements based on lists of commodities (sometimes quite lengthy) and quantities of goods to be exchanged. The prices and implicit exchange rates for the bartered goods were often different from market prices. As a rule, the amounts exchanged fell far short of the amounts originally agreed upon for a variety of reasons (Konovalov 1994), and the importance of the agreements and their scope declined drastically over time. They were supposed to have been terminated within CIS at the end of 1996, but some agreements appear to be still in place (see below) and the manner of their operation raises a number of questions.

All of them had attachments with lists of commodities that the signatories were obliged to ship to each other on a barter basis via specified trading companies. In Russia the main beneficiary of such agreements has been the company Roscontract. In fact, this company was established in 1992 as a private enterprise to be operated on a profit basis specifically in order to intermediate intergovernmental barter agreements from the Russian side. At the time it also received a loan from the federal budget for this purpose — whose repayment to date is unknown.

Strictly speaking, the commodity lists in these agreements were not binding, and in fact, in most cases the targets set were not achieved. However, articles of the agreements do provide for foreign trade privileges: specific companies are explicitly nominated by the government as its exclusive agents. So, at least in the part that they are fulfilled, activities of companies explicitly designated in these agreements could be construed to fall under Article XVII. It appears from personal interviews with Roscontract and MFER officials that Roscontract has stopped its involvement in the interstate barter deals as of the beginning of 1996. Unfortunately, we have to express caution with respect to such a conclusion, because the language of Russia's intergovernmental agreements with Georgia and the Kyrgyz Republic for 1996–1997 is absolutely identical to that of previous ones, including both explicit nomination of Roscontract for intergovernmental barter intermediation and the inclusion of lists of commodities to be shipped in agreed volumes to and from Russia.

As late as Spring 1997, Russia signed two barter agreements with Uzbekistan and confirmed shipments under the "sugar-oil" agreement with Cuba[10]: one for to exchange 18.2 thousand tons of cotton for 100 thousand tons of Russian wheat in 1997; the second, a three-year contract to exchange Russian fuel, non-ferrous metals, and agricultural equipment for Uzbek cotton. Two Russian trading companies, Rostekstil and Contex, participating in the first barter deal were explicitly named. Although it is not clear what privileges these companies obtained[11], some concessions seem likely to have been granted. Otherwise, the naming of these companies in the agreements would have been meaningless and nobody would have tried to participate in the deal, which was not the case.[12]

A particular concern from the standpoint of efficiency for the economy as a whole is whether these barter deals involve the exchange of commodities at less than world prices. This had been a prevalent practice in earlier periods, but in principle has been abandoned. However, as these transactions are not transparent, there is a concern that exchanges at less than world prices continue, which could result in distortions in other parts of the economy as well. For example, in the above transaction, if both Uzbek cotton and Russian oil are underpriced, this would spread the distortion to the Russian textile industry and to energy users in Uzbekistan.

The Situation in 1996–1997

An effort was made to develop a quantitative estimate of the extent of state trading in Russia in 1996 relative to the total turnover of trade (the value of exports plus imports) for that year, as well as to make some judgements on the evolution of the situation since then. Table 1 presents a summary of our analysis. The estimates presented on the FTOs and Roscontract should be considered as orders of magnitude subject to a considerable margin of error. On the whole, an effort was made to include the activities of all state-owned or -controlled firms which could be considered to be extended privileges of some kind and thus fall under the purview of Article XVII of the GATT.

Table 1. State Trading in Russia – 1996 (in US$ billion)

Type of State Trading Enterprise	Value of International Trade Transactions
Gazprom	14.1
FTOs (listed in Annex)*	10.2
Roscontract	7.2
Oil exports for state needs	3.3
Electric Utilities	0.7
Total State Trade	35.5
Total Exports plus Imports	148.1

*Excludes Rosvooruzhenie (approximately US$ 3.5 billion); total also excludes Transneft, which could be viewed as a "privileged" monopoly
Source: Roscomstat, Ministry of Foreign Economic Relations (MFER), Authors' estimates.

The total value of state trading activity in Russia for 1996 is estimated at US$ 35.5 billion or 24 percent of Russia's total world trade (i.e., exports plus imports). For reasons discussed below, this estimate is a maximum — and the actual value of Russian state trading is likely to be considerably smaller. Of this total, the largest amount (US$ 14.1 billion) involves the activities of Gazprom. Another US$ 10.2 billion is accounted by the turnover of FTOs listed in the Annex, including the diamond export monopolies. Again, this figure is probably a maximum for this category of firms, as many of them are operating on a commercial basis, even if state-owned. The estimate for Roscontract is based on the 1996 turnover of CIS interstate barter and is also probably a maximum, as some of the activities that it undertook may have been on a strictly commercial basis. The state needs program for oil exports accounts for another US$ 3.3 billion. Finally, there are smaller amounts involving the fees of Transneft (state-owned oil pipeline monopoly) which are not included, and exports by RAO UES, the state-owned electric grid monopoly.

With the exception of the trade under intergovernmental agreements, the bulk of the trading activities involved exports rather than imports; and in energy and raw materials the "privileges" enjoyed by the exporting organizations did not involve subsidies. Rather, these companies do not have to pay export taxes, which typically caused the domestic price of energy to be lower than the international price. Since there are no export taxes in Russia at the moment, such privileges, in principle, do not exist.

Assuming announced government policies are implemented, the total state trading for 1997 is likely to decline for a number of reasons. First, the oil exports for state needs are supposed to have been eliminated. Second, the role of state-owned FTOs can be expected to decline as more start to function on a commercial basis. And third, the role of Roscontract and other FTOs as intermediaries in intergovernmental agreements is supposed to be terminated (but note the caution on this issue above). If all this is accomplished, the total state trading as a percent of total volume of trade would fall to about ten to fourteen percent.

4. Implications

The main implication of this analysis is that while Russia has made tremendous progress in privatizing its economy and operating enterprises on a commercial basis, at least ten percent and perhaps as much as twenty percent of trade is still controlled by the state. The problem is not so much the absolute size of the share — which predominantly involves exports of energy and a few raw materials (diamonds) — but the lack of transparency in the relations between the state and enterprises engaged in international trade, whether formally privatized or not. This is a problem which, unfortunately, is more general and not limited to firms involved in trade. The system is especially opaque in trade with the other CIS and a few centrally planned economies. Moreover, the problem is compounded by a general weakness in governance which results in weak enforcement of announced government policies.

The implications of these findings for Russia's accession to the WTO are twofold: (a) the Russian government would need to take urgent steps to clarify the status and privileges of a number of firms engaged in international trade — e.g., Gazprom, Roscontract and some of the FTOs; and (b) it would need to provide appropriate explanations to the WTO working party dealing with Russia's accession. Otherwise, the accession process could be delayed.

The broader implications of these findings for Article XVII of the GATT is that the Article and the notification mechanism under it were clearly not meant to cope with the complex and non-transparent relations between the state and the private sector now evolving not only in Russia but in some of the other CIS countries as well. Questions thus arise as to whether an effort should be made to amplify the practices covered by the Article to cover more subtle aspects of state involvement in trade.

At the same time, questions also arise as to the standards that transition economies should meet regarding state trading and whether in some cases countries seeking accession should be given some time to meet certain standards. To do this now, however, raises other questions regarding former centrally planned economies which have already gained entry into the WTO (e.g., Bulgaria) without meeting any specific standards or gaining any special deferments. These questions are made difficult to answer by the lack of previous experience and the abysmal record of most members of the GATT in notifying state trading practices in the past.

Finally, a few comments are appropriate on the implications of these findings for the designation of Russia as a non-market economy in the context of determination of dumping in the United States and the EU, two very important markets for Russia's exports. As noted earlier, this designation may not have been significantly more detrimental to Russia's exports than the inherently protective characteristics of antidumping or threat of antidumping actions. However, the designation carries with it the potential for damaging action and the introduction of non-transparent processes — ironically in this case on the part of the major industrialized countries. Moreover, the designation tends to encourage both the EU and the United States to enter into cartel-like price and quota understandings with Russia — the EU-Russia arrangements on steel and the U.S. agreements with several CIS countries on uranium and aluminum are just two examples (Michalopoulos and Winters 1997). This reinforces existing monopolistic tendencies within Russia and intensifies the problem of creating competitive market conditions.

There is little doubt that today Russia is a market economy and should be treated as such, although many of its markets are characterized by significant imperfections. Even if the highest of the various estimates is used for state trading — twenty-four percent, this is certainly consistent with the share present in other economies with significant public sector involvement in production and exports of raw materials and energy. For example, the state enterprise sector of countries such as Egypt, Tunisia, Venezuela, and Zambia accounted for about twenty-three to thirty percent of total GDP, in Algeria and Sudan the ratio was even higher — in excess of forty-five percent (World Bank 1997). Yet none of these countries has ever been treated as a non-market economy. By comparison, the share of the public sector in Russia in 1995 was estimated at forty percent of GDP (EBRD 1996) and following recent privatizations, is probably on the order of twenty-five to thirty percent.

A similar conclusion can be reached regarding the other criteria that the United States uses in classifying "non-market economies" (see above). First, there is little doubt that Russia meets the test of currency convertibility as it has been recognized by the IMF to meet obligations under IMF Article VIII for full current account convertibility. Second, there are clearly no wage controls or significant government interference in wage setting. Third, there are few limitations on joint ventures, and those that exist (in defense, banking, and insurance) would have to be dealt with in the context of Russia's commitments under the GATS.

More specifically, regarding the issue of dumping, which involves firms selling abroad at prices less than in domestic markets, government interference (with the possible exception of intergovernmental barter deals) has focused on having exporting firms raise their export prices to international levels.

It is of course possible, although it would be odd indeed, that Russia will become a member of the WTO but will continue to be designated a non-market economy by the United States and the European Union for purposes of antidumping (Michalopoulos and Winters 1997). Common sense and coherence in policy, however, would suggest that upon accession to the WTO — if not before — Russia and many other CIS countries be designated as market economies to reflect the progress they have made in privatizing their economies and in terminating one of the last vestiges of the Cold War.

5. Recommendations

State trading has the potential to introduce significant distortions in trade. The Russian government should make all efforts to accelerate market reforms and minimize state trading activities within the meaning of Article XVII of the GATT and otherwise.

Particular emphasis should be placed on: (a) reducing the role of monopolies in state trading, through bona fide privatization and elimination of barriers to entry created through special privileges accorded to individual companies; (b) creating transparent relations between the state and individual companies or agencies that enjoy special privileges notifiable under Article XVII; (c) taking steps to immediately and effectively terminate the state trading aspects of the intergovernmental agreements as called for by existing policy. Such policies would be both beneficial to Russia's economy and would expedite accession to the WTO.

Consideration should be given to expanding the scope of state trading practices notifiable under Article XVII to cover a variety of state trading activities and relations between the state and the private sector emerging in Russia and other transition economies.

The European Union, the United States and other members of the WTO should consider terminating the designation of non-market status in the context of antidumping measures for Russia as soon as possible and not later than the date of its accession to the WTO.

In the meantime, these countries should monitor carefully the progress made by Russia in introducing market-oriented reforms and reducing state trading, to ensure its fair treatment in antidumping cases. In particular, the monitoring should ensure that the designation of Russia as a non-market economy does not result in a less favourable treatment than for "market" economies.

NOTES

1. The annual notification obligation follows a three year cycle: in the first year, a new and full notification (i.e., a complete response to the questionnaire issued by the WTO Secretariat) is due; in the second and third years, an updating notification is due, indicating any changes since the most recent notification.

2. But see the Canadian Liquor Board panel (BISD 358/37).

3. In the United States there were a few cases where it was argued that an enterprise was judged to be functioning within a market environment even the though the country as a whole was judged a non-market economy (Ehrenhaft 1997).

4. European Union 1994, Article 18 and joint declaration in relation to Article 18. It should be noted in this connection, that Russia wanted to be assured that in antidumping actions, its comparative advantage would be taken into account, as reflected in the above passage; and the Russian negotiators viewed the language in this passage as a small step forward. But implementation of the phrase is to date unclear. One interpretation that could be given is that if the EU continues to use a surrogate country procedure, it would at least chose a country whose cost structure is similar to that of Russia's.

In late 1997 the EU Commission announced proposals for liberalizing EU policy toward Russia and China, terminating the two countries' designation as "non-market economies" at the country level. Instead, permit determinations would be made on a case-by-case basis, taking into account the market conditions prevailing in each commodity for which dumping has been alleged (Croft 1997).

5. For a discussion of the trade regime during this period (Konovalov 1994).

6. Access rights to oil pipelines with a constrained capacity — meaning all Russia's export pipelines apart from the Druzhba line going to Eastern Europe — are allocated on a pro-rata basis among oil producing companies. Yet, since (according to the government ruling) exports for state needs are automatically granted priority in allocation of the access rights, only the capacity left after the fulfilment of contracts for state needs is actually distributed.

7. Two types of export quotas and licenses still exist in Russia: firstly, export quotas are still in place for commodities for which exports are restricted by Russia's various international obligations — such as VERs or U.S. and EC import quotas for steel, textiles, satellite launchers, etc.; secondly, licenses are required for hazardous exports — weaponry and goods dangerous to human health.

8. Strictly speaking, what has been said in the previous footnote with respect to hazardous exports is valid for imports of a similar nature. Yet since such licensing does not employ any quantitative restrictions or price setting, it does not fit the definition used for purposes of Article XVII.

9. CIS consists of Armenia, Azerbaijan, Belarus, Georgia, Kazakstan, the Kyrgyz Republic, Moldova, Russia, Tadjikistan, Turkmenistan, Ukraine, and Uzbekistan, i.e., all the independent states that emerged from the breakup of the Soviet Union except the Baltics.

10. According to MFER, six million tons of Russian oil should be exchanged for two million tons of Cuban raw sugar in 1997.

11. At least on the Russian side there were no export or import duties applicable to such deals with the CIS in 1997, so on this ground companies selected by the government remained on a level with all other traders.

12. Of course, one should also note in the same connection that Gazprom is involved in a large number of state trading relationships with many countries in the CIS and Eastern Europe, e.g., the Czech Republic.

REFERENCES

Croft, A. 1997. "EU Body Seeks New Russia, China Dumping Policy." Reuters, Brussels, 16 December 1997.
Ehrenhaft, P.D. 1997. "U.S. Policy on Imports from Economies in Transition." In Peter D. Ehrenhaft et al., eds. *Policies on Imports from Economies in Transition.* Washington, D.C.: World Bank.
European Bank for Reconstruction and Development (EBRD). 1996. "Transition Report." London: EBRD.
European Union-Russian Federation. 1994. "Agreement on Partnership and Cooperation."
Hindley, B. 1997. "The Regulation of Imports from Transition Economies by the European Union." In Constantine Michalopoulos and Alan Winters, eds. *Policies on Imports from Economies in Transition.* Washington, D.C.: World Bank.
Konovalov, Vladimir. 1994. "Russian Trade Policy." In Constantine Michalopoulos and David Tarr. *Trade in the New Independent States.* Washington, D.C.: World Bank.
Michalopoulos, Constantine and Alan Winters. 1997. "Summary and Overview." In Peter D. Ehrenhaft et al., eds. *Policies on Imports from Economies in Transition.* Washington, D.C.: World Bank.
Tarr, David. 1992. "Problems in the Transition from the CMEA: Implications for Eastern Europe." Communist Economies and Economic Transformation 4/1: 23–43.
U.S. General Accounting Office (GAO). 1995. "State Trading Enterprises." GAO/GGD-95-208.
U.S. General Accounting Office (GAO). 1996. "Canada, Australia and New Zealand: Potential Ability of State Trading Enterprises to Distort Trade." GAO/NSIAD-96-94.
World Trade Organization (WTO). 1996. "Report (1996) of the Working Party on State Trading Enterprises." G/L/128. Geneva: WTO.
World Bank. 1997. "World Development Indicators - Table 5.4." Washington, D.C.: World Bank.

ANNEX

List of state-owned/-controlled trading firms (FTOs), as of June 1997

Name	Ownership status	Area of specialization
Almazyuvelir Export	State-owned	Diamonds
Atomenergoexport	Privatized (golden share*)	Nuclear energy equipment
Avtopromimport	Approved for privatization	Motor vehicles
Diamonds of Russia-Sakha	State-owned	Diamonds
Lenfintorg	Approved for privatization	
Litintern	Privatized (golden share)	
Litsenzintorg	Approved for privatization	Licenses and patents

Mashinoexport	Approved for privatization	Machine-building industry products
Mashinoimport	Approved for privatization	Machine-building industry products
Nafta-Moskva	Privatized (golden share)	Petroleum
Novoexport	Approved for privatization	Miscellaneous exports
Prodintertorg	State-owned	
Prodintorg	State-owned	Food industry products
Promexim	Approved for privatization	Miscellaneous industrial goods
Prommashimport	Approved for privatization	Industrial machine building
Promsiryoimport	Approved for privatization	Industrial raw materials
Raznoimport	Privatized (golden share)	Miscellaneous imports
Roscomagenstvo	Privatized	
Rostehexport	Privatized	
Rosvneshtorg	Approved for privatization	Miscellaneous external trade
Rosvooruzhenie	State-owned	Armaments
Selkhozpromexport	State-owned	Agricultural goods
Sojizpromexport	Approved for privatization	
Sojuzpushnina	Approved for privatization	Furs
Sudoimport	Approved for privatization	Vessels, ships
Sojuztranzit	Privatized (golden share)	Transit transportation
Tekhmashimport	Approved for privatization	Technical machinery, equipment
Tekhnointorg	Approved for privatization	Technology transfer
Tekhnopromexport	State-owned	Industrial technology, equipment
Tekhnopromimport	Approved for privatization	Industrial technology, equipment
Tekhnostroyexport	Privatized (golden share)	Construction
Tyazhpromexport	Approved for privatization	Heavy industry products
Vneshintorg	Privatized	Miscellaneous trade
Vneshstroyimport	Approved for privatization	Construction, construction materials
Zarubezheconomservice	Approved for privatization	

*"Golden Share" involves continued government control of company operations through ownership of such a special share.

Source: MFER

CHAPTER 16

National Experiences in State Trading: Comments

Ichiro Araki[*]

To paraphrase what Tolstoy said about families, all free trade regimes are alike, but each state trading regime is different reflecting each country's specific situations. However, if one were to extract one common element in these different regimes, I would say that it is the political sensitivity involved. As is evident from the presentations by various authors, there is no denying that state trading enterprises are used as a tool for protecting domestic industries from foreign competition. To be able to benefit from such protection, those particular sectors must possess political clout. Thus, it is not surprising to see many state trading activities occur in the agricultural sector, which has a strong influence in the political process of any country.

Political factors are clearly at play in the case of formerly centrally planned economies. In recent years, these economies have undergone a drastic change in respect of the way in which states regulate the flow of trade in goods and services. As Will Martin and Christian Bach observe in *State Trading in China*, prior to the economic reforms, China's trade regime was one of pure state trading. Now only a small set of products (mainly agricultural products and oil) remains subject to state trading. The change may have been less drastic compared to Russia for instance, but it certainly involves a political will toward the reform of the economy. Judging from the result of the Fifth Communist Party Congress held in September 1997, the reformists appear to be taking control of the economic policy making in China (Harding 1997a). Thus there are reasons to believe that further economic liberalization will be achieved under the current political leadership. However, this does not mean that the role of state trading in China will be diminished in the future. I would note that there is a close resemblance between the lists of products covered by state trading and those subject to state pricing (grain, cotton, tobacco, tea, crude oil, refined oil, fertilizers, etc.).[1] One of the major reasons why state trading is maintained in these sectors must be the need for price control, and the price control is maintained precisely because these are politically important sectors. The rationale behind the selection of these sectors might be that of central planners (the Chinese

[*]Legal Affairs Officer, World Trade Organization. The comments presented here are personal and should in no way be attributed to the World Trade Organization.

political leadership undoubtedly considers it their duty to secure stable supply of basic foodstuff, clothing, heating oil, and other essentials for their nationals) and it may not necessarily indicate the political influence of producers in these sectors. However, it can be easily imagined that politically important individuals and organizations are directly involved in the production of these essential goods. I think it is unlikely that state trading in these sectors would be abolished in the near future, and the issue will continue to be on the agenda of China's accession to the WTO.

The situation is very similar in the case of Russia. According to Vladimir Drebentsov and Constantine Michalopoulos in *State Trading in Russia*, assuming the announced government policies are implemented, the trade volume subject to state trading as a percentage of total trade will fall to about ten to fourteen percent in 1997. Sectors subject to state trading are also similar, i.e., agricultural commodities and foodstuff on the import side and oil, gas, and diamonds on the export side. It is clear that these are politically sensitive areas for Russia.

Drebentsov and Michalopoulos present another interesting question regarding the application of antidumping duties on goods exported from "non-market" economies, a subject also dealt with by David Palmeter in *The WTO Antidumping Agreement and the Economies in Transition*. In view of the progress in economic reforms in Russia (and probably China also), it is high time that the user governments of antidumping mechanism reviewed the blanket designation of "non-market" status. It is reported that the European Union is moving toward that direction and that China and Russia are, naturally, welcoming the move (Harding 1997a). Does this mean that we no longer have to worry about what John Jackson calls "the interface question" (Jackson 1997:248)? It seems to me that it is too early to draw that conclusion at this juncture. The interface question extends far beyond the narrow question of state trading and antidumping duties. In my view, the question was there as early as 1955, when Japan sought accession to the GATT. Many European countries then were opposed to Japan's accession because it was feared that once becoming a contracting party to the GATT Japan might revert to the pre-war practice of "social dumping" (making use of low wages and long work hours). The issue was eventually solved by invocation of GATT Article XXXV against Japan by these countries in the short term and by the establishment of special arrangements for textiles in the longer term. However, it was the biggest obstacle to Japan's accession process at the time. As long as similar sentiments are shared among importing countries, the interface question is bound to be debated in the accession process of China and Russia. It would especially be the case when the sectors involved are subject to state trading in view of the political sensitivity both in the exporting countries and in the importing countries.

Both Jacques Bourgeois (*EC Rules on State Monopolies and Public Undertakings*) and André Sapir (*The Role of Articles 37 and 90 ECT in the Integration of EC Markets*) focus on Article 90 of the EC Treaty. As both authors acknowledge, it is difficult to arrive at any definitive conclusions regarding the implications for the WTO rules on state trading because the development of Article 90 jurisprudence has been supported by a strong political will towards harmonization and economic integration, coupled with strong, supranational enforcement mechanisms, evidently a different setting from the background against which the WTO rules are applied. Nevertheless, I would note that active enforcement of Article 90 only started in the 1980s, after those enforcement mechanisms had accumulated enough experience and self-confidence over actions taken by Member States. This would underscore my previous point that sectors where state trading enterprises or state monopolies operate are often dominated by political interests. I also note that most discussions on state monopolies within the EC are concentrated on the telecommunications sector. It would have been interesting to see the experiences in other sectors, particularly in agriculture, in view of the experiences in other countries. Perhaps the answer is that the Common Agricultural Policy operates in areas which are totally divorced from the principles of Article 90. Then, my next questions would be: why is that the case in EC? Why does state trading not play as important a role in the Europeans' agricultural policy as it does in many other countries? A comparative study of state trading in the agricultural sector could provide a useful material in the future negotiations on agriculture in the WTO.

Robert Howse in *State Trading Enterprises and Multilateral Trade Rules* surveys a wide range of sectors which are subject to state trading in Canada — liquor, electric power, telecommunications and broadcasting, financial services, and agricultural marketing boards. As is the case with all other economies, these appear to be politically sensitive sectors, particularly in view of the tension between the federal government and the provincial governments. It is not a coincidence that Canada has often experienced trade disputes in the GATT/WTO in these sectors. Howse analyzes in detail a series of liquor cases between Canada and the United States. In addition, disputes involving the operation of agricultural marketing boards in Canada are now reaching the panel stage.[2] In my view, these are healthy developments in the sense that those vested interests cannot hide behind the veil of state trading to escape the scrutiny by the multilateral trading system.

In Japan, discussed by Mitsuo Matsushita in *State Trading in Japan*, there seems to exist a general perception that state trading can provide a powerful tool of protection despite the 1988 *Agricultural Items* case. According to an expert on this subject, many agricultural economists in Japan mistakenly believe that overseas agricultural production does not affect

Japanese agriculture either in terms of volume or price because state trading is maintained in the key sectors (Saeki 1997a:59). The same expert, while rejecting this simplistic notion, concludes that there will be little, if any, over-quota trade in areas where the in-quota trade is monopolized by state trading agencies (Saeki 1997b:48). Thus, the above-mentioned perception prevailing in Japan is not without a factual basis. Ironically, as a result of the Uruguay Round, the very practice which was condemned in the *Agricultural Items* case as a violation of Article XI has been kept intact so long as it is in compliance with the tariffication formula under Article 4 of the Agreement on Agriculture. The powerful agricultural lobby is happy with the status quo, and it is unlikely that changes will come from within Japan, judging from the extreme judicial passivism demonstrated in the *Silk Necktie* case. While I do not disagree with Matsushita's conclusion that it is foreseeable that the role of state trading in the agricultural sector will be decreased, I would note the process will take a very long time under the current political situation in Japan.

In *State Trading in the United States*, Diane Wood observes that the role of state trading in the United States, in contrast to Japan, is negligible for most sectors. Nevertheless, I cannot help but noticing the influence of political process in the selection of the sectors which are subject to state trading. The Commodity Credit Corporation is a case in point. Without the political influence of the agricultural producers, the scheme would not have been operated the way it is as part of the broader web of regulations administered by the Department of Agriculture. Even the Federal Helium Program, whose *raison d'être* is rather dubious today, must have been established under a heavy political pressure. In the 1920s and 1930s, helium was regarded as a substance of strategic importance for the United States. One of the reasons why the airship Hindenburg ended up in flames over the mooring mast in Lakehurst, New Jersey in 1937 was the refusal by the U.S. Government to sell helium to Nazis Germany despite the repeated requests from the latter. This is also an example of how long a protectionist system can persist after the rationale for it has been lost due to political inertia.

Finally, Stilpon Nestor in *Privatisation in the OECD Area* describes various challenges and difficulties faced by a privatization programme in the OECD countries. Again, I note that various political factors are at play, not the least of which is the perceived fear of unemployment and social friction. This is why state trading enterprises remain operational in many countries despite the criticisms against them.

I can safely conclude that all authors who contributed chapters about national experiences in state trading are sceptical about the rationale for maintaining the system because of its lack of transparency and certain level of inefficiency. However, state trading persists for various political reasons.

Should we accept it as a political necessity? Could we ignore it because it only plays a marginal role (or a diminished role in countries like China or Russia) in the overall trade? To answer these questions, we need more information regarding the operation of state trading enterprises in different sectors. Although it is difficult to assess the overall impact of state trading enterprises in the multilateral trading system, one could hope that the global trend of regulatory reform (Kawamoto 1997) would bring about more competition in areas which traditionally have been protected by state trading.

NOTES

1. Compare footnote 4 with table 3 in Martin and Bach's chapter.

2. In February 1998, the United States requested the establishment of a panel on "Canada - Measures Affecting the Importation of Milk and the Exportation of Milk Products" (WT/DS103/4). New Zealand also requested consultations with Canada on the same issue (WT/DS113/1).

REFERENCES

Harding, James. 1997a. "Pro-business Reformers Strengthen Grip in China." Financial Times, September 20, 1997.
Harding, James. 1997b. "China Hails EU Gesture over Dumping Duties." Financial Times, December 18, 1997.
Jackson, John. 1997. *The World Trading System, Second Edition.* Cambridge, MA: The MIT Press.
Kawamoto, Akira. 1997. "Regulatory Reform on the International Trade Policy Agenda." Journal of World Trade, 31: 82-116.
Saeki, Naomi. 1997a. "WTO Nôgyô Kyôtei to Nôsanbutsu Bôeki (WTO Agreement on Agriculture and the Agricultural Trade), Part 1." Bôeki to Kanzei (Trade and Customs) 45/8: 58-69.
Saeki, Naomi. 1997b. "WTO Nôgyô Kyôtei to Nôsanbutsu Bôeki (WTO Agreement on Agriculture and the Agricultural Trade), Part 2." Bôeki to Kanzei (Trade and Customs) 45/9: 42-53.

Part IV: Conceptual Issues

CHAPTER 17

State Trading: Rule Making Alternatives for Entities with Exclusive Rights

*Bernard M. Hoekman and Patrick Low**

1. Introduction

From the inception of the General Agreement on Tariffs and Trade (GATT), governments have been unconstrained in terms of the ownership of productive assets or the regulation of domestic production.[1] However, it was recognized that enterprises granted exclusive trading rights and privileges would be able to restrict trade and/or avoid liberalization commitments. They might do so in a number of ways. First, state trading enterprises (STEs) could circumvent the most-favored nation (MFN) principle (GATT Article I) by discriminating among trading partners in their purchasing and selling decisions. Secondly, they could limit quantities of imports or exports in contravention of the GATT Article XI prohibition on quantitative restrictions. Third, they might impose price mark-ups that exceed permitted (i.e., bound) tariff levels. Fourth, they could contravene the national treatment principle by discriminating against imported products in matters affecting, for example, the internal conditions of distribution or sale. Fifth, STEs might engage in non-transparent cross-subsidization activities or benefit from various forms of assistance from governments that distort competition. Finally, STEs might affect competition on export markets if their exclusive privileges allow them to undercut other suppliers.

In view of these possibilities, a number of GATT provisions establish rules of behavior for STEs. These have played only a minor role in practice, in large part because the main sectors/countries where STEs are significant were effectively excluded from multilateral disciplines (agriculture; services; centrally-planned economies). This has now changed and the prominence of state trading as a policy issue has consequently been increasing. The World Trade Organization (WTO) now covers services and agriculture (sectors where exclusive rights and privileges are quite prevalent in many countries).

*Bernard Hoekman is with the World Bank and CEPR. Patrick Low is with the World Trade Organization. We are grateful to Damien Neven, Will Martin, and other conference participants for helpful comments and suggestions and to Francis Ng for excellent research assistance. The views expressed are personal and should not be attributed to the World Bank or the WTO.

Moreover, many former centrally-planned economies are in the process of accession to the WTO, and many members appear to be concerned with the apparent prevalence of state trading in such countries.[2]

This chapter discusses alternative approaches to multilateral rule-making for STEs. Section 2 discusses issues of defining the "STE problem" and its impact on international trade. Section 3 describes existing WTO rules and approaches. These include regulating the behavior of STEs, restricting the scope/extent of state trading, and allowing the trade-distorting effect of STEs to be contested in WTO fora. Section 4 identifies and evaluates a number of possible rule-making alternatives for STEs. We argue in favor of a hybrid approach that aims at reducing the scope for WTO members to use STEs with the further development of behavioral and procedural disciplines for those STEs that governments wish to maintain. Section 5 concludes.

2. Conceptual Issues

In evaluating existing multilateral rules for STEs as well as possible alternative disciplines, it is necessary first to determine how the term STE should be defined. This will depend on the concerns that governments have regarding the economic consequences of activities by enterprises that are sheltered from market forces. There are numerous reasons why governments might be concerned about the existence and behavior of such entities when negotiating commitments to liberalize trade. Most obviously, if an entity is a monopoly, controls bottleneck facilities, or has significant power to affect downstream activities such as distribution, trade policy may be irrelevant in market access terms. Even with zero tariffs, no formal quotas, and full national treatment, a STE may be able to foreclose the market to potential foreign entrants. More generally, a firm with exclusive rights may be able to control the price at which it sources from domestic suppliers and distributes imported goods. If prices paid for inputs are below market clearing levels, the entity will effectively enjoy a subsidy which may reduce market access opportunities for foreign goods. Similarly, the entity may be able to impose high mark-ups on imported goods, thereby reducing domestic demand for foreign products. In all these situations, the activities of STEs will have an effect equivalent to a tax (tariff) or subsidy (Lloyd, 1982).

The definition of STEs found in Article XVII GATT is a relatively broad one:

> Governmental and non-governmental enterprises, including marketing boards, which have been granted exclusive or special rights or privileges, including statutory or constitutional powers, in the exercise of

which they influence through their purchases or sales the level or direction of imports or exports.[3]

Note that the definition is not limited to entities with exclusive rights with respect to trade; the emphasis is on exclusivity arrangements that have an effect on trade. This effect must be realized through purchase or sales activity. Note also that Article XVII is not restricted to entities that are owned or controlled by the state. Public ownership is not what matters; instead, the focus is on the behavior of firms granted exclusive rights. Entities that have in effect been granted exclusive rights or privileges are also covered by Article XVII, and any WTO member may notify the existence of foreign entities that are deemed to act as STEs on a *de facto* basis.[4]

There are many types of exclusivity arrangements that could have an effect on trade. They range from total monopoly/monopsony control — under which an entity is granted a monopoly right to import/export — to situations where an entity is obliged to compete with domestic buyers/distributors on both the domestic and foreign markets. Governments may allow certain enterprises ("STEs") to affect trade flows through the pursuit of regulatory controls that create (or permit) the exercise of market power. They may also pursue policies that have effects analogous to direct subsidies. More generally, any enterprise with a "dominant" position may exercise its market power and distort competition, independent of any action by government to support its activities. The question therefore arises where the line should be drawn between STEs — however defined — and regulatory policy more in general (Kostecki, 1982). As it stands, Article XVII is worded quite broadly and potentially covers a wide range of activities. We would argue that it is important that the "STE issue" be defined as narrowly as possible in order to ensure that any multilateral rules are targeted at those areas that cannot be addressed through the application of general WTO rules and disciplines. In this connection one can question the usefulness of the extension of STE disciplines to entities that "in effect" act like STEs. As argued below, we believe that *de facto* exclusivity claims are something that should be dealt with under generally applicable national competition policy rules.

Many governments intervene in the functioning of the market, often to achieve non-economic objectives. Sometimes this takes the form of granting exclusive rights and privileges that restrict competition. From an economic perspective a key issue is that such interventions are efficient — are the least cost way of attaining the social objective. Trade negotiators are generally concerned with the market access implications of government intervention. In the case of STEs, this is reflected in the "trade effect" criterion that is embodied in the Article XVII definition of STEs. This "trade effect test" is again very broadly worded. It could be made more consistent with an efficiency-based criterion by restating it as a "least trade distorting test", similar to what is found in Article XX GATT. That is, the question that could be posed is whether the trade distortions that are implied by the activities of a STE are necessary to achieve the government's objective. Alternatively, an attempt might be made to rank order the "types" of STEs depending on their potential for distorting trade flows. These types of approaches are currently lacking in the WTO's STE disciplines. Increasing the economic content of the multilateral rules that apply is one of the major challenges confronting the trading system.

In principle, one input into the rule-making process should be information regarding the major distortions that are currently implied by the activities of STEs. Unfortunately, little is known about the effect of STEs on trade. Indeed, no comprehensive data is available about the extent of STEs outside of agriculture.[5] This makes it impossible to determine how important state trading is as an economic issue, or to identify the countries where state trading is significant. Even if data were available on the prevalence of STEs, information would also be needed on their behavior, as what is of concern is not state trading per se, but the magnitude of the trade distortions that are associated with STEs. In this respect the situation is similar to that arising in the current discussions on the need for a multilateral agreement on competition policy: the empirical basis for evaluating the likely benefits of alternative options is very weak. This in turn makes it more difficult to establish focal points for negotiations.

Table 1. Share of State Trading Enterprises in GDP, 1978-91 (unweighted averages, %)

	1978-1985	1986-1991	1978-1991
Developing countries:			
Africa	13.1	12.2	12.9
East Asia	8.8	9.8	9.8
South Asia	6.3	9.7	7.6
Europe and Middle East	30.7	26.5	28.8
Latin America	9.4	10.6	10.2
65 Developing countries	13.0	12.8	12.8
10 Industrial countries	5.6	6.6	6.1

Source: World Bank, Bureaucrats in Business 1995.

Nonetheless, in order to obtain a sense of the magnitude of the "problem", the extent of public ownership of industry can be used as a proxy. As indicated in table 1, state-owned enterprises — defined as entities with a majority state-owned equity share — accounted for thirteen percent of GDP in a sample of sixty-five developing countries in the late 1980s and early 1990s, as compared to six percent in a group of ten OECD members. What role, if any, these enterprises have on trade is unknown. Schmitz (1996) notes that state-owned enterprises in low income countries are much more concentrated in manufacturing activities than is the case for high income nations, suggesting that their role in trade may be much greater than is indicated by their share in national output. In OECD countries, state-owned enterprises are largely found in services. Such entities may have both formal exclusive rights and *de facto* exclusivity (e.g., monopoly control of bottleneck or essential facilities in the case of telecommunications).

3. Existing Approaches Towards STEs in the WTO

There are a number of alternative approaches towards STEs in the WTO. The first consists of horizontal rules that impose behavioral norms that apply to all STEs in all WTO Members. The second comprises specific commitments that are made by WTO members regarding the existence of enterprises with exclusive or special rights or privileges. These can be found in sector-specific commitments under the General Agreement on Trade in Services (GATS). Increasingly, they may also be found in the accession protocols of recent WTO members. Thirdly, the WTO allows members to invoke dispute settlement procedures if STEs nullify liberalization commitments.

Horizontal Commitments

Articles II and XVII GATT and Article VIII GATS embody generic, horizontal disciplines on STEs. Article XVII requires that STEs act consistently with the general principles of non-discriminatory treatment, and that in giving effect to this requirement, purchases and sales are solely based on commercial considerations, giving enterprises of other contracting parties adequate opportunity to compete in such purchases and sales. Article II:4 requires that mark-ups imposed by import monopolies not exceed tariff bindings (if these have been scheduled), and that STEs satisfy domestic demand for imports.[6] Considering the different ways in which STEs can undermine the most basic GATT rules, it is perhaps surprising that the "commercial consideration" requirements of Article XVII are established only with respect to non-discrimination,[7] which in turn refers only to MFN treatment.[8] This is a major weakness in the disciplines of Article XVII. If national treatment were an integral part of the GATT's STE disciplines, it could do much to help foreign firms in situations where STEs control markets, as it would constrain attempts to discriminate against foreign goods.

An effort was made in the Uruguay Round to address some of the perceived limitations of Article XVII. The resulting Understanding on the Interpretation of Article XVII did little more than establish the working definition of STEs mentioned earlier and strengthen transparency provisions (e.g., notification requirements).[9] The apparent laxity of GATT disciplines on state trading can at least partly be explained by the limited degree to which the original signatories of GATT relied on state trading.[10] It is also the case, however, that a large part of the state trading in the merchandise area takes place in agriculture — marketing boards and related institutions being a prime example. Given the magnitude of distortions created by agricultural policies since the establishment of GATT, it is questionable whether governments would have been willing to see problems in the sector addressed through tighter disciplines on state trading.[11]

Article VIII GATS is similar to Article XVII GATT in that monopoly or exclusive supply of services is allowed in principle. As under the GATT, monopoly suppliers and STEs are prohibited from abusing their market power to nullify any specific commitments relating to activities that fall *outside* the scope of their exclusive rights. But GATS goes further than GATT because Articles XVI and XVII allow countries to enter into negotiations to reduce or eliminate the existence of exclusive rights granted to STEs in specific sectors by subjecting them to market access and national treatment commitments. However, as discussed further below, these are conditional on the willingness of members to undertake such commitments.

Specific Commitments

Two types of specific commitments are currently found in the WTO with respect to state trading: agreements to limit the scope of STEs (including through privatization); and acceptance of national treatment and market access commitments for service sectors.

Commitments to Limit the Scope of State Trading
Given that tariff concessions by economies where the role of the state in the economy is large can be of limited value, WTO members may seek assurances regarding the role of STEs in a country's trade regime. In the past, GATT Contracting Parties negotiated global import commitments with centrally-planned economies (e.g., Poland and Romania) when such countries sought accession. These commitments were included in their protocols of accession. For example, Poland agreed to increase the total value of its im-

ports from GATT members by at least seven percent per year (Hoekman and Kostecki, 1995). In general, it may be argued that up until recently, the inclusion of centrally-planned economies within GATT was probably more to do with political expediency than with a desire to see trade relations with the economies concerned governed by the market-based mechanisms of GATT. Thus, in addition to import expansion targets or similar undertakings designed to compensate for the limited value of tariff commitments, special safeguard mechanisms were designed to allow GATT contracting parties to restrict imports from the centrally-planned economies on a discriminatory basis. Special antidumping procedures were also contemplated[12], and the relevant protocols of accession contained special provisions for withdrawal from GATT obligations that rendered the effective use of mainstream dispute settlement involving a centrally-planned economy unlikely. In this way, the absence of market mechanisms was accommodated within the GATT framework, and no attempt was made to induce structural reform.

More recent accession negotiations involving former centrally planned economies reveal a very different approach to that used in connection with the East Europeans, such as Poland, Romania, Hungary, and Yugoslavia. Countries seeking accession today are considered to be "in transition" and WTO members are seeking assurances that substantial progress has been made in privatizing enterprises and establishing competitive market structures, and that further progress in this direction will be pursued where necessary. Demands made on countries such as China, Bulgaria, Latvia, Estonia, Lithuania, and other former Soviet Union countries are focusing more on market structure than ownership. Thus, commitments on the trading rights of enterprises have become a crucial part of the accession negotiations. Typically, acceding countries are being asked to guarantee the rights of individuals and enterprises to import and export goods, unless otherwise provided for in WTO agreements. What such a commitment does is ensure market entry, thereby eliminating the exclusivity associated with STE arrangements. Countries negotiating accession may be able to secure a phase-in timetable for the structural changes implied by such a commitment, and perhaps also to exclude certain subsectors or activities, but the basic thrust of the demand is clear.

As far as privatization is concerned, acceding countries are being asked to provide details of their divestiture programs, both during the accession negotiations and on a regular basis thereafter. The implication of this is that acceding countries are committed to privatization, but the reporting requirement falls short of a firm commitment to privatization targets. This approach has blurred the distinction between supplying information and undertaking commitments in accession protocols, and seems intended to have the effect of exerting pressure in a situation where concrete commitments are unobtainable. These developments are noteworthy in that they imply that new members are being asked to undertake commitments that do not apply to existing members, some of which continue to have a significant degree of state trading. Although acceding countries remain adamant that they are not adopting a "WTO-plus" approach involving commitments relating to the ownership of assets in the economy, in practice it appears that a certain degree of asymmetry may be created between the commitments of WTO members.

Sector-Specific Commitments on Services

There are two so-called specific commitments in the GATS, market access and national treatment. These obligations apply *only* to services that are included in the schedules of specific commitments of members, and then only subject to whatever qualifications or conditions are listed. Six types of *market access limitations* are prohibited, unless a member indicates otherwise. Indeed, if a member inscribes a service sector in its schedule, market access limitations can only be listed in terms of one these six elements. The six consist of limitations on: (i) the number of service suppliers allowed; (ii) the value of transactions or assets; (iii) the total quantity of service output; (iv) the number of natural persons that may be employed; (v) the type of legal entity through which a service supplier is permitted to supply a service (e.g., branches vs. subsidiaries for banking); and (vi) participation of foreign capital in terms of a maximum percentage limit of foreign shareholding or the absolute value of foreign investment. *National treatment* is defined as treatment no less favorable than that accorded to like domestic services and service providers.

The introduction of the market access article in the GATS reflects one of the distinguishing characteristics of service markets — namely, that their contestability is frequently restricted by non-discriminatory measures. The presence of a STE in a sector would typically involve a limitation on at least one of the six elements listed above — that relating to a limitation on the number of suppliers. In the course of negotiations, WTO members are free to seek specific commitments for STEs if these exist. If no STEs exist and a government has bound itself to apply the national treatment and market access commitments for a specific sector, it will have to offer compensation to WTO members if it seeks to introduce STEs at a later date.

Dispute Settlement

Both GATT and GATS allow WTO members to invoke dispute settlement procedures in instances where they perceive that a STE has violated, respectively, Article XVII or Article VIII (e.g., by discriminating among foreign products). Cases alleging violations of the rules on STEs have so far been rare in the GATT/WTO system. This may reflect tacit agreement not to throw stones for fear of retaliatory counter charges (Horlick and Heim Mowry, 1997), or it may reflect the fact that STEs have not been a major issue. As noted above, GATS Article VIII includes explicit disciplines regarding *new* STEs, whose creation may give rise to compensation claims if specific commitments are violated in the process. In the GATT context, governments would be forced to invoke non-violation dispute settlement procedures in such situations.[13] This is a provision under which it can be argued that the establishment of a STE — although it does not violate any WTO rule — nonetheless nullifies or impairs concessions obtained in earlier trade negotiations. Non-violation disputes have mostly centered on subsidies, as the WTO allows members to continue to use various kinds of subsidies. The non-violation dispute settlement option appears to be straightforward to apply in cases where a government establishes a new STE. This is clearly a government "measure" that could not be "reasonably" foreseen by a trading partner. A problem, however, is that STEs cannot be attacked directly. Because the measure does not violate a WTO obligation (by definition), the remedies that may be suggested by a WTO panel cannot affect the existence or behavior of STEs. At best, a complainant country will be offered compensation in another area. Non-violation therefore does little to deal with the market access problems that arise as a result of STEs.

4. Alternative Rule-Making Options

Summarizing, three distinct approaches currently are pursued in the WTO as regards STEs. The first is to subject the behavior of such entities to multilateral disciplines such as nondiscrimination and transparency, enforced through WTO dispute settlement. The second is to negotiate on national treatment and market access on a case-by-case basis. Finally, non-violation dispute settlement procedures may be used to address the impact of new STEs.[14] In seeking to impose greater discipline on STE-type activities within the multilateral trading system, the choice is between building upon existing approaches and/or adopting new ones. The following options can be identified: (i) maintain the principle of "STE freedom" but expand behavioral rules for STEs, complemented by domestic enforcement mechanisms; (ii) expand the GATS specific commitments approach to STEs that control trade in goods as well as services; (iii) circumscribe the existing principle of "STE freedom" by seeking agreement that certain types of STEs and supporting policies should be prohibited; (iv) introduce the possibility of subjecting the actions of STEs to countervailing actions; (v) apply generally applicable competition or antitrust principles to the activities of STEs; and (vi) strengthen the ability of market participants to contest the exclusive rights granted to STEs — both through the adoption of criteria to ensure that STEs are efficient (e.g., via regular competitive bidding for exercising the exclusive rights) and through judicial enforcement of whatever rules of the game are agreed on concerning the behavior of STEs.

Behavioral Norms for STEs

The rules contained in Article XVII of GATT and Article VIII of GATS impose limited constraints on STEs, and have little impact in terms of the conditions of market access. From a market access perspective, it would appear necessary that at the very least STEs be subject to the national treatment rule. Of course, such an obligation should apply to both products and producers if it is to be effective. In many cases the inputs or outputs that are required from the STE will be services — e.g., interconnection services by or information on the subscriber base of a telecom operator.[15] However, competition from domestic entrants may also be circumscribed. Increasing market access opportunities in industries or activities that are controlled by STEs will then require that the relevant barrier to entry is directly attacked at its source — in other words, the exclusivity arrangements that stem from the regulatory decisions of a government. This implies that multilateral negotiations would need to center more directly on an aspect of domestic regulatory policies traditionally regarded as beyond the purview of the GATT (see option 2 below).

A national treatment obligation — and behavioral rules more generally — should apply only to formal, *de jure* STEs. *De facto* situations are most appropriately regarded as a subset of the more general question as to whether and how to introduce competition policy disciplines in the WTO (see option 5 below). The various behavioral and procedural rules could be embodied in a stand-alone agreement along the lines of those that emerged from the Uruguay Round on a variety of issues. In addition to stronger transparency and reporting requirements, one element of such a state trading agreement (STA) could be that signatories bind mark-ups of all their STEs controlling the import of goods. Consideration might also be given to introducing concepts that are analogous to those found in the Agreement on Government Procurement. This agreement, for example, contains provisions requiring international competitive bidding, as well as a bid protest (challenge) mechanism. The latter is crucial, as effective enforcement of procedural and behavioral norms must occur locally. There are many other aspects of the GPA that could be emulated, in particular its due process and transparency requirements, including the obligation to submit annual statistics on the activities of STEs.[16]

Negotiate Reductions in the Scope of STEs

Largely because of the inclusion of investment in GATS[17], market access has been tackled head-on, making such factors as entry conditions, market structure, and number of suppliers the key and explicit determinants of market access. And these access barriers are supposed to be negotiated down over time. In the GATS, traditional state trading concerns have therefore been subsumed into a broad framework defining international market access commitments. This can be regarded as a possible model for dealing with *all* state trading and exclusivity arrangements. It implies little in the way of general behavioral rules (except discrimination in the MFN sense). The emphasis is instead on negotiating away state trading (as well as other market access restrictions) over time. Abstracting from possible concerns about excessive gradualism in the GATS market access context, there is no doubt that unhindered market access in the GATS sense, plus full national treatment, would eliminate many of the problems associated with state trading and exclusive rights.

The way GATS Article XVI is structured, and given its relationship to national treatment, the GATS approach allows market access commitments to be articulated in a manner that does not distinguish between foreigners and nationals. Thus, the conditions of competition in the market (insofar as these turn on entry conditions) can be defined in universal terms, without distinguishing between subsets of economic agents (i.e., domestic versus foreign). This differs from most WTO approaches to rule-making, but is consistent with the nationality-blind nature of antitrust law and competition policy. If this approach were to be generalized to cover goods as well as services, it would mean the establishment of schedules or timetables for the elimination of STE arrangements, combined with a prohibition on the introduction of new STE rights. There is no ban in GATT on attempts to seek elimination of STEs in the context of a multilateral trade negotiation. To the extent that STEs are perceived to be a problem they can therefore be attacked directly.[18]

Impose Constraints on the "STE Freedom" Principle

Rather than negotiate on STEs on a case-by-case basis, an alternative approach would be to seek agreement to declare STEs illegal or to prohibit the use of certain types of STEs (e.g., public monopoly). This is not only very unlikely to be feasible in the WTO context given the differences across members in economic systems, but is also undesirable from an economic perspective. There may well be situations where "outlawed" STE-types are an efficient mechanism through which to achieve a particular social objective. Although it appears that to some limited extent the EU may be moving toward constraining the ability to employ public ownership of undertakings through the use of Article 90 ECT, this is not an option for the WTO.[19]

The Remedy Approach

Another option is to pursue a remedy approach. Rather than attacking anti-competitive behavior at source through rules setting out behavioral restraints, or through head-on prohibitions of certain practices, injured parties would be able to countervail anticompetitive actions by STEs. As in the Subsidies Agreement, a two-track approach might be considered, allowing either a legal challenge of the policy or practice itself, or actions to countervail the consequences. Under the countervail route, the subsidy equivalent of the anticompetitive policies or practices would need to be determined. One could also envisage an attempt to classify STEs into green, amber, and red categories, along the lines found in the WTO Subsidies agreement. This would imply that some types of STEs would be permitted, some would be countervailable, and some would be prohibited.[20]

In general this is an approach that has little to recommend itself. Problems associated with the behavior of STEs are much better addressed at their source through agreed rules, whether these focus on behavioral restraints or on circumscribing the practices themselves. Although the granting of an exclusive privilege or right may be equivalent to a subsidy in an economic sense, quantifying the subsidy equivalent would be difficult and potentially controversial, as would be agreement on defining a tolerance level for trade distortions arising from STE behavior. Subsidies, and appropriate measures to counter their impact on trade, have been a contentious issue in the GATT system. In the Uruguay Round, agreement was reached that a subsidy is deemed to exist if there is a financial contribution by a government (or public body). This in turn may involve either a direct transfer of funds (e.g., grants, loans, and equity infusion), potential direct transfers of funds or liabilities (e.g., loan guarantees), or government revenue foregone (e.g., tax concessions or credits). Reopening the discussion of what constitutes a countervailable subsidy is unlikely to be productive. More generally, if it is accepted that STEs can be considered equivalent to subsidies, the path is opened to more general attempts to consider the subsidy equivalent of government regulations and policies. This would be a dangerous direction for the trading system, opening the door to greater tolerance of trade-distorting policies, combined with trade-restricting self-help remedies.

Apply Generic Competition Rules to STEs

Given their status as enterprises, STEs can in principle be subject to competition law. This is the case in the EU: Article 90 of the ECT prohibits public undertakings and entities with exclusive privileges from maintaining measures that violate the rules of the Treaty of Rome, especially the rules on competition, unless this is *necessary* to achieve the tasks required by the government. An advantage of the Article 90 approach is that it does not distinguish between STEs and other firms: the same competition rules apply to all. The main area of attention therefore centers on the "necessity" test. For such an approach to be emulated in the WTO it will be necessary to agree on a common set of competition rules.

Noteworthy here is that Article XVII of GATT and Article VIII of GATS pertain not only to formally granted exclusivity arrangements, but also to entities that have been granted exclusive rights *in effect*. The need to address such *de facto* rights calls for consideration of what role competition policy might play in dealing with the behavior of STEs. STE-like practices that governments do not directly support through de jure exclusivity arrangements could be of two kinds. Either they can result because governments indirectly and in effect give independent economic agents the ability to behave anticompetitively because of some policy intervention, such as a tariff or a badly designed technical standard. Alternatively, they can arise purely from market structure, unaided by any government policy. For those practices indirectly supported by other government interventions, the offending policy should be dealt with as the first-best option. If, however, there is some overriding reason for maintaining the offending policy (e.g., governments must apply discriminatory taxes to obtain revenue), behavioral norms and restraints may be an appropriate option. Similarly, behavioral restraints may be called for where STE-like practices are made possible by the structure of a market alone.

More generally, state trading falls within the ambit of concerns typically associated with competition policy — that is, there are market entry and/or exit barriers which prevent competition from occurring in the market. Unfortunately, suggestions to introduce competition or antitrust policy norms and remedies for STEs run into the problem that formal, *de jure* exclusivity arrangements derive from government-granted privilege. Antitrust cannot play much of a role in reducing the anticompetitive impact of formal STEs, as these will by definition be exempt from national antitrust law. It is for this reason that a multilateral set of competition disciplines will be needed. The relevance of national antitrust disciplines could be greater in addressing market entry and exit barriers that are supported by "informal" exclusive rights. Recent accession negotiations have revealed that such "informal" situations are a cause for concern for WTO members.

The issue of whether to pursue a multilateral agreement on competition policy is of course a general one, and is the subject of the deliberations of the Working Group on the Interaction of Trade and Competition Policy. Opinions differ regarding the need for and feasibility of negotiating an agreement.

As far as de jure STEs are concerned, it is likely that one or more of the alternative approaches noted in this chapter will be pursued by WTO members.

Contestability and Efficiency Norms

A final approach is more economic in nature. It is built on the premise that behavioral and procedural rules should be complemented by mechanisms to increase the probability that STEs, when used, will be efficient in attaining whatever non-economic objectives are pursued by a government. This applies especially to instances where *service publique* considerations predominate and it is argued that restrictions on trade and/or violations of national treatment are necessary to achieve the objectives. One possibility in this connection would be to grant WTO members the right to ask for determination that the operation of and rights granted to a STE are such that no alternative methods exist to achieve the objectives at equal or lower cost, while reducing the trade distorting impact. Another possibility would be to impose a requirement that STEs report data that allow the WTO Secretariat to determine the tariff or subsidy equivalent of their operation. This is of course not a trivial matter, and consideration could be given to requiring the use of alternative methods both to generate data and to increase the likelihood that STEs are operating efficiently. Here one enters into the realm of regulation and regulatory control mechanisms. There are many options, and clearly a great deal of thought is required to explore the various possibilities. The point to be made is that there may well be a need to address the question of designing mechanisms to monitor the behavior of STEs as part of a State Trading Agreement, and that the welfare payoff of doing so can be large.

5. Conclusions

State trading has been poorly attended to in the history of GATT, not least because it was considered a relatively minor aspect of policy among the original signatories of the GATT, and in any event was most prevalent in agriculture — a sector that remained largely outside the purview of multilateral discipline until the Uruguay Round. This situation has changed with the introduction of services into the WTO and the prospective accession to the WTO of many economies in transition. In effect, state trading is part of a much bigger complex of policy questions to do with the conditions of competition in markets.

The sources of market access problems arising from state trading include: (i) explicit privileges granted by government; and (ii) *de facto* obstacles arising incidentally from government policies which aim at objectives other than the insulation of privileged suppliers. These impediments to competition can be dealt with in a number of different ways. First, behavioral disciplines could be further developed. These would apply to *de jure* privileges and should pertain to those STEs that governments regard as non-negotiable and wish to continue to maintain. This behavioral approach can be complemented by efforts to introduce greater economic content into WTO rules by adopting a set of regulatory principles that seek to ensure that STEs will operate in an efficient and least-trade distorting manner. It should also be complemented by requirements regarding domestic enforcement mechanisms, perhaps along the lines of the bid-protest or challenge mechanisms foreseen in the GPA.

An alternative is to pursue negotiations to eliminate state trading in the style contemplated by GATS. This is a more direct approach than the imposition of behavioral restraints, and would certainly address *de jure* arrangements effectively. It is the "revealed preferred" approach in the context of current accession negotiations, through emphasis on the trading rights of enterprises and privatization commitments. While straightforward in principle, this approach is inherently limited in the sense that governments will differ regarding the extent to which they are willing to negotiate away their rights to grant exclusive rights and privileges in the pursuit of *service publique* objectives.

The issue of addressing *de facto* exclusivity is best seen as a more general matter. To the extent that STE-like behavior is facilitated by other government interventions, these should be the focus of attention. Where government policy *per se* is not the root of the problem, competition policy questions enter the picture. These, however, would be more adequately addressed in the broader context of the current debate on trade and competition. It is difficult to envisage an effective approach to dealing with *de facto* exclusionary behavior on the part of enterprises[21] without a willingness by governments to delve deeper into regulatory issues (both trade- and non-trade-related), and also to contemplate policy activism to deal with exclusionary or anticompetitive behavior that does not feed on government intervention.

Addressing STE-related problems, whether *de jure* or *de facto* in origin, through countervailing mechanisms of a self-help nature would be a bad idea. It would further open the door to an approach that tolerates trade distortions in exchange for the right to impose additional restrictions on trade. Quite apart from the scope for sanctioning suboptimal policy interventions, experience shows that this approach lends itself to a range of definitional problems and to various kinds of abuse that can be difficult to control. Finally, reliance on remedies to STE-like behavior via the WTO's dispute settlement mechanism is limited by the nature of the underlying rules themselves, and by the narrow range of circumstances in which non-violation complaints would prosper.

NOTES

1. The same applied to government consumption. GATT signatories agreed that public purchases or procurement of goods for government use would not be subject to the national treatment rule, which requires that once foreign products have entered a market they are treated no less favorably than similar domestic goods. A side agreement on government procurement (the Agreement on Government Procurement) negotiated in the Tokyo Round (1973–1979) establishes rights and obligations that only apply among the signatories to this agreement. For a wide-ranging analysis of the treatment of procurement in the GATT/WTO system, see Hoekman and Mavroidis (1997).

2. See Drebentsov and Michalopolous (1998) and Martin and Bach (1998) for empirical assesments of the extent and impact of STEs in Russia and China.

3. Understanding on Article XVII.

4. Article XVII talks of rights or privileges that are granted "formally or in effect". The Uruguay Round Understanding on STEs foresees counter-notifications by trading partners.

5. See Ingco and Ng (1997) for an assessment of the impact and prevalence of state trading in agriculture.

6. A supporting note to Art. II:4 states that Article II GATT will be applied in light of the provisions of Article 31 of the Havana Charter. Art. 31 *inter alia* required that STEs must satisfy the full domestic demand for imports and provided for binding of the level of protection imposed by import monopolies (Davey, 1997). Thus, under the GATT, the margins charged by importing STEs (their mark-ups) may be bound similarly to tariffs. While extensive commitments have been made to bind tariffs, commitments to bind mark-ups by STEs have been rare. In 1952 Italy undertook not to exceed a fifteen percent mark-up on wheat and rye imported by the Italian government or its agencies. France made a similar commitment regarding wheat imports by the "Office National Interprofessionel des Cereals", and undertook a minimum import commitment with respect to lead, tobacco, and cigarettes imported by France's tobacco monopoly from countries other than those of the French Union. Both concessions lapsed with the formation of a common tariff schedule for the EEC (Hoekman and Kostecki, 1995).

7. This interpretation was given in a 1984 legal finding on Canada's administration of its Foreign Investment Review Act.

8. Jurisprudence in GATT has extended national treatment obligations to STEs, but on the basis of violations of Article III, not Article XVII.

9. Indirectly, however, the Uruguay Round led to greater control on state trading activity through increased coverage of tariff bindings and the elimination of quantitative restrictions. This will ensure that the Article II:4 provision disallowing mark-ups on imports in excess of tariff bindings has wider application. In addition,

the Agreement on Agriculture contains a general prohibition on the use of nontariff barriers in agriculture, including those maintained through state trading enterprises (Article 4.2).

10. It is worth noting that in the mid 1950s public enterprises accounted for twenty-five to thirty percent of gross fixed investment in Austria, France, Italy, and the United Kingdom (Milward, 1992:38).

11. Dixit and Josling (1997) have pointed out that many agricultural STEs could be defended in the past on the basis that they administered legal quotas justified under Article XI:2 GATT. This greatly limited the applicability of Article II:4.

12. These related to procedures and methodologies associated with the determination of dumping.

13. Except in the circumstance that involve a mark-up on import prices by a STE in excess of a bound level of mark-up or tariff, as envisaged in Article II:4, which would entail a violation case.

14. Of course, all the other WTO rules and disciplines apply, e.g., on the use of quantitative restrictions, subsidies, etc. See Horlick and Heim Mowry (1998) on the link between subsidy and STE disciplines.

15. To give just one illustration of the need for national treatment, take the case of a telecom operator that provides data on phone numbers and addresses for the universe of subscribers to a domestic firm publishing a Yellow Pages at a much lower cost than what it charges a foreign firm that wishes to contest the yellow pages market. Without a national treatment requirement, entry may be prohibited.

16. GPA members must submit data on a number of key procurement-related activity indicators, including the share of contracts that are below certain thresholds and the share of foreign sourcing (see Hoekman and Mavroidis, 1997). Analogous reporting requirements could be envisaged under an STA.

17. Trade in services is defined in terms of four modes of supply under GATS. These are cross-border supply, consumption abroad, commercial presence (investment), and the presence of natural persons.

18. This point was made at the conference by Crawford Falconer and Gary Horlick.

19. On this issue see Mavroidis and Messerlin (1998) and Bourgeois (1998).

20. This has been proposed by Dixit and Josling (1997).

21. It should be recalled that both the GATT and the GATS use the formulation of "formally or in effect" when dealing with these questions.

R E F E R E N C E S

Bourgeois, Jacques. 1998. "EC Rules on State Monopolies and Public Undertakings: Lessons for the WTO." In this volume.
Davey, William. 1998. "Article XVII GATT: An Overview." In this volume.
Dixit, Praveen and Tim Josling. 1997. "State Trading in Agriculture: An Analytical Framework." Mimeo.

Drebentsov, Vladimir and Constantine Michalopoulos. 1998. "State Trading in Russia." In this volume.

Hoekman, Bernard and Michel Kostecki. 1995. *The Political Economy of the World Trading System: From GATT to WTO.* Oxford: Oxford University Press.

Hoekman, Bernard and Petros C. Mavroidis, eds. 1997. *Law and Policy in Public Purchasing: The WTO Agreement on Government Procurement.* Ann Arbor: University of Michigan Press.

Horlick, Gary and Kristin Heim Mowry. 1998. "The Treatment of Activities of State Trading Enterprises Under the WTO Subsidies Rules." In this volume.

Ingco, Melinda and Francis Ng. 1997. "Distortionary Effects of State Trading in Agricultural Trade: Policy Issues for the 1999 Round." Mimeo.

Kostecki, Michel. 1982. "State Trading by the Advanced and Developing Countries." In M. Kostecki, ed. *State Trading in International Markets.* New York: St. Martin's Press.

Lloyd, Peter. 1982. "State Trading and the Theory of International Trade." In M. Kostecki, ed. *State Trading in International Markets.* New York: St. Martin's Press.

Martin, Will and Christian Bach. 1998. "State Trading in China." In this volume.

Mavroidis, Petros C. and Patrick Messerlin. 1998. "Has Art. 90 Prejudged the Status of Property Ownership?" In this volume.

Milward, Alan. 1992. *The European Rescue of the Nation-State.* Berkeley: University of California Press.

Schmitz, James. 1996. "The Role Played by Public Enterprises: How Much Does it Differ Across Countries?" Federal Reserve Board of Minneapolis Quarterly Review, 20: 2–15.

World Bank. 1995. *Bureaucrats in Business.* Washington, D.C.: World Bank.

CHAPTER 18

Has Article 90 ECT Prejudged the Status of Property Ownership?

*Petros C. Mavroidis and Patrick A. Messerlin**

I. Introduction

This chapter examines the recent jurisprudence of the European Court of Justice (ECJ) in the field of state enterprises. More specifically, it aims at decodifying the philosophy of the ECJ on the following issue: to what extent the ECJ has prejudged the extent of state involvement in economic activities through its jurisprudence?

Normally, the starting point should be the European Community Treaty (ECT) itself. However, one can deduce no clear answer on this issue by merely examining the ECT. Article 222 ECT unambiguously establishes a neutral approach with respect to property ownership in the Member States of the European Community (EC). Articles 90*ff.* ECT regulate the modalities of government involvement in economic activities by subjecting, in principle, such involvement to the EC rules on competition and only exceptionally liberating them from this obligation. Thus, in the ECT system, there is implicitly the recognition that, in principle, respecting competition laws can prejudge decisions on property ownership. Moreover, recent amendments to the ECT seem to underline the primacy of the EC competition laws. Hence the interpretation of the relevant ECT general provisions and exceptions is crucial: this is precisely why one should turn to the ECJ case-law in this field.

We aim to present a comprehensive framework of the ECJ case-law in this field from both the legal and the economic perspectives. By doing so, we leave aside what is likely to be a crucial aspect of the problem: the political aspect. State enterprises have been one of the most blatant manifestations of the post-war European (Member) state power. Almost all the European state enterprises have been created for political purposes — from "nationalisation" to state ownership as a sanction on vanquished people (such as the French car maker Renault in 1945).

*Respectively, University of Neuchâtel, Law Faculty, and Institut d'Etudes Politiques de Paris. We thank very much the participants at the conference, particularly Damien Neven, for very helpful criticisms and comments.

In the early years of the Community, this political aspect was not at odds with the then-existing microeconomic foundations of state-owned enterprises (anyway, it is highly unlikely that economics played any notable role in the decision to create such firms). Hence, the above-mentioned dual (public ownership vs. competition) structure of the ECT was not perceived as a source of serious conflicts until the 1980s. The experience of the state-owned enterprises and the evolution of economic analysis have changed this situation. State-owned enterprises have been increasingly perceived as a source of political benefits and economic costs — at least when compared to private firms operating in more competitive markets. This perception has generated increasing strains on the interpretation of the ECT which is, by nature, a set of legal commitments on economic issues aiming at creating a political entity. These tensions are mirrored by the ECJ rulings. These rulings try to favor economic considerations, but they carefully avoid any discussion of the basic political issue of state power. As a result, they consist of decisions worded in such a way that they can contribute to an erosion of the state-owned enterprises — but only to the extent that the public opinion in the concerned Member State is ready to listen the message.

The chapter is organized as follows. Section 2 examines the ECT provisions dealing with state-owned enterprises. Section 3 analyzes the relevant ECJ case-law, and Section 4 concludes.

2. The ECT Provisions on State Enterprises

There is always the twin dangers of seeing the ECT as a logical construction starting from scratch and of perceiving the economic analysis of competition issues as a set of immutable rules.

The ECT mirrors a one-time compromise between vested interests and emerging forces. It was struck at a time when Western European economies were relatively simple, catching up with the U.S. economy — all factors relatively favorable to state intervention — and not under the pressure of massive and rapid technical progress. Indeed, in most of the EC Member States of the late 1950s, few people were convinced of the superiority of the market economy over central planning — not to mention the ultimate triumph of the "mixed economy" and "indicative planning". One had to wait for the fall of the Berlin Wall to get a majority of Europeans (and maybe even all the EC Member States) convinced of the relative merit of markets.

Economists were not much more enlightened than non-economists. In the late 1950s, many of them accepted the idea that a planned economy could successfully mimic a market economy [Lange, 1936], that ownership was totally irrelevant for efficiency, and that state-owned monopolies could follow optimization rules better and more easily than private monopolies (close to what microeconomic theory suggested, such as pricing at marginal cost) [Boiteux, 1956]. It took some time for the economists to recognize that these arguments may be correct, but that they disregard crucial points, such as the exact scope of scale economies, externalities and market failures, the numerous alternative ways to deal with these factors, or the role of dynamic incentives and rent-seeking behavior. Progressively, these latter points have revealed their full importance — particularly when technical progress became strong and when existing state-owned enterprises involved a large percentage of the labor force (creating huge coalitions of vested interests).

All this explains that in the late 1950s the ECT was seen as having the rare virtue of being *both* a politically acceptable and an economically consistent set of rules. Article 222 ECT acknowledged the existence of state-owned enterprises which were not seen as a threat to microeconomic optimization rules consistent with competitive markets. Article 37 ECT was available for eliminating the intra-EC discriminatory impact of state-owned monopolies of a commercial character. Article 90(1) ECT confirmed the dominant role of competition, and as will be argued, Article 90(2) ECT was a "safeguard" valve. In this structure, Article 90 ECT is the most ambiguous piece: as a result, it deserves attention first.

An Overview of Article 90 ECT

On its face, Article 90 ECT does not seem to prejudge property ownership in the Member States. It states that in principle, any public undertaking has to observe the ECT rules on competition. Public undertakings are exempted from this obligation only insofar as the conditions mentioned in Article 90(2) ECT are fulfilled. Article 90 ECT reads as follows:

1. In the case of public undertakings and undertakings to which Members States grant special or exclusive rights, Member States shall neither enact nor maintain in force any measure contrary to the rules contained in this Treaty, in particular those rules provided for in Article 6 and Articles 85 to 94.

2. Undertakings entrusted with the operation of services of general economic interest or having the character of a revenue producing monopoly shall be subject to the rules contained in this Treaty, in particular the rules on competition, insofar as the application of such rules does not obstruct the performance in law or in fact of the particular tasks assigned to them. The development of trade must not be affected to such an extent as would be contrary to the interests of the Community.

3. The Commission shall ensure the application of the provisions of this Article and shall where necessary address the appropriate directives or decisions to Member States.

Contrary to the first impression of neutrality with respect to property ownership in the Member States, we argue that the system of the ECT is prepared to accommodate the needs of public undertakings, and thus to facilitate state intervention, as Article 90(2) ECT states.

On its face, when subjecting all public undertakings to the EC competition laws, Article 90 ECT follows the neutrality of the ECT with respect to property ownership unambiguously established in Article 222 ECT which states, "[t]his Treaty shall in no way prejudice the rules of the Member States governing the system of property ownership".

Article 90 ECT does not require the elimination of state-owned monopolies (state-owned firms having special or exclusive rights) — thus implicitly recognizing their legitimacy. The ECT takes the view that one state-owned producer can behave as a competitive firm: Article 90 ECT imposes disciplines on the Member State (not to enact or maintain in force any anti-competitive measure) and Articles 85–86 ECT impose disciplines on the producer itself. This is essentially why for a long time the legal system of the EC was perceived as neutral with respect to property ownership.

It is interesting to note that Article 37 ECT puts additional limits on public monopolies on behalf of "pure" competition, with its first and third paragraphs:

> 1. Member States shall progressively adjust any State monopolies of a commercial character so as to ensure that when the transitional period has ended no discrimination regarding the conditions under which goods are procured and marketed exists between nationals of Member States. . . .
>
> ***
>
> 3. . . . If a product is subject to a State monopoly of a commercial character in only one or some Member States, the Commission may authorize the other Member States to apply protective measures until the adjustment provided for in paragraph 1 has been effected; the Commission shall determine the conditions and details of such measures.

Prices are certainly among such "conditions of providing and marketing the goods". As a result, Article 37(1) ECT limits price discrimination by public state-owned monopolies when based on the nationality of the consumers. In other words, Article 37(1) ECT is a specific antidumping provision for state-owned enterprises: it is a wider antidumping clause than the corresponding Article 91(1) ECT for private firms because discrimination is prohibited *per se*, without any specific consideration for prices or costs in the home and export markets of the state-owned enterprise. In this respect, one can argue that the ECT introduces *too much* "pure" competition. It ignores the fact that state-owned monopolies, as private firms, could have economically sound reasons for "dumping" or price-discriminating. Differences among consumers' demand elasticities could flow from the fact that nationals from one Member State have more confidence in their national state-owned enterprise or that the domestic monopoly better fits the taste of its nationals.

This "excessive" competition constraint is confirmed by the antidumping procedure allowed by Article 37(3) ECT quoted above. This paragraph authorizes "protective" measures which do not refer to the so-called "boomerang" antidumping procedure under Article 91(2) ECT (allegedly dumped goods must be admitted back in the exporting Member State without any barrier). In other words, the ECT more severely restricts dumping by state monopolies of commercial character than it restricts dumping by private firms. This confirms not only the apparent neutrality of the ECT with respect to the ownership issue, but also the fact that in 1958 all the provisions of the ECT could only be seen as perfectly in line with the perception of ideal pure competition prevailing during the early days of the Community.

Article 90(2) ECT

Forty years later, our understanding of competition has evolved for reasons briefly evoked at the beginning of this section. These changes have been exacerbated by more circumstantial reasons. Many EC Member States run substantial debts: in order to reach the Maastricht disciplines and qualify for integration in the monetary union, they have to minimize state involvement in economic activities. As a result, it seems that the scope for state-owned enterprises consistent with competition has almost completely evaporated. Privatization is seen as a necessary (though it is not sufficient) ingredient to competitive markets.

At a first glance, this conclusion suggests focussing on Article 222 ECT as the key stumbling block and the most obvious remnant of the past. However, this should not be the case. If a Member State is stuck in old ideological beliefs and wants to keep state-owned enterprises, it essentially hurts *itself* — not its EC partners. Since competition from private firms will be progressively substituted for state-owned firms, why bother about Article 222 ECT? There are many other provisions in the ECT which do not play any noticeable role. In one, two, or three decades — depending on the rapidity of Member States in breaking with the past and from the strength of competition — an inter-governmental conference will eliminate Article 222 ECT.

However, there is a limit to this lax attitude with respect to Article 222 ECT: the possibility that the state-owned enterprises are so unsuccessful that they have to be subsidized. This possibility has been — and still is — a real problem in the Community, particularly in services (air transport, banking, etc.). However, this is not sufficient to consider Article 222 ECT as a key issue: it simply means that the harm of keeping Article 222 ECT depends on the Community's disciplines on state aids.

The real obstacle to the evolution required by our new understanding of competitive markets is Article 90(2) ECT. Whereas Article 90(1) ECT refers to all public undertakings, Article 90(2) ECT refers to some of them, namely those that are entrusted with the operation of services of general economic interest. Viewed from this angle, Article 90(2) ECT is *lex specialis* to Article 90(1) ECT.[1] It explicitly liberates some public undertakings from the obligation to respect EC competition rules. Arguably, such respect could eventually put into question the very existence (or establishment) of the public undertakings covered by Article 90(2) ECT. The *ratio legis* of Article 90(2) ECT consequently, could be the will to ensure that this is not the case. One could speak of EC "affirmative action" in this respect in order to ensure neutrality with respect to property ownership as Article 222 ECT mandates. For this reason, the rest of the chapter will pay comparatively more attention to the ECJ case-law in the field of Article 90(2) ECT.

In a GATT/WTO context, it seems reasonable to interpret Article 90(2) ECT as a safeguard clause. It implicitly refers to some kind of harm or "injury": it assumes that, without the use of services of general economic interest, certain interests will be hurt in some way. It relies on a concept (services of general economic interest) at least as vague as the "injury" concept embodied in the GATT safeguard provision. This *ad hoc* concept (with no other mention in the ECT) is all the more vague in that it has no equivalent in the legal order of Member States. The closest concept is the *service public* in French law (that today no French lawyer is able to define). Indeed, the wide variation of the estimated costs of service public in telecoms (from almost zero in Britain to five billion francs in France) suggests that service public *de facto* has a lot to do with the political environment of the country. This is close to a safeguard clause which relies on vague concepts in order to provide the degree of freedom necessary for trading partners to deal with political pressures from vested interests.

Recent Evolution

One should take into account though, that the aforementioned articles are not the only relevant ones for the purposes of our analysis. A contextual interpretation requires a thorough examination of at least the rest of the Treaty.

First, we note that Article 5 ECT prohibits Member States from taking any action that might frustrate the attainment of the objectives assigned to the ECT, including those espoused in Articles 85 and 86 ECT (the EC competition rules). Hence, the tension between regulated monopolies that can, in principle, operate beyond the reach of EC competition laws (Article 90 ECT) and the obligation of Member States not to frustrate the objectives of the ECT (including those on competition).

Second, over time, there has been some encroachment on the freedom of Member States regarding public ownership. Article 3 of the Treaty on Economic Union (TEU) states:

> . . . the activities of the Members States and the Community shall include . . . the adoption of an economic policy which is based on the close coordination of Member States' economic policies, on the internal market and on the definition of common objectives, and conducted in accordance with the principle of an open market economy with free competition.[2]

Article 3 TEU is part of the "principles" of the Treaty and, arguably, should be of higher hierarchical value than the rest of the Articles.[3] At any rate, the obligations imposed in the main body of the TEU have to be interpreted against this background. Such an interpretation would be consistent with the general rule of interpretation embodied in Article 31 of the Vienna Convention on the Law of Treaties (VCLT). (We remind the reader that there is no serious allegation anymore against the thesis that Article 31 VCLT codifies customary international law.) Article 3 TEU constitutes at least part of the context of Article 90 ECT and consequently, according to Article 31 VCLT, has to be taken into account whenever Article 90 ECT is interpreted. Gardner (1995) based, *inter alia*, his conclusion that ". . . the neutrality towards public and privileged enterprises in the text of the Treaty of Rome as signed in 1957 has now been supplanted by a presumption of illegality" on the recent amendments.

3. The ECJ Case-law in the State Enterprise Field

Recent ECJ case-law on Article 90 ECT illustrates the rising challenge to state ownership.[4] In the early case-law in this field, the ECJ essentially attacked the "abusive" exercise of special or exclusive rights. More recent case-law suggests that even the mere existence of a monopoly can constitute an abuse of dominant position and thus violate the ECT. Indeed, the ECJ appears to have set limits regarding the permissible extent of regulated monopolies.

Article 90(1) ECT

At first the ECJ demonstrated in an unambiguous way its intentions to avoid treating Article 90(1) ECT as dead letter when it ruled in the *France v Commission* case [C-202/88] that:

... it should be noted that even though that article presupposes the existence of undertakings which have certain special or exclusive rights, it does not follow that all the special or exclusive rights are necessarily compatible with the Treaty. That depends on different rules, to which Article 90(1) refers.[5]

Subsequently, the ECJ contributed some very interesting clarifications explaining its attitude with respect to Article 90(1) ECT. In *Port of Genoa* [Case C-179/90], the ECJ found that an undertaking was abusing its dominant position by pricing excessively. In the *ERT* case [C-260/89], the ECJ found that the likelihood that the existence of the special or exclusive right would lead to abuse was enough to take action. In *Höfner* [C-41/90], the ECJ concluded that Members States will violate Article 90 ECT if the undertaking enjoying special or exclusive rights cannot avoid abusive behaviour when exercising such rights. In this case, the German Government had granted the Federal Employment Office an exclusive right to conduct job placement. No other private or public undertaking was permitted under German law to perform similar functions. The Federal Employment Office was unable to satisfy demand, leading the ECJ to find against it. Edward and Hoskins (1995) correctly insist on reproducing the French text which better reflects the ECJ's approach on this issue:

[the Court decided that] . . . serait incompatible avec les régles du traité toute mesure d'un Etat membre qui maintiendrait en vigueur une disposition légale créant une situation dans laquelle un office public pour l'emploi serait nécessairement amené a contrevenir aux termes de l'article 86.[6]

It is the "inevitability" captured in the word "*nécessairement*" that probably led the ECJ to formulate its position.

The line of reasoning in *Höfner* is certainly more restrictive than that in *ERT*. The approach followed in *Höfner* seems to be confirmed in the recent ECJ decision in the recent *La Crespelle* case [C-323/93]. There the Court decided that:

A Member State contravenes the prohibitions contained in those two provisions only if, in merely exercising the exclusive right granted to it, the undertaking in question cannot avoid abusing its dominant position.[7]

In the same judgment, the Court further clarifies this point when it states the relevant question to be addressed in order to establish compatibility (or, as the case may be, incompatibility) with Article 90(1) ECT. The opinion states, "[t]he question to be examined is therefore whether such a practice constituting the alleged abuse is the direct consequence of the national law".[8]

Thus, it seems that the "inevitability" mentioned in *Höfner* is confirmed. Were one to make a synthesis of the aforementioned case-law, one would therefore conclude that in the context of Article 90(1) ECT, the ECJ will outlaw public undertakings any time that their establishment will inevitably lead to disrespect of the ECT Articles mentioned in the context of Article 90(1) ECT. There is consequently a condition of direct causality between the establishment of the public undertaking and the disrespect of the relevant ECT rules that has to be satisfied for the ECJ to proceed in the outlawing of state intervention in this context.

Article 90(2) ECT

With respect to Article 90(2) ECT, the situation is presented as follows. In *Corbeau* [C-239/91], the ECJ was presented with the case of Paul Corbeau, a delivery services provider in the city of Liège, Belgium. He specialized in rapid delivery (within one day). It was alleged that this interfered with the monopoly of the Belgian *Régie des Postes* and proceedings against Mr. Corbeau were instituted in the competent Belgian court. The ECJ, to which the case was submitted by the Belgian court, observed at first that: ". . . it cannot be disputed that the Régie des Postes is entrusted with a service of general economic interest . . . ".[9]

It then goes on to state that:

> However, the exclusion of competition is not justified as regards specific services *dissociable* from the service of general interest which meet special needs of economic operators and which call for additional services not offered by the traditional postal service, such as collection from the senders' address, greater speed or reliability of distribution or the possibility of changing the destination in the course of transit, in so far as such specific services, by their nature and the conditions in which they are offered, such as the geographical area in which they are provided, do not compromise the economic equilibrium of the service of general economic interest performed by the holder of the exclusive right.
>
> It is for the national court to consider whether the services at issue in the dispute before it meet those criteria.[10]

And based on such considerations, the ECJ goes on to conclude that:

> It is contrary to Article 90 of the EEC Treaty for a legislation of a Member State which confers on a body such as the Régie des Postes the exclusive right to collect, carry and distribute mail, to prohibit, under threat of criminal penalties, an economic operator established in that

State from offering certain specific services dissociable from the service operated of general interest which meet the special needs of economic operators and call for certain additional services not offered by the traditional postal service, in so far as those services do not compromise the economic stability of the service of general economic interest performed by the holder of the exclusive right. It is for the national court to consider whether the services in question in the main proceedings meet those criteria.

This decision, unfortunately, presents us with more problems than those it tried to solve. Although it might be perceived as a direct attack on the extent of the state, a closer look will take away some of the first impressions. Let us first of all see what is at stake.

Mr. Corbeau collects mail in Liège, Belgium from the senders' home and promises to have it delivered by noon on the following day. This promise, however, is valid only for mail delivered within Mr. Corbeau's self-defined district, namely the City of Liège and the surrounding areas. As far as the rest of the mail is concerned, Mr. Corbeau still collects it from the senders' home but sends it by post. We are basically facing here a niche market and consequently, the ECJ's decision should be appreciated within the correct *ordre de grandeur*. One could hardly, for example, compare the ECJ's activities in this field with the U.S. Department of Justice (DOJ) attack on the telecoms sector in the early 1980s. Of course, and in order to keep things in perspective, the ECJ is part of the judiciary whereas the U.S. DOJ is part of the executive and arguably, the latter is better legitimized to address such issues.

For the Article 90(2) ECT rule to come into play, one important question has to be answered, namely whether the service in question is of general economic interest — hence, the importance of the question: who defines whether a service is of general economic interest? The ECJ neither explicitly assumes nor explicitly refuses such responsibility. On the one hand, it states that it cannot be disputed that the *Régie des Postes* is entrusted with a service of general economic interest, thus giving the impression that it is competent to define whether a service is of such interest. Moreover, when it mentions "dissociable" services in the cited passage, one begins to get the impression that the ECJ is competent to define the extent of such services. However, one paragraph later the ECJ decides that it is up to national courts to decide whether a service is or is not dissociable from a service of general interest. And then the question becomes: does the ECJ provide national courts with enough guidance in this endeavor?

We conclude that, unfortunately, this is not the case. The criteria offered by the ECJ resemble very much the sayings of Pythia in Delphi and hardly promote legal security. The Court accepts that the mailing service is in the general interest since it has "the obligation to collect, carry and distribute mail on behalf of all users throughout the territory of the Member State concerned, at uniform tariffs and on similar quality conditions, irrespective of the specific situations or the degree of economic profitability of each individual operation".[11] According to the ECJ, it is then up to national courts, using this definition, to define which are the dissociable services. The national court can use as criteria essentially (i) whether such services are (or are not) offered by traditional postal service and (ii) whether some economic operators need greater speed and reliability. The national court, when defining whether a service is dissociable, should keep in mind, however, that its performance should "not compromise the economic equilibrium of the service of general economic interest". In other words, it should ensure that no creaming-off of the gains in the profitable segments of the market should occur; the guarantee that no creaming-off will occur is, in the Court's analysis, the necessary precondition for cross-subsidization of the less profitable sectors.

Our argument is that the ECJ's decision is based on dubious economics. Let us first though turn on to some peripheral problems. First, traditional postal services, like all traditional services, are changing every day. Besides the on-going discussion on privatization lies another on-going discussion, namely trade liberalization. As markets gradually open up, monopolies gradually disappear. Second, how can anybody besides the actual consumer possibly define what level of reliability or speed is desirable when it comes to postal services? Essentially, consumers so far did not have a choice: postal services have been entrusted to national monopolies. Courier services are a recent phenomenon. Market indicators show that this is a growing market: more and more consumers prefer or need the reliability/speed provided by courier services. It seems a quixotic test to try to define how many consumers do prefer or need such services. It depends on a series of parameters, like their availability, their cost, etc. Some of them are easy to quantify, some are not. A national court however, more likely than not, simply lacks the resources to proceed to this type of analysis. As a result, were one to follow the ECJ's decision on this point to refer to national courts, one would most likely end up with arbitrary results. Maybe subsidiarity-driven considerations led the ECJ to this decision. But the theory of optimal intervention presupposes the right choice of the organ as well; courts are rather ill-suited for such an exercise.

Yet, the basic problem with this decision is the wrong economic premise that to a large extent defines the legal ruling. In three paragraphs, the ECJ essentially explains its economic philosophy in this field:

The question which falls to be considered is therefore the extent to which a restriction on competition or even the exclusion of all competition from other economic operators is necessary in order to allow the holder of the exclusive right to perform its task of general interest and in particular to have the benefit of economically acceptable conditions.

The starting point of such an examination must be the premise that the obligation on the part of the undertaking entrusted with that task to perform its services in conditions of economic equilibrium presupposes that it will be possible to offset less profitable sectors against the profitable sectors and hence justifies a restriction of competition from individual undertakings where the economically profitable sectors are concerned.

Indeed, to authorize individual undertakings to compete with the holder of the exclusive rights in the sectors of their choice corresponding to those rights would make it possible for them to concentrate on the economically profitable operations and to offer more advantageous tariffs than those adopted by the holders of the exclusive rights since, unlike the latter, they are not bound for economic reasons to offset losses in the unprofitable sectors against the profits in the more profitable sectors.

These quotes underline the two key criteria of the ECJ *Corbeau* ruling for relieving the services of general economic interest from the scope of competition laws. The problem is, neither criteria are economically very sound.

The first criterion is the existence of "specific needs", defined by both a demand component ("special needs") and a supply component ("additional services not offered by the traditional postal service"). At a given point of time, the consumers' demand and the supply from the state enterprise never match perfectly — raising the above-mentioned issue of who should define the threshold where the extent to which supply and demand do not match is "unusual". This criterion is a crude definition of market relevance which is likely to be *de facto* biased against incremental changes: the institutions which are likely to be state-related (including if they are competition authorities or tribunals) would be inclined to risk-averse *ad hoc* definitions. This criterion is likely to open markets *slowly* where state-owned firms operate — except if technical progress favors product or service differentiation, as it does in telecoms.

Indeed, the ECJ *Corbeau* ruling is ambiguous enough to raise the question of the possible reversibility of the first criterion. If the supply or the demand (or both) component of the special needs disappears, is it conceivable that the service — now "normalized" — will come back to the general interest box of the state-owned firm? There is nothing in the ECJ *Corbeau* ruling to exclude the possibility that the special need, once satisfied by the public *Poste*, could not be satisfied again under the clause of a service of general economic interest.

In its second criterion, the ECJ imposes that the opening of the niche to competition should not "compromise the economic equilibrium of the service of general economic interest performed by the holder of the exclusive right". It is hard to interpret this key criterion which raises at least two sets of issues.

First, it is assumed that the service of general economic interest should have an economic equilibrium *per se*. Every term is ambiguous. Does "economic" mean financial? or does it refer to market clearance — the demand-supply equilibrium? Behind all these questions, the ECJ seems to have implicitly chosen one way of providing a loss-making service of general economic interest, whereas there are two ways. The first possibility is to keep a public firm combining the loss-making production of the service of general economic interest with the production of other products or services — the rents over the latter paying for the losses of the service of general economic interest. The second possibility is to allow for profit-making firms, but having them pay a direct subsidy in order to provide the alleged service of general economic interest — this solution being generally preferred by the "theory of distortions" [Bhagwati, 1963]. The ECJ condition tends to exclude this second solution.

In this respect, the *Corbeau* case illustrates the inconsistency of an international approach based on two partly inconsistent principles: a ban of subsidies on the basis of competition principles, and disciplines on state enterprises perceived as competitive firms (except when providing services of general economic interest). Subsidies can be perfectly acceptable on competition grounds. If they have to be disciplined, it is above all on the basis of their costs and benefits for the whole economy. Such an approach is likely to eliminate most of the reasons to exclude services of general economic interest from the scope of competition: the only price to be paid for the elimination of Article 90(2) ECT would be economically-sound disciplines on state aids.

Second, though it seems to confine the issue to a market-price dimension, the ECJ condition ignores all the complications related to the substitution and complementarity between the competitive service, the service of general economic interest, and the other goods or services produced by the state-owned firm. For instance, the situation examined in the *Corbeau* ruling includes at least three services: the service of general economic interest which is the Belgian *Poste*'s normal mail (based on an inexpensive stamp supposed affordable for everybody, hence loss-making); the service which "pays" the first product, say the Belgian *Poste*'s fast mail (paid by a more expensive stamp which is assumed to compensate the loss-making normal mail); and the competitor's service (the Corbeau express mail). The ECJ ruling states that Corbeau's express mail service should not compromise the financial equilibrium of the two first types of services. In addition to the above-mentioned problem (the possibility to finance the normal mail by subsidies), this approach raises questions because it takes the *Poste*'s behavior as exogenous. But, in fact, the *Poste*'s behavior is endogenous on an *ex ante* and *ex post* basis. It is endogenous on an *ex ante* basis in the sense the *Poste*'s price for its fast mail is a factor determining the entry of private firms. And it is endogenous on an *ex post* basis in the sense the *Poste*'s prices charged for both its normal and fast mail after the entry of competitors determine the *Poste*'s financial equilibrium.

4. Conclusion

The mid-1990s have witnessed an increasingly large ditch between the European Treaties and the regulatory reforms introduced in many non-(continental) European industrialized economies. Whereas the latter favor the functioning of markets without direct state economic regulations (but requiring disciplines, law enforcement, and social regulations when necessary), the European Treaties have tended to reaffirm the direct role of the state in the economic life — in terms of industrial policy, labor relations, etc. On October 2, 1997, the Treaty of Amsterdam was signed. A new Article 7 was introduced which reads as follows:

> Without prejudice to Articles 73, 86 and 87, and given the place occupied by services of general economic interest in the shared values of the Union as well as their role in promoting social and territorial cohesion, the Community and the Member States, each within their respective powers and within the scope of application of this Treaty, shall take care that such services operate on the basis of principles and conditions which enable them to fulfil their missions.

Article 7 was accepted with mixed emotions. Louis [1997] qualifies it as part of many "*déclarations essentiellement symboliques*". The Commissioner for Competition, Karel van Miert, seems to see more into it [Rodrigues, 1998]. At any rate, the vagueness of the Article 7 terms reinforces the opinion that the EC is more comfortable with the retreat of the jurisprudence as evidenced in the post-*Höfner* case-law of the ECJ — and particularly in the *Corbeau* case. Precisions are not advanced at the regulatory level and it is difficult to imagine how such provisions could come into play only through the ECJ.

NOTES

1. A state, however, does not get involved in economic activities only to pursue general economic interest: public choice theory has helped remove the veil of "benevolent governments". In this sense, there is a parallel between Art. 90(1) ECT and Art. 222 ECT, since the first requests respect of the EC competition rules without prejudging property ownership.

2. This has led some observers to conclude that competition policy is of higher hierarchical value than either trade or industrial policies. See Bourgeois and Demaret (1995).

3. This is the approach adopted by Bourgeois and Demaret (1995).

4. For an excellent overview, as well as a very original classification of the ECJ case-law in this field, see Edward and Hoskins (1995).

5. See [1991] ECR I-1223 at §22. Edward and Hoskins based on this passage conclude that "Member States have not retained complete sovereignty in relation to the creation of legal monopolies. Rather, the creation of such monopolies must be balanced with the principle of free competition. However, the precise point at which the balance is to be struck is less clear". See Edward and Hoskins (1995:160).

6. See Edward and Hoskins (1995:161).

7. See ECR (1995) I-5097 at §18 of the Court's judgment. The two provisions that the Court is referring to in this passage are those contained in Articles 86 and 90(1) ECT.

8. Id. at §20.

9. [1993] ECR I-2533 at §15.

10. Id. at §§19–20 (emphasis supplied).

11. Id. at §15.

REFERENCES

Bhagwati, Jagdish. 1963. "The Generalized Theory of Distortions and Welfare." In J. Bhagwati, R.W. Jones, R.A. Mundell, and J. Vanek, eds. *Trade, Balance of Payments, and Growth: Papers in Honor of C.P. Kindleberger*. Amsterdam: North Holland Publishing Company.
Boiteux, Marcel. 1956. "Sur la gestion des monopoles publics astreints à l'équilibre budgétaire." Econometrica 24.
Bourgeois, Jacques and Paul Demaret. 1995. "The EC Trade, Competition and Industrial Policies." In A. Jacquemin, P. Buigues, and A. Sapir, eds. *The EC Policies on Competition, Trade and Industry: Complementarities and Conflicts*. United Kindom: Elgar.
Case C-260/89, ERT v Dimotiki, 1991, ECR I-2925.
Case C-41/90, Hofner and Elser v Macrotron, 1991, ECR I-1979.
Case C-179/90, Corsica Ferries v Corpo dei Piloti del Porto di Genova, 1991, ECR I-5889.
Case C-320/91, Criminal Proceedings against Paul Corbeau, 1993, ECR I-2533.

Case C-323/93, Société Civile Agricole du Centre d'Insémination de la Crespelle v Coopérative d'Elevage et d'Insémination Artificielle du Département de la Mayenne, 1995, ECR I-5097.

Edward, David and Mark Hoskins. 1995 "Article 89: Deregulation and EC Law: Reflections Arising From the XVI FIDE Conference." Common Market Law Review 32:157–86.

Lange, Oskar. 1936. "On the Economic Theory of Socialism." Review of Economic Studies 4:53–71.

Louis, Jean Victor. 1997. "Le Traité d'Amsterdam: une occasion perdue?" Revue du Marché Unique Européen, 7 (July):9.

Rodrigues, Stephane, 1998, "Les services publics et le Traité d'Amsterdam." Revue du Marché commun et de l'Union européenne, 414 (January):37–46.

CHAPTER 19

Comments

Damien J. Neven

The paper by Hoekman and Low, *State Trading: Rule Making Alternatives for Entities with Exclusive Rights*, offers a lucid analysis of the current state of affairs towards state trading enterprises in the GATT and an insightful discussion of current policy options. The authors convincingly argue that Article XVII GATT is not powerful enough and they consider three ways in which it could be improved. First, they suggest that non-violation dispute settlement mechanisms should be applied to the establishment of state trading enterprises. One can only concur with this suggestion.

Hoekman and Low also consider broadening the scope of specific commitments regarding state trading enterprises in sectoral negotiations and subjecting the behaviour of these enterprises to multilateral discipline. Overall, they argue that specific commitments offer a better route than behavioural discipline. They shy away from this last option partly because the introduction of competition policy in the WTO is itself a contentious matter. Whether competition rules at the WTO should encompass the behaviour of state trading organisations is thus, in their view, a further delicate issue regarding a regulation which is itself unlikely to be established in the short-term. Their political judgement may be sound, but it is nonetheless interesting to pursue the matter a little further. Indeed, what the Community has done with Article 90 is precisely to make state trading enterprises subject to competition rules at some supranational level. The paper by Mavroidis and Messerlin which reviews the use of Article 90 and analyses its effectiveness thus offers a particularly useful evidence for the debate on the appropriate scope of antitrust rules in the WTO.

The first observation of Mavroidis and Messerlin in *Has Article 90 Prejudged the Status of Property Ownership* is that the second paragraph of Article 90 (allowing for an exceptions to the principle that regulated enterprises are subject to competition rules) is too general to be readily applicable. They argue that the courts have not been particularly good at clarifying the scope of this exception.

Mavroidis and Messerlin refer at length to the *Corbeau* case and argue that this decision is both bad law and bad economics. In their view, the *Corbeau* decision is based on dubious economic principles because it recommends an explicit cross-subsidy between the tasks undertaken by regulated enterprises. Restrictions of competition in the provision of services that could be fully liberalised are then justified by the need to generate a surplus which compensates for the loss that regulated enterprises make when meeting public service obligations. The authors rightly suggest that the optimal arrangement would entail full liberalisation of the competitive services together with a subsidy for public service obligations. However, they point out that the legal framework of the Community might not easily accommodate such a solution because the EC's strict regulation of state aids might not consider public service obligations as an adequate justification.

It is not clear whether the first best is the appropriate benchmark in this context. The distortions associated with taxation might easily dominate the distortions induced by a restriction of competition. In addition, the budget constraints imposed on the regulated enterprise may be more credible when resources are granted through a restriction of competition rather than a general subsidy. The former would be typically enshrined in a regulation which can only be changed at great political cost, whereas the latter is presumably negotiated every year and could be part of rather obscure budget procedures.

Hence, it seems that when additional distortions and the political economy of subsidies are taken into account, the case against the economic principles underlying the *Corbeau* decision is not as tight as Mavroidis and Messerlin make it. But it is nonetheless clear that cross-subsidisation should not be seen as the preferable arrangement for financing public service obligations in all circumstances and the *Corbeau* decision does indeed create a presumption in its favour which should be resisted.

According the authors, the *Corbeau* decision is also bad law because it has entrusted national courts with the responsibility of evaluating the appropriate scope of the restrictions of competition that are necessary to ensure the viability of regulated enterprises. Surely, however, the point is broader; it is not that *Corbeau* is bad law, but rather that no good law could be expected. What the *Corbeau* case is illustrating is that the task of designing and fine-tuning a regulatory framework should not be left to the judiciary. The reason is simply that regulation involves a set of complex and fairly technical issues for which the courts have little competence. This is well illustrated by recent experiments across Europe in the regulation of utilities, a field where public service obligations often arise. The restructuring of these industries involves the vertical separation of different activities which often were performed by a single entity, and extensive regulation of the interaction between disintegrated parts (typically a network operated as a natural monopoly and the competitive provision of services on that network). Regulation of this interaction has proven very difficult, and in many instances the power of the incumbent to circumvent regulation has been underestimated. In other instances, like the U.K. rail sector, regulation may not have provided incentives for the owner of the network to undertake adequate investments. If, despite substantial resources and expertise, regulatory agencies have found it difficult to implement their tasks and have had to undertake many adjustments on the way, it seems that courts are hardly well suited to substitute for regulatory agencies.

In my view, the importance of this issue is underplayed by the authors. The *Corbeau* case is only the tip of the iceberg, and the current arrangement might lead to substantial conflicts across jurisdictions if Article 90 were to be interpreted by national courts. Consider for instance network industries, where services of economic interest take the form of universal services being imposed on the incumbent firm. In the current situation, both incumbents and third parties who argue that adequate universal services are not provided might have an incentive to challenge domestic regulatory provisions in court, attempting thereby to reduce the scope of services opened to competition. Admittedly, this is not an issue for telecommunications, where the scope of universal services has been defined in a directive. But it may be an issue for the other industries like postal services, rail, electricity, and water. Entrants might also consider challenging the national regulations, gambling on what could turn out to be a highly favourable outcome. As a result, domestic courts could challenge domestic regulations on the basis of EC law. The cases could also be handled by the EC court if the parties can show that trade between the Member States is affected. Given the very open attitude of the jurisprudence on this issue, it will not take long for the European Court of Justice to handle a case where, for instance, a French firm challenges the universal service provisions of a U.K. regulation. Serious conflicts could thus arise between national regulators, national courts, and the Community.

In this context, the authors would like to do away with Article 90 altogether — given that in their view the scope for public services is narrow and shrinking. It is not clear whether such a drastic attitude is warranted. Rather, a sensible way forward would be for the Commission to make use of its power to legislate (under Article 90(3)). In the case of telecommunications, the Commission has used this power to define the universal services. This could be done in other industries. Given the wide variety of universal service provisions that could arise across industries, however, it may be more effective for the Commission to issue a directive, or at least guidelines, outlining some principles.

What could be a sensible definition of "services of general economic interest" is a difficult issue. Efficiency as well as equity considerations come into play, and it is not always easy even to disentangle these aspects. A working definition has been provided recently by Henry (1996). He suggests that beyond the existence of market failures, it is useful to consider the essential character of particular services. In turn, services can be deemed essential when they prevent (or reduce) exclusion or contribute to social cohesion. This approach, which is applied by Henry to various industries (including rail and postal services), seems fruitful and it could form a sensible starting point for the Commission.

REFERENCES

Henry, C. 1996. "Concurrence et service publics dans l'Union Européenne." DEEP DP 9608.

CHAPTER 20

Auctions as a Trade Policy Instrument

Toni Haniotis[*]

1. Introduction

An auction is a market institution with an explicit set of rules determining resource allocation and prices on the basis of competitive bids from the market participants (McAfee and McMillan 1987:701). A government can use auctions to sell any goods or assets it owns or any rights it may define. Moreover, the government can set up a competitive bidding procedure for awarding public procurement contracts. Governments can use auctions to implement a variety of policies such as competition, environmental, industrial, and trade policies. In recent years, auctions have become increasingly popular policy instruments all over the world, particularly in privatisation, franchising, licensing, public procurement, and for awarding rights for the exploitation of natural resources.

Standard trade policy analysis concentrates mainly on tariffs and quotas as trade policy instruments. Other instruments such as taxes, subsidies, or non-tariff measures are also considered. But until recently, the use of auctions as a trade policy instrument has played a marginal role in both legal and economic trade policy analyses. This picture is now changing gradually. Auctions are becoming more important in practice (see, e.g., Bergsten et al., 1987) as an increasing number of legislators discover auctions either as a domestic or a foreign trade policy instrument.

This chapter surveys the main findings on auctions in the international trade theory literature and reports on some recent practical experience with auctioned quotas in Switzerland. The result derived in the appendix and parts of the reasoning on the (non-) discriminatory nature of auctioned quotas and tariff-quotas (developed in Section 3) are new. The purpose of this chapter is not to argue that auctions are always the best trade policy instrument, but rather to illustrate how auctions can serve as a useful trade policy instrument under certain circumstances.

[*]Federal Office for Foreign Economic Affairs, Berne, Switzerland. The views expressed in this article are the author's own views. I am grateful to Henrik Horn, Christian Häberli, Serge Pannatier, and in particular Will Martin for their useful comments.

The arguments are developed along three broad lines. First, since an important purpose of auctions is to raise revenue, Section 2 compares auctioned import quotas and tariffs as revenue raising devices. It is shown that under certain circumstances, a government can raise revenue more effectively through auctioned quotas than through tariffs. This result is new and is derived analytically in the appendix. Secondly, Sections 3 and 4 discuss the non-discriminatory nature of auctions. In Section 3, it is argued that auctions constitute, in principle, a non-discriminatory method for the allocation of quotas and tariff-quotas. Of course, an auction can be discriminatory if it explicitly grants a preference to domestic bidders. In practice, such discrimination does often occur in government procurement auctions. An indication of the close relation between government procurement and trade policies is also the conclusion of the plurilateral Agreement on Government Procurement (GPA), which is managed under the auspices of the World Trade Organization (WTO). The GPA's main goal is to foster transparent and non-discriminatory procurement practices among its members. Although this goal is not generally contested, a reasoning has been developed in the literature which can justify discriminatory auction rules in certain circumstances (Section 4). Another role of auctions for trade policy is illustrated in Section 5. Several authors have shown that in a heterogeous product market, an overall import quota involves inefficiencies. The reason for this is that no price mechanism is available for determining the optimal import shares of each product variety within the same market. Such a price mechanism can be introduced either in the form of a secondary market for import licences or in the form of an auction for allocating these licences. In both cases, an arbitrage mechanism is introduced which guarantees an optimal mix of imports. Finally, Section 6 reports on recent experience with auctions in Swiss foreign trade policy, illustrating the practical use of auctions for allocating tariff-quotas.

2. Auctions as a Rent Extraction Device

An important feature of auctions is that they can be used by the government to extract monopoly and other rents from either domestic or foreign market participants. Although this fact is well-known, many economists, politicians, and negotiators tend to neglect it when evaluating quotas or tariff-quotas as trade policy instruments. Unlike other quantitative restrictions, auctioned quotas or tariff-quotas have the advantage of being based on competitive bids, the efficiency properties of which are discussed in Section 4. The present section concentrates on the rent extraction effect of auctions.

There is a strong presumption among economists that price-based measures, as policy instruments, are superior to quantitative measures. Price-based measures tend to be less distortionary because they leave quantitative choices to economic agents. In a trade policy context this presumption translates into a preference for tariffs relative to quotas. This presumption is reflected explicitly in the international trade rules of the GATT/WTO. In particular, according to Article XI of GATT, quantitative trade restrictions are generally prohibited. The main rationale for the preference for tariffs under the GATT/WTO system is based on the fact that *ad valorem* tariffs can be compared more easily across countries. This is, of course, an important characteristic in international tariff negotiations. On the other hand, there exists a large literature in economics comparing tariffs and quotas on social welfare grounds. Although there is no robust, general result, most of the literature tends to support the presumption in favour of tariffs. This presumption is based on the intuition that quotas normally do not provide for sufficient arbitrage and competition, thus they involve inefficiencies (see, e.g., Anderson, 1988).

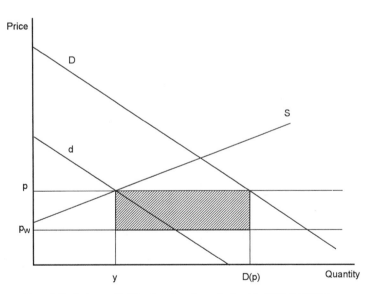

Figure 1: Equivalence of tariff and quota under perfectly competitive conditions

Domestic production y, domestic price p, imports D(p)-y, and government revenue (shaded area) are the same under, either a tariff t=p-p$_W$, or an auctioned quota q=D(p)-y (see, e.g., Anderson, 1988).

The presumption in favour of tariffs is valid when, under a quota regime, no mechanism is available for allocating import licences optimally. This occurs when the latter are awarded either arbitrarily, or using some fixed rule. If, however, a market for import licenses is created in the form of an auction, then the comparison between tariffs and quotas as trade policy in-stuments becomes more interesting.[1]

It is well-known that under perfectly competitive conditions, appropria-tely chosen import tariffs and quotas lead to equivalent outcomes, except for the fact that the government does not raise any revenue with a quota (see, e.g., Anderson 1988:3–4). The quota, a quantitative restriction, creates a domestic shortage and drives the domestic price level up to a level above the world market price. Thus, an importer is willing to pay a charge up to the difference between the world market price and the domestic price for one unit import licence. This difference is equal to that tariff level which re-stricts imports to the same level as under the quota.

In an auction, competitive bidding for import licences will drive the pri-ce for one unit import licence up to that level. Again, this implies perfect equivalence of tariff and quota (see figure 1).[2]

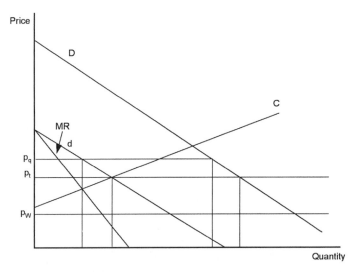

Figure 2: Non-equivalence of tariff and quota under monopolistic conditions

Domestic production is lower, while domestic price and government revenue are higher under a quota than under a tariff which yields the same quantity of imports (see Bhagwati, 1965).

As Bhagwati (1965) has shown in his celebrated article, this equiva-lence breaks down under imperfectly competitive conditions.[3] He has shown that a monopolised domestic market will be exposed to less competition with the imposition of an import quota than under a tariff implying the same level of imports. The reason for this result is that under a tariff, a domestic monopolist loses market share when raising the price, while this cannot happen under a quota (as long as the quota is binding). Thus, the domestic producer faces a more elastic demand schedule (has less market power) under a tariff than under a quota. This implies that the price level will be higher under a quota. In terms of Marshallian national welfare, tariffs are thus unambiguously preferred to quotas (see figure 2, and Helpman and Krugman 1989:33–34).

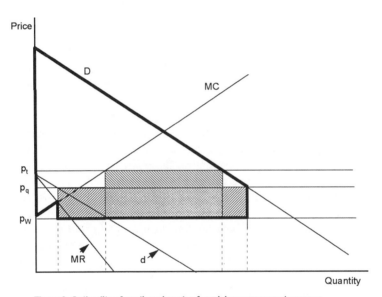

Figure 3: Optimality of auctioned quotas for raising government revenue

The bold polygon represents domestic social welfare under an auctioned quota. It is strictly greater than domestic social welfare under the tariff which yields the same government revenue. Domestic price is lower and imports are higher under the quota than under the tariff (see appendix).

This assessment changes radically when the purpose of the government's trade policy is to raise revenue. This is just what happens in many developing or transition countries. For this purpose, the government can use auctions to award import licenses. It is shown in the appendix, below, that it may be strictly preferrable for the government to use a quota rather than a tariff. The intuition for this result is the following: as a quota tends to preserve — at least to some extent — the domestic producer's monopoly power, such a producer is able to limit her output and to increase the price. Thus, somewhat paradoxically, under a quota imports will obtain a relatively large share of the domestic market (see figure 3). Together monopoly pricing and the high market share of imports imply a large rent for importers. The government can extract this rent by auctioning off import licences. In contrast to this, a tariff forces the domestic supplier to behave competitively and, therefore, allows imports only a relatively small market share. This explains why tariff revenue will be less than the corresponding auction revenue. Or, alternatively, it explains why the same revenue can be raised more efficiently under an auctioned quota than under a tariff.

Campos e Cunha and Santos (1996) consider a similar case. They, however, use a quota that is not perfectly divisible. They show that the monopolist will have an incentive to buy some or all of the quota licences herself, in order to pre-empt competition.[4] They do not, however, study the effect of the monopolist bidding at the auction on auction revenue. Therefore, the question remains open whether the fact that the monopolist might participate in the auction would make auctioned quotas a less efficient means for raising government revenue.

Krishna (1990) has shown that tariffs are preferable to quotas for raising government revenue under foreign (instead of domestic) monopoly. In that case, the value of an import license to the foreign monopolist is either zero or relatively small, depending on the restrictiveness of the quota, and the resulting auction revenue will also be relatively small.

Dasgupta and Stiglitz (1977) and Young (1980a,b) compare tariffs and auctioned quotas as revenue-raising devices under competitive conditions when there is uncertainty about the foreign price and about domestic supply and demand functions. In this context, no general preference for one or the other instrument can be established. Tariffs are superior to quotas in terms of expected import costs and because they permit imports to respond to changes in domestic supply and demand conditions. On the other hand, tariffs are inferior to quotas in terms of the risks which have to be borne by domestic producers and consumers. Analysing the resulting trade-off, Young (1980a) shows that a quota will be preferred to a tariff when the amount of funds the government has to raise (and the required tariff rate) is large relative to the degree of uncertainty. Otherwise, a tariff will be preferred to a quota. Dasgupta and Stiglitz (1977) argue, moreover, that a two-tier tariff schedule (i.e., a tariff-quota) would generally be superior to both a uniform tariff rate and a uniform quota.

3. Auctions and Non-discriminatory Allocation of (Tariff-) Quotas

In many situations, administrators possess considerable discretion in the implementation of trade policies. This is the case, for example, in the administration of import licences or in the selection of contractors for public works. Legislators can limit such discretion by setting certain allocation rules. If such rules are too crude and inflexible, however, their implementation may become very costly. To avoid such a cost, legislators can require import licences or procurement contracts to be awarded by means of auctions. Thus, the administrator's discretion is limited while a high degree of flexibility is maintained. At the same time, to the extent that the auction rules are non-discriminatory, the overall policy will also be non-discriminatory. The purpose of this section and the following one is to review the argument that auctions represent a non-discriminatory means for administering quantitative import measures (i.e., quotas and tariff-quotas) as well as government procurement.

Consider first the situation where some country has an import quota in place, allowing only imports up to some fixed quantity per year of a particular product. There are basically four ways to implement such a measure:

1. the country may reserve *equal shares* of import licenses for each trading partner;

2. import licenses may be allocated according to some formula based either on *historical import shares,* or on an *agreement with the main supplying countries*;[5]

3. the country may allow imports on a *"first-come, first-served"* basis;

4. finally, import licenses may be *auctioned* off.

From an economic perspective, the four methods are in principle equivalent — in the sense of implying the same quantity of imports — as long as the quota is fully used.[6] Yet, as not every product is produced in all countries, it can happen that under the equal share method, (1), a substantial part of the licences will not be used. Moreover, these methods are not equivalent from the legal perspective of the WTO agreements. Discrimination has many facets and can take various forms. With each of these measures, clearly some units of the good may be denied entry into the domestic market while other units of the same (or similar) product will be allowed to enter. In this sense, any method will necessarily be "discriminatory".

The most favoured nation principle of the GATT refers to one particular type of discrimination. It requires that goods originating from one country are treated equally to similar products originating from another country.

Taking the non-discrimination requirement of Article XIII:1 of GATT, which re-phrases the most-favoured nation principle in the context of licence allocation, the following test should be applied: if discrimination is present, does it involve the product being discriminated against solely on the basis of its origin? That is, all other things being equal, would that particular item have been granted a licence, if it had been of some other origin? If the answer to this question is "yes", then the method is discriminatory. If the answer to this question is "no", then any discrimination exists independently of the product's origin. It is easy to verify, based on this test, that methods (1) and (2) can lead to violation of the non-discrimination principle[7], while methods (3) and (4) are non-discriminatory with respect to the origin of the product in question.

Method (3) discriminates on the basis of the date of importation, while method (4) discriminates on the basis of the price bid for the licence. In this sense, the auction method (4), may be classified as a price-based measure which is non-discriminatory in the sense of GATT. Moreover, the "first-come, first-served" method (3), is more likely to produce distortions, while an auction can reasonably be expected to produce "a distribution of trade in such product approaching as closely as possible the shares which the various contracting parties might be expected to obtain in the absence of such restrictions", a criterion introduced in the chapeau of Article XIII:2. As will be argued in Section 5, auctioning (similar to a uniform *ad valorem* tariff) does not alter relative prices from their free trade values. Auctioning, therefore, produces the same import shares, for all product varieties on which the same overall quota is applied, as would prevail under free trade.

These appear to be convincing GATT-legal arguments favouring auctions as a method for allocating import quotas. It should be emphasised at this point that the above arguments do not deal with the WTO-compatibility of the existence *per se* of the quota. Only the method of allocation has been assessed with respect to its (non-)discriminatory nature.[8]

The GATT-compatibility of auctioned tariff-quotas is a more intricate issue (see Rom, 1980, for a related discussion). Unlike quotas, tariff-quotas are in principle permissible under the GATT. The reasoning developed above for the case of import quotas also applies to tariff quotas, with one additional issue arising in the latter context. If the country applying the tariff-quota has explicitly bound such tariff-quota in its schedule of concessions, the auction outcome will have to conform with that commitment.[9] In particular, such commitment implies that a certain quantity of imports should be admitted being charged only up to the low (within-quota) level of duties and other charges. The crucial question in this case is whether the price paid at the auction for acquiring a licence is to be regarded as part of "all other duties or charges of any kind imposed on or in connection with the importation" in the sense of Article II:1(b) of GATT. If the answer to this question was "yes", then the ordinary within-quota tariff together with the auction payment would not be permitted to exceed the within-quota binding, as contained in the importing country's schedule of concessions.[10] Article VIII:1(a) of GATT is quite clear about the fact that no additional fees may be charged for revenue purposes. It states that

> All fees and charges of whatever character [. . .] imposed by contracting parties on or in connection with importation or exportation shall be limited in amount to the approximate cost of service rendered and shall not present [. . .] a taxation of imports or exports for fiscal purposes.

Article VIII, however, still does not clearly answer the question whether it applies to auction payments or not.[11]

From an economist's perspective, one might argue that there is a difference between a "price" (such as the auction payment) on the one hand and a "duty" (as referred to in Articles II and VIII of GATT) on the other hand. A "price" is defined as an exchange ratio. That is, the buyer acquires some benefit *in exchange for* a payment. A "duty" does not involve the notion of reciprocity. But this does still not resolve the legal issue, because the provisions of Articles II and VIII of GATT also refer to "fees for services rendered", which clearly involves reciprocity. Unfortunately, the question whether the auction payments are to be viewed as "other duties or charges" remains a matter of interpretation. This issue may well have to be resolved one day under the WTO's dispute settlement mechanism.

Taking a broader view than a strictly legalistic one, there seem to be three main reasons why auctions should not be regarded as trade restrictive or protectionist measures: first, the auction *per se* does not lead to a reduction of imports, as long as all licences are sold at the auction; second, neither the domestic price level, nor the overall quantity of imports are likely to be affected by the auction[12]; thirdly, what is sold at the auction is not the right to import a particular article, but the right to import it at the lower (within-quota) tariff rate (in other words, what is sold at the auction is a privilege and this privilege is sold in a non-discriminatory manner). No individual importer has an *a priori* right derived from GATT to such preferential treatment. It can, therefore, be regarded as legitimate for the government to sell this right to those importers which have the highest willingness to pay, instead of giving such privilege away for free, using some fixed or *ad hoc* alloction rule. In the light of all their economically and legally desirable properties, it can be argued that — contrary to quantitative restrictions or discriminatory rules — auctions as such do conform with the general philosophy of the multilateral trading system. Auctions as price-based, non-discriminatory methods for the administration of (tariff-) quotas will probably remain important as long as quantitative measures are in use.

4. Auctions in Government Procurement

Another policy area where international non-discrimination disciplines have been established regards the purchase of goods and services by public agencies. In government procurement, the benefits of auctions have already been clearly recognised: governments can use auctions to reveal information held by individual market participants. For example, typically the public agency does not know a contractor's cost structure for the provision of the required services. A procurement auction helps the government select the most efficient provider. At the same time, the government can impose any environmental or safety regulations or any other regulations which might be necessary in the public interest. The advantages of competitive market institutions can be combined with the possibilities of regulatory intervention.

In this context, however, auctions will only be non-distortionary with respect to trade if: (i) no tariffs are levied on the products or services procured; and (ii) no price-preference is accorded to domestic bidders (see Mattoo, 1996). In practice, such policies are quite widespread. Apart from the existence of tariffs, most governments tend to favour domestic over foreign bidders in their procurement auctions. Such discrimination is generally regarded as protectionist and inefficient. The GPA, which was signed together with the Uruguay Round agreements, constitutes an attempt to limit such discrimination in auctions.[13]

On the other hand, discriminatory procurement policies, favouring domestic high-cost contractors over foreign low-cost suppliers, have been rationalised under certain conditions in McAfee and McMillan (1989) and in Branco (1994), along the following lines: favouring high-cost bidders on the one hand increases the expected production cost, because the probability of them being awarded the contract is increased. But at the same time, more fierce competition among bidders is induced, thus lowering the expected price. McAfee and McMillan (1989) show that with a small degree of discrimination, the second effect will outweigh the first. Therefore, if the domestic firms have a cost disadvantage, the government will minimise its expected procurement cost by offering them a preference at the procurement auction. A more popular view of (and justification for) discrimination is developed by Branco (1994). Based on the fact that the government is only interested in the profits of domestic firms and not in those of foreign firms, Branco shows that the government will be ready to incur a higher cost for domestic purchases. The government will only select a foreign candidate if the latter's bid is sufficiently lower than the lowest domestic bid, such that the cost saving outweighs the "loss" of the funds paid to the foreign supplier.

As mentioned in Mattoo (1996), those articles do not take into account the (domestic) economy-wide misallocation of resources which results from such discrimination. Since high-cost firms will be more likely to be awarded the contract, domestic resources will be deviated to sectors of absolute and possibly also comparative disadvantage. In a general equilibrium perspective, such discrimination may therefore not be beneficial.

The second source of discrimination in government procurement stems from the existence of tariffs. Kim (1994) argues that tariffs and price preferences are equivalent, both in terms of the government's procurement costs and the domestic and foreign bidders' profits. Yet Kim's reasoning does not take into account the following elements: first, a tariff applies to *all* imports of the same product and not only to government purchases (this implies that — even if a cost saving can be achieved through the discriminatory effect of the tariff on the outcome of the procurement auction — it also induces an economy-wide distortion); second, as Mattoo (1996) points out, tariffs will only have an effect on procurement auctions if the procurement agency does not consider the tariffs to be paid by foreign bidders as revenue. This may be the case for a procurement agency belonging to a sub-federal government and thus not directly benefiting from federal tariff revenues, for instance. From this, one may conclude that if the government wants to discriminate against foreign bidders, it should do so in the form of a price-preference rather than through a tariff.[14] Moreover, it should take into account the intersectoral distortion caused by its discriminatory procurement policy.

5. Auctioned (Tariff-) Quotas and Allocation Efficiency

We now turn back to the role of auctions in the administration of quotas and tariff-quotas. In many cases, administrators are responsible for allocating import licences across different products or across different varieties within a heterogeneous product class. In fulfilling their task, administrators are very likely to use some practical but inefficient rule. It is normally not possible for administrators to know the optimal (sub-) quota for each type of product by taking into account supply and demand conditions in every single segment of the market. Several authors have shown that in such circumstances a tariff is superior to a quota (see, e.g., Bhagwati and Srinivasan 1983, or Dixit 1985). The basic reasoning behind this result is best expressed in Anderson (1988:5–6), where he argues:

In practice, protection is granted for a product class: autos, cheese, oil, etc. An aggregate number of units, e.g., 1.85 million Japanese cars, is authorized. The distribution of licenses across members of the controlled group is left to an administrator. Instead of using the market system to price the licenses, the administrator allocates according to some simple rule [. . .]. In general, this system will not imply rent earned on a unit license being the same across products, so long as resale is frustrated (which it usually is) or is inefficient.

In contrast to this, through a uniform *ad valorem* tariff, imports can be restricted to the desired level while preserving the domestic relative prices (among the protected sectors) equal to those on the world market. This implies that under a uniform *ad valorem* tariff, the import shares among protected varieties will be chosen optimally by the market participants.

If, instead of allocating import quotas according to some administrative rule, the administrator uses an auction, then the equivalence of tariffs and quotas can be restored. Even if the class of products being subject to the same quota is very heterogeneous, the competitive bidding process will lead to an efficient outcome. To see why this must be the case, consider the situation where the government auctions off the right to import any product variety from the class in question up to a certain monetary amount. This means that one such *ad valorem* licence entails the right to import a quantity of, for instance, cars worth one monetary unit. If p_i denotes the domestic price and p_{iW} the world market price of a particular car i from this class, then a licence holder will choose to import type i cars as long as his rent on such imports is higher than on the imports of any other type j. That is, as long as

$$[p_i - p_{iW}] / p_{iW} > [p_j - p_{jW}] / p_{jW} \qquad \text{Eq. 1}$$

As more type i cars are imported the domestic price p_i tends to fall, until equality holds in (eq. 1). This, in turn, implies that relative prices under the value quota will be the same as under free trade, i.e., $p_i/p_j = p_{iW}/p_{jW}$. The government can implement the desired degree of import restriction in an optimal manner by issuing precisely that amount of *ad valorem* licences which equals the value of imports under the optimal *ad valorem* tariff. In this case, an importer's rent earned on one *ad valorem* import licence, $[p_i - p_{iW}] / p_{iW}$, will be precisely equal to the optimal *ad valorem* tariff rate. In a competitive auction, bidders will offer to pay precisely this amount for one *ad valorem* import licence. This demonstrates the equivalence of optimal tariff and auctioned value quota and illustrates that product heterogeneity is not sufficient for establishing a preference for tariffs relative to auctioned quotas.[15]

6. Swiss Experience

This section reports on recent experience in Switzerland with auctions for allocating import licences.[16] For certain agricultural products, Switzerland maintains tariff-quotas as part of its agricultural policy. Recent experience with the allocation of tariff-quotas in the Swiss wine market is particularly interesting.

As a result of the Uruguay Round negotiations, Switzerland fixed its previously existing quota on wine imports at 170 million litres per year and transformed it into a tariff-quota. The within-quota rate of 0.50 francs per litre has been bound under the WTO. Outside the tariff-quota, the rate was bound at five francs per litre. The tariff-quota was sub-divided as follows: 162 million litres of red wine and 7.6 million litres of white wine.[17]

In the first year, 1995, the Swiss authorities used a complicated system for allocating within-quota import licenses to individual importers. The licenses were allocated based on the importers' previous years' shares. The system was rather costly and impractical. In 1996, it was replaced by a "first-come, first-served" rule. At the same time, the tariff-quota for white wine was doubled to 15 million litres. The total tariff-quota for wine remained at 170 million litres.[18]

The result was striking. On 1 January 1996, huge queues had built up at the Swiss customs, consisting of hundreds of lorries carrying white wine. On 3 January 1996, the authorities announced that the 1996 tariff-quota had been fully utilised and that further imports would be liable for the higher tariff.[19] The consequence was a political outcry which forced the government to authorize additional imports during the year and to reduce the above-quota tariff from five to three francs per litre. Another economically foreseeable effect was that the tariff-quota was mainly used by importers of low quality white wines, as the cost saving under the lower, within-quota, (specific) duty rate was relatively more important for the lower price segment.[20] Almost the entire upper range of white wines paid the above-quota tariff rate. In addition, it turned out that large importers had reacted more flexibly and more quickly than smaller ones, such that the five biggest importers realised more than three-quarters of the within-quota imports.

After such a negative experience, the Swiss government decided to introduce a new mechanism. For 1997, the quota for white wine was further increased, and an auction was organised for allocating the rights to the preferential rates. It was announced that each importer will be allowed to submit up to five sealed bids — consisting of a quantity of white wine and a price offer — and those bids with the highest offers would receive the right to import at the lower rate.[21] Of the 2185 bids submitted, 1430 were accepted, with the lowest successful bid offering 0.51 francs per litre. The government's total auction revenue amounted to fourteen million francs. This means that the average price paid for the right to import at a tariff of 0.50 francs per litre, was 0.89 francs per litre. A balanced mix of imports of high and low quality wines was realised. The same picture resulted from the auction for 1998 imports. The tariff-quota was increased again (from sixteen to seventeen million litres) and was allocated in the same way as in the previous year. The bids were slightly lower than for 1997. The average price paid for 1998 was at 0.60 francs per litre.

The auction has been both an economic and political success. It has been demonstrated that the auction method offers several advantages compared to the "first-come, first-served" method. These advantages are particularly relevant when the quota is relatively small and restrictive. In this case, the economic rent created by the quota will be high. Although the auction method does extract such rents from importers, the latter had to admit that the method is both effective and efficient. It has provided a predictable trading environment. Critics of the auction method (who were to be found mainly among importers) had predicted that the domestic market prices would be driven up by the use of auctions. In accordance with economic theory, however, practice has proven them wrong, as no price changes were observed compared to the previous years' prices.[22] This practical illustration complements the theoretical arguments developed above and should encourage legislators to make more use of auctions as a trade policy instrument.

7. Concluding Remarks

This chapter reviews some basic features of auctions as a trade policy instrument. It illustrates that auctions are particularly useful when the main goal of trade policy is to raise government revenue, and the theoretical considerations are supported by experience recently gained in Switzerland with the administration of import licenses for white wine. This is a vital policy objective in many developing and transition countries where other sources of government revenue are not very effective or practicable, due to various reasons such as administrative or social problems. But also in developed countries, where liberalisation, recession, and globalisation put increasing strains on public budgets, governments have to find effective ways for raising revenue. At the same time, however, Article XI of GATT stipulates the general elimination of quantitative restrictions, implying that auctioned quotas will, in general, not be a WTO-compatible trade policy instrument. The advantages of auctions will, thus, remain confined to the administration of tariff-quotas and to those specific cases in which quotas are exceptionally permitted.

Due to the heterogeneity of products, a fixed quota in general will induce inefficiencies due to the absence of arbitrage possibilities. It is argued that the auctioning of quotas restores the allocation efficiency of quotas as well as the standard equivalence of tariffs and quotas. Despite the existence of the quota, an auction still leaves the actual allocation to the competitive market forces. Another advantage of auctions is related to the fact that they limit the discretion of administrators in the context of the allocation of import licences. At the same time, a high degree of flexibility is maintained. To the extent that auction rules are non-discriminatory, the overall policy will also be non-discriminatory and conform to GATT/WTO disciplines.

NOTES

1. While not all types of auctions are equivalent, and a careful study of the strategic considerations of every auction participant is required in order to derive the equilibrium outcome for each set of auction rules, there is a range of circumstances under which the commonly used auction types are equivalent (see McAffee and McMillan, 1987). By disregarding information asymmetries, the precise auction type does not need to be specified here.

2. For the ease of exposition, linear supply and demand functions are shown in all figures in this chapter. None of the arguments relies on this assumption, though.

3. Following Bhagwati's article, "On equivalence of Tariffs and Quotas", a large literature has emerged, identifying cases of non-equivalence of tariffs and quotas. See, e.g., Rodriguez (1974); Fishelson and Flatters (1975); Pelcovits (1976); Young (1980b); and Anderson (1980 and 1988).

4. This argument assumes that licence holders are not required to actually use all their licences for imports. Otherwise, the monopolist would not benefit from acquiring import licences.

5. For the present purpose, this type of measure can be regarded as a residual category, subsuming any other algorithm for allocating import shares. Thus, the list is exhaustive.

6. As emphasized in the previous section, one important difference is that auctioning is the only method by which the government will raise revenue.

7. Methods 1 and 2 establish fixed country (or firm) quotas. When such a quota is full, no more imports from that particular origin are admitted, while similar goods from other origins may still be admitted. This constitutes a discrimination by origin in the sense of Article XIII:1 of GATT. It should be noted, however, that Article XIII:2(d) does explicitly provide for the possibility of using method 2, provided that *all* other WTO Members with a *"substantial interest in supplying the product concerned"* are duly considered.

8. It should also be noted that the arguments developed here apply, in principle, to industrial products as well as to agricultural products. The Agreement on Agriculture

(particularly Parts II and III), however, contains some specific provisions for agricultural products.

9. If that particular item does not appear on the country's schedule, the auctioned tariff-quota only needs to be compatible with the provisions mentioned above in relation to a pure quota.

10. If, on the other hand, the answer was "no", then a auctioned tariff-quota could be regarded as compatible with GATT.

11. Article VIII:4 only states that "The provisions of this Article shall extend to fees, charges, formalities and requirements [. . .] including those relating to [. . .] quantitative restrictions [and to] licensing".

12. While introduction of a (tariff-) quota creates an economic rent by restricting the supply and, hence, raising the price of the goods that are subject to the (tariff-) quota, the auction itself does not further increase the prices. It only transfers the rent from the importer to the government.

13. The GPA is reprinted and analyzed in Hoekman and Mavroidis (1996). More specifically, on the issue of discriminatory procurement. See Mattoo (1996).

14. This finding is derived from economic considerations and does not take into account the legal requirements under the GPA.

15. If, as might be the case under a different set of assumptions, a uniform specific (rather than *ad valorem*) tariff was optimal, then it can be shown that the equivalent quota policy would be for the government to auction off specific import licences in an amount equal to the quantity of imports under the optimal specific tariff.

16. Examples of administrative procedures for the allocation of quotas and tariff-quotas in other countries are reported in Rom (1980); see also references therein.

17. In the white wine segment, domestic production accounts for seventy-nine percent of the market, while for red wine, domestic production accounts only for twenty-seven percent.

18. From the year 2001 on, all wine (whether red or white) will be administered under one overall tariff-quota.

19. Similar experiences are made in the European Union where the "first come, first served" method is widely used for allocating tariff-quota.

20. Under *ad valorem* (instead of specific) tariffs, such distortion effect would not have occurred.

21. Slightly different rules apply for the auctions of sausages and ham tariff quotas. In that case, every successful bidder makes the same payment, equal to the lowest successful bid.

22. It is interesting to note in this context that a Swiss importer of dried meat recently challenged the Swiss quota allocation system. Due to the change from the previous system — which was based on historical import shares — to the auction method, that particular importer lost his guaranteed privilege, namely the right to preferential imports and to the associated monopoly rent. The fact that the auction method was challenged by an importer who has lost his privilege is already an indication that the new method leads to more competitive outcomes. One of his arguments was that the auction was not compatible with Switzerland's commitments

under the WTO. He claimed that the auction payment together with the tariff would exceed Switzerland's binding according to her schedule of concessions. Moreover, the auction would have to be regarded as a non-automatic licencing procedure which was violating the WTO Licensing Agreement. In its ruling of 14 July 1997, the Swiss Federal Court did not see a violation of WTO law. It regarded auctions as a non-trade-restrictive method for allocating a tariff quota, which did not violate the provisions of the WTO Agreement on Import Licensing Procedures.

REFERENCES

Anderson, James E. 1980. "The Relative Inefficiency of Quotas: The Cheese Case." American Economic Review 75: 178-190.
Anderson, James E. 1988. *The Relative Inefficiency of Quotas.* Cambridge, MA: MIT Press.
Anderson, James E. and Leslie Young. 1982. "The Optimality of Tariff-Quotas." Journal of International Economics 13: 337-351.
Bergsten, C. Fred, Kimberly Elliott, Jeffrey Scott and Wendy Takacs. 1987. "Auction Quotas and United States Policy." *Policy Analysis in International Economics 19*, Washington, D.C.: Institute for International Economics.
Bhagwati, Jagdish. 1965. "On the Equivalence of Tariffs and Quotas." In R. Caves et al., ed., *Trade, Growth, and the Balance of Payments.* Chicago: Rand-McNally.
Bhagwati, Jagdish and T. N. Srinivasan. 1969. "Optimal Intervention to Achieve Non-Economic Objectives." Review of Economic Studies 36: 27-38.
Bhagwati, Jagdish and T. N. Srinivasan. 1983. *Lectures in International Trade.* Cambridge, MA: MIT Press.
Branco, Fernando. 1994. "Favoring Domestic Firms in Procurement Contracts." Journal of International Economics 37:65–80.
Campos e Cunha, Luis and Vasco Santos. 1996. "Sleeping Quotas, Pre-emptive Quota Bidding and Monopoly Power." Journal of International Economics 40:127–148.
Cassing, James H. and Arye L. Hillman. 1985. "Political Influence Motives and the Choice between Tariffs and Quotas." Journal of International Economics 19:279–290.
Dasgupta, Partha and Joseph E. Stiglitz. 1977. "Tariffs vs. Quotas as Revenue-Raising Devices under Uncertainty." American Economic Review 67:975–981.
Dixit, Avinash. 1985. "Tax Policy in Open Economies." Alan Auerbach and Martin Feldstein, eds. *Handbook of Public Economics.* Amsterdam: North Holland.
Finkelshtain, Israel and Yoav Kislev. 1997. "Prices versus Quantities: The Political Perspective." Journal of Political Economy 105:83–100.
Fishelson, G. and F. Flatters. 1975. "The (Non-)Equivalence of Optimal Tariffs and Quotas under Uncertainty." Journal of International Economics 5:385–393.
Helpman, Elhanan and Paul R. Krugman. 1989. *Trade Policy and Market Structure.* Cambridge, MA: The MIT Press.
Hoekman, Bernard and Petros Mavroidis, eds. 1996. *Law and Policy in Public Purchasing. The WTO Agreement on Government Procurement.* Ann Arbor: University of Michigan Press.

Kim, In-Guy. 1994. "Price-preference vs. Tariff Policies in Government Procurement Auctions." Economics Letters 45:217–222.
Krishna, Kala. 1990. "The Case of the Vanishing Revenues: Auction Quotas with Monopoly." American Economic Review 80:828–836.
Mattoo, Aaditya. 1997. "Economic Theory and the Procurement Agreement." In Bernard M. Hoekman and Petros C Mavroidis, eds. *Law and Policy in Public Purchasing. The WTO Agreement on Government Procurement.* Ann Arbor: University of Michigan Press.
McAfee, Preston and John McMillan. 1987. "Auctions and Bidding." Journal of Economic Literature 25:699–738.
Pelcovits, M. G. 1976. "Quotas vs. Tariffs." Journal of International Economics 6:363–370.
Rodriguez, Carlos A. 1974. "The Non-Equivalence of Tariffs and Quotas under Retaliation." Journal of International Economics 4:295–298.
Rom, M. 1980. *The Role of Tariff Quotas in Commercial Policy.* London: McMillan.
Young, Leslie. 1980a. "Optimal Revenue-Raising Trade Restrictions under Uncertainty." Journal of International Economics 10:425–440.
Young, Leslie. 1980b. "Tariffs vs. Quotas under Uncertainty: An Extension." American Economic Review 70:522–527.
Young, Leslie and James E. Anderson. 1980. "The Optimal Instruments for Restricting Trade under Uncertainty." Review of Economic Studies 10:425–440.

APPENDIX

This appendix provides the analytical reasoning and assumptions which underlie the result stated in section 2. In the model developed below, auctioned quotas are more effective than tariffs in raising government revenue when the domestic market is monopolistic. The relevant question can be stated as follows: *given that the government wants to raise a given amount of revenue G, should it use a tariff or an auctioned quota?* The precise type of auction does not need to be specified here, since the model does not assume any information asymmetries. Under this assumption, it follows from the revenue equivalence theorem (see Mc Affee and Mc Millan 1987) that all of the auctions used in practice will lead to the same outcome.

The Model

Consider the following partial equilibrium framework. Suppose that domestic demand is represented by a (strictly) downward sloping function D(p), where p denotes the domestic price in the market under consideration. Let domestic production be characterised by a (strictly) upward sloping marginal cost function MC(y), where y denotes the domestic monopolist's output. The same good is also available in sufficient quantity on the world market at price p_W. The two instruments are compared in terms of domestic social welfare which is measured by the sum of consumer's surplus and producer's surplus. (The question how government revenue should enter social welfare does not arise here because government revenue is the same in both regimes considered. This approach separates the determination of the optimal amount of government revenue G from the optimal method of collection. Only the latter issue is studied here. The welfare approach taken here is the same as in Dasgupta and Stiglitz (1977)). Producer's surplus is equal to the monopolist's profit. Consumer's surplus is measured by the area below the domestic demand function and above the domestic price level.

First, notice that under free trade the domestic price level will be equal to p_W. If a (specific) import tariff t is levied, the domestic price p_t will be equal to p_W+t, the monopolist will extend production up to the point y_t where $MC(y_t)=p_W+t$, and the remaining demand (if any) will be satisfied from imports, $I_t(t)=D(p_W+t)-y_t$. Notice next that the monopolist's output y_t is an increasing function of t, and $I_t(t)$ is a decreasing function (see figure 3 in the main text).

If an import quota q is established, the domestic supplier will be able to raise the price p_q above marginal cost. As shown in Bhagwati (1965), facing the residual demand function $RD(p_q)=D(p_q)-q$, the monopolist will extend output up to the point where marginal revenue is equal to marginal cost, i.e., $MR=MC$, whereby revenue is $R(p_q)=p_q.RD(p_q)$, and importers will make full use of the quota such that $I_q(q)=q$.

Notice also that in any case consumer's surplus CS(p), measured by the area below D(p) and above p, is a decreasing function of the domestic price. Producer's surplus PS(y,p) is equal to the monopolist's profit $p.y-C(y)$, where C denotes the monopolist's cost function, i.e., the integral of MC(y). Government revenue is, in any of the two regimes, equal to the quantity of imports multiplied by the domestic price mark-up above the world price level, i.e., $G=I.(p-p_W)$. (It is assumed that under the auction quota regime, bidders behave competitively, knowing p_W and forming rational expectations about p. Then, the price paid at the auction for one unit import license will be equal to $p-p_W$. In order to simplify, it is also assumed that all import licenses acquired at the auction have to be used. This ensures that the monopolist will not have an interest in participating in the auction.)

Suppose now that the government raises a given revenue G through a tariff on imports of the particular good under consideration. Since $G=t.I(t)$, and I(t) is decreasing, there may exist several tariffs yielding the same revenue. It can be shown that among those, it is always the lowest one which yields the highest domestic welfare. Denote that tariff level by $t^*(G)$, the optimum tariff for raising revenue G. Starting from $G=0$ which implies $t^*=0$, an increase in G implies a higher t^*. There exists, however, a tariff level beyond which a further increase will not yield more revenue. The reason for this is that, as t is increased, the level of imports $I_t(t)$ falls. This, in turn, tends to reduce tariff revenue. This means that there exists an upper bound G^{max} to the revenue that can be collected with a tariff, and a corresponding tariff level t^{*max}. If the tariff is increased beyond t^{*max}, import elasticity will be so high that tariff revenue, $G_t=t.I_t(t)$, will fall. Ultimately, imports will cease completely, namely at the point where domestic demand can be satisfied entirely by the domestic monopolist at a marginal cost below p_W+t (see figure 3 in the main text).

The purpose of the remainder of this appendix is to show that domestic social welfare will always be higher when G is raised through an auctioned quota. This can be seen by starting from a situation where G is raised through a tariff t^*, yielding domestic price $p_t^*=p_W+t^*$, imports $I_t(t^*)$ and national welfare $W_t^*=CS(p_t^*)+PS(p_t^*)$. Define now q^* as that quota which yields the same domestic price level as under t^*, i.e., $p_q(q^*)=p_W+t^*$. It can be shown that $q^*>I_t(t^*)$. This, in turn, implies that more revenue is raised with q^* than with t^*, i.e., $G_q(q^*)>G_t(t^*)$.

Since the price level is the same in both regimes, CS will also be the same in both regimes. Producer's surplus, however, may either be higher, equal or lower. If $PS_q(q^*)>PS_t(t^*)$, then the result is established. If, on the other hand, $PS_q(q^*)<PS_t(t^*)$, then one more step is required. Suppose that q is further increased beyond q^*, up to the point q^{**} where $G_q(q^{**})=G_t(t^*)$. The resulting national welfare is then $W_q^{**}=CS(p_q^{**})+PS(p_q^{**})$, where p_q^{**} denotes the domestic price which results under a quota q^{**}. In the new outcome, PS will be lower, but the increase in CS will more than compensate for it, if MC(y) is everywhere above p_W. (This condition is sufficient but not necessary for the result) To see that $W_q^{**}>W_t^*$, notice that $p_q^{**}<p_t^*$. This means that the economy will be able to consume more of the good while incurring less production costs. In figure 3, $W_q^{**}+G$ is represented by the boldly marked area. It strictly contains the area representing W_t^*+G. This establishes that $W_q^{**}>W_t^*$, which in turn means that under an auctioned quota q^{**}, the required government revenue G is raised with a higher national welfare than under a tariff which raises the same government revenue.

CHAPTER 21

Comment on Toni Haniotis' "Auctions as a Trade Policy Instrument"

Henrik Horn

1. Introduction

The general claim of Haniotis' chapter — that auction quotas are socially superior to tariffs under empirically plausible circumstances — is partly, but not entirely, surprising to an economist. As pointed out in the chapter, there is a strong presumption among economists that price-based policy interventions are generally preferable to those that regulate quantities. However, the claim does not refer to quotas in general, but rather to auction quotas. Auctions are price-based mechanisms of allocation for which economists have a particular affection, partly because of the often desirable efficiency properties of their outcomes. It does not seem implausible *a priori* that because of these properties, quotas may be socially preferred to tariffs. The author indeed argues very well for his case, providing not only theoretical economic arguments (that is, a coherent explanation for their superiority), but also defends them as being in conformity with the GATT, and even tries to give some empirical evidence on their superiority.

I find the chapter very interesting reading, both because it makes an interesting theoretical observation, and because it seeks to support the policy conclusions resulting from this theoretical analysis with an empirical vindication and with an analysis of their legality under GATT. In my opinion, the chapter makes an important contribution in pointing out the fact that quotas can have very different properties when auctioned compared to when distributed in other, and empirically more common, ways. The purpose of this comment is to briefly discuss the robustness of this argumentation, concentrating on the economic theory.

2. The Model in Section 2

The model in Section 2 demonstrates one reason why a government might prefer auctioned quotas to tariffs. The result rests on a number of convenient but special assumptions, as is the case with any type of economic model. It seems that some of the assumptions could be straight-forwardly generalized, whereas other assumptions are somewhat more special.

The Social Value of Government Revenue

One of my few concerns regarding the economic analysis is the role played by government revenue. Strictly speaking, the chapter assumes that the government is only concerned with the sum of consumer and producer, but has to collect an exogenously fixed level of revenue (G), regardless of whether it employs a tariff or an auction quota. But the results are more general than this, and might in particular also hold in circumstances where government revenue is a source of welfare and where the government chooses the amount of revenue to collect in the two trade regimes. Underlying the analysis, however, is an assumption that revenue in the hands of the government in some sense is socially more valuable than when in the hands of the private sector.

The simplest way of seeing this is to generalize the welfare maximization problem facing the government as having to choose either a tariff or an auctioned quota in order to maximize welfare. This is represented by the equation:

Consumer Surplus + Producer Surplus + (a+1) x Government Revenue

Government revenue here reflects the social value of public spending, and enters the picture in the same way as does private consumption. The only difference is that the weight attached to this spending, $a + 1$, differs from the unitary weight put on private consumption whenever the parameter a differs from zero.

Haniotis' assumed objective function would arise as a special case when $a = -1$, and his government maximizes this objective under the constraint that the resulting government revenue equals some exogenous level G, a level which is the same with a tariff and an auction quota. This formulation has the virtue of analytical convenience, since the more general formulation suggested above would complicate the comparison of welfare in the two regimes (as government revenue would typically differ in the case of a tariff and with an auction quota).

Another special case of interest arises when $a = 0$. Government revenue is then assumed not to have any intrinsic value — for instance, a (non-distortionary) tax that decreased producer surplus by \$1 and increased government revenue by the same amount — would leave welfare unaffected. Assuming for simplicity that the demand and marginal costs are linear, as in figure 3 in the chapter, it is straightforward to show that in this benchmark case *free trade* is optimal regardless of whether the government can use a tariff or an auctioned quota.[1] Hence, the rationale for the departure from free trade, and for the auction quota to be preferred to a tariff are the assumptions that revenue is socially *more* valuable in the hands of the government than in those of the private sector (formally, that $a > 1$), and the assumption that there is no alternative source of tax revenue.

This reasoning above is overly restrictive in that it assumes that a dollar is more valuable in the hands of the government than in those of the private sector *regardless* of the level of government consumption. There is an alternative generalization of the analysis in the chapter, one that at least from a theoretical point of view requires a less stringent assumption. This reinterpretation, which views the analysis from the perspective of the theory of public goods, is slightly more involved, however. Along the lines of this literature, one could assume welfare to be a concave function V of the consumption of a private good, as represented by consumer and producer surplus, and the consumption of a public good, financed by the trade tax.[2] This representation differs from the trade theory representation in that the assumed objective function of the government is not the simple sum of these surpluses, as in expression (1). The central assumption that would be required would then be that in a situation where there is *no* provision of public goods, the provision of one unit of this good increases welfare by more than the associated cost in terms of reduced private consumption. Hence, strictly speaking, a dollar need not be more valuable in the government's hands than in those of the private sector for *all* levels of government consumption, as is implicitly assumed in (1). Maintaining this modified assumption, one could show that an auction quota is preferable to a tariff for *any* identical strictly positive level of G, and *a fortiori* also in situations where it can be allowed to differ with auction quota from what is optimal with a tariff.

Haniotis' findings can be evaluated from two different perspectives. As a contribution to economic theory, the chapter represents a significant contribution. But I have small question mark concerning the other perspective — the practical relevance of its policy conclusions. For the analysis to be of empirical interest it must be assumed that a dollar is more valuable in the hands of the government than in those of the private sector for a *large* range of government revenue levels, and not only for the first unit. I am not convinced that this is descriptive of countries that typically are said to lack other tax bases — economies in transition and least developed countries. On the contrary, I think that there are often reasons to distrust governments' propensity to spend the proceeds in a socially desirable manner in these types of economies, in particular in cases where governments are not democratically elected. Furthermore, it should also be noted that even if revenue were more valuable in the hands of the government than in those of the private sector, the gain of moving from a tariff regime to an auction quotas regime would be proportional only to the *difference* between these two values. Hence, even if positive, these gains can still be very small. Other considerations, such as the political economy aspects of the two regimes, might then become much more decisive in a ranking of the two regimes.

Alternative Policy Instruments

A typical feature of most economic policy analyses is that the outcome to a large extent is dictated by the policy instruments assumed to be at the government's disposal. In any particular analysis, provide the government with a wide enough arsenal of instruments and almost any established policy result will vanish. An interesting aspect of the present analysis is that it seems to be robust to the inclusion of at least some instruments that are usually believed to be superior to most other instruments. For instance, a profit tax, even if non-distortionary, does not serve the purpose of the quota in the case under consideration: because of the inefficient production technology of the monopoly, there will be no profits to tax absent a trade barrier. Hence, the profit tax only becomes efficient when applied *jointly* with the trade policy instruments. But, even if the profit tax collected *all* profits in this case, the quota would still be preferred to the tariff when some extra weight is attached to government revenue, at least in the linear case above. Relatedly, it can also be noted that some form of competition policy intervention that increased the degree of competition in the domestic industry would erode the tax base, and might thus reduce welfare.

The Auction

The model makes a number of simplifying but restrictive assumptions concerning the format of the auction:

1. Bidders behave *competitively* in the auction. Typically, however, bidders have incentives to collude in the bidding just as they would profit from collusion in the product market. This raises the question of whether collusion among foreign suppliers is more or less likely under an auction quota regime than under a tariff.

2. The domestic firm does *not* bid. However, and as also pointed out, the licenses may be more valuable to the domestic firm. It may therefore want to acquire the license for pre-emptive purposes. In order to avoid this, the auction must discriminate against the owner of the monopoly.

3. Bidders have *full information* concerning their own and competitors' production costs, market demand, and so forth.

Among these three assumptions, it seems as if the full information assumption is the most debatable, and for certain products is clearly inadequate. This is problematic, since (as noted in the chapter), the property of an auction will often be very sensitive to its exact procedure once information is imperfect. General statements about efficiency properties, like those underlying the chapter, are then not possible.

A Monopolistic Domestic Firm, Perfectly Competitive Foreign Firms

The chapter makes the extreme assumption that there is one domestic firm that faces competition from perfectly competitive foreign suppliers. One possible interpretation of the assumption is that it is a simple way of capturing the notion that firms often have more market power in their home markets than abroad. But, the question is whether this is an innocuous approximation. That is, does the present model approximate one where there is more than one home firm and where the foreign firms are less than perfectly competitive, even if more competitive than home firms? This question is of relevance, since it has been shown in the literature that in the opposite case — where there are a competitive domestic industry and a foreign monopolist — quotas are not desirable. Presumably, it would be possible to have a domestic oligopoly and obtain similar results, but it would be more problematic to introduce oligopolistic behavior among foreign firms.

3. The GATT Compatibility of Auctions

The purpose of Section 3 is to argue that "auctions are the least discriminating way to administer quantitative import measures". I find the discussion very interesting, but I am not well enough versed in law to judge its credentials. However, from an economics point of view one can a make a general remark: the discussion implicitly assumes that an "auction" is a well-defined concept, with an outcome that fulfils a number of economically desirable criteria. Yet, as pointed out both above and in the chapter, the properties of auction outcomes are very sensitive to the circumstances under which the auctions are conducted (for instance, whether informational asymmetries are important or not, or whether the bidding is competitive or not). Hence, for practical purposes it will be difficult to claim that auctions *in general* have certain superior features to other modes of distribution of quotas.

In addition, according to the chapter there are "basically four ways" of allocating quotas: equal shares across trading partners; according to previous shares; first-come, first-serve; or auctions. The chapter makes the general claim that "auctions" is the least discriminatory method among the four. But, under what circumstances are these comparison made? For instance, if the auction allows a dominant buyer to purchase all the quotas and thus completely monopolize the market, whereas such monopolization would not be possible under free trade, can we then say that the auction replicates the free trade outcome more closely than some of the other methods of distribution of quotas? Or, even more obviously, what if the authorities explicitly or implicitly award certain firms advantages in the bidding?

4. The Empirical Support

The theoretical analysis was motivated by the lack of tax bases in less developed countries and in transition economies, but the empirical support relies on the example of Swiss tariff-quotas on wine. This gives rise to at least two questions:

1. To what extent is the theoretical analysis concerning traditional quotas relevant to tariff-quotas?

2. What is the *appropriate criterion* for evaluating the "degree of success" of the Swiss wine quota auctions?

Switzerland is hardly the first country to come to mind that fits the description of a country that lacks other tax bases. It would require some argumentation to assume that money in the hands of the Swiss government has a larger social value than money in the hands of the private sector. In what sense, then, can quota auctions be said to work well? I want to stress that I do not dispute the possibility that the auctioning was better than the methods employed in previous years. But if we are to evaluate the performance of the previous tariff-quota system, and in particular to compare the auction quotas system with other systems, it is necessary to take into consideration the purpose of the trade barriers in the first place. For instance, if the main purpose is not to collect revenue *per se* but to maintain a certain level of domestic wine production, one might want to compare the auctioned quota with income support for farmers.

5. Concluding Remarks

Haniotis' chapter makes a serious attempt to restore the credentials of quotas as trade policy instruments. The chapter discusses their usefulness from the point of view of economic theory and empirical economics, as well as arguing for their legality under the GATT. I find the chapter very interesting even though I have some question marks regarding some aspects of the argument. I am convinced that there is considerable scope for further fruitful research on the usefulness of auction quotas. For instance, it would be very interesting to investigate the robustness of the conclusions of this chapter to the full information assumption, and to allow for tariff-quotas.

N O T E S

1. Formally, the problem analyzed in the paper could be seen as a special case of maximizing expression (1), assuming that the parameter a was very large for all values of government revenue less than G, and equalled -1 for larger values.

2. The assumption about concavity implies that for a given level of private consumption, the marginal utility of consumption of the public good is lower, the larger the level of consumption of this good.

Part V: Conclusions

CHAPTER 22

Conclusions: The Reach of International Trade Law

Thomas Cottier and Petros C. Mavroidis

1. Constitutional Choices and Challenges

The various contributions to the first World Trade Forum Conference and this volume address a fundamental issue both of constitutional and international trade law: the issue of state trading in the twenty-first century. In particular, the contributors examined the scope and grant of exclusive or privileged production and marketing rights within the broad relationship of government and economic operators.

State trading is one aspect of a broader picture: the proper relationship between governments and economic activities. Which of these activities may or should be reserved to state monopolies either exercised by public entities or granted to private operators? In all the World Trade Organization (WTO) members, defining the proper scope and role of exclusive rights is at the center of constitutional law and debate. In all countries and members of the WTO, this is a matter of fundamental political choices in defining the relationship of the state, the economy, and society at large. The reports in this volume depict a large variety, ranging from minimal state trading in the United States, to mixed constellations in Canada and Europe, to traditions of extensive monopolies in Japan and even exclusive state trading in China and Russia, two potential and important future members of the World Trade Organization.

The issue of state trading, however, is equally a fundamental and unresolved constitutional issue of the international trading system. To what extent does and should international trade law define and prescribe that relationship in a uniform manner? How far should it reach? How can it find and define an appropriate balance between proper choices in the pursuit of providing essential goods, services, and facilities and the interest of enhancing market access for foreign competitors? We are faced with the question of to what extent national or regional constitutions, stemming from different historical backgrounds in different quarters of the globe, should be shaped in this point by international trade law. Moreover, how far should it determine capital formation and ownership? In other words, how and to what extent should the WTO prescribe such a relationship from a perspective of facilitating international trade in goods and services? To what extent should it prescribe competition, at least between foreign and domestic producers and service providers?

These issues need to placed in a context where the WTO, as much as the European Community before it, increasingly assumes constitutional functions. No longer is it simply a matter of liberalizing trade and market access. With the advent of an increasing number of trade-related issues, it becomes more apparent that there must be a balancing of governmental goals, both economic and non-economic, in order to achieve the wide-ranging social goals of the WTO enshrined in the Preamble of the Marrakesh Agreement ("raising standards of living, ensuring full employment and a large and steadily growing volume of real income and effective demand, and expanding the production of and trade in goods and services, while allowing for the optimal use of the world's resources in accordance with the objective of sustainable development, seeking both to protect and preserve the environment and to enhance the means for doing so in a manner consistent with respective needs and concerns at different levels of economic development"). It is in to that perspective that the problem of state trading and monopolies needs to be addressed to shape rules for the twenty-first century.

2. From Neglect to Prominence

World trade law assumes that the goals of WTO can best be achieved by letting markets work, and the principles and rules of the WTO are written from a presumption that the WTO members have market economies with only minor state trading activities. This explains why for many years little attention has been paid to the subject. Difficulties encountered in the area of state trading were dealt with in accession protocols rather than through the application of general rules. With the existing members dedicated to managed trade, state trading enterprises posed conceptual difficulties, yet without causing too much concern over the relatively unimportant trade flows. This has been changing with the impending accession of the People's Republic of China and the Russian Federation.

However, while these developments brought renewed attention to the neglected subject of state trading, the conceptually difficult issues found in the present papers lie *within market economies* and thus within longstanding members of the WTO/GATT system. Problems encountered with remaining fields of classical state trading in China and Russia will need to be addressed in accession protocols. They will result in substantial commitments to dismantle exclusive rights of state trading entities to the extent that this is not done by way of unilateral policies in these countries. The main issues with these prospective members relate to enforcing the rule of law in societies where law has played a different role as an instrument of governance, rather than as an instrument for the allocation rights and entitlement. Yet the inclusion of trade in services into the disciplines of international trade regulation has opened new dimensions in the field of essential utilities, of which many have been operating under exclusive rights in open market economies, such as telecommunication, postal services, public transportation, and electricity. The challenges of the twenty-first century are within this field.

3. Four Recommendations in a Nutshell

How far should international trade law reach into these complex areas? The authors to this volume all operate from common underlying economic assumptions and insights. They share the conviction that competition among domestic and foreign suppliers of goods and services generally is best suited to providing efficient services and to pursuing the goals of international trade law in WTO. The reader may thus expect recommendations supporting stringent prescriptive rules on dismantling state trading regimes in Members States of the WTO. On balance, however, our recommendation is less ambitious. It is based on past experience, insights into the limitations of prescriptive international law, and the potential of future market failures induced by current economic prescriptions and models. In a nutshell, we draw the following four conclusions inspired by the contributions to this volume:

• first, WTO law should not take sides in prescribing basic choices in organizing the economy of Member States. It should be neutral regarding the formation and ownership of capital, whether private or public. If countries choose to operate on the basis of exclusive rights, they should be able to do so. Such rights exclude or limit domestic and foreign competitors alike. The approach is inherently discriminatory. International tradelaw cannot overcome such discrimination in principle at its current stage of progress, but it should provide effective remedies against the abuse of exclusive rights with a view to avoiding excessive or unnecessary discriminations of foreign goods and services suppliers;

• second, international trade law should provide incentives to negotiate the de-monopolization of exclusive and preferential rights both in goods and services. Such an option, however, should remain a domestic constitutional issue. This will be more effective than issuing prescriptive rules;

• third, to the extent that countries choose to de-monopolize, or reduce or relinquish exclusive or preferential rights, either unilaterally or in the context of negotiations, the WTO needs to develop appropriate competition rules to prevent and remedy de facto monopolies, both of state-owned and privately-owned competitors. Such disciplines need to include the fields of subsidies, in particular in services, and general rules on government procurement;

• fourth, the control of exclusive rights, subsidization, and government procurement practices need to be subject to efficient dispute settlement and enforcement. Standing in WTO dispute settlement in this areas should be extended to affected private operators.

The currently existing legal framework of the WTO cannot respond adequately to these requirements.

4. A Framework of Analysis: Three Layers of State Activities

Broadly speaking, the relationship of the state to economic activities can be defined on three different levels. In market economies, the main state activity is regulatory. It brings about framework conditions of competition for private operators. Ideally, it seeks to establish level playing fields. Competition essentially excludes the concept of exclusive or preferential rights, precluding or limiting market access per se. Nevertheless, preferential rights exist on this first level and are sometimes necessary (albeit not sufficient) conditions of competition. This is the case of intellectual property rights, where limited monopoly rights are granted to private or public operators with a view to stimulating and protecting investment. It is equally true in the case of tariff quotas which are preferentially allocated to competing importers, creating preferential, albeit not exclusive, rights.

Within the general regulatory framework, state trading entities may compete with private operators. They do not enjoy exclusive rights. So far they operate within the first (regulatory) level. State ownership, however, may bring about subsidization, distorting benefits on the market. This the law should address. This brings us to the second level. Here, state trading mainly amounts to a problem of disciplines on cross-subsidization of the production and export of goods and services. Privileged rights may result from such subsidization, and it is necessary to address the scope and limits of such rights. Similarly, purchasing activities of public entities should be allocated to this level. Given the powerful position of purchasing government entities, public procurement tends to distort competition among private operators in the absence of disciplines and procedural rights of competitors.

The main field of state trading, however, is be found at a third level. By law, exclusive rights to produce, distribute, import, or export are granted to a single entity. Such entities may be state-owned or privately-owned corporations enjoying monopoly rights. They inherently result in market access restrictions for potential domestic and foreign competitors alike. Unlike levels one and two, competition is per se excluded and goods and services are typically provided by a single chartered operator in a given market. Alternatively, exclusive rights may be limited in scope and limited to a certain percentage of the market while leaving the rest to competition. The nature of exclusive rights, however, is not altered by this variation.

The three levels of state activities cannot be entirely separated. Regulations may work in favor of state enterprise and bring about discrimination. Subsidies may in effect bring about privileged positions and come close to exclusive marketing rights. Similarly, the allocation of quotas may produce comparable results. State trading therefore cannot be addressed solely on the third level. All three are closely interrelated. The process of liberalization of state trading typically moves the matter up from level three to level one. To what extent does or should international trade law influence and support this process? A number of interesting observations can be made.

5. The Scope and Limits of Prescriptive Law

Various chapters of this book analyze the shortcomings in regulating complex areas of state trading, in particular in the context of GATT. They usually deal with politically sensitive and essential areas from a point of view of securing basic public goods and services: food, utilities, transportation, infrastructure, cultural identities. The analysis of state practice in relation to Article XVII GATT decodifies the essential characteristics but also reveals tensions. In particular, the scope of the provision has not been fully explored in case law. Panels refrained from applying the provision if solutions could be based on other ones. The impact of national treatment remains unresolved. While it does not formally apply to Article XVIII GATT, state trading activities had been frequently defined to fall under the terms of governmental measures in Article III of the General Agreement. There is a basic inconsistency within the compromise of allowing exclusive rights while making them at the same time subject to the obligation of non-discrimination. Moreover, little is known about the implications of general exceptions to the field, in particular Articles XX and XXI GATT. They have not played much of a role so far.

Similar observations can be made with respect to Articles 37 and 90 of the Treaty Establishing the European Community (ECT). The provisions did not bring about a substantial dismantlement of state trading in the European Community (EC) to the benefit of market access and competition among private operators, domestic and in particular foreign. The changes introduced were much more due to technological developments, in particular in telecommunications, than to shifts in the basic philosophy relating to the proper relationship of the state and the economy. Even within advanced levels of regional integration, some issues are of high political sensitivity. Courts have been reluctant to intervene forcefully due to such sensitivity and due to the technical complexity of these regulatory areas. While it may be argued that EC laws prescribe de-monopolization to some extent, no such basis can be found in WTO law. Therefore, it is likely that panels and the Appellate Body are even less equipped to bring about fundamental shifts on the basis of Article XVII GATT and Article VIII GATS, given the absence of explicit delegation of such powers to the WTO and in light of a much lower degree of integration at the WTO as compared to the European Community.

The relative weakness and insignificance of these rules leads to the question, to what extent are prescriptive rules and approaches enshrined in GATT and the GATS and in Article 90 ECT the proper avenue, even if improvements (for example in transparency and access to dispute settlement) can be achieved. The fundamental issue is to what extent a reinforced prescriptive approach could assist in defining a proper common global triangle of market regulation, market access, and the provision and securing of essential public goods and services. In prescriptive terms, international trade law is of limited reach. If high expectations are raised, rules are likely to fail.

Instead, WTO rules cannot and should not attempt to address the formation of capital. Whether or not state trading is undertaken by means of public or private capital formation should not be legally relevant. Whether exclusive rights are allocated and exercised by public entities or licensed to private but exclusive operators should not matter. Indeed, different members of the WTO employ different means of capital formation. The WTO is and should remain colorblind on this issue. As much as it is a matter for governments to decide upon nationalization under international law, it should remain their choice to privatize nationalized industries.

Similarly, basic decisions as to the granting of exclusive rights are fundamental choices of domestic policy making. International law cannot, nor should it, prescribe such basic choices. It is important to realize that the reach of international trade law needs to be contained if it is to remain effective. Exclusive rights are a matter of high political importance, and regulations depend on different traditions of government. The WTO is not in a position to bring about harmonized regimes for different public utilities. This is difficult to achieve in the context of regional integration. It is even more difficult under the current state of affairs in global integration.

Since the prescriptive functions of the law are limited in the present context, what is the role for judges, panels, and the Appellate Body? As basic decisions on de-monopolization are matters left to national or regional constitutional decisions, international rules are and should be limited to containing excessive use and to preventing and remedying the abuse of existing exclusive rights and privileges. Prescriptive rules on non-discrimination can hardly reach beyond this point. In fact, even this is a daunting task, requiring courage from judges and panels. It is not a coincidence that little is known about the concept of abuse of rights in contemporary WTO law. In terms of sovereignty, it amounts to one of the most sensitive issues. Yet, we believe that, based on general precepts and principles of law, such doctrine could be developed on a case-by-case basis. This implies effective procedural remedies and bodies of dispute settlement strong enough to make such assessment.

We doubt whether the present ad hoc panel system and the Appellate Body review are in a sufficient position to make these decisions effectively. Structural and procedural devices should therefore be strengthened. In this context, private operators should be in a position to challenge abusive practices of public entities and private operators vested with exclusive or privileged rights in light of the experience that governments have traditionally been reluctant to mutually challenge their own prerogatives. We conclude that private standing should be examined in the field of exclusive rights and subsidization.

6. Toward Negotiations

With prescriptive rules being of complex and limited potential impact, the more interesting approach to bring about a proper balance of market access and "service public" lies in exploring and developing the procedural, or negotiating, approaches enshrined in the General Agreement on Trade in Services (GATS). International law should provide a procedural framework and incentives to bring about mutually beneficial liberalization and market opening in sensitive areas. Gradual liberalization of essential facilities and utilities, such as energy and transportation services, can be achieved in a more balanced and nuanced manner on that basis. It is hardly a coincidence that the agreement on telecommunications could be reached within the flexible framework of GATS and not by way of prescriptive rules. This is not only true for services, but also for goods for which such approaches are currently lacking. Tariff protection has been widely dismantled except in agricultural sectors, and other instruments of gradually opening markets are in principle not available under a strict application of national treatment. The application of strict non-discrimination to liberalized sectors may impede rather than promote the process of improving international market access in politically sensitive sectors, such as foodstuffs. It will therefore be necessary to bring about coherent and uniform approaches to negotiating and securing market access and non-discrimination in areas subject to exclusive rights. Procedures and methods developed for services may equally pertain to goods. The question needs further exploration whether the negotiating approaches of GATS should not equally apply to state trading in essential goods and that the two areas should be combined and interfaced. It is a task for the future to develop a comprehensive system applicable both to goods and services in the various fields of exclusive rights.

7. Five Points on Competition Rules

To the extent that the liberalization of monopolies and companies enjoying exclusive or preferential rights is brought about in the wake of unilateral policy measures in accordance with economic prescriptions, or in the wake of multilateral, mutually beneficial negotiations, it is necessary to stabilize market access. It is at this stage that levels one and two of regulatory state activities are achieved, and at which regulatory prescriptions become necessary to secure competition among different competitors. In fact, the demonopolization of core public services cannot be envisaged on a global scale before corresponding disciplines against abuse of dominant positions both of state-owned and private competitors are not being developed both domestically and on a global scale.

Progressive liberalization of public utilities — reflecting current mainstreams in economic thinking and policy-making — may eventually lead to the formation of new de facto monopolies and dominant positions in the relevant market. If left unchallenged, they may undo what is being sought by liberalization — competitive pricing and cheapening of services. From the point of view of the consumer, it does not matter who provides a service as long as dominant positions are not being abused. From this perspective it would seem reasonable to develop prescriptive rules which are applicable both to dominant state trading entities as well as to dominant market operators. Five points emerge from our discussions of this issue:

- first, state trading monopolies have a habit of continuing their behavior after liberalization. They also are often in the position of controlling essential facilities. It is therefore necessary to oblige WTO members to implement and enforce a competitive environment;

- second, it is of equal importance to prevent and avoid de facto monopolies by private operators. In the wake of liberalization, core facilities may end up being controlled by single providers in a relevant market. While formerly the concept of exclusive rights has been abandoned, it could reemerge by the backdoor, and economic benefits may be nullified and impaired;

• third, it is important to strengthen disciplines in the field of subsidies. Cross-subsidization of state trading entities results in the bringing about of special privileges which may distort competition and nullify and impair market access in the wake of liberalizing companies enjoying exclusive rights. The same effects occur in the subsidization of private domestic operators, and it will be necessary to assess the scope and reach of subsidization, in particular in the field of services. Work undertaken in WTO on service-related subsidies therefore is of utmost importance, and may also provide further insights in refining disciplines in the sector of goods from a point of view of securing competition;

• fourth, we need to include and address an issue which has not received much attention in the papers of this volume. State trading cannot be looked at only in the context of providing good and services. State trading is of equal importance on the part of buying goods and services. State trading, in all forms, has to be accompanied by effective general disciplines on government procurement. Existing plurilateral commitments are not adequate to avoid the abuse of purchasing power by government. De facto monopolies and companies enjoying exclusive rights may well be the results of arbitrary and selective purchasing practices on the part of governments to the benefit of state trading entities or privileged private operators. Even with formal state trading entities and exclusive rights absent, public procurement may bring about similar effects of foreclosing markets and competition by granting privileged access to governmental purchases of goods and services from private operators;

• finally, it will be necessary to look more closely into the relationship of state trading rules and dispute settlement. What has been said on assessing abuses of exclusive rights in the context of legal monopolies is equally, or even more, true for dominant positions in a de-monopolized regime. Structures and procedures need to be adequate to prevent and remedy de facto monopolies, both public and private. The studies undertaken in this volume reveal that governments seem to be reluctant, for fear of reciprocal challenge, to submit public sector economic activities to dispute settlement. It does not take a theory of conspiracy to understand such behavior. Similar experiences can be observed in the process of mutually controlling subsidization practices and disciplines of government procurement. These are constellations where authoritative dispute settlement and enforcement mechanisms, including private standing, will need to be further explored.

8. Final Remarks

In conclusion, it is submitted that WTO rules relating to capital formation and property ownership, public or private, and exclusive rights should be colorblind in the WTO. Exclusive rights are neither good nor bad. They are legitimate in the WTO under different titles (including, in particular the TRIPs Agreement) as long as they are not abused, and as long as they serve legitimate governmental goals that the WTO is called upon to protect as much as liberalization and enhanced market access for foreign competitors. Whether or not they are enjoyed by public or private operators, whether they stem from the implementation of public interests, or whether they are granted to protect investment and good will, they all should be subject to coherent disciplines preventing and remedying abuse of such rights. Whether or not such abuses exist is an issue to be settled on a case-by-case basis. Additional prescriptive rules emerge from disciplines on subsidies and government procurement.

As for the process of improving market access and bringing about competition, this is a matter which should be left, due to political interests at stake, rather to the negotiating process, in particular in the framework of GATS. It is submitted that the rules of GATS on progressive liberalization, and the possibilities of conditioning market access and national treatment in a tailor-made fashion, are more suitable for this purpose than the search for detailed prescriptive rules which seek to protect legitimate public interest goals and competition rules at the same time.

Given the current drive for liberalization, de-monopolization, and dismantlement of exclusive trading rights around the world, the main challenge consists of bringing about adequate rules on competition, including services and subsidies, which are equally applicable to private and public entities and which do not depend on qualifications of ownership. Again, structures and procedures of dispute settlement and enforcement need to be developed that are fully capable of dealing with such challenges. Indeed, given current geo-economic trends, effective and enforceable rules on competition are more pressing and will be more important than specific prescriptive rules on state trading and as important as procedural avenues to bring about mutually agreed liberalization. The twenty-first century is likely to start with a host of newly privatized utilities. It is premature to assess as to whether the current movement to abandon state monopolies, and in particular in the field of essential and core facitilities, will be successful in the longer run. Market failures may occur, as they occurred before many of these facilities were nationalized in the first place. The nineteenth century history of railways may be repeated in the age of cyberspace. Private capital formation led to disarray and disruptions and states ended up buying private and bankrupt lines in order to ensure essential public services. The trading system therefore should remain flexible and allow for adjustments as they seem appropriate to nations in the twenty-first century.

Annexes

The Legal Texts

Article XVII

State Trading Enterprises

1.*   (a)   Each contracting party undertakes that if it establishes or maintains a State enterprise, wherever located, or grants to any enterprise, formally or in effect, exclusive or special privileges,* such enterprise shall, in its purchases or sales involving either imports or exports, act in a manner consistent with the general principles of non-discriminatory treatment prescribed in this Agreement for governmental measures affecting imports or exports by private traders.

(b)   The provisions of sub-paragraph (a) of this paragraph shall be understood to require that such enterprises shall, having due regard to the other provisions of this Agreement, make any such purchases or sales solely in accordance with commercial considerations,* including price, quality, availability, marketability, transportation and other conditions of purchase or sale, and shall afford the enterprises of the other contracting parties adequate opportunity, in accordance with customary business practice, to compete for participation in such purchases or sales.

(c)   No contracting party shall prevent any enterprise (whether or not an enterprise described in sub-paragraph (a) of this paragraph) under its jurisdiction from acting in accordance with the principles of sub-paragraphs (a) and (b) of this paragraph.

2.   The provisions of paragraph 1 of this Article shall not apply to imports of products for immediate or ultimate consumption in governmental use and not otherwise for resale or use in the production of goods* for sale. With respect to such imports, each contracting party shall accord to the trade of the other contracting parties fair and equitable treatment.

3.   The contracting parties recognize that enterprises of the kind described in paragraph 1 (a) of this Article might be operated so as to create serious obstacles to trade; thus negotiations on a reciprocal and mutually

advantageous basis designed to limit or reduce such obstacles are of importance to the expansion of international trade.*

4.   (a)   Contracting parties shall notify the CONTRACTING PARTIES of the products which are imported into or exported from their territories by enterprises of the kind described in paragraph 1 (a) of this Article.

(b)   A contracting party establishing, maintaining or authorizing an import monopoly of a product, which is not the subject of a concession under Article II, shall, on the request of another contracting party having a substantial trade in the product concerned, inform the CONTRACTING PARTIES of the import mark-up* on the product during a recent representative period, or, when it is not possible to do so, of the price charged on the resale of the product.

(c)   The Contracting Parties may, at the request of a contracting party which has reason to believe that its interests under this Agreement are being adversely affected by the operations of an enterprise of the kind described in paragraph 1 (a), request the contracting party establishing, maintaining or authorizing such enterprise to supply information about its operations related to the carrying out of the provisions of this Agreement.

(d)   The provisions of this paragraph shall not require any contracting party to disclose confidential information which would impede law enforcement or otherwise be contrary to the public interest or would prejudice the legitimate commercial interests of particular enterprises.

Interpretative Note *Ad* Article XVII from Annex I

Paragraph 1

The operations of Marketing Boards, which are established by contracting parties and are engaged in purchasing or selling, are subject to the provisions of sub-paragraphs (a) and (b).

The activities of Marketing Boards which are established by contracting parties and which do not purchase or sell but lay down regulations covering private trade are governed by the relevant Articles of this Agreement.

The charging by a state enterprise of different prices for its sales of a product in different markets is not precluded by the provisions of this Article, provided that such different prices are charged for commercial reasons, to meet conditions of supply and demand in export markets.

Paragraph 1 (a)

Governmental measures imposed to insure standards of quality and efficiency in the operation of external trade, or privileges granted for the exploitation of national natural resources but which do not empower the government to exercise control over the trading activities of the enterprise in question, do not constitute "exclusive or special privileges".

Paragraph 1 (b)

A country receiving a "tied loan" is free to take this loan into account as a "commercial consideration" when purchasing requirements abroad.

Paragraph 2

The term "goods" is limited to products as understood in commercial practice, and is not intended to include the purchase or sale of services.

Paragraph 3

Negotiations which contracting parties agree to conduct under this paragraph may be directed towards the reduction of duties and other charges on imports and exports or towards the conclusion of any other mutually satisfactory arrangement consistent with the provisions of this Agreement. (See paragraph 4 of Article II and the note to that paragraph.)

Paragraph 4 (b)

The term "import mark-up" in this paragraph shall represent the margin by which the price charged by the import monopoly for the imported product (exclusive of internal taxes within the purview of Article III, transportation, distribution, and other expenses incident to the purchase, sale or further processing, and a reasonable margin of profit) exceeds the landed cost.

WTO UNDERSTANDING ON THE INTERPRETATION OF ARTICLE XVII OF THE GENERAL AGREEMENT ON TARIFFS AND TRADE 1994

Members,

Noting that Article XVII provides for obligations on Members in respect of the activities of the state trading enterprises referred to in paragraph 1 of Article XVII, which are required to be consistent with the general principles of non-discriminatory treatment prescribed in GATT 1994 for governmental measures affecting imports or exports by private traders;

Noting further that Members are subject to their GATT 1994 obligations in respect of those governmental measures affecting state trading enterprises;

Recognizing that this Understanding is without prejudice to the substantive disciplines prescribed in Article XVII;

Hereby *agree* as follows:

1.   In order to ensure the transparency of the activities of state trading enterprises, Members shall notify such enterprises to the Council for Trade in Goods, for review by the working party to be set up under paragraph 5, in accordance with the following working definition:

"Governmental and non-governmental enterprises, including marketing boards, which have been granted exclusive or special rights or privileges, including statutory or constitutional powers, in the exercise of which they influence through their purchases or sales the level or direction of imports or exports."

This notification requirement does not apply to imports of products for immediate or ultimate consumption in governmental use or in use by an enterprise as specified above and not otherwise for resale or use in the production of goods for sale.

2.   Each Member shall conduct a review of its policy with regard to the submission of notifications on state trading enterprises to the Council for Trade in Goods, taking account of the provisions of this Understanding. In carrying out such a review, each Member should have regard to the need to ensure the maximum transparency possible in its notifications so as to permit a clear appreciation of the manner of operation of the enterprises notified and the effect of their operations on international trade.

3.   Notifications shall be made in accordance with the questionnaire on state trading adopted on 24 May 1960 (BISD 9S/184–185), it being understood that Members shall notify the enterprises referred to in paragraph 1 whether or not imports or exports have in fact taken place.

4.   Any Member which has reason to believe that another Member has not adequately met its notification obligation may raise the matter with the Member concerned. If the matter is not satisfactorily resolved it may make a counter-notification to the Council for Trade in Goods, for consideration by the working party set up under paragraph 5, simultaneously informing the Member concerned.

5.   A working party shall be set up, on behalf of the Council for Trade in Goods, to review notifications and counter-notifications. In the light of this review and without prejudice to paragraph 4(c) of Article XVII, the Council for Trade in Goods may make recommendations with regard to the adequacy of notifications and the need for further information. The working party shall also review, in the light of the notifications received, the adequacy of the above-mentioned questionnaire on state trading and the coverage of state trading enterprises notified under paragraph 1. It shall also develop an illustrative list showing the kinds of relationships between governments and enterprises, and the kinds of activities, engaged in by these enterprises, which may be relevant for the purposes of Article XVII. It is understood that the Secretariat will provide a general background paper for the working party on the operations of state trading enterprises as they relate to international trade. Membership of the working party shall be open to all Members indicating their wish to serve on it. It shall meet within a year of the date of entry into force of the WTO Agreement and thereafter at least once a year. It shall report annually to the Council for Trade in Goods.[1]

Note 1: The activities of this working party shall be coordinated with those of the working group provided for in Section III of the Ministerial Decision on Notification Procedures adopted on 15 April 1994.

GATS Provisions

Article VIII

Monopolies and Exclusive Service Suppliers

1.   Each Member shall ensure that any monopoly supplier of a service in its territory does not, in the supply of the monopoly service in the relevant market, act in a manner inconsistent with that Member's obligations under Article II and specific commitments.

2.   Where a Member's monopoly supplier competes, either directly or through an affiliated company, in the supply of a service outside the scope of its monopoly rights and which is subject to that Member's specific commitments, the Member shall ensure that such a supplier does not abuse its monopoly position to act in its territory in a manner inconsistent with such commitments.

3.   The Council for Trade in Services may, at the request of a Member which has a reason to believe that a monopoly supplier of a service of any

other Member is acting in a manner inconsistent with paragraph 1 or 2, request the Member establishing, maintaining or authorizing such supplier to provide specific information concerning the relevant operations.

4.   If, after the date of entry into force of the WTO Agreement, a Member grants monopoly rights regarding the supply of a service covered by its specific commitments, that Member shall notify the Council for Trade in Services no later than three months before the intended implementation of the grant of monopoly rights and the provisions of paragraphs 2, 3 and 4 of Article XXI shall apply.

5.   The provisions of this Article shall also apply to cases of exclusive service suppliers, where a Member, formally or in effect, (*a*) authorizes or establishes a small number of service suppliers and (*b*) substantially prevents competition among those suppliers in its territory.

Article IX

Business Practices

1.   Members recognize that certain business practices of service suppliers, other than those falling under Article VIII, may restrain competition and thereby restrict trade in services.

2.   Each Member shall, at the request of any other Member, enter into consultations with a view to eliminating practices referred to in paragraph 1. The Member addressed shall accord full and sympathetic consideration to such a request and shall cooperate through the supply of publicly available non-confidential information of relevance to the matter in question. The Member addressed shall also provide other information available to the requesting Member, subject to its domestic law and to the conclusion of satisfactory agreement concerning the safeguarding of its confidentiality by the requesting Member.

Treaty of Rome Provisions

Article 37

1.   Member States shall progressively adjust any State monopolies of a commercial character so as to ensure that when the transitional period has ended no discrimination regarding the conditions under which goods are procured and marketed exists between nationals of Member States.

The provisions of this Article shall apply to any body through which a Member State, in law or in fact, either directly or indirectly supervises, determines, or appreciably influences imports or exports between Member States. These provisions shall likewise apply to monopolies delegated by the State to others.

2.   Member States shall refrain from introducing any new measure which is contrary to the principles laid down in paragraph 1 or which restricts the scope of the articles dealing with the abolition of customs duties and quantitative retrictions between Member States.

3.   The timetable for the measures referred to in paragraph 1 shall be harmonized with the abolition of quantitative restrictions on the same products provided for in Articles 30 to 34.

If a product is subject to a State monopoly of a commercial character in only one or some Member States, the Commission may authorize the other Member States to apply protective measures until the adjustment provided for in paragraph 1 has been effected; the Commission shall determine the conditions and details of such measures.

4.   If a State monopoly of a commercial character has rules which are designed to make it easier to dispose of agricultural products or obtain for them the best return, steps should be taken in applying the rules contained in this article to ensure equivalent safeguards for the employment and standard of living of the producers concerned, account being taken of the adjustments that will be possible and the specialization that will be needed with the passage of time.

5.   The obligations on Member States shall be binding only insofar as they are compatible with existing international agreements.

6.   With effect from the first stage the Commission shall make recommendations as to the manner in which and the timetable according to which the adjustment provided for in this article shall be carried out.

Article 90

1.   In the case of public undertakings and undertakings to which Member States grant special or exclusive rights, Member States shall neither enact nor maintain in force any measure contrary to the rules contained in this Treaty, in particular to those rules provided for in Art. 7 [prohibiting discrimination on the basis of nationality] and Arts. 85–94 [the competition rules].

2.   Undertakings entrusted with the operation of services of general economic interest or having the character of a revenue-producing monopoly shall be subject to the rules contained in this Treaty, in particular to the rules on competition, in so far as the application of such rules does not obstruct

the performance, in law or in fact, of the particular tasks assigned to them. The development of trade must not be affected to such an extent as would be contrary to the interests of the Community.

3.   The Commission shall ensure the application of the provisions of this article and shall, where necessary, address appropriate directives or decisions to Member States.

Transcript of Roundtable Discussion

13 September 1997, Gerzensee, Switzerland

C. Ehlermann*:   I propose to structure the discussion by addressing the following three broad subjects. First we might take up the very last contribution of Damien Neven and ask ourselves whether there is a justification for STEs in the world as it is today, and special rights (in addition to just companies being state-owned) from the economic point of view. The underlying assumption in many interventions was that they are losing importance and are going away, so perhaps one doesn't have to deal with them. Is there justification for them to remain with us — in particular in certain parts of the world that are less developed?

The second question might be: are the existing WTO rules sufficient to deal with this phenomenon? Instead of discussing provisions which we have not discussed, we might concentrate on Article XVII GATT. We could distinguish between WTO Members in general, and state trading countries in particular, and concentrate on the example which has been most with us: China.

Finally, we could discuss the question of what should be done (or what could reasonably be done) in order to improve the situation.

J. Bourgeois: As to your first question, Chairman, would it be possible to expand it? When state trading enterprises are being privatized, public monopolies may become private monopolies. Moreover, those that were in charge of the public monopoly may remain in charge of the private monopoly.

C. Ehlermann: I'm afraid if we do that, if we don't have a special right, an exclusive right we would move into the area of pure competition law, and that is not the subject of the day. Underlying your question is, of course, what is more important — structure or ownership? Is ownership relevant?

---

*Chairperson of the Roundtable Discussion.

P. Messerlin: I would like to also relate your first question to what Jacques said yesterday: we don't have figures, and one thing will be to try to find figures about how *service publique*, which is a kind of vague definition of this state-owned enterprise, is defined in telecoms and in air transport today in the open community. We have figures now, and those figures are relatively small — in a range of zero to five percent of the sales of the activity. I don't know exactly the basis of the percentage. So, the answer could be: maybe we have the result of justification of the state-owned enterprise or exclusive privileges, but maybe the justification does not affect as huge a portion of the economy as feared. That would be point number one.

And second, your question has raised what to do with this remaining part, which is an empirical answer. We can either react by state enterprise or we could react by other schemes like subsidies, which means that we shift from Article XVII GATT to the article on subsidies and countervailing duties in the WTO, because we need better disciplines on subsidies if we want to support *service publique* by this special scheme of subsidization.

D. Wood: I want to ask whether, as we think of both your first and second question with an Article XVII GATT focus, we are clear which state trading enterprises definition we mean. Because you mentioned the possibility of looking at ownership or control, I would suggest we also might want to think about asking about market impact. There could be a state-owned or local-owned enterprise that didn't have the slightest effect on international trade issues, and my understanding of Article XVII GATT is (at least traditionally) that has not been thought to be a concern. I just want to keep this definitional issue in front of us because our conclusions might be quite different on your first question depending on what we want to do.

T. Cottier: I'm very glad we are able to take this question up front. My impression was, from the papers, that the problem of state trading was very much approached through the glasses of the WTO lawyer and economist who says, "I am interested in improving market access, therefore, the monopoly should be reduced or should go". I think the fundamental question really is about *service publique* — to what extent do our societies need *service publique* to have an equitable share of services around the country?

It is of no help to the WTO if all the remote areas, for example, in this country become aggressive against it because they are constantly

losing out to the benefit of the centers. In my view, this is the fundamental question. Then we should ask, what does it mean for WTO?
How far could we go? Should we try to design rules which are neutral,
which apply to both private and public entities? Or should we have
special rules for public entities? Or, should we even encourage moves
toward privatization and liberalization in terms of WTO rules? I think
the starting point really should be a clarification as to the justification
of these services. We have not heard really much about why these monopolies came about in the nineteenth century and in the twentieth
century — what they were intended to remedy and what may be the
drawbacks we are running into now when we dismantle all of them. It
is a matter of intellectual honesty to clarify this point. Personally, I
would like to place a note of caution of simply looking at the issue
from a trade lawyer's or a trade economist's point of view. Because in
the end, when it comes to the big political battle (and it was never
contested that this is politically a very very sensitive issue), it is not the
nations and the national governments who are going to lose, but it is
the world trading system because that is the more feeble part of the
game. So, I would like to invite you to express your views on how you
see this — I'm very reluctant to conclude, "well, economists now tell
us this will go away" — perhaps the opposite will be true.

C. Ehlermann: In the debates in Brussels about the liberalization of telecoms, there was a common understanding that the monopoly is not necessarily, particularly not the public monopoly, is not the only way to
guarantee public service or general service functions. That contrasts
with what Damien Neven has said, that public service necessarily is
combined with exclusivity. It might in certain sectors, but in others it
might not be necessary.

R. Howse: I think before one can understand what the legal constraints are that one might want or not want, one should approach the
problem of the essential public services from an instrument choice
point of view. First of all defining what the goal is. I presume that at a
minimum, certain services are considered essential in the sense that
everyone — regardless of their ability to pay a price that might be
charged in the competitive market — should have access to those services. Then, if that's the goal, we could imagine a wide range of instruments. One possibility is the government guarantees the provision
of these services to everyone, but then goes on the market and purchases them from various kinds of providers or enters into contracts. There the legal constraints might be non-discrimination at a minimum as

between different providers, and you get into a government procurement type of issue.

A second possibility (which has happened in some jurisdictions with respect to telecommunications) is that you de-monopolize and, if necessary, privatize. But then you impose upon the competing entities some kind of regulatory obligations — say, to provide the basic telecommunications service at some price and also on some terms (for example, if somebody has not paid their bill in fifteen days, you cannot simply cut off the telephone, and that sort of thing). So there you are using regulation to impose some kind of obligation on enterprises to provide the service.

And, of course, another traditional alternative is to simply integrate everything in the government. The government guarantees the services to everyone, then plans them and delivers them using its own employees and inputs. And there it seems to me that, first of all, one can't theoretically exclude the possibility that that would always be an inefficient or an inappropriate way to deliver certain services: I did some work on the establishment of the new Canadian food inspection agency and looked at various delivery alternatives of contracting some of the inspection functions to the private sector. It turns out we found (and the private sector agreed) that with respect to food inspection, certain of the agency costs that will be introduced by external contracting of the certification of food as safe are sufficiently grave to give a sound justification for the result that the agency that has been established is a public monopoly.

On the other hand, the agency may eventually start competing with private services in certain areas like labelling, which again raises another issue: the relationship between the monopoly element, where the government is the provider and areas where the government is the same government agency, maybe competing with private firms to provide the service. And that, I think, is a different kind of issue in terms of the legal constraints that you would want, because there you don't want the agency using or abusing its power as a monopolist (which may be justified with respect to some dimensions of the services it's providing) to compete unfairly with private providers in the portion of the market where there is actual competition. So, once we start disaggregating the instruments that are available to deliver essential public services, we will see that there are different kinds of legal issues and possible legal constraints we might want to consider.

S. Nestor: Thank you. Actually, a lot of what I wanted to say was just said by Professor Howse, so I will not repeat it. The distinction between the enterprise providing a service in the public sector and the service itself is at the core of the reform we are talking about. Now, why is that? In my mind, at least, the main reason is that new technologies have made possible (and much cheaper) an arms-length regulation instead of state ownership. We can now regulate what we previously could not have in terms of transaction costs and administrative costs. This makes it cheaper sometimes to actually have private providers of public services and a state regulator (something that was in the past very expensive). What does that mean? and here I come back to Professor Messerlin's point on subsidies. That basically means that the firms (even state-owned firms) are subject to competition disciplines. International disciplines like WTO disciplines focus on states: the subjects are the states, not the enterprises, not even the state trading enterprises. And that is because subsidies are now the way to actually ensure that the public services are being provided — not the creation of state-owned firms.

C. Ehlermann: That seems to me the fundamental question.

S. Nestor: There is a variety of factors which all lead us to the same conclusion: that the old instruments, the traditional instruments, are no longer efficient, therefore necessary. We achieve the same results by injecting some degree of competition.

F. Abbott: It seems to me that the question Thomas asked was whether the WTO somehow implies a preference for private capital formation. The question we have been discussing is to what extent the WTO should be regulating public service entities. But to address what I understood to be Thomas' principle question, there are at least two reasons why a society might opt for public capital formation. You may have a defective private capital market, so that buses don't get built and telephones don't ring, or you may have a social preference for public capital formation. So, for example, to take the case of China, for many years that society preferred public capital formation as a matter of choice. Is there a WTO preference for private capital formation and ownership? My intuition is that the answer to that question is "no". Part of Thomas' question, it seemed to me, is whether the WTO is an organization like the OECD that says, "We are going to tell you how to create your capital market structure". My belief is that, at least historically, the WTO has not been taking a position on that.

That leads to the second question: do you need a separate set of rules for the public and private systems? That is what Gary Horlick was talking about, and to a certain extent Bill Davey yesterday. If we don't care who owns the capital because we accept that social preferences may differ, why doesn't the GATT Article III non-discrimination provision work as well for Chinese state trading in toys as it does for General Motors trading in automobiles?

A. Sapir: To come back to the question, is there a danger that this WTO-type liberalization will turn against us, and people will sort of rebel: I think if one talks about trade liberalization, one has to separate trade and liberalization. The first question here is, should a particular service, since that is what we are talking about, be provided on a monopoly basis or on a competitive basis? If it is provided, if we agree (and I'll come back to that) that it should be provided on a competitive basis, then I think we can go to the next step: should it be provided on a competitive basis only among actors that are located domestically or should the liberalization encompass also actors that are outside our jurisdiction? This is really, I think, the way one has to think about this. Should this be a monopoly or should it be liberalized? and if it is liberalized, should it be liberalized simply domestically or should it be liberalized in a global manner?

So the real question indeed is, we have seen that in a number of activities that used to be provided on the monopoly basis there has been liberalization. Is that a good thing? Now, what can I say about that? Some of the changes that do come (this is very clear in telecommunications), come from changes in technology. In the end it seems to me, that the onus is on those who want to impose a monopoly. Maybe the monopoly should be kept, but it should be demonstrated that this monopoly, this fashion of providing the service, is in the public interest. And, well, maybe in some instances there is indeed a natural monopoly. Maybe certain segments of the industry are characterized by natural monopoly. That is what we need to look at. And maybe even in instances where there is a decision that monopoly provision is first best, one can see also how one allocates this monopoly. Maybe it should be by auction. Maybe it is not a monopoly forever — maybe it is a monopoly for a certain period of time. There are all kinds of ways to introduce competition, even in instances of monopoly.

We first have to make a decision whether monopoly provision is right or whether we need liberalization. It is only then we can talk of WTO

— if people are convinced that monopoly provision is first best, then there is no point talking about trade liberalization. It makes no sense.

D. Wood: Yes, thank you. Maybe part of what I am saying is following up on what André has just said. Because I think in answering your first question, the first point is whether there is any need for an STE, maybe because it is a natural monopoly, maybe because it's a public service that we don't want to risk somehow having the market provide in a supply that is too short or in a supply that is too selective. But, I think that Robert Howse's comments showed that even in that case there is no strict need for a state trading enterprise: it could be contracted out, it could be franchised, it could be provided in a number of ways. So then we come to deciding which way we want to provide it, and there, logically, you first asked whether there is any harm to using the state trading enterprise mechanism: what are the down sides? There are some: STEs are much harder to look behind, they can conceal in some ways discriminatory practices or anti-competitive practices or other kinds of manipulations of the market a little more successfully than something more open might do. So there may be some reason to have at least a bias in the system against them, even if we are not going to abolish them altogether.

Are there any benefits that would cause us to hesitate to have such a bias? I think in most developed countries the answer is probably "no". There aren't any particular benefits to doing it this way. It is possible though, that in some developing countries, maybe capital markets are not sufficiently developed. Or maybe the rest of the infrastructure isn't strong enough, such that we might want to take a broader view about this mechanism for achieving these goals. But it is just a mechanism in the end: unless we analyze it through those kinds of steps, I don't think we will have a good grip on when we might want at least to tolerate them.

P. Low: I don't know if it helps the discussion in terms of where the WTO is coming from, but I think we should have at least introduced the distinction between supplying through cross-border sales, and getting into a market by establishing a commercial presence. Although the WTO does not deal with investment as a horizontal issue, the GATS is largely about investment. The question about the attitude towards public ownership has been much more prominent in the services area than it has in the goods area precisely for this reason. When you look at the terms upon which governments negotiate access to markets, the question of ownership, or equity participation, receives considerable attention. Obviously, this changes the attitude of potential market players to the question of ownership.

M. Bronckers: I would like to take up the point of André Sapir when he says we have to make a distinction. First, we have to decide the policy question of whether or not we need a monopoly; and secondly, when we decide that question one way or the other, only then do we get into the trade or WTO-type question. That is also how I understand the traditional approach of WTO (or the GATT at least) to be — that is to say, let the governments decide their policies and once they have decided what they want to do, then GATT comes in and helps you to discipline the implementation. But I see a distinction between the GATT (which might be to that extent more value-neutral) and the GATS. In the GATS, it is possible to lock in the decision to abolish monopolies. And so to that extent, I wonder whether we see a different aim, a different type of philosophy, under the same heading of "the WTO".

C. Ehlermann: I have not heard any arguments in favor of maintaining monopoly. We are talking about now and the future. In services where we have public service, there might be a case for maintaining monopoly rights, but it would be a case that has to be justified. The burden of proof is on the side of those who argue for them.

This introduces subject number two. Let's concentrate on the terms "appropriate, adequate, sufficient" in the light of the experience of the EC, where part of the daily work is dealing with public companies under a heading that we have not discussed: subsidies.

J. Bourgeois: I would like to take this opportunity to indirectly comment on what Damien Neven has said in his paper. The question of the adequacy of the present rules in the European Community context could also arise in the WTO context. The point raised by Damien was about review of the decision of regulating authorities. That is an issue that we are going to face: we already face this problem at the national level, we have faced it already at the European Community level, and we will probably have to face it some day at the WTO level.

Let me take an example. Damien said it is difficult to contemplate that there would be some sort of review of the decision of regulating authorities, certainly at the WTO level, and I see difficulties at the EC level. I have a concrete example: the Belgian telecoms operator charged a certain price for basic data to be used by the established publisher of the "Yellow Pages". It started charging a higher price when its subsidiary began publishing "Yellow Pages" as well. The Belgian Telecom regulator found nothing wrong with this higher price.

The established publisher filed a complaint under the EC competition rules. It requested the European Commission to review these rates. Following a fairly thorough investigation, the European Commission found that this price was too high.

This shows that there is a need for review of what the national regulators do whenever there is an impact on trade within the European Community and on the competition within the European Community. It also shows that it is possible to do so.

T. Haniotis: If the question is whether Article XVII GATT is sufficient to deal with the issue of state trading or not, I think we should agree on the question of what we want the WTO to do: what is the role of the WTO? And there I think that many of the issues that we have discussed (capital/ownership structure, *service publique*, etc.) can be resolved within each country, because there does not need to be a global consensus on what sort of *service publique* we want in each country or what capital structure and ownership structure is considered optimal. Is there a need for a global harmonization on these issues? I think there is not. So, maybe a lot of issues can be dealt with unilaterally. Then the question is, what do we need to deal with on the multilateral level? And there, I'm just raising this question. From a purely economic point of view, I think, there are very few externalities or trade effects of ownership and I would think that all of them could be dealt with under the existing provisions of the WTO. If subsidies is an issue, then we have the Subsidies Agreement. I agree that transparency of subsidies may be a bigger problem under public ownership than under private ownership. But there is an underlying conceptual issue of what is a subsidy, and this applies to both state trading and to private trading. So, if there needs to be conceptual clarification, this could be addressed regardless of the ownership structure.

But, more fundamentally, we should agree on what we need to do on the multilateral level. Maybe the WTO builds on some sort of "Weightwatcher's effect": if you do something good for you, I do something good for me. Paul Krugman wrote an article in the World Economy (1992) arguing essentially along these lines. Unilaterally, from a social point of view, every country would liberalize, but because of the capturing and the pressure groups, they don't. So they need to have a sort of a Weightwatcher scheme, where each one looks at the other one and says if you lose weight, I will lose weight; if you liberalize, I will liberalize. Maybe that is the role of the WTO — but I just raise the question.

G. Horlick: For at least the mid-term — say five-year — future, we are not likely to see any changes in the text of either Article XVII GATT, or the Understanding, or the Agreement on Subsidies, so it is not an issue of what we would like it to say, it is there. It is an unusual situation with Article XVII GATT in particular, and with some of the other texts as well, there is actually no interpretation (very few cases or none), so I would think that the "commercial considerations" language in particular (which arguably may exhibit a slight bias in favor of private ownership, which I'll explain if anyone cares) still gives you a lot of work with. And it is one of the many areas (like others in the WTO) where panels can certainly come up with reasonable solutions. There's nothing, or very little, in Article XVII GATT that is a barrier to sound policy choices, without prejudging what those are. I think it really does become more questions of underlying theology, ideology, than what's wrong with the text of Article XVII GATT.

The subsidy issues, I think, are probably more defined and choices have been made for better or worse in the Subsidies Agreement. But there again, at risk of repeating myself from yesterday, with both Article XVII GATT and subsidies and a number of other areas, you don't actually have an enforcement mechanism. So I would focus some attention on this example of wine-coolers in Ontario. The WTO panels are not going to do it — and more important, you don't have citizens' complaints. You don't have anyone who is complaining. Another government is not going to complain because it has its own wine-coolers (I've shifted from governments living in glass houses, to living in glass wine-coolers, I fear). So, some attention should be given to setting up some incentive structure for getting these issues resolved. I don't think we are anywhere close to a private access situation, much less a GATT procurator general. So, what is missing are incentives for governments to take action. Thank you.

J. Bourgeois: I have a small follow-up question to one of your interventions. Basically, we don't really need anything more than what we have nowadays, so I am returning to my example of the rates set by the Belgian telecom's operator for use of the information to be published by a

Yellow Pages publisher. Imagine now that the Yellow Pages publisher is a company from Malaysia and it wants to rely on the GATT to attack that. It cannot rely on the GATS to attack it on its own, so let's assume that the Malaysian government is willing to do something about it. Are we confident that under the GATT as it stands, there are provisions that would allow the Malaysian government to challenge the rate setting by the Belgian telecom's operator? I have my doubts about that. Thank you.

T. Cottier: I think your example and also the preceeding interventions show that we have to look at Article XVII GATT in context. Perhaps most of the problems with state trading could be solved on the basis of Article III national treatment. You may not have to go much further. Maybe the Yellow Pages could be approached on the same grounds, I don't know. I am only suggesting that we have to look at this in context and to ask what the other provisions of the GATT and the GATS are doing here.

I was impressed, Jacques, by your argument on the phone listing, and I think we should also focus on the procedural side. Maybe the incentives in this case are indeed, as Gary said, lacking because states don't fight each other as little as they like to do on national security exceptions. National security has very little precedent and that is not an accident. Maybe state trading is a case where selectively private companies should have a greater say.

P. Mavroidis: I want to go back to Jacques Bourgeois' point because I like your point very much, Jacques — we have it in our paper but we have not made it clear. In Article 90 (ECT) you say, you have a general state trading enterprise, you take it out of the application of basic competition law. In the GATT, all you talk about in state trading is MFN (within the parameters of Article II:4 GATT, of course). That's all. Moreover, if my market is closed, which could theoretically be closed, I have no defense. Because all a state trading enterprise has to do is behave in a non-discriminatory way. There is absolutely no defense. That is where I see the problem. We have made one assumption which could be absolutely false: it could very well be the case that you have state trading enterprises in a very closed market, why not?

J. Bourgeois: Let me just inject a consideration based on EC experience. I don't want to speculate about what's GATT or GATS or whatever. It is likely that the picture would change with the introduction of a competition clause. Article 90(1) ECT with respect to states has been used in combination with Article 86 ECT, which is a competition rule. If you transpose that to the GATT situation, you would assume that Article 37 ECT equals Article XVII GATT. Gary Horlick says, "Let's use it fully. Then we will see whether it is sufficient." GATS plus a competition for the future would achieve what Article 90 ECT has achieved.

W. Martin: I'm struck by the importance of way the question has been posed to us by the chairman: the justification for STEs and then the question of whether Article XVII GATT does effectively discipline state trading organizations. It seems to me terribly important to make that separation. Because the justification question is the normative one of what the country ought to do in terms of its own economic interests. Article XVII GATT, and the GATT more generally, should focus on the question of what damage the country will do to other people. The second one is legal, the first one is much more an economic question. I think to try to answer the two together will lead to a terrible mess for the interpretation of Article XVII GATT.

One thing I'm a little confused about, particularly in Petros Mavroidis' comment about Article XVII GATT focusing on the MFN principle rather than national treatment: I understood Bill Davey to say yesterday that the protection given by an STE could not exceed the binding and the Havana Charter also requires the STE to meet demand at that price. That seems a fairly tight requirement for national treatment. I have always thought it wasn't tight because an STE could always charge a low mark-up but still sell a restricted quantity. State traders could limit their imports, but sell them on to someone else who then took the really large profit associated with their scarcity value and then cover up the fact that they were restricting trade by pointing to their low margin. But the point that Bill Davey made yesterday was that they must meet the demand at their selling price — ruling out this form of disguised protection. There may still be information problems in ensuring compliance with this rule, of course. I'd be interested in Bill's views on it.

M. Bronckers: I'm struck that we seem to be seeking new norms again. I would like to expand on what Gary Horlick said for GATT Article XVII. There is already quite a bit of content in Article XVII GATT (and the new WTO Understanding) that could be usefully applied. And I think the same is true for GATS. Article VIII of the GATS says quite clearly as a norm that the Members shall make sure that the monopoly service providers shall not abuse their monopoly. What more do you want? That's Article 90 and 86 ECT in one neat little sentence.

Again, as far as I am concerned, perhaps to make a brief reference to what I said before the break, enforcement matters a lot here. This could be as Gary said, a sort of idealistic "let's have a private right of access to WTO"; another perhaps less idealistic formula might be "let's have direct effect" like Thomas said; or the third possibility as I suggested before was "let's tack on to Article XVII of GATT, let's tack onto Article VIII of the GATS, something like the TRIPs enforcement provisions, something like the government procurement enforcement provisions". Then you let these private companies fight it out. Let's not try and regulate all of that again at the WTO level.

W. Davey: On the need for and adequacy of Article XVII GATT, I suppose if you look at it from the market access side, if you are talking about import monopolies, the provisions of Article II GATT that Will Martin has mentioned apply. There is also an interpretive note that says that you cannot make quotas effective through state trading enterprises. So Article XI may apply to the behavior of state trading enterprises. With respect to discrimination, of course, Article XVII GATT is limited to MFN, but there have been no Article XVII GATT cases per se. Panels have in some cases applied Article III because there was a sufficient government connection that you could say what was taking place was governmental. So you did solve the national treatment problem in those cases. So in that sense, there is a lot in the arsenal that I suppose might be used to solve distortions caused by state trading enterprises.

The concern of the United States when they made amendment proposals in the Uruguay Round, was to it make it clear that the rules on national treatment applied and that the rules on subsidies applied. And I think those are the two areas where there is a little ambiguity, because if you cannot show a sufficiently close connection to a governmental measure you may not be able to use Article III. And I think the problem with subsidies is exactly what is the complete relationship between some state trading enterprises and the government: do you know enough about it so you can decide whether not there are in fact subsidies?

Overall, Article XVII GATT has not done badly in dealing with the cases that have been presented, but there haven't been very many cases presented. There does seem to be a general lack of knowledge about the problem, and that's why disputes over the adequacy of the notification form have taken so long to resolve. There, some like the United States would like to know a lot more (particularly in the agricultural sector), in part to figure out whether not there are these subsidy problems. So to answer your question, I think Article XVII GATT is not in bad shape, but there are a couple of areas where there are problems. And the problems go back to the fact that if a government makes a commitment, you want to make sure the government cannot evade the commitment. With the state trading enterprises there is just more of a feeling that the government may reneg indirectly on the commitment. That's why you need the rules and why we talk about their effectiveness.

C. Falconer: Just a couple of observations. On the first point: is there really such a large question-mark as to why Article XVII GATT has not had cases fought under it? I am not sure that it is in fact the case that this is an Article which should have been invoked more often, and that there must be some political reason to explain why this has not happened. Is there really a large number of concerns out there which could have been addressed through Article XVII GATT, or should have been addressed through Article XVII GATT, but have been precluded because of concerns about reciprocal actions? I am not sure. What accounts for the situation? I am inclined to think that Bill is on the right track. Part of it is, I think, that there is genuine lack of clarity of how far Article XVII GATT might go. So it reflects that genuine uncertainty about its operational value. I do accept, however, that there is one exception to that: the agricultural sector. Non-use of Article XVII GATT may well be at least partly explained by the fear of having action taken against you in that case. But even then, only partly. The other major factor is that parties got satisfaction using other means anyway, particularly going to Article XI. There was a long period of time when actions under Article XVII GATT did not take place, and suddenly they did, and by and large people got satisfaction there, so the question was why would one need to bother going anywhere else. So I think that has a lot to do with why Article XVII GATT was not invoked.

The other reason why I am inclined to follow Bill's view on this is because there has always been, in any case, the capacity to negotiate on state trading arrangements to liberalize them. Nothing ever precluded parties in any negotiation from having an ad hoc negotiation about state trading enterprises if they'd wanted to. And if there really was a demand out there from the market for liberalization, but a concern that it might result in actions taken against yourself legally, the way in which you would have dealt with that would have been to negotiate. After all, the Uruguay Round agricultural negotiations eventually reflected that dynamic. You wanted to have a negotiated outcome which led to a balance without being expanded to litigation and counter-litigation. That way you got a politically satisfactory deal. But it didn't happen on state trading. So I'm inclined to the view that maybe in goods, at least, there isn't that much pent-up problem outside agriculture.

My second point is that maybe — just maybe — there are more difficulties with the Article than we have realized. This goes to the question of whether there might be more to Article XVII GATT than the implicit concensus of what it is about suggests. This would be related to the question of what those "exclusive rights" might be that can be mandated to private enterprises and entities. And this, it seems to me, is a much more interesting (and difficult) question. It raises issues which could parallel somewhat comments that have been made about the way in which the European treaty has been applied. If the view we have heard expressed — that there is a wider scope to Article XVII GATT — is correct, how would a panel in the WTO be capable of dealing with ascertaining whether "commercial considerations" have been made? To put it another way, I don't get the impression that, based on jurisprudence to this point, panels have many established or reliable benchmarks for making reliable judgements about whether private firms are "acting in accordance with commercial considerations". Panels tend to be obliged to make judgements, rather, about governmental measures. Perhaps they have difficulties attributing particular measures to governments or describing to which they belong. But this is quite a different matter from judging whether enterprises are following "commercial" considerations. I think this would be very very difficult (I'm not saying it would be impossible) for a panel to deliberate on. That seems to me to be somewhat parallel to what was discussed this morning about the European experience.

One final remark. I'm struck by the thought that maybe there is less difference in all of this, structurally between services and goods as far as the WTO is concerned than we often assume. After all, in services you have national treatment if you make a commitment. If you make a negotiated commitment, then the national treatment obligation applies. If you don't make the commitment, it doesn't apply. You could argue that in the case of goods you are in effect free to make commitments on state trading enterprises in a negotiation. You could have negotiated, in an ad hoc way, national treatment obligations with state trading enterprises if you had wanted to, should you have had doubts about what the coverage of Article XVII GATT was. I would also venture the view that has not been, to this point at least, a driver of liberalization when it comes to privatization-type issues. And I think that is reflected in the GATS to this point. It is about contractually consolidating and binding what has already been achieved. In other words, the liberalization impulse has been domestic. GATT has been more about providing a legal certainty for that in a multilateral framework. Yet that too is what the framework for goods provides for. The emphasis in the article on freedom to negotiate binding commitments automatically leaves the way open for this to take place in a similar manner to the GATS.

C. Ehlermann: You just allow me to take two elements of my own experience. There is one difference between private-owned and public companies: that is the transparency issue. It is not for nothing that earlier in the 1980s the Article 90 (ECT) activities started with a directive on transparency for public enterprises. This directive was violently opposed by those who had a large public sector. But they lost that case before the Court. Secondly, you are totally unable to run a subsidy control with respect to public companies if you do not efficiently apply the capital market principle of commercially-oriented action. You have to use that, with all the large gray zone which is around it. That is daily bread in Brussels. To what extent it could become daily bread elsewhere remains to be seen.

R. Howse: Following up on the logic of the last intervention, I think it is worth noting that not only does Article XVII GATT actually permit negotiations on a reciprocal basis, it foresees it, and the language, I believe, is Article XVII:3 GATT. First of all, it seems to state that even if one applies Article XVII GATT, there will remain the possibility of serious obstacles to trade being created by these enterprises that will have to be negotiated on a reciprocal basis. This, of course, is itself an interesting provision in terms of interpreting the scope of Article XVII GATT since it is suggested that in the first place the drafters thought that it wasn't going to be sufficient, whatever it meant, to deal with all the serious obstacles to trade that might be thrown up by these enterprises.

The second point is, it really goes to the comment about WTO panels applying ideas such as "commercial considerations". As you know from my own paper, I think this is one of the major explanations why panels have not been willing to touch Article XVII GATT. Their tendency to formalistic, traditional analysis has made them very cautious about employing these kinds of concepts. Perhaps the answer is institutional change, bringing more economic analysis into the panel process. I think one should reflect on what kinds of institutional innovation — whether in who's chosen for panels or what kinds of expert advice they can rely on in terms of market analysis — might be necessary if one is either going to breathe life into Article XVII GATT or indeed move to any kind of controls that involve the application of ideas about how a competitive market functions or ought to function.

R. Quick: I would like to present an argument in favor of the establishment of new rules and question somewhat Gary's and Marco's positions on applying the existing rules, because I see some difficulties in those positions. I would like to make two points. First, in a dispute settlement case involving Article VIII GATS, the panel might have as many difficulties as the European Court of Justice had with respect to Article 90(2) (ECT). Would the parties not argue that they provide a public service or a service of general interest? This morning we said that the European Court of Justice had quite some difficulties in making any decision on the issue of public service or service of general interest. The suggestion to rely on enforcement and dispute settlement will create an enormous pressure on the WTO system since its rulings do not (yet) receive as strong a general acceptance as the rulings of the European Court of Justice. So, I wonder whether it would be a good idea to rely on enforcement and dispute settlement only without having recourse to rule-making. I prefer Thomas Cottier's suggestion that in order to gain acceptance by the public we need to develop the rules.

Second, the differences between Article XVII GATT and Article VIII GATS need to be taken into account. Again the dispute settlement system might not overcome these differences and therefore one should not totally discard the idea of establishing new rules. If it is true that the success of Article 90 ECT was due to the existence of Article 86, then we should consider an Article 86-type clause also for the WTO.

P. Mavroidis: I will make three brief points, *court mais bref* as we say in French. First point, with all due respect to Bill Davey who taught me much of my trade, I think that the GATT panels that refer to national treatment were referring to import and distribution monopolies. If I have no distribution monopoly, why do I have to respect national treatment? I buy at five, I respect non-discrimination, I sell at twenty billion. Nobody can do anything against it (as long as Article II:4 is respected of course).

Now, two points for you. First, I think there is a fundamental difference between Article VIII GATS and Article XVII GATT. And the fundamental difference is the following. The example I gave you before: I buy at five and I sell at twenty billion. If it was a GATS issue, as Marco Bronckers pointed out before, this could be abuse of dominant position, so it could be a violation case. If it is a GATT issue it is at best a non-violation case, because there is no violation. Maybe I undo your legal expectations in this way, but it is no violation.

My second point is about "commercial considerations" which is, I think, one of the reasons why you did not have much case law on Article XVII GATT. It is precisely because of the difficulty in interpreting such terms. How can you interpret "commercial considerations" unless you do a case-by-case analysis? It is different in Canada, different in the United States, different in the EC, I guarantee to you that it is very different in Switzerland, n'est-ce pas? Now, if you start doing something like that case-by-case, the limits between arbitrariness and discretion are extremely thin. And you can trespass these limits if you are the European Court of Justice or if you are the U.S. Supreme Court. But can you trespass those limits if you are the WTO panel, which is not perceived as having the same degree of legitimacy as the aforementioned ajudicating bodies?

G. Horlick: I would like to add two observations into the mix. First, we should not lose sight of the linkage between state trading and government procurement. And indeed, I think probably the sins in government procurement may be even more widespread than in state trading at the present. I see the same lack of transparency, the same problems of hidden subsidization. The market participant doctrine is a good example, and the government procuring — acting as state trader — is in fact not acting as a market participant because there is no discipline from profit and loss. If a private enterprise wants to buy purely domestic goods and pays a price for it, eventually (at least in theory) the shareholders could reverse that if it is too painful; whereas a political body doing that usually does not face the same discipline. So, I don't think in dealing with state trading we should bear in mind the so far very partial success of the WTO in dealing with public procurement.

Second is a rather unusual aspect of the influence of the state trading enterprises on the trade system which I observed during the Uruguay Round, thanks to some of Reinhard Quick's colleagues in the German chemical industry explaining to me why a certain tariff liberalization had failed in the Round because their colleagues in a neighboring country, being state-owned, were in a better position to block it. It really interferes with the lobbying. If you are state-owned and the minister, say because of agricultural concerns, has taken a certain position, you can't lobby that minister, you certainly can't pressure him publicly. It really had quite an impact on some very important tariff negotiations in the Uruguay Round. Certain state-owned companies had preferred access to their governments. So, to some extent state trading interferes not only with the market for goods and services, but also the market for political choice. Thank you.

D. Palmeter: Just a couple of comments stimulated by Rob Howse's discussion of the need to ground these cases in XVII:3 GATT with Article XVII GATT and why it is not happening. I think one reason would simply be because the complaining parties would want to win. If you have a factual situation that is ostensibly covered by Article XVII GATT which is also under Article III, or some other provision where there is existing jurisprudence and you can fit there, you are certainly going to ground your request for a panel in that. Article XVII GATT may be tossed into it, and therefore might be within the terms of reference, but I would suspect the panels would react the same way. And they would therefore prefer to decide a case in line with an already-existing line of cases, simply to establish legitimacy for the decision. There would be an enormous reluctance on the part of anybody, I would think, to go off into new territory if you don't have to. So, probably the only way that Article XVII GATT will be construed is if somebody brings a case on the grounds of Article XVII GATT only. That may not happen anytime soon.

T. Hanoitis: I just want to react quickly to the examples of Petros Mavroidis and of Jacques Bourgeois. In these two examples — the one where a state company has bought at five and sells at twenty billion and the Malaysian telecom monopoly — I think we should trust more in the national governments' powers and in unilateralism as well. I mean, if a government is so irrational as to accept such a thing or to implement such policies, then at some point the domestic consumers will raise up their voice and say, "let's stop this". Why do we need the WTO to do this? Why do we need the WTO to run around all over the world to eliminate every single inefficiency that they see? I think if this sort of inefficiency is at the cost of consumers, it will disappear in the medium run.

W. Martin: Just an observation. The long run, it seems to me, could be fairly long and the rate of protection can be quite high. I think if you look at the agricultural protection created by state trading controls in the case of Japan, in some cases it got up over 600 percent, and stayed there for a sustained time period. I think internal pressures might not be enough to discipline these forces.

C. Ehlermann: One has seen over the last years in Brussels numerous cases which should have been solved by the national legislatures or administrations, where the center of gravity was clearly French or German or Belgian, but which were brought to Brussels under Community rules because apparently there was no national solution. In this situation you find yourself in a rather awkward position, particularly if the principles of subsidiarity are high on the agenda, because you solve a problem for somebody in France, in Germany, or in Belgium where redress should really be given by the national authority. So one can expect problems which are fundamentally local, national, to be brought to the international level because the way political power is distributed works differently in different places.

F. Abbott: Two questions, and they are directed to other people in the room. When we were asked to discuss the problem of state enterprises and state trading, I had assumed that a large measure of what we were doing or were thinking about was the prospective entry of China into the World Trade Organization. Will Martin has presented a tremendously interesting paper on this subject, and what that tremendously interesting paper says is, even with the great changes, fifty-three percent of exports and forty-four percent of imports are controlled by FTCs and seventeen percent of exports and eight percent of imports are controlled by state-owned enterprises. So, in the aggregate, we are looking at seventy and fifty-two percent of Chinese external trade being controlled by companies directly or indirectly owned by the government and controlled by governmental entities. I don't recall the exact numbers, but something also to the effect that by 2005 China will be the second largest economy in the world, and so-forth. At least in my own mind, this was a really central reason why we were looking at state trading at this particular point in time. The two questions it raised for me were: one, to ask Will Martin again, based on these numbers, what is it the WTO cares about with respect to the STEs, other than that they compete on a non-discriminatory basis under Article III, for example. And the second question turns to Bill Davey and maybe Gary Horlick as well: there is a second part of Article XVII:1(b) GATT after "commercial considerations" that refers to "and shall afford the enterprises of the other contracting parties adequate opportunity", and then the important clause "in accordance with customary business practice to compete for participation in such purchases or sales". What does the qualification that you need to do this "in accordance with your customary commercial practices" — perhaps this is to be understood in the context of local business practices — add to the mix of Article XVII GATT? Those are my two questions. Thank you.

C. Ehlermann: You raised correctly something which I should have raised: what does that all mean for China?

D. Wood: I wanted us to go back to what you were just saying about local problems and the need to move up to the international level, because I think it returns us again to the theme of which things have an effect on international markets. My colleague Frank Easterbrook wrote an article some years ago about the Parker v. Brown issue in U.S. antitrust law, and he suggested that there should be a very simple test for when we might need federal regulation and when you should leave it at the State level: you should just look to see if there are externalities that the State is imposing on other States or other foreign countries. If the State is doing something idiotic locally and only the State citizens pay for it, so be it. They've made the political decision. But if the State is, for example, running a raisin cartel and 90 percent of the raisins are sold outside of the State, that is unacceptable and you should step in. I think that kind of approach to the STE issue would be very useful too.

T. Cottier: Thank you very much, Claus, for chairing the meeting so far. Sorry you have to leave. I think we can focus now perhaps on the particularities raising from the accessions ahead, in particular of China and maybe further down the road also of Russia. And here the question I would like to inject for your consideration is the following: should we go towards a regime of géometrie variable as it seems or should we go for a regime which has the same rules and which essentially follows the philosophy of the Uruguay Round (which means no special and differential treatment but just transitional arrangements). I think this is a major policy question. And maybe you could also explore whether there are further options to associate such countries short of full membership, if the latter might overstrain the system. If within the last part we could address these questions, that would be most interesting.

G. Horlick: As to Russia, we had a very good paper that I would simply add to from observation. I have been spending a lot of time doing rather less state trading than even the paper reflects. More than half of the twenty-four percent cited is oil and gas, and I can assure you that those companies — whatever else they may be doing — are not state-controlled. And indeed it raises an interesting situation where some of these countries' situations are extremely different, for example Ukraine and Byelarus. In Russia itself you're headed for a situation where you have rather less state trading (because they're a very weak state) than in much of the West. This does raise an interesting question in accession negotiations when you try to lock that in. I would add that as recently as 1985 or maybe 1986 the United States, as Diane said (where there is very little state trading), didn't really bring cases under Article XVII GATT, or even discuss them. There was pressure not to do so because it was understood that state trading enterprises were much too sensitive a subject within the GATT because the strong reaction it would bring from such GATT members such as New Zealand and the United Kingdom, even as late as 1985, so it just wasn't worth it. I remember the discussions: the Reagan Administration thought state trading was awful but people in the U.S. government were not going to spend their chips on it — and this was only ten or eleven years ago. So, seize the moment and use the Russian accession deal to set up a pattern that you can then replicate with others with less bargaining power.

J. Bourgeois: Yes, thank you very much. The point made by Gary brings me again to the question as to what the Contracting Parties were assuming when they agreed to Article XVII GATT. Was the assumption, "we need to have that special provision on state trading companies because state trading companies simply do not react according to the laws of the market"? My question is whether in countries like Russia, and to certain extent already in countries like China, state trading or former state trading companies were acting according to rules that are not the rules of marketing economy? I have had a few experiences with Chinese companies, and I am not sure that a Shanghai company is listening to what Beijing is telling them. In the end, the problem could very well be not market distortions created by state trading companies in a command economy, but distortions by state trading companies that have become private monopolies. And with respect to this, at present, there are no rules at the international level except Article VIII of the GATS, and it applies only to those sectors where there have been concessions.

S. Nestor: There is a question I want also to put forth following both Jacques Bourgeois' and Fred Abbott's interventions. I totally agree with the comments on Russia by Gary Horlick. But, to limit ourselves to China, there are a few thousand foreign trade enterprises there. To what extent do those few thousands have any exclusive rights or any monopoly rights in trading because they are state-owned? They are foreign trade companies, but do they have any sort of market power given the enormous amount of trading that goes on in China these days? So that is the first question, and the second question is to follow Jacques Bourgeois' question: would there be any scope for a non-foreign trade company to be controlled by Article XVII GATT if it has market power? and what would the scope be? For example a joint venture company which is, in the Chinese context, a very common form of investment by some very powerful companies.

W. Martin: In time-honored tradition, I think I'll answer the last question first. So, as far as it is concerned, there are some commodities where the state trading system remains intact in its original form. We estimate those to be about eleven percent of imports based on 1992 imports. It's chemical fertilizers, a lot of agriculturally-related commodities, sugar, tobacco, and oil products. There is a different set for imports and exports. They are listed in the paper. For these commodities, the system is the very old system. I think in that it's a very inefficient and costly sort of system. It is non-transparent, and costly in a static sense, and creates a serious risk that protection will take off the way it has in the other East Asian countries. It was only the Uruguay Round that started the process of bringing those barrier down. So, in terms of the economic question of this article system, the answer is very clear.

The question of its GATT legality is much harder. The issue here is the eleven percent of imports covered by the exclusive trading system as well as the designated trade where you have a larger number of firms for each commodity. Looking forward, China has agreed to phase out the designated trading system. So once China has acceded, the explicit state trading will be the issue.

I think the full force of Frederick Abbott's question was devoted to the question of general trade in China's case. Now he points to the second column of table 2: the shares of exports by the government. There are very large shares of exports. In the case of exports it is seventy percent. This is being handled by foreign trade corporations and state-owned enterprises; fifty-two percent of imports being handled by those. Now, if this were just a classical monopoly it would be very clear that there was a serious problem with state trading. But I guess, it needs to be very carefully examined. When we look at this extraordinary number of firms, there are 9400 foreign trade corporations and 8700 that are importing. So, there is a very very large numbers of enterprises to try to control in the traditional sort of way of simply telling the monopoly how much it can import. That's okay with one, if there are three or four you can sort of divide it up very quickly and it is not an issue. But once you get to 9400, it is pretty difficult to control trade in this way.

My judgement is that this particular sort of state trading, with the large number of firms, is actually quite decentralized and is operating essentially according to commercial principles. When I talk to the policy makers, they make the point that the trading enterprises, the foreign trade corporations, are profit motivated and are quite decentralized. And it is clear they are run by all sorts of different organizations: governmental organizations; some of the old original ones are still run by the Ministry of Foreign Trade; then you've got ones run by provincial governments, local governments; you've got others run by the PLA; and so on. And these things all have subsidiaries (they talk about daughter firms and granddaughter firms — there is a huge number). It becomes difficult to see how they could be controlled without something like an explicit policy.

The logical way it has seemed to me to deal with that if you did want to exert quantitative control would be to set up a quota system or a licence system. And that's what has been done. There's a quota or a licence system there that's quite explicit and is used to control the volumes of those products which are subject to non-tariff barriers. And of course the phase-out for those is part of the on-going negotiations on accession and there is agreement to phase them out in several batches over a maximum period of eight years. So, I guess, by looking at the official position and seeing whether that seems to square with what has actually happened, and if you ask yourself how could it be done if you wanted to exert control, you say there are explicit mechanisms for doing it. It is conceivable that there is some deep-down backdoor plan of control for doing it. Certainly, there is no visible evidence of it. But to make sure over the long term, the key to deal with this would be to open up trading rights and to phase out the restrictions on entry. And that is part of the terms of accession agreed to date. Given that China is starting from a decentralised system of trading points including many state-owned enterprises and many joint ventures and so on, it doesn't seem such a big step in terms of actual policy — it just seems like a very useful step in terms of safeguarding the situation in a long term.

F. Abbott: This is a big battle we are going to have in the United States, hopefully six months from now, maybe ten years from now. What I hear from you is that if we said those companies under Article XVII GATT will act in accordance with ordinary commercial considerations, then from a world trading system standpoint (provided that their behavior isn't coupled with quotas which we don't like for the European Community or the United States or others), you are not suggesting that we need to add anything beyond behaving "according to ordinary commercial considerations" with respect to those firms. You would be more or less satisfied assuming that that was the accepted interpretation of Article XVII GATT.

W. Martin: I think that would seem to be sufficient if you have got a large number of state enterprises who are directed to be profit motivated, who are able to retain their profits. In fact its now pretty much the rule that the state enterprises that don't succeed go out of business. They have to operate according to commercial principles. They are doing something in a zero-profit/equilibrium situation, which leaves few excess profits with which to subsidize non-commercial activities. So the situation should create the sort of behavior that's mandated and applied by Article XVII GATT.

T. Cottier: Could I just put one more question? Given the data and facts, would you think that what accession negotiations should achieve is simply an in-phasing of the ordinary regime or is there still need for special rules in a protocol of accession as we had it under the GATT?

P. Mavroidis: I think you want to say, China and Russia stay out. My point was much more general.

S. Nestor: I have just an ancillary point. If you look at it from another point of view, what basically has been said here is that all these firms that look to us as state trading firms have been unofficially privatized. And that's what has been happening in China for a long long time now. Now, most of the rents are being captured by private individuals that are basically insiders. And that is what happened in many other countries in transition from central planning.

W. Martin: With your very specific issue, Thomas, on the negotiations, it would not seem sensible to introduce a set of quantitative controls such as voluntary import expansions as they have been used in the past for centrally planned economies. It would seem to me to be a backward step to look at doing that. I mean, in China the planning process back in 1978 involved planning physical quantities of every unit which was transacted. Then later some commodities were let out: there was value planning for the so-called "category two commodities". And then in the World Bank's 1994 report, we looked at the situation in 1992. And the thing that was really left was the foreign exchange plan. And we were very critical of that. But all of that has now gone, except for those commodities in the state trading and categories where there are strong restrictions on trade, and designated trading where there are restrictions on entry. So, when we are looking outside the state trading sector, eleven percent of imports, there are no quantitative instruments there except the ones which are going to be abolished. It would seem undesirable to add to that kind of trade regime requirements to have quantitative minimum levels of imports.

G. Horlick: The China and Russia accession negotiations represent possibly the extreme case of enforcement questions. Marco's suggestion won't work. I am not sure if you want to bring a hundred cases against China in the WTO — the Chinese will not take it in the proper spirit, I am sure. I am not offering any solution, but it is certainly a big problem. The issue is not the language of Article XVII GATT. And indeed it is not limited to Article XVII GATT with China as a whole. There is a substantial question about China's ability (if not intention) to comply with WTO commitments. I think a lot of thought has to be given to enforcement mechanisms that do not consume the entire energy of Bill Davey's office.

W. Davey: I guess that was a question about what the second half of Article XVII:1(b) GATT means. The question is what are "customary business practices". There is a record of a discussion in the subcommittee that indicates that it was intended to cover business practices customary in a respective line of trade. The other thing to say about Article XVII:1(b) GATT, I suppose, is that it has been interpreted to only apply in the case of MFN discrimination, which limits its overall coverage. There have been a couple of cases that have said that. But there has been otherwise no interpretation of that part of Article XVII:1(b) GATT, to my knowledge.

T. Cottier: Thank you very much. Is there anybody who would like to further address the accession issues, or could we move on to the end of the agenda?

P. Mavroidis: I have a point about Ehlermann's third point: what could reasonably be done. I mean basically it's a question. If I understand Ehlermann and Neven correctly, and I think, Jacques, we are on the same wavelength. There is considerable reticence in the EC in allowing the Court of Justice to address issues related to Article 92 ECT. By definition, it would be much more difficult to see WTO Members acknowledge such a role to the WTO panels. So another institution is probably better placed. Now, the crucial difference between the European Community and the WTO is the presence in the European setting and the absence in the WTO setting of an institution like the Commission. We have no Commission. There is no institution comparable to the Commission in the WTO. Everything is intergovernmental. Taking into account on top of it, that the WTO panels lack, to put it bluntly, the legitimacy the ECJ enjoys, I wonder what could be the body at the WTO that could play a role equivalent to the role of the Commission. Basically it is a question. André, maybe you have some more ideas.

T. Cottier: It seems to me, it's like the prayer "God please give me the insight what I can change and also what I cannot change". And maybe this is something we might take along for the end. I think dealing with issues in the GATT particularly in these areas where you have a lot of politics involved we always should ask the question of what can we reasonably achieve and what we may not be able to achieve. And that's a consideration we certainly have to bear in mind in this peculiar context. Jacques, please.

J. Bourgeois: This is a very very partial reply to Petros' question. I think that, as Claus Ehlermann made clear, one should not overstate the role played by the European Commission in these developments. However, there is one important element (i.e., the very fact that the Commission had this power). The Council of Ministers plus the European Parliament took under Article 100(a) ECT a number of decisions that would never have been taken, involving difficult political issues, but for the fact that they realized that the Commission might take them. I agree with Thomas that one always has to think very carefully about what is politically possible in a framework such as the WTO. But a framework such as the WTO probably sometimes needs some machinery to generate a consensus. If one leaves to the consensus of the WTO Members in their collective wisdom the generation of an impulse, one runs the risk of having blockages. The advantage, as I see it, in the European Community system is that a body can be a "loose cannon" in the eyes of the Members and where one of the ways of controlling that body is taking the decisions by the collectivity to preempt action by the "loose cannon".

M. Bronckers: To follow up on what Jacques said, I wonder whether someone should take the place of the Commission in the WTO context. Again, I think, the question is what do you want to achieve. The Commission has been very useful in the EC in bringing about structural change (notably to reduce monopolies). But what has been said during this discussion is that that is not what the WTO should do — the WTO should perhaps record domestic liberalization moves, lock them in. Yet it should not be seen as driving towards privatization, etc. So the fact that there is no "Commission" in WTO is not really of great concern in this respect.

On the other hand, if what you are really looking for is more supervision of the behavior of enterprises that are still somehow state-controlled, state-owned or whatever, then I would suggest the Commission has not been all that important. There are cases like the case that Jacques has referred to, this ITT case, but they are fairly exceptional. Most of these behavior questions are litigated and are solved domestically. So I would suggest to you the fact that such behavioral supervision cannot be done at the WTO level is probably just as well. There is no pressing need for a "Commission" in the WTO in this respect, either, if you make sure that domestic enforcement possibilities exist.

T. Cottier: I think this brings us to the end of our discussions. I would like to thank you indeed for your participation. To me, it was a very illuminating discussion, and I learned a lot about the complexities and about the problems involved. Thank you very much.

J. Bourgeois: In the name of everybody, I would like to congratulate the organizers because it has been a marvellous experience. They have organized it well, efficiently, and thoroughly. We enjoyed it all. Thank you very much.

STUDIES IN INTERNATIONAL TRADE POLICY

Studies in International Trade Policy includes works dealing with the theory, empirical analysis, political, economic, legal relations, and evaluations of international trade policies and institutions.

General Editor: Robert M. Stern

John H. Jackson and Edwin Vermulst, Editors. *Antidumping Law and Practice: A Comparative Study*

John Whalley, Editor. *Developing Countries and the Global Trading System.* Volumes 1 and 2

John Whalley, Coordinator. *The Uruguay Round and Beyond: The Final Report from the Ford Foundation Project on Developing Countries and the Global Trading System*

John S. Odell and Thomas D. Willett, Editors. *International Trade Policies: Gains from Exchange between Economics and Political Science*

Ulrich Kohli. *Technology, Duality, and Foreign Trade: The GNP Function Approach to Modeling Imports and Exports*

Stephen V. Marks and Keith E. Maskus, Editors. *The Economics and Politics of World Sugar Policies*

J. Michael Finger, Editor. *Antidumping: How It Works and Who Gets Hurt*

Horst Herberg and Ngo Van Long, Editors. *Trade, Welfare, and Economic Policies: Essays in Honor of Murray C. Kemp*

David Schwartzman. *The Japanese Television Cartel: A Study Based on* Matsushita v. Zenith

Alan V. Deardorff and Robert M. Stern, Editors. *Analytical Perspectives and Negotiating Issues in the Global Trading System*

Edwin Vermulst, Paul Waer, and Jacques Bourgeois, Editors. *Rules of Origin in International Trade: A Comparative Study*

Alan V. Deardorff and Robert M. Stern, Editors. *The Stolper-Samuelson Theorem: A Golden Jubilee*

Kent Albert Jones. *Export Restraint and the New Protectionism: The Political Economy of Discriminatory Trade Restrictions*

Alan V. Deardorff, James A. Levinsohn, and Robert M. Stern, Editors. *New Directions in Trade Theory*

Robert Baldwin, Tain-Jy Chen, and Douglas Nelson. *Political Economy of U.S.–Taiwan Trade*

Bernard M. Hoekman and Petros C. Mavroidis, Editors. *Law and Policy in Public Purchasing: The WTO Agreement on Government Procurement*

Danny M. Leipziger, Editor. *Lessons from East Asia*

Tamin Bayoumi. *Financial Integration and Real Activity*

Harry P. Bowen, Abraham Hollander, and Jean-Marie Viaene. *Applied International Trade Analysis*